Conflict, Order

and Action

Readings In Sociology

edited by

Ed Ksenych
and David Liu

Control, Order and Action: Readings in Sociology

First published in 1992 by
Canadian Scholars' Press Inc.
339 Bloor Street West, Suite 220
Toronto, M5S 1W7
Canada

Canadian Cataloguing in Publication Data

Main entry under title:

Conflict, Control and Action

ISBN 0-921627-81-5

1. Sociology. I. Ksenych, Edward. II. Liu, David, 1957-.

HM51.C6   1992   301   C92-093299-1

Book Layout by The Dancing Puffin Co.

Conflict, Order

and Action

Readings in Sociology

Canadian Scholars' Press   **Toronto**   **1992**

Table of Contents

III — Action and Interaction

IV — Socialization

V — Work and Organizations

IX — Deviance and Social Control

X — Field Projects

Preface

While general introductory textbooks provide a useful overview of research, concepts and theories within sociology, they tend to describe the field rather than exemplify the activity of doing sociological inquiry. This reader aims to offer students a clearer idea of the practice of sociology.

This book has been designed for an introductory sociology course at a post-secondary level. It grew out of our experience of teaching community college students on the fast track to jobs primarily in the field of health care. The collection reflects a particular approach to teaching that has successfully managed to integrate the practical interests and needs of our students with our desire to expose them to sociology as a form of inquiry. At the heart of this pedagogy is the presentation of familiar topic areas as a series of problems, and sociology as a practice that is brought to bear on the problems that it poses.

While some of the articles do focus on the medical professions, our intention has been to invite students to examine a broad range of areas and issues in contemporary society. In addition the readings represent a variety of theoretic styles and research methods. We have included examples of conflict theory, the structural-functionalist tradition, and the symbolic interactionist perspective, as well as more recent approaches to sociological inquiry. Our aim in this regard has been to have these abstract concepts come to life within the context of group conflict, social order and human action.

The selections vary in orientation and complexity. They range from classical to more contemporary works. While several of the readings will be challenging, we have found that students are capable of benefitting from challenging material if they have been appropriately prepared. As a guide, each selection has been prefaced by remarks which serve to highlight important concerns, raise questions or suggest further research.

The selections are not intended to comprehensively cover the field of sociology. They are meant to stand as an introduction, and as such, an opportunity for both student and teacher to begin a shared examination of their own conduct and embeddedness in the web of social relations and meanings we call modern society.

Ed Ksenych and David Liu
Toronto, Ontario

Acknowledgements

I — The Sociological Perspective

Vernon Boggs and William Kornblum, "Social Interaction in Times Square,"
adapted from "Symbiosis in the City," *The Sciences*, January/February,
1985: 25-30 [as reprinted in Peter Morrill (ed), *Societies: A Cultural
Reader*, Harper Collins, 1991: 8-9.

C. Wright Mills, "The Promise," from *The Sociological Imagination*, New
York: Oxford University Press, 1959: 3-13.

William Levin, "Ideal Type, Model and Paradigm," from *Sociological Ideas*
(2nd edition) Wadsworth, 1988: 21-24.

Patricia Marchak, "Ideology and Social Organization," from *Ideological
Perspectives On Canada* (3rd ed) Toronto: McGraw-Hill Ryerson, 1988
[as reprinted in Lorne Tepperman and James Curtis (ed) *Readings in
Sociology: An Introduction*, Toronto: McGraw- Hill Ryerson, 1988: 49-57.

C. D. Naylor, "Medical Aggression," *Canadian Forum* April, 1981: 5-9; 31.

II — Culture

Northrop Frye, "Sharing the Continent," *Divisions on a Ground: Essays on
Canadian Culture*, Toronto: House of Anansi Press, 1982: 57-70 [as
reprinted in Eli Mandel and David Taras (ed), *A Passion for Identity: An
Introduction to Canadian Studies*, Toronto: Methuen,1987: 206-216.

Horace Miner, "Body Ritual Among the Nacirema," *American Anthropologist*
50(3): 503-507.

Jean Paul Sartre, *Anti-Semite and Jew* (Trans. by George J. Becker),
Schoken Books, 1948.

Arthur Asa Berger, "Sex and Symbol in Fashion Advertising," from *Media
Analysis Techniques*, Sage Publications, 1982:135-146.

III — Action and Interaction

Herbert Blumer, "The Nature of Symbolic Interactionism," from *Symbolic Interactionism: Perspective and Method,* Englewood Cliffs: Prentice-Hall, 1969: 1-5 [as reprinted in Joel M. Charon (ed), *The Meaning of Sociology: A Reader* (2nd ed), Englewood Cliffs: Prentice-Hall, 1987: 324-326.

"Goffman: Rituals of Interaction," as prepared by *Saul Geiser* for Leonard Broom and Philip Selznick, *Essentials of Sociology* (2nd ed), New York: Harper and Row, 1979: 28-33.

Barney G. Glaser and Anselm L. Strauss, "The Ritual Drama of Mutual Pretence" from *Awareness of Dying*, Aldine, 1965 [as reprinted in Edwin Shneidman (ed), *Death: Current Perspectives* (3rd edition) Mayfield, 1984: 161-171.

Pamela Fishman, "Interaction: The Work Women Do," *Social Problems*, 1978, 25: 397-406 [as revised and reprinted in B. Thorne, C. Kramarac and N. Henley (ed) *Language, Gender and Society*, Newbury/Harper and Row, 1983: 89-101].

IV — Socialization

"Mead: Mind, Self and Society," a summary and interpretation of George H. Mead, *Mind, Self and Society*, Chicago: University of Chicago Press, 1934, from *Leonard Broom and Philip Selznick, Essentials of Sociology* (2nd ed), New York: Harper and Row, 1979: 28-33.

Stanley Milgram, "Behavioural Study of Obedience," *Journal of Abnormal and Social Psychology*, 1963, 67: 371-378 [as reprinted in Amy Halberstadt and Steve Ellyson, *Social Psychology Readings*, McGraw Hill, 1990: 362-372.

Jack Haas and William Shaffir, "The Professionalization of Medical Students: Developing Competence and a Cloak of Competence," *Symbolic Interaction* Volume 1, Number 1 (1978) [as reprinted in Lorne Tepperman and James Curtis (ed), *Readings In Sociology: An Introduction*, Toronto: McGraw-Hill Ryerson, 1988: 139-147.

Lillian Breslow Rubin, "And So They Were Wed," from *Worlds of Pain: Life in the Working-Class Family,* Basic Books, 1976: Chapter 4 [as reprinted in William Feigelman (ed), *Sociology Full Circle: Contemporary Readings On Society* (4th ed), New York: Holt, Rinehart and Winston: 1985: 277-291.

VII — Gender Relations

"The 'Facts of Life' As Usually Written Contrasted With A Matriarchal Culture Perspective" adapted from *Ruth Herschberger, Adam's Rib,* New York: Harper and Row, 1948 [as reprinted in Laurel Richardson, *The Dynamics of Sex and Gender: A Sociological Perspective* (3rd ed) New York: Harper and Row, 1988: 125.

Steven Goldberg, "Reaffirming the Obvious," *Society*, 23 (6), 1986 [as reprinted in Kurt Finsterbusch and George McKenna (editors), *Taking Sides: Clashing Views of Controversial Social Issues* (6th edition), Dushkin, 1990: 78-82.

Cynthia Fuchs Epstein, "Inevitabilities of Prejudice," *Society*, 23 (6), 1986 [as reprinted in Kurt Finsterbusch and George McKenna (ed), *Taking Sides: Clashing Views on Controversial Social Issues* (6th edition), Dushkin, 1990: 83-87.

Carol Gilligan, "Woman's Place In Man's Life Cycle," from *In A Different Voice*, Harvard, 1982.

VIII — Family

Christopher Lasch, "The Children of Narcissus," *Design for Arts in Education*, May/June, 1987: 45-48.

Meg Luxton, "Thinking About the Future" from K. L. Anderson, et al., *Family Matters,* Nelson Canada, 1988: 237-260.

Claude Levi-Strauss, "The Family," in Harry Shapiro (ed), *Man, Culture and Society*, Oxford: 1956: 142-170 [as reprinted in Arlene Skolnick and Jerome Skolnick (editors), *Family In Transition*, Little, Brown, 1971.

Section I

The
Sociological
Perspective

Social Interaction in Times Square

Vernon Boggs and William Kornblum

In this article, Boggs and Kornblum's observations of New York City's Times Square give us a glimpse of sociology's subject matter—the orderly nature of everyday life. Amid the apparently unrelated and disorganized activities of people going about their daily business, the authors show us a clearly defined social structure with demarcated roles and statuses.

A warm summer night on "the Deuce," West Forty-second street, the southern boundary of Manhattan's theatre district. It is past midnight, and the Broadway audiences are long gone. Dope dealers muttering, "Smoke, smoke," stand in the glare of movie marquees touting *Dirty Radio Sex* and other films. Some alcoholic derelicts—a "bottle gang"—weave along the broad sidewalk, on their way to a darker side street where they can sit and pass a pint. Men in business suits wander in and out of store-fronts whose flashing lights promise pornographic thrills. At the corner of Eighth Avenue, a prostitute begins arguing with her pimp, then tears away and heads east on Forty-second toward the intersection where Seventh Avenue crosses Broadway—the Great White Way—and forms Times Square.

To European and Asian tourists, and to many American out-of-towners as well, such sights are to be expected in any major city. But if the outsider sees Forty-second Street as a place where violent and exotic creatures tear at one another and at a victimized public in a fierce struggle to survive, those who make their homes there experience a way of life that is ordered, predictable, and controlled. There is a human ecology in Times Square that is at least as elaborate and as fascinating as the ecology of the tropical jungle to which the area has often been compared. What appears to be chaos and confusion is actually a complex interaction of social groups, each with its codes and rituals.

The literature of social science has long recognized that great urban centres create "natural areas" like Times Square where very different kinds of people come in contact. Robert Park observed in his seminal 1921 essay "The City," that people come together in cities "not because they are alike, but because they are useful to one another. This is particularly true in great cities, where social distances are maintained in spite of geographical proximity, and where every community is likely to be composed of people who live together in relationships that can best be described as symbiotic rather than social."

Street people are all around Manhattan, but the Times Square area is among the few places where they have staked out territories. Prostitutes, drug dealers, and bottle gangs all have their "strolls," or regularly travelled routes, each with its "stations," or oases of rest. Liquor stores, dark corners, and doorways serve as stations for the alcoholic derelicts who haunt the narrower,

less populous side streets. Corners where a waiting woman can pick up a trick
are the stations along the prostitutes' stroll on the west side of Eight Avenue,
north of Forty-second street. For the drug peddlers, whose stroll is the Deuce
itself, the stations are recesses and courtyards where their transactions can be
made out of sight.

Another type of turf is the hustling spot, set up, like a nomad's camp, only
when conditions are right. People with a hustle to pull off, such as three-card
monte or the con known as the Murphy (an elaborate scheme to persuade the
mark to turn over his savings), will not stage such shows along the strolls of
those selling drugs or sex. Working in small teams, hustlers play their trade with
an eye always out for "the man," in both his uniformed and plainclothes guises.
Periods of stepped-up police work, like times of bad weather, are viewed as
natural obstacles to be overcome with cunning and luck.

Different territories in Times Square mark not only different occupations
but different levels of status as well. Through the city, street people rank
themselves according to a hierarchy. Alcoholics and the mentally ill occupy the
bottom rungs. The young men who hustle for their living are further up. And
the pimps who set up shop in bars, safe from arrest and other dangers outside,
are at the top—in the street world, an admired elite. The members of each of
these status groups share rituals and norms learned in prisons and on the mean
streets of the city's ghetto neighbourhoods. A prostitute who has chosen a pimp
knows she must "give up choosing cake"—turn over a lump sum that the pimp
accepts as a kind of dowry. An older man wise in the ways of straight society
will be respectfully consulted as a "wisdom brother." Even the gangs of drinkers
at the bottom of the hierarchy have rituals to determine who buys a bottle and
who drinks from it last. Before anyone takes a swig, a few drops are poured on
the pavement, in memory of those who have died or gone to jail.

By far the largest and most complex of these status groups is the hustlers.
Hustling in Times Square involves running con games, selling phony jewellery,
shoplifting, and a host of other activities requiring good street sense and an
aptitude for calculating the risks of arrest, injury, or being taken in by
somebody else's "game." Large numbers of passers-by offer a ready market for
a wide variety of goods and services that the hustler can provide.

Hustling zones often overlap, and the various players sometimes try to
hustle one another. But not all the relationships of hustlers are exploitative.
Regulars on the street know and depend on one another. Some drug dealers
are related by family ties, others are acquaintances from prison; a number live
in the same buildings nearby. Though at a glance it may seem that every hustler
on the stroll is fiercely competing with every other, hustlers actually belong to
identifiable cliques, whose members can be seen sharing drugs, loaning one
another money, and calling out one another's names. They often arrive at a

station on their stroll the same time every morning, as if they were going to an entirely routine job.

Though prostitutes, drug dealers, and con men are well dispersed throughout Manhattan, their concentration in Times Square creates a permanent marketplace, the likes of which exists nowhere else in the city. Times Square is more than a home for groups of street people; it is also visited by thousands from the mainstream of society—office workers, garment-district employees, tourists, theatre-goers, retail merchants, restaurateurs, entertainers, and the middle-class and working-class people of Clinton, the residential neighbourhood to the west. Some 113,000 people use the subway stations every day, and another 100,000 arrive at and depart from the bus terminal. Most of these trips occur during the morning and late-afternoon rush hours, but in the evening, too, the area is crowded with people seeking entertainment, from Broadway plays and first-run movies to live sex shows and twenty-five-cent glimpses at silent pornographic shorts. As theatre-goers and seekers of sexual thrills head home and most of the city descends into the dark quiet of the early-morning hours, West Forty-second Street remains one of New York's liveliest streets.

The Promise

C. Wright Mills

Mills' introduction to the sociological imagination is an essay to be studied rather than skimmed for information. In it, Mills highlights significant characteristics of the sociological imagination and exercises this imagination in a study of the central issues of contemporary North American society. Some guiding questions for the reader are: What is the sociological imagination? What is the difference between a personal trouble and a public issue? What is the key issue of our times according to Mills? And what are the societal and historical roots of this issue?

Nowadays men often feel that their private lives are a series of traps. They sense that within their everyday worlds, they cannot overcome their troubles, and in this feeling, they are often quite correct: What ordinary men are directly aware of and what they try to do are bounded by the private orbits in which they live; their visions and their powers are limited to the close-up scenes of job, family, neighbourhood; in other milieux, they move vicariously and remain spectators. And the more aware they become, however vaguely, of ambitions and of threats which transcend their immediate locales, the more trapped they seem to feel.

Underlying this sense of being trapped are seemingly impersonal changes in the very structure of continent-wide societies. The facts of contemporary history are also facts about the success and the failure of individual men and women. When a society is industrialized, a peasant becomes a worker; a feudal lord is liquidated or becomes a businessman. When classes rise or fall, a man is employed or unemployed; when the rate of investment goes up or down, a man takes new heart or goes broke. When wars happen, an insurance salesman becomes a rocket launcher; a store clerk, a radar man; a wife lives alone; a child grows up without a father. Neither the life of an individual nor the history of a society can be understood without understanding both.

Yet men do not usually define the troubles they endure in terms of historical change and institutional contradiction. The well-being they enjoy, they do not usually impute to the big ups and downs of the societies in which they live. Seldom aware of the intricate connection between the patterns of their own lives and the course of world history, ordinary men do not usually know what this connection means for the kinds of men they are becoming and for the kinds of history-making in which they might take part. They do not possess the quality of mind essential to grasp the interplay of man and society, of biography and history, of self and world. They cannot cope with their personal troubles in such ways as to control the structural transformations that usually lie behind them.

Surely it is no wonder. In what period have so many men been so totally exposed at so fast a pace to such earthquakes of change? That Americans have not known such catastrophic changes as have the men and women of other societies is due to historical facts that are now quickly becoming "merely history." The history that now affects every man is world history. Within this scene and this period, in the course of a single generation, one sixth of mankind is transformed from all that is feudal and backward into all that is modern, advanced, and fearful. Political colonies are freed; new and less visible forms of imperialism installed. Revolutions occur; men feel the intimate grip of new kinds of authority. Totalitarian societies rise, and are smashed to bits—or succeed fabulously. After two centuries of ascendancy, capitalism is shown up as only one way to make society into an industrial apparatus. After two centuries of hope, even formal democracy is restricted to a quite small portion of mankind. Everywhere in the underdeveloped world, ancient ways of life are broken up and vague expectations become urgent demands. Everywhere in the overdeveloped world, the means of authority and of violence become total in scope and bureaucratic in form. Humanity itself now lies before us, the super-nation at either pole concentrating its most coordinated and massive efforts upon the preparation of World War Three.

The very shaping of history now outpaces the ability of men to orient themselves in accordance with cherished values. And which values? Even when they do not panic, men often sense that older ways of feeling and thinking have collapsed and that newer beginnings are ambiguous to the point of moral stasis. Is it any wonder that ordinary men feel they cannot cope with the larger worlds with which they are so suddenly confronted? That they cannot understand the meaning of their epoch for their own lives? That—in defence of selfhood—they become morally insensible, trying to remain altogether private men? Is it any wonder that they come to be possessed by a sense of the trap?

It is not only information that they need—in this Age of Fact, information often dominates their attention and overwhelms their capacities to assimilate it. It is not only the skills of reason that they need—although their struggles to acquire these often exhaust their limited moral energy.

What they need, and what they feel they need, is a quality of mind that will help them to use information and to develop reason in order to achieve lucid summations of what is going on in the world and of what may be happening within themselves. It is this quality, I am going to contend, that journalists and scholars, artists and publics, scientists and editors are coming to expect of what may be called the sociological imagination.

I

The sociological imagination enables its possessor to understand the larger historical scene in terms of its meaning for the inner life and the external career of a variety of individuals. It enables him to take into account how individuals, in the welter of their daily experience, often become falsely conscious of their social positions. Within that welter, the framework of modern society is sought, and within that framework the psychologies of a variety of men and women are formulated. By such means the personal uneasiness of individuals is focused upon explicit troubles and the indifference of publics is transformed into involvement with public issues.

The first fruit of this imagination—and the first lesson of the social science that embodies it—is the idea that the individual can understand his own experience and gauge his own fate only by locating himself within his period, that he can know his own chances in life only by becoming aware of those of all individuals in his circumstances. In many ways it is a terrible lesson; in many ways a magnificent one. We do not know the limits of man's capacities for supreme effort or willing degradation, for agony or glee, for pleasurable brutality or the sweetness of reason. But in our time we have come to know that the limits of "human nature" are frighteningly broad. We have come to know that every individual lives, from one generation to the next, in some society; that he lives out a biography, and that he lives it out within some historical sequence. By the fact of his living he contributes, however minutely, to the shaping of this society and to the course of its history, even as he is made by society and by its historical push and shove.

The sociological imagination enables us to grasp history and biography and the relations between the two within society. That is its task and its promise. To recognize this task and this promise is the mark of the classic social analyst. It is characteristic of Herbert Spencer—turgid, polysyllabic, comprehensive; of E.A. Ross—graceful, muckraking, upright; of August Compte and Emile Durkheim; of the intricate and subtle Karl Mannheim. It is the quality of all that is intellectually excellent in Karl Marx; it is the clue to Thorstein Veblen's brilliant and ironic insight, to Joseph Schumpeter's many-sided constructions of reality; it is the basis of the psychological sweep of W.E.H. Lecky no less than of the profundity and clarity of Max Weber. And it is the signal of what is best in contemporary studies of man and society.

No social study that does not come back to the problems of biography, of history and of their intersections within a society has completed its intellectual journey. Whatever the specific problems of the classic social analysts, however limited or however broad the features of social reality they have examined, those who have been imaginatively aware of the promise of their work have consistently asked three sorts of questions:

1) What is the structure of this particular society as a whole? What are the essential components, and how are they related to one another? How does it differ from other varieties of social order? Within it, what is the meaning of any particular feature for its continuance and for its change?
2) Where does this society stand in human history? What are the mechanics by which it is changing? What is its place within and its meaning for the development of humanity as a whole? How does any particular feature we are examining affect, and how is it affected by, the historical period in which it moves? And this period—what are its essential features? How does it differ from other periods? What are its characteristic ways of history-making?
3) What varieties of men and women now prevail in this society and in this period? And what varieties are coming to prevail? In what ways are they selected and formed, liberated and repressed, made sensitive and blunted? What kinds of "human nature" are revealed in the conduct and character we observe in this society in this period? And what is the meaning for "human nature" of each and every feature of the society we are examining?

Whether the point of interest is a great power state or a minor literary mood, a family, a prison, a creed—these are the kinds of questions the best social analysts have asked. They are the intellectual pivots of classic studies of man in society—and they are the questions inevitably raised by any mind possessing the sociological imagination. For that imagination is the capacity to shift from one perspective to another—from the political to the psychological; from examination of a single family to comparative assessment of the national budgets of the world; from the theological school to the military establishment; from considerations of an oil industry to studies of contemporary poetry. It is the capacity to range from the most impersonal and remote transformations to the most intimate features of the human self—and to see the relations between the two. Back of its use there is always the urge to know the social and historical meaning of the individual in the society and in the personal in which he has his quality and his being.

That, in brief, is why it is by means of the sociological imagination that men now hope to grasp what is going on in the world, and to understand what is happening in themselves as minute points of the intersections of biography and history within society. In large part, contemporary man's self-conscious view of himself as at least an outsider, if not a permanent stranger, rests upon an absorbed realization of social relativity and of the transformative power of history. The sociological imagination is the most fruitful form of self-consciousness. By its use men whose mentalities have swept only a series of limited orbits often come to feel as if suddenly awakened in a house with which they had only supposed themselves to be familiar. Correctly or incorrectly, they often come to feel that they can now provide themselves orientations. Older decisions that once appeared sound now seem to them products of a mind unaccountably dense. Their capacity for astonishment is made lively again. They acquire a new way of thinking, they experience a transvaluation of values; in a word, by their reflection and by their sensibility, they realize the cultural meaning of the social sciences.

II

Perhaps the most fruitful distinction with which the sociological imagination works is between "the personal troubles of milieu" and "the public issues of social structure." This distinction is an essential tool of the sociological imagination and a feature of all classic work in social science.

Troubles occur within the character of the individual and within the range of his immediate relations with others; they have to do with his self and with those limited areas of social life of which he is directly and personally aware. Accordingly, the statement and the resolution of troubles properly lie within the individual as a biographical entity and within the scope of his immediate milieu—the social setting that is directly open to his personal experience and to some extent his wilful activity. A trouble is a private matter: values cherished by an individual are felt by him to be threatened.

Issues have to do with matters that transcend these local environments of the individual and the range of his inner life. They have to do with the organization of many such milieux into the institutions of an historical society as a whole, with the ways in which various milieux overlap and interpenetrate to form the larger structure of social and historical life. An issue is a public matter: some value cherished by publics is felt to be threatened. Often there is a debate about what that value really is and about what it is that really threatens it. This debate is often without focus if only because it is the very nature of an issue, unlike even widespread trouble, that it cannot very well be defined in terms of the immediate and everyday environments of ordinary men. An issue, in fact, often involves a crisis in institutional arrangements, and often too it involves what Marxists call "contradictions" or "antagonisms."

In these terms, consider unemployment. When, in a city of 100,000, only one man is unemployed, that is his personal trouble, and for its relief we properly look to the character of the man, his skills, and his immediate opportunities. But when in a nation of 50 million employees, 15 million men are unemployed, that is an issue and we may not hope to find its solution within the range of opportunities open to any one individual. The very structure of opportunities has collapsed. Both the correct statement of the problem and the range of possible solutions require us to consider the economic and political institutions of the society, and not merely the personal situation and character of a scatter of individuals.

Consider war. The personal problem of war, when it occurs, may be how to survive it or how to die in it with honour; how to make money out of it; how to climb into the higher safety of the military apparatus; or how to contribute to the war's termination. In short, according to one's values, to find a set of milieux and within it to survive the war or make one's death in it meaningful. But the structural issues of war have to do with its causes; with what types of men it throws up into command; with its effects upon economic and political, family and religious institutions, with the unorganized irresponsibility of a world of nation-states.

Consider marriage. In a marriage a man and a woman may experience personal troubles, but when the divorce rate during the first four years of marriage is 250 out of every 1,000 attempts, this is an indication of a structural issue having to do with the institutions of marriage and the family and other institutions that bear upon them.

Or consider the metropolis—the horrible, beautiful, ugly, magnificent sprawl of the great city. For many upper-class people, the personal solution to "the problem of the city" is to have an apartment with private garage under it in the heart of the city, and forty miles out, a house by Henry Hill, garden by Garrett Eckbo, on a hundred acres of private land. In these two controlled environments—with a small staff at each end and a private helicopter connection—most people could solve many of the problems of personal milieux caused by the facts of the city. But all this, however splendid, does not solve the public issues that the structural fact of the city poses. What should be done with this wonderful monstrosity? Break it all up into scattered units, combining residence and work? Refurbish it as it stands? Or, after evacuation, dynamite it and build new cities according to new plans in new places? What should those plans be? And who is to decide and to accomplish whatever choice is made? These are structural issues; to confront them and to solve them requires us to consider political and economic issues that affect innumerable milieux.

In so far as an economy is arranged that slumps occur, the problem of unemployment becomes incapable of personal solution. In so far as war is inherent in the nation-state system and in the uneven industrialization of the world, the ordinary individual in his restricted milieu will be powerless—with or without psychiatric aid—to solve the troubles this system or lack of system imposes upon him. In so far as the family as an institution turns women in to darling little slaves and men into their chief providers and unweaned dependants, the problem of a satisfactory marriage remains incapable of purely private solution. In so far as the overdeveloped megalopolis and the overdeveloped automobile are built-in features of the overdeveloped society, the issues of urban living will not be solved by personal ingenuity and private wealth.

What we experience in various and specific milieux, I have noted, is often caused by structural changes. Accordingly, to understand the changes of many personal milieu we are required to look beyond them. And the number and variety of such structural changes increase as the institutions within which we live become more embracing and more intricately connected with one another. To be aware of the idea of social structure and to use it with sensibility is to be capable of tracing such linkages among a great variety of milieux. To be able to do that is to possess the sociological imagination.

III

What are the major issues for publics and the key troubles of private individuals in our time? To formulate issues and troubles, we must ask what values are cherished yet threatened, and what values are cherished and supported, by the characterizing trends of our period. In the case both of threat and of support we must ask what salient contradictions of structure may be involved.

When people cherish some set of values and do not feel any threat to them, they experience well-being. When they cherish values but do feel them to be threatened, they experience a crisis—either as personal trouble or as public issue. And if all their values seem involved, they feel the total threat of panic.

But suppose people are neither aware of any cherished values nor experience any threat? That is the experience of indifference, which, if it seems to involve all their values, becomes apathy. Suppose, finally, they are unaware of any cherished values, but still are very much aware of a threat? That is the experience of uneasiness, of anxiety, which, if it is total enough, becomes a deadly unspecified malaise.

Ours is a time of uneasiness and indifference—not yet formulated in such ways as to permit the work of reason and the play of sensibility. Instead of troubles—defined in terms of values and threats—there is often the misery of vague uneasiness; instead of explicit issues there is often merely the beat feeling that all is somehow not right. Neither the values threatened nor whatever threatens them has been stated; in short, they have not been carried to the point of decision. Much less have they been formulated as problems of social science.

In the 'thirties there was little doubt—except among certain deluded business circles that there was an economic issue which was also a pack of personal troubles. In these arguments about "the crisis of capitalism," the formulations of Marx and the many unacknowledged re-formulations of his work probably set the leading terms of the issue, and some men came to understand their personal troubles in these terms. The values threatened were plain to see and cherished by all; the structural contradictions that threatened them also seemed plain. Both were widely and deeply experienced. It was a political age.

But the values threatened in the era after World War Two are often neither widely acknowledged as values nor widely felt to be threatened. Much private uneasiness goes unformulated; much public malaise and many decisions of enormous structural relevance never become public issues. For those who accept such inherited values as reason and freedom, it is the uneasiness itself that is the trouble; it is the indifference itself that is the issue. And it is this condition, of uneasiness and indifference, that is the signal feature of our period.

All this is so striking that it is often interpreted by observers as a shift in the very kinds of problems that need now to be formulated. We are frequently told that the problems of our decade, or even the crises of our period, have shifted from the external realm of economics and now have to do with the quality of individual life—in fact with the question of whether there is soon going to be anything that can properly be called individual life. Not child labour but comic books, not poverty but mass leisure, are at the centre of concern. Many great public issues as well as many private troubles are described in terms of "the psychiatric"—often, it seems, in a pathetic attempt to avoid the large issues and problems of modern society. Often this statement seems to rest upon a provincial narrowing of interest to the Western societies, or even to the United States—thus ignoring two-thirds of mankind; often, too, it arbitrarily divorces the individual life from the larger institutions within which that life is enacted, and which on occasion bear upon it more grievously than do the intimate environments of childhood.

Problems of leisure, for example, cannot even be stated without considering problems of work. Family troubles over comic books cannot be formulated as problems without considering the plight of the contemporary family in its new relations with the newer institutions of the social structure. Neither leisure nor its debilitating uses can be understood as problems without recognition of the extent to which malaise and indifference now form the social and personal climate of contemporary American society. In this climate, no problems of "the private life" can be stated and solved without recognition of the crisis of ambition that is part of the very career of men at work in the incorporated economy.

It is true, as psychoanalysts continually point out, that people do often have "the increasing sense of being moved by obscure forces within themselves which they are unable to define." But it is not true, as Ernest Jones asserted, that "man's chief enemy and danger is his own unruly nature and the dark forces pent up within him." On the contrary: "Man's chief danger" today lies in the unruly forces of contemporary society itself, with its alienating methods of production, its enveloping techniques of political domination, its international anarchy—in a word, its pervasive transformations of the very "nature" of man and the conditions and aims of his life.

It is now the social scientist's foremost political and intellectual task—for here the two coincide—to make clear the elements of contemporary uneasiness and indifference. It is the central demand made upon him by other cultural workmen—by physical scientists and artists, by the intellectual community in general. It is because of this task and these demands, I believe, that the social sciences are becoming the common denominator of our cultural period, and the sociological imagination our most needed quality of mind.

Ideal Type, Model, and Paradigm

William Levin

One of the basic problems that has faced sociology is how to integrate social inquiry, which is a moral inquiry by nature of its subject matter, with the requirements of science, which rejects moral judgments in its claim to objectivity. In this article Levin outlines three approaches to establishing sociology as a social science which form the basis of sociology's investigation into social life. Do any of the three approaches manage to resolve the problem successfully?

In high school biology we students were shown diagrams of microscopic plants and animals and their internal structures. These pictures were either in our textbooks or drawn on the chalkboard by the teacher. They were marvels of complex draughtsmanship—all those little cell walls and nuclei, all those different colours showing where one part ended and another began. We copied everything in our notebooks just as clearly. Then we went to the laboratory microscopes to identify the same things the diagrams had shown us, only "for real" this time. But they never looked the same. In fact, sometimes they were barely recognizable from the pictures we had been shown. Under my microscope, when I could focus it at all, was something with no apparent nucleus, or something with lots of little dots where there should have been only a few, or something not round enough. My biggest problem was that I wanted the structures I saw in the lab to match perfectly with the picture drawn on the board. I didn't understand the concept of the *ideal type*.

When we wish to understand the character of some object, we rarely describe one unique object. Instead, we speak about a category of such objects that have characteristics in common. Red blood cells, for example, are generally disk-shaped with dished (concave) centres and a yellowish colour. But all the cells are not exactly alike in reality. Categories of objects have characteristics in common but also differ from one another. To explain, or define, such a grouping to a person who has had no experience with it, we must ignore the differences that occur and develop an ideal type, a description focusing on characteristics typically held in common among otherwise differing cases. The dictionary is filled with such ideal types. My dictionary has wonderful illustrations and photographs for selected definitions. The drawings of the flowers are of perfect, idealized flowers, and the photographs of the dogs are of breed champions who represent the ideal for the specific animal. Every concrete example of an ideal type will differ from the theoretical definition, but having the definition in mind makes the common features of the real world examples stand out clearly.

Ideal Types in Sociology

The concept of ideal types has existed for as long as people have been able to group things that have some qualities in common. It seems likely that this was applied first to physical objects such as flowers, dogs, and (when microscopes extended our vision) red blood cells. By the end of the nineteenth century, the developing field of sociology had focused our attention on patterns of behaviour and ways of thinking that, like physical objects, could also be seen as having characteristics in common. The German sociologist Max Weber (1864-1920) coined the term *ideal type* (Weber, [1925] 1946) as an aid in describing such regularities in patterns of social behaviour.

As an example let us take the concept of minority group. American sociologist Louis Wirth (1897-1952) developed a famous definition of a minority as a group of people who "because of physical or cultural characteristics are singled out from others in the society in which they live for differential and unequal treatment, and who therefore regard themselves as objects of collective discrimination" (Wirth, 1945:347). As an ideal type, Wirth's definition should fit the experiences of all minority groups to some degree, but we should not expect it to fit any single minority group perfectly. Not all minorities need be physically or culturally distinctive in the exact same ways to fit the definition. They need not have experienced the same kind of discrimination, nor do they have to express the same kind of collective consciousness of discrimination. For example, blacks in the United States have experienced a very different history of discrimination from women, yet both are good examples of minority groups. The cultural characteristics by which Jews are identified are entirely different from those of Vietnamese-Americans, but both are examples of minority groups as well. The elderly have only recently begun to see themselves as objects of collective discrimination. Before this self-awareness developed, the elderly had only a kind of negative group consciousness that led them to avoid association with the status of old people. Yet this negative group consciousness is a form of awareness of collective discrimination, so the elderly should also be defined as a minority group. The ideal type fits all these groups, but in different ways. Although they are different from one another in some ways, they all still share the essential characteristics of minority groups as spelled out in the definition.

When we begin to pay attention to patterns in social life, a wide variety of such ideal types appear. Family, friendship, social class, bureaucracy, even major types of societies (such as hunting-gathering, horticultural, agrarian, and industrial) are all examples of ideal types. By observation, you could develop an ideal type for some common experience of your own. For example, what are the minimum, abstract characteristics of a college class? Are there certain necessary participants? How many are needed? Can there be too many? What are the essential relationships that must be present? What forms of behaviour, exhibited at what times, in what order, and in what kind of setting are required? When you begin to think of such questions, the existence of some underlying order can be discovered and eventually described.

Ideal Types and Models: "What If"

The attempt to discover order in the social world involves roughly equal parts of observation and speculation. We watch, listen, and make guesses from moment to moment about whether what we have seen is a genuine pattern or a chance event. For example, is it just in my classes that a certain thing happens, or is it true of other college classes also? That kind of speculation is what leads us to test our ideas against reality and eventually to develop stable ideal types for describing social order.

Another type of speculation that helps us in this process is "what if" speculation or *model* building. Assume that we have come to some agreement about how a specific part of the social world operates—for example, we have agreed that the family is primarily a unit of kinship in which a number of tasks are accomplished, such as procreation; care, socialization, and education of the young; sexual access between adults; and consumption of goods. Based on this ideal type, we can speculate what shape the family would take in American society under a variety of conditions. What if war broke out, the men left to fight, and the women had to do what had been considered "men's work" (as occurred during World War II)? Or what if the economy suddenly developed a greatly increased demand for the work skills that women traditionally have provided and simultaneously diminished the need for traditionally male work skills? What if housing became much more difficult to obtain, and several generations of parents and children were required to live together in extended families? What changes in the family could we expect under any of these conditions? Model building allows us to guess, based on our assumptions about how the social world currently operates, how a variety of circumstances would influence that social order. Not only does model building have the practical consequence of helping us to plan, but it also clarifies the ideal types on which we depend for our normal examination of social order.

I want to make it clear that this definition of the term *model* has been chosen for two specific reasons. One is that in many texts the terms *ideal type, model*, and *paradigm* (which is discussed next) are used interchangeably. They have lost their usefulness as separate terms. I want the distinctions among them to be clear. The second reason is that *model* is used in a similar way in other fields. Engineers build models of physical objects to test their behaviour under a variety of conditions (such as car tests in wind tunnels). Urban planners build computer models of vehicle and pedestrian movements to test the effect of changes in street patterns on their mobility. Planners in various segments of the federal government build models of population demands for foods, housing, fuel, and so on. (The military even has models for the various outcomes of war under a variety of, we hope, theoretical conditions.) So I chose this definition of *model* to fit with those in other fields.

Paradigms

Ideal types and models are fairly concrete statements about the way things work and, therefore, lend themselves to testing against reality. For example, we can observe how well various groups fit our ideal type for minority group. Or, using a model, we can speculate about the influence various conditions might have on the structure of the American family. But underlying both ideal types and models are sets of very broad assumptions that often go unexamined, even though these assumptions shape the kinds of ideal types and models we are capable of developing. We can call this collection of broad assumptions a *paradigm* (Gouldner, 1970).

Two opposing paradigms that have shaped much of our thinking about social order deal with the question of how order itself develops. The *conflict* paradigm argues that social order is the result of a balance of contending forces, each struggling against the other for some valued good. The result of such a struggle is either domination of one group by the other or a balance of contention between them. In either case, a sort of orderliness is the consequence of the conflict. By contrast, the *consensus* paradigm argues that social order is the result of agreement among groups and individuals about what the distribution of valued goods should be. Accordingly, order is seen as the consequence of a consensus (whether conscious or not) about what is in everyone's best interests.

Very often my students are surprised to discover that they have held one of these paradigms in preference to the other without awareness that they were doing so. The kind of paradigm a person holds can be traced, in turn, to even more basic assumptions about the nature of human beings, such as their capacity for cooperation and generosity or the degree of their natural competitiveness. Whatever the origins of paradigms, they inevitably shape how we think about the character of social order. A person holding the consensus paradigm would likely develop an ideal type for the family that stresses the agreements among its members about what each is to do as a family member. By contrast, a person holding the conflict paradigm would probably see the family as a social unit in which the differing aims of members produce a relatively stable balance of contending forces. Does one of these views seem more likely than the other to you? If not, then you might hold a different paradigm, which would lead to the development of alternative ideal types and models. Or perhaps the consensus and conflict paradigms are not in complete disagreement. At times consensus might be possible, while at other times conflicts contribute to stable social order. They may be complementary processes.

The usefulness of concepts such as paradigm, ideal type, and model is that they cause us to examine the way we study and think about the social world. As you read material in sociology (or any other discipline), keep in mind how broad assumptions, especially unexamined ones, shape the ideal types and models we can produce.

References

Gouldner, Alvin W. 1970. *The Coming Crisis of Western Sociology*. New York: Avon Books.

———. 1925. From *Max Weber: Essays in Sociology*, trans. and ed. Hans H. Gerth and C. Wright Mills. New York: Oxford University Press.

Wirth, Louis. 1945. "The Problem of Minority Groups." In *The Science of Man in the World Crisis*, ed. Ralph Linton, 347-72. New York: Columbia University Press.

Ideology and Social Organization

M. Patricia Marchak

The concept of ideology and its significance in the organization and understanding of collective life is the focus of Marchak's article. She provides us with a basic overview of competing ideologies that we draw upon to describe and justify how society is or should be organized.

Ideologies

Dominant and counter-ideologies grow out of the same social organization. They take the same economic arrangement, the same territorial boundaries, the same population as their units of analysis. But they posit different relationships between these units and different relationships between these units and different organizations within them. Although the two major ideologies of our time—which we will label liberalism and socialism—claim to explain society in historical and comparative perspective, they both originate in the period of the European Industrial Revolution, and both are unmistakably locked into industrial society as it emerged in Europe at that time.

Because they grow out of the same organization, they have much in common. They are the two sides of a single coin: one describing how the entire structure looks to one who accepts it and expects it to survive; the other, how it looks to one who rejects it and anticipates its demise....

Ideologies are explanations for the social organization, but they are, as well, evaluations of it. These evaluations tend to be circular: the social organization gives rise to certain beliefs about what is right, appropriate, and desirable, that is, to certain values. These values are then assumed, and the society judges itself by those values. The liberal democracy gave rise to positive evaluations of equality, individualism, material prosperity and personal freedom. The society is then judged within that framework: does it allow for the realization of these values? The dominant ideology rests on an affirmative answer: yes, this society provides the necessary conditions for equality, material prosperity, and personal freedom. Where there are deficiencies, these are often not recognized. Where the deficiencies are recognized, they are explained not as symptoms of a system that fails but as aberrations or temporary problems in a system that succeeds.

Widespread acceptance of an ideology creates an incapacity for judgment of its truth. There is comfort in believing what so many others appear to believe, in accepting conventional wisdom. There is fear in doing otherwise. Sometimes there are, as well, serious social consequences. To many minds, the person who admits to a deviant perspective is out of bounds, somehow dirty and unacceptable.

Counter ideologies involve a good deal of imagination. They provide a critique of the present society and a creative vision of an alternative. Both socialism and the "new right" provide these critiques and creative visions; and whether we agree with them or despise them, we are indebted to their proponents for enabling us to imagine other ways of doing things.

Counter ideologies generally begin with a critical perspective which arises from recognition of inconsistencies between what the dominant ideology portrays as truth and what the senses suggest is reality. They begin, then, as reform movements and their members are social critics. Equality, material prosperity, and personal freedom may be assumed as "right" values, but the society it judges as deficient in providing for their realization. The negative judgment leads to an analysis of social organization which diverges from that propagated by those who hold the dominant ideology and believe it to meet its own objectives. Gradually the analysis turns into a fully developed counter ideology, and an entirely different way of viewing the society.

Some people think that ideology is something that happens to others, and generally to somewhat deranged others. That is not the sense in which the term is used here. We are all immersed in ideological understandings of our world.

We define ideology as shared ideas, perceptions, values, and beliefs through which members of a society interpret history and contemporary social events and which shape their expectations and wishes for the future.

A dominant ideology is defined as that particular set of ideas, perceptions, values, and beliefs which is most widely shared and has the greatest impact on social action at any particular time in any particular society.

A counter ideology is defined as a set of ideas, etc., which is held by a substantial minority and which has noticeable impact on social action. There may be many or few counter ideologies in any society at any historical period.

There is another definition of ideology: the ideas and values of the ruling class, disseminated through agencies controlled by that class in ways that obfuscate class realities for subservient classes. We are not using this definition here.

Ideology and theory are different entities, though they grow out of the same womb. Theory consists of explicit assumptions, a reasoning by which the assumptions are demonstrated to be linked to conclusions on the one hand, and such material evidence as can be gathered on the other. It is, by definition, open to challenge through the presentation of more complete or contesting evidence, or by a refutation of the logic that links assumptions to conclusions. It is not a faith. It is not unexamined.

In some ways, theories are rivals and enemies of ideologies because they tend to dissect them. Someone begins by saying, "Hmmm, I believe this and that, I think I'll write it all down in some systematic way so that others will think as I do." Then, in the writing of it, the author begins to see some inconsistencies, some flaws in logic, some mismatch between theory and evidence. And the reader, perusing the manuscript, says, "but this isn't good enough." Theories evolve over time, moving further and further away from their ideological base, becoming more sophisticated, more logical, more consistent—but often moving so far from their beginnings that they leave the majority of believers far behind.

Ideologies normally attract some people who want to make them public and systematic. In addition to theorists, there are scribes and prophets who define ideologies, trying to demonstrate how their particular beliefs are unique and true. For this reason, we can examine such ideologies through the writings of the scribes and the speeches of the prophets. And, as we begin to see which values they emphasize, which utopian visions they advance, we can label the ideologies and identify them relative to one another with reference to specific values. But for the same reason that we need to distinguish between theory and ideology, we need to recognize the possible differences between what the scribes and prophets say and what a majority of believers accept.

Ideologies may be phrased in terms we would recognize as political, that is, they are about the political world and how the public arena should be governed. Other ideologies may also have political implications but may be phrased as religious belief systems. Although the language of discourse may seem very different, there are usually close ties between what people believe about the meaning of human existence or the properties of nature and gods, and what they believe about political governance in the temporal world.

We are concerned here with the major ideologies of our society, the dominant and the counter ideologies which motivate large numbers of people. And we are concerned primarily, though not exclusively, with how these ideologies link up with economic and political events. There are, in addition to these central ideologies, other versions of the world espoused by smaller numbers of people. Some of these other versions take political forms, some take religious forms.

Political ideologies ultimately boil down to the relative emphasis placed on individualism versus collectivism, and on egalitarianism versus elitism. It is in these terms that we can identify the differences between one ideology and another. We have political labels for various positions in our own society, along two continuums: the first, from extreme individualists (society has absolutely no claims on the individual, and there should be no rules, government, or constraints on individual actions) to extreme collectivists (society always has precedence over individuals, and the right to demand conformance with rules for the public good): and the second, from extreme elitism (there should be rulers and the rulers should have complete power) to extreme egalitarianism (all people should be absolutely equal in condition, not just opportunities). The differences between these labelled positions can be noted by referring to the theories, scribes and prophets, but as observed above, we must be wary of assuming that all adherents to labelled positions are consistent in their beliefs.

Individualist and Market-Based Ideologies

Anarchism, libertarianism, and to a lesser degree, liberalism, treat society as a collection of individuals. Society does not exist in and of itself, it is not an organic whole. Individuals each strive to manufacture the necessary conditions for life, and the market mechanism has emerged as a means of coordinating their separate strivings without applying force. The preservation of individual liberty and of the "free market" becomes the major concerns of advocates of these positions.

Anarchism and Libertarianism

The individualist position is taken to the extreme in anarchist and libertarian ideologies; all other values become subordinate. Anarchists would do away with all government and social restrictions on personal liberty; libertarians (though with some differences between various groups) generally accept the necessity of government, but would restrict its functions to the defence of persons and property. Anything which prevents individuals from fully exercising their initiative, entrepreneurial skills, and talents is harshly judged: thus democracy and the welfare state are deemed to be impediments to individual growth. Inequality is viewed as inevitable because people are genetically unequal, and as necessary because the most talented provide the leadership which permits others to survive. Libertarians believe that "pure" capitalism is an ideal social and economic system because it includes a genuinely free market for absolutely all good and services.

Liberalism

Liberalism has a somewhat different meaning in Canada than in the United States. In Canada, it is an approach which emphasizes the individual but combines that emphasis with concern for the preservation of law, order, and public well-being in the society, and includes some concern for equality between citizens. In the United States, its connotation is more strongly connected to social and collective values, closer to what Canadians regard as "social democratic." It differs from the Canadian social democratic view in that while both take equality to be a positive value, the liberal view is that equality is largely achieved within the present social system. Social democrats argue in favour of greater equality of condition and perceive great inequalities of both opportunity and condition in the present social system.

Like libertarians, liberals believe in the virtues of a free enterprise market, in which all sellers and buyers compete on equal terms for the attention of consumers. Unlike libertarians, liberals temper this belief by acknowledgement of some services and goods which "ought" to be in the public realm. The free enterprise market is rarely called "capitalism" in liberal ideology; the phrase "free enterprise" becomes the euphemism for capitalism. Consonant with the belief that society is made up of individuals, liberals deny the existence of classes in capitalist society. A great deal of emphasis is placed on the education system because liberals believe that individuals have equal opportunity in that sphere, each achieving there what their innate talents and hard work permit and thus moving upward or downward in the social system according to ability.

The role of government is to regulate the market place and to ensure that the rules are fair and equitable; government is not itself an economic actor in a truly "free" enterprise system. Further, since there are no classes, government cannot be seen as the agent of any particular class; and since there is no ruling class, it cannot be seen as acting on behalf of that class.

Liberalism has been the dominant ideological perspective adopted by Canadians throughout the past 40 years. One political party is called "Liberal" but when we speak of liberalism, we do not refer exclusively to this party. In fact, throughout this period, the two major alternative parties, the Progressive Conservative and the New Democratic Parties, have shared much of the liberal version of Canadian society.

Collectivist Positions

Collectivist positions begin with the argument that the society is an organic whole. Society exists independent of the individuals who happen to live in it at any time. But there is enormous difference in the conclusions and policy positions taken by collectivists of the "left" and of the "right." The basic difference occurs between those who believe that society ought to be more egalitarian (social democratic, socialist, communist) and those who believe it should be more hierarchically ordered (conservative, corporatist, and fascist).

Social Democratic

Social democrats accept the basic values of liberalism but place more emphasis on equality. As well, they recognize the existence of classes, of class barriers, and of governments acting in the interests of a dominant or ruling class. They thus share some of the understandings of socialists. They are committed to the gradual and democratic evolution of a socialist society, which they understand to be a more egalitarian organization within which workers have decision making control over production, and private ownership rights over industrial units and natural resources are abolished. This is the position of various democratic socialist parties throughout the world, and of the CCF and NDP parties.

Socialist

Socialists perceive capitalism as a system where a ruling class extracts wealth from a subordinate class (or classes), sells products made by labour, and uses the profits to invest in more properties and new technologies which displace or further enslave labour. Classes exist, inequalities are essential to the system, and individual freedom is highly circumscribed by the fundamental requirements that labour must produce goods and services for capital. For the socialist these conditions are unacceptable.

Socialism involves a version of the future which differs markedly from that of liberalism. For liberals, the future is a continuum of the past and present. It is a highly optimistic ideology, assuming eternal progress and gradual elimination of imperfections in the social system. But socialism, identifying capitalism as an oppressive and exploitative system, involves the belief that only through the destruction of capitalism can a more egalitarian and humane system emerge. Capitalism is expected to self-destruct, because its internal contradictions must eventually cause a fatal blockage in the capacities of capitalists to continue accumulating new profits (this is called "a crisis of accumulation" in the socialist literature).

For the liberal, capitalism is necessary reality and critiques of it are ideology. For the socialist, the liberal version of capitalism is ideology. It is understood by socialists as an essential feature of the capitalist system, because it induces workers to consent to their own exploitation. They are persuaded, rather than forced (although force may on occasion also be necessary), to believe that the system is fair even if it leads to extremely unequal distributions of material wealth and economic power. Part of the key to this persuasion is, in the opinion of socialists, the nature of democratic governments. These are either so constrained by the economic decisions of private capital (there are different theories on this) that they can do little more than facilitate private accumulation. They mediate class conflict by developing rules for employment, hours, welfare and the like, because the system could not continue with persistent or violent class conflict, but the appearance is of governments acting in the general public interest. As well, since governments are formally elected by the population at large, there is a widespread belief in their neutrality and representative character. The ideology of democracy, then, and the mechanics of democratic elections are important features of capitalism because they "legitimate" the economic system and provide the pretence of impartiality.

Conservatism

Conservatism—like liberalism not to be interpreted as necessarily coincident with a particular political party—shares with socialism a belief that there are classes, that capitalism necessarily involves inequality, and that the marketplace should not be the locus of most important social decisions. But unlike socialism, conservatism gives a high positive value to class inequalities: they are necessary because society requires leadership, and well established leaders look after less well established workers. Conservatism thus values a "natural" hierarchy, paternalistic relations between capital and labour. For the conservative, government properly has the right to establish norms for the conduct of social life, though it should have a restrained role in the economy.

The chief difference between conservatism and liberalism is in their respective views of society: conservatives viewing it as an organic whole within which individuals have assigned places; liberals as a collection of individuals each striving for personal goals. Thus true conservatives should be concerned with the collective moral fabric as well as the permanence of a dominant class. Logically, liberals would be less concerned with social and moral issues except where society infringes on individual rights.

Corporatism

Corporatism shares with conservatism the belief in a natural hierarchy of human beings, the importance of planning the economy, and the positive evaluation of social classes. It goes beyond conservatism in arguing that economic units—corporations—should make the decisions about the conduct of economic life. Democratic procedures typical of liberal societies are viewed as unacceptable, because they allow uninformed and unpropertied individuals and groups to choose leaders and policies and thus inhibit social progress.

This position is associated with Italy under Mussolini, and has not had much of a history in Canada though some Canadians flirted with it during the 1930s. At the present time, some Canadians are again flirting with it, and there are curious alliances between some of its advocates and libertarians.

Fascism

Fascism is an extreme form of corporatism, going beyond it in accepting the necessity for force in controlling dissidents. We usually associate it with Nazi Germany in the 1930s and 1940s, but there was a fascist party in Canada during the 1930s, and a very small group of followers have persisted throughout this century.

Dominant Ideology

If we identify the dominant ideology as the values and beliefs held in common by a majority, we would include the liberal, social democratic, and conservative positions as falling within its compass. Although they differ in the degree to which they emphasize individualism and egalitarianism, they share a number of assumptions. To begin with, proponents of these positions assume the legitimacy of private property rights, but at the same time recognize legitimate constraints on these. They accept (with varying degrees of approval) the economic drive for profits, but again, place limits on its capacity to drive the entire social system. They accept differential rewards for work associated with numerous social factors (education, skills, talent, etc.), but reject differences associated with gender, ethnicity, religion, or other "non-economic" attributes of individuals. Although both the conservative and social democratic positions include acknowledgement of the reality of class divisions in capitalist society, and liberalism does not, all three tend to explain social events in terms of individuals or non-class groups (e.g., men and women, ethnic groups, particular interest groups) more than in terms of classes. All positions involve notions of social progress toward a "better" society to be achieved through gradual evolution.

Political parties espousing these points of view make many more distinctions between the positions. It is in their interests to do so, of course, since they have to make their party appear to be the unique champion of individual rights or equal opportunity or whatever.

All societies arrive, whether through conscious political activity or tacit agreements and traditional activities, at some position between individualism and collectivism, egalitarianism and elitism. There is another set of values which cross-cuts these, providing a third dimension to social organization. It is attitudes toward nature.

Societies dependent on hunting and gathering, and some societies dependent on cultivation of foods, have developed understandings of people as components of nature on the same level with other animate beings. Most such societies also hold the view that there are unseen spirits guiding and judging their activities. Within these perceptions, animals and land are highly valued, and destruction of either is unacceptable behaviour. Thus the hunter must apologise to the beast he has killed, explaining his need for food and his sincere appreciation for the sacrifice made by the animal.

By contrast, the industrial society treats animals and humans as qualitatively different entities, with humans having the right to kill and conquer all other living things. Land is but a space where human activity takes place: it has no spiritual quality.

Within the past decade, new social movements have arisen within industrial societies opposed to the destruction of our environment. Some of these have taken on political aspects, organizing as political parties or as pressure groups. The anti-nuclear movement, the Green Party, and numerous groups devoted to the saving of particular territories are among these. To date, these groups have not developed consistent positions on individualism-collectivism, egalitarianism-elitism. They are, in a sense, outside the mainstream of public discourse, and adherents to environmentalist ideologies could, conceivably, place themselves anywhere within the other political spectrums.

Similarly, religious movements sometimes exist outside the main discourse of industrial society. While the major religions in Canada—Christian Catholicism and Protestantism and Judaism—have generally adopted and supported the dominant ideology, smaller and often sectarian groups have challenged these views. Some support highly individualistic positions (salvationist religions), others more collectivist positions (cultural renewal religions).

The industrial society is not a static social organization. The processes set in motion by the development of urban populations and competitive capitalism destroyed the feudal aristocracy and the peasantry. They created new forms of government. They destroyed societies and created new ones in far-off colonies. Change occurred at many levels simultaneously: at the level of the family unit, at the level of education. The liberal ideology explains these changes as cumulative growth. Society is always progressing, always adjusting to new conditions. Its growth is limitless, its perfection is a viable goal. The analogy is to a wheel turning over new territory and adding always to its conquest of distance.

Marx posited quite a different kind of change—cumulative, still, but fraught with internal contradictions. The growth in competitive capitalism would give rise to monopoly capitalism. The growth of wealth at the top would create the growth of poverty at the bottom. The more successful the capitalists were in developing technology and organizing the work-force for their own ends, the faster they brought about their own demise by an organized, efficient proletariat. The wheel in this analogy spins ever faster only to break down from over-use, and its riders are obliged to make a new wheel out of the parts. Marx envisioned the final stages in these words:

> One capitalist always kills many. Hand in hand with this centralization, or this expropriation of many capitalists by few, develop, on an ever-extending scale, the cooperative form of the labour process, the conscious technical application of science, the methodical cultivation of the soil, the transformation of the instruments of labour into instruments of labour only usable in common, the economizing of all means of production by their use as the means of production of combined, socialized labour, the entanglement of all peoples in the net of the world market, and with this, the international character of the capitalistic regime. Along with the constantly diminishing number of the magnates of capital, who usurp and monopolise all advantages of this process of transformation, grows the mass of misery, oppression, slavery, degradation, exploitation; but with this too grows the revolt of the working-class, a class always increasing in numbers, and disciplined, united, organized by the very mechanism of the process of capitalist production itself.[1]

Whether one takes the progressional view of history or the dialectic view, one is struck by the observation that cumulative growth in any respect of social organization eventually becomes destructive of that organization. Whether we eventually arrive in a different town by riding the wheel from one place to another, or whether the journey itself transforms the travellers, the fact is that the industrial society of the 1980s is not the industrial society of the 1920s or the 1880s. It is qualitatively a different society. The technology has changed dramatically. The social organization has changed. The population balance has changed. The relations between nation states have changed. What has noticeably failed to change is the ideology.

The ideologies at the popular level are very much the same as they were in these other times. Speeches to the Chamber of Commerce reflect the same abiding faith in progress, material prosperity, and general affluence; the same evaluation of private property, individualism, and achievement; the same belief in the existence of equality and opportunity. The slogans of the Left are remarkably similar to those uttered in the trade union struggles of the turn of the century. There is the same belief in massive exploitation by a ruling class, the same faith in the nobility of labour, the same conviction that pervasive equality is both yet to come and highly desirable.

In Canada, for example, feudalistic values remained into the early twentieth century. While these were tinged by the values of liberalism as it was expressed in the United States and Britain, liberalism in its classic form did not emerge as a dominant ideology until very late in history by comparison with these other countries. Nearly a century after the American War of Independence had spawned the notion that individuals should pursue happiness and that this was a legitimate basis for social organization, as long again after the French Revolution had bannered the words "liberty, equality, fraternity," Canada continued to be ruled by a landed aristocracy which gained its wealth through the fur trade, export-import businesses, and banking. Its values were not those of industrial capitalists. It was not engaged in competitive enterprise, and was not generating new wealth out of the production of goods for a market. At the other end of the social scale, the larger part of the population was engaged in farming rather than manufacturing, and Canada was largely a rural country before World War I; indeed, it remained predominantly rural until the 1930s. The slow development of industry and of an industrial urban labour force retarded the development of liberalism as an ideology.

Conservativism, then, has not been absent in Canada, but in the past half-century it has not been a dominant ideology either.

Liberalism and socialism can interpret one kind of society, one form of industrial organization. This is the society in transition within the political framework of nation states. Neither is suited to providing a popular interpretation or appropriate set of values for maintenance of a multi-national or non-national capitalism in which wage work is not available to many people, surplus is not created out of labour, communications technology becomes more central to political control, and corporations are the chief social as well as economic organizations. Those of us who continue to live in the "old world" like the peasant of the feudal period or the colonials of an imperial empire, are unable to envision or make sense of the developments around us which lead in such a direction. We attempt to interpret them through the ideological perspectives of a society already in decline. Subtly, scarcely intruding on our consciousness, a new set of perceptions and beliefs and their appropriate justifying values will develop around the new technologies and within the corporate empires. Some of this will be transmitted to the generations now living out what may well be the last state of national states and a social organization which divides the political, economic, and religious realms. These transmissions are phrased clumsily, to fit existing belief systems. Thus we have insights on what might be called "liberal corporatism" and we are puzzled by where the Soviet form of corporatism fits in to our theories of history. But if the past is an indication of the future, it will not be the case that liberalism as an ideology imperceptibly becomes corporatism; nor that socialism becomes totalitarianism, bur rather that both are superseded by new ideologies emanating from a new society that has already grown within the old and destroyed its foundations.

Endnotes

1.   Karl Marx, *Capital* (1867), translated by Samuel Moore and Edward Aveling (New York International Publishers, 1967), Vol. 1, pp. 762-763.

Medical Aggression

C.D. Naylor

Naylor's article challenges both the authority of medicine and our trust in it through an examination of medical intervention that is actually not in the patient's best interests. In so doing the author demonstrates how unnecessary intervention results, not from some flaw, but from the medical system working exactly as it was set up and intended to work.

There can no longer be much doubt that modern medicine is out of control. For a decade, well-documented anti-doctor books have been dotting the newsstands and bookstores of Canada, the United States and Europe. While these accounts have show the toll of medicine, historical epidemiology has cast considerable light on medicine's role through the centuries in decreasing mortality rates. The historical record is clear: better housing, better nutrition and a more equitable income distribution have been the key factors in reducing death rates—*not* medical heroics. Nor, for that matter, are iatrogenic deaths a purely modern phenomenon arising from medical technology gone wild. A glance at medical history reveals that the profession has been doing as much harm as good for hundreds of years. In fact, it was during the nineteenth century, a period of unprecedented medical mayhem, that the profession began its climb to the top of the wages and incomes pyramid in North America and Europe by gaining control of the medical services marketplace. But, to paraphrase Oscar Wilde, excess and success go hand-in-hand in a market society. And from my point of view, it is medical excess—an aggressive approach to the patient based on an interventionist ethic—that has made medicine dangerous, even as it has allowed doctors to increase their earnings.

If we define medical aggression as *an intervention by a physician or surgeon that is not in the patient's best interest*, three main questions arise. First, granted that there is a massive and growing literature on American medical aggression, what evidence is there that Canadian doctors are playing the same game as their colleagues south of the forty-ninth parallel? Second, what are the causes of the interventionist ethic? Greed is part of the problem but many other factors must be taken into account. And third, what—if anything—can be done about the ongoing problem of iatrogenesis?

At the outset, we should abandon any idealistic notions of Canadian doctors as resistant to the malaise which afflicts American medicine. Many of our current crop of medical educators took segments of their advanced training at American teaching hospitals, and this will be even more common in the next generation as Canadian medical schools insist that their staff be super-specialists or, as Ortega Y. Gasset described them, "learned ignoramuses." Canadian medical students are weaned on the *New England Journal of Medicine* and other American publications. In short, the two brands of medicine are indistinguishable. Hence whatever complaints can be made against the American head office are likely to apply equally to the Canadian branch plant.

But before drawing on evidence of abuses in the American medical marketplace, nationalism dictates that we examine our own backyard. Here, therefore, are some examples of medical aggression at work in Canada.

Tonsillectomy is an operation of very dubious merit. Tonsils atrophy in adolescence and adult tonsillitis is quite rare. Although the death rate from tonsillectomy is low, inadequate anaesthetic techniques and sloppy surgery once made it a more dangerous operation. But any surgery at any time has its risks. With this in mind, tonsillectomy rates prove interesting if disturbing. Per ten thousand children under the age of 15, the operation rate in Uppsala, Sweden, was 17. In Liverpool, England, it was 26 and in the New England States—70. British Columbia, however, had a tonsillectomy rate of 107 while Ontario's rate was 200.[1] I can assure the reader that Canadian children are not suffering from raging and recurrent epidemics of tonsillitis unheard of in Europe, nor are the complications sometimes attributed to recurrent tonsillitis more prevalent in Sweden. What then are the criteria used to justify this excessive scalpel-wielding?

A little-publicized experiment carried out at a New York free clinic in 1934 sheds some light on that question. In a random fashion, 1000 children were selected. A substantial proportion had already undergone tonsillectomy and were set aside. Those remaining were presented for examination to a group of respected doctors who picked a little less than half of them for tonsillectomy. The designated group was set aside and the remaining group presented at the clinic again. Once more, just under half were chosen for operation. And to prove conclusively that the physicians were arbitrarily choosing about half of all children for surgery on a near-random basis, the experimenters produced the now much reduced group for screening again, with exactly the same results.[2] That was medical science in a *free* clinic. What happened when financial incentives were added is anybody's guess. However the lesson is clear: the scientific status of tonsillectomy as a legitimately helpful and worthwhile operation has been in doubt for decades. Canadian doctors, however, continue to snatch tonsils at rates unheard of in other nations.

There are other examples of knife-happy behaviour by Canadian doctors. In 1974, Dr. F. Dyck found that about 40 percent of hysterectomies carried out in Saskatchewan were unjustified on medical grounds.[3] Dyck's report was prepared for the Saskatchewan College of Physicians and Surgeons and is therefore likely to err, if at all, on the side of underestimation.

Gall bladder removal (cholecystectomy) is another area of abuse. Canadian cholecystectomy rates are five times as high as those in the United Kingdom.[4] Differences in diet and variations in gall stone formation rates between ethnic groups are nowhere near large enough to explain the difference. Furthermore, although Canadian medical students may be taught that a gall stone—even if asymptomatic—should be considered for removal because it increases the risk of subsequently developing cancer of the gall bladder, there is no significant difference in gall bladder cancer incidence between the United Kingdom and Canada. Again, we must look beyond science and safety for an explanation of these surgical habits.

What of radiology? At a meeting of the Canadian Association of Radiologists in the early '70s, it was suggested that X-rays were taken 30 percent more often than they needed to be.[5] If my observations in Toronto teaching hospitals are any indicator, this figure is conservative to say the least. Yet X-rays have been linked to a vast array of common and not-so-common diseases. Thyroid tumours, leukaemia, and other forms of cancer are simply the well recognized tip of the radiation iceberg. X-rays have also been implicated in the acceleration of cell aging: diabetes, heart disease, strokes and high blood pressure may therefore all be associated.[6]

Drug prescribing patterns are—or should be—an embarrassment to the profession. Something like one third of all visits to family physicians in Canada have to do with upper respiratory infections of various kinds—colds, sore throats and so forth. Only an infinitesimal fraction of these conditions are caused by bacteria, the majority being due to viruses for which antibiotics do not constitute effective treatment. Still, penicillin and tetracycline compounds are shovelled out by doctors in massive amounts for these ailments. The result: allergic reactions which may lead to hospitalization and are occasionally fatal, bacterial resistance which makes antibiotics less effective when really needed, and wasted money.

Nor do abuses end there. Minor tranquilizers are handed out freely—especially to women with any complaint that smacks in the least of psychosomatic or psychiatric etiology. High blood fat is another racket, one that allows doctors to cash in on the widespread fear of heart attacks. The diagnosis of high blood fat or hyperlipemia is often made on the basis of a single laboratory test, and the patient is consigned to lifetime medication and medical supervision on these dubious grounds. Furthermore, the evidence linking the most common types of hyperlipemia to hardening of the arteries is not all that strong, and the standard lab test does not detect the specific patterns of elevated fat in the blood that represent a risk for heart disease. Finally, the array of drugs used in hyperlipemia is of questionable efficacy. Simply put, it is not clear that the risks from their use can be justified when the benefits are as yet unproven. Nevertheless, these drugs are very commonly prescribed in Canada.

The overall estimates for the number of patients in hospital at any one time because of adverse drug reactions vary, but the figures fall mainly around the

4 to 5 percent mark. And thousands of Canadians beside those actually requiring hospitalization can look forward to suffering from some of the constellation of side effects that all drugs have. Nor, in this discussion, have I paid any attention to cancer chemotherapy, another area for dangerous heroics. Even though substances such as Laetrile and Essiac may be quack nostrums, there is little to recommend many of the chemicals being shoved into cancer victims across Canada. In many instances, these interventions are justified because they bring an extra few weeks or months of survival. The patient meanwhile lives with false hope, nauseated by drugs which may also cause hair to fall out, or the blood count to fall with the result that he is confined to hospital away from his family. Death with dignity has no meaning to the oncologists. For them, cancer—and death with it—is some enemy to be overcome. Hence success is measured exclusively in mean survival rates, and human notions of life quality are debased into statistical games predicated on life quantity alone.

Earlier, it was suggested that medical aggression was not a new phenomenon. Certainly bleeding, purging, and dosing with poisons such as strychnine and mercury remained commonplace throughout the eighteenth and nineteenth centuries. Doctors opened the patient's veins and bowels with the same avidity they showed in emptying his billfold. Partly in response to this mania for heroic purges and poisons in the medical mainstream, other healing schools sprang up or—if they already existed—gained in strength: homeopathy, osteopathy, chiropractic, herbalism, and eclecticism were among the "irregular" factions. There were then, and continue to be now, elements of charlatanry in these healing cadres; but the same is true of "regular" medicine. Particularly in the last century, these groups were far safer and less elitist in their attitudes than their allopathic or mainstream rivals who struggled so mightily to bar them from the medical services marketplace. Furthermore, females were treated on a more nearly equal footing by the "irregulars," and women seeking medical training were more likely to find their way into an alternative healing sect. Hence links can be made between regular medicine's rise to power, its male domination and its therapeutic aggressivity.

To underscore medicine's history of dangerous interventions, a brief backward look is indicated.

In the 1950s, enlargement of the thymus gland was blamed for infant crib deaths, and radiation treatment was given to babies whose gland appeared on screening to be outside the "normal" range of glandular size. That correlation has since been shown to be entirely false and a considerable percentage of the irradiated babies grew up to develop cancer of the thyroid.

In the 1920s, in the wake of the bacteriological revolution, medicine had fallen into bizarre prescribing patterns, with all manner of complex, expensive and dubiously effective remedies being suggested by doctors in their new "scientific" furore. A prominent Quebec physician, alarmed by this development, included this warning in a pamphlet on practical problems facing the profession: "Pourquoi avoir tant oublie la Natura medicatrix! L'expectation est souvent un act de foi scientifique et raisonne dans une evolution favorable du mal." But the real reason to avoid unnecessary drugs had nothing to do with the patient's well-being: "Le client ne peut solder le cout d'une ordonnance dispendieuse, et l'honoraire du medecin reste impaye."[7]

In the 1880s, Sir William Osler began in earnest his long battle to reform medical diagnostics and therapeutics. He demonstrated, for example, that all the extant remedies for pneumonia were useless, and became the advocate of an outlook sometimes referred to as "therapeutic nihilism": unless a treatment could be proven in clear-cut fashion to have a positive effect on the course of disease, no treatment, or symptomatic relief only, should be undertaken. Some prescriptions in Osler's time had as many as 43 different ingredients, and many of the remedies in common use have since been recognized as exceedingly dangerous.

In 1847, Dr. Ignaz Semmelweis was disgraced and ostracized by his Vienna colleagues for daring to suggest that they were killing maternity patients by infecting them with unwashed hands carrying germs taken from the dissecting room. Women cared for by midwives survived; women cared for by doctors and medical students were contracting fatal puerperal fever and dying. Semmelweis contended that simple hand-washing would rectify the problem and supported his case with mortality figures. The good doctors ignored his advice, women went on dying, and Semmelweis ended up in a lunatic asylum.

Shift back to Canada for a final example: in 1785, Dr. James Bowman was employed by then Governor-General Hamilton, to visit the region of la Baie St. Paul where a disease resembling syphilis was endemic. Bowman was to try to control the spread of the infection. Not only was Bowman later found to have defrauded the government by claiming to have seen ridiculous numbers of patients in impossibly short periods of time, but he also was merrily dosing the habitants with highly toxic levels of mercury. Symptoms of syphilis in its end-stage and signs of mercury poisoning are very similar, and we will never know how many Canadians were poisoned by Bowman and others like him.[8] Judging however from the doses used, the numbers would be considerable.

One could go on in this vein indefinitely, but the thrust of my argument should be clear. Despite an appalling historical record of dangerous and foolhardy practices, medicine appears bent on learning nothing from the past. Indeed, Canadian medical historiography has been tailor-made to support the mythology of heroism on which professional egos thrive. The profession, still riding the crest of the technological boom of the 1950s, still dazzled by transplant techniques, chemotherapeutic interventions of all kinds, and the rash of medical cybernetic devices is, as usual, out of touch with science, safety and social reality. But the more powerful medical technology becomes, the greater the dangers medical aggression will pose. As Bertrand Russell said: "One of the troubles of our age is that habits of thought cannot change as quickly as techniques, with the result that as skill increases, wisdom fades."

We now come to the second main area to be explored: Why have these practices persisted? Greed is part of the explanation. Canadian physicians and surgeons are paid on a fee-for-service basis that encourages interventions: the more they do to the patient, the more they are paid. Hence it is no surprise to find that surgeons in a salaried system operate less than their counterparts on fee-for-service payment schemes. Certainly this would help explain why Canadians are so much more likely than Europeans to leave a gallbladder or a pair of tonsils in the operating room.

The financial benefits from knee-jerk prescription drugs are less obvious. If a physician minimizes the amount of time spent with each patient by doling out prescription panaceas, the patient turnover can be increased with a corresponding increase in profits. But in many cases, the physician prescribes simply to pretend omnipotence. Just as the predictions of the Zande oracle were magical in that they could not be falsified, so also are the prescriptions of the modern medicine man magical in that they are often written where the physician is unwilling to admit to the patient that his drugs are useless. If the oracle predicts correctly, credit accrues to him and his magic. Similarly, if the patient gets better, credit accrues to the doctor and his "magic" when in fact the drug may have had nothing whatsoever to do with the outcome of the illness and simply imposed an unnecessary risk of side effects. When, however, the oracle's prediction is inaccurate, he may blame the community for breaking a taboo; or he may claim either that the rites of divination were performed incorrectly or that they were interpreted wrongly. So, too, with the physician: if the patient does not get well, it may be because he did not "comply" properly with the treatment plan; or it may be that there was a diagnostic error. Blame is spread between magic and magician, among medicine, patient and physician—*but the overall system remains inviolable.*

The prescription pad also hides the fundamental inability of many doctors to communicate with their patients. Since the discovery of antibiotics, there has been a "magic bullet" philosophy in medicine that focuses on disease in abstraction from individuals. The very term, "patient," has a connotation of passivity; and the impression emerges of the doctor doing battle against disease in the patient's body while this latter unfortunate watches and applauds his physician's heroic struggle. The recent re-emphasis on holistic—or "holistic"—healing methods has begun to smack of faddish and profitable quackery, but nevertheless points up the ongoing failure of the medical mainstream to temper a mechanistic approach that ignores the interactions among illnesses, individuals and environments.

Social and socialization factors exacerbate the failure of communication that goes hand-in-glove with the interventionist ethic. Medical students are culled from the middle class. They spend a minimum of five or six years leaning the medical jargon from a host of scientists and specialists before they proceed into practice. They are taught to take histories from patients on a rigid and formulaic basis. They memorize the steps to be taken in any given circumstance and spew them back to their mentors on ward rounds and in oral examinations. They take written tests of multiple-choice format which are hardly conducive to fostering a mentality which grasps the nuances of some scientific dispute or the subtleties of a social situation. And at the end of this process, it is a miracle if the fledgling physician can think, let alone think independently or communicate with a patient—especially one with class origins different from his own.

The dogmatic and interventionist approach is especially highlighted in the university teaching hospitals where "academic interest" and "completeness" justify a plethora of unnecessary, painful and dehumanizing tests and procedures. Nor are the clinical instructors who inculcate their young charges with this mindset necessarily a collection of ogres. In the teaching hospital where I took a year of training in internal medicine, one of the pleasantest staff physicians had a near-fetish for penetrating the body from either end with an awesome array of rigid and flexible viewing devices. One day, when he proposed a sigmoidoscopic examination on an 80-year-old woman with an inflamed bowel for the third time in a week, I questioned his reasons. It rapidly emerged that there was no justification save a child-like curiosity on the clinician's part. An elderly woman was to be put through a painful and humiliating experience to satisfy his jejune whim for amusement.

Medical aggression often arises out of such conflicts of allegiance as the foregoing where the physician's interests are put ahead of the patient's. Doctors may want to treat or test a patient to complete a series of cases for a research paper. Worse yet, a given procedure may be carried out simply to give the resident physicians and surgeons who are training in a specialty the opportunity to perform the required allotment of sigmoidoscopies, colonoscopies, liver biopsies, cardiac catheterizations, laparotomies and so forth. The patient in this setting is not a person: he or she is a research subject, a teaching tool, a case of this or that to be poked and prodded in the name of medical science and medical education. He or she is shuffled from one specialist to another, as each team of experts reifies its narrow realm of expertise. Those who complain about the pernicious aspects of teaching hospital practice are ignored. In fact, complaints about the specialist-to-specialist hand-off, so often heard today, have been conspicuous in Canada since the first world war.[9] Caught up in "the self-propelling will to technology,"[10] the doctors refused to listen then, and refuse to listen now.

Those on the receiving end of medical aggression have seldom protested, at least not until recently. Thus, without playing the tired old game of "Blame the Victim," one might say that a *folie à deux* has existed with doctor and patient doing a dangerous dance together. But the point is that the patient, not the doctor, is the one who stands to lose the most; the doctor, if worst comes to worst, has to face a discipline committee composed of colleagues who are likely to be sympathetic to his plight. As in any relationship between a client and a consulting expert, the patient tends to fall into dependence upon his doctor. Maverick psychiatrist and social philosopher Thomas Szasz sums this situation up neatly:

> Because in the case of illness, the client fears for his health and for his life, it is especially dramatic and troublesome in medicine. In general, the more dependent a person is on another, the greater will be his need to aggrandize his helper, and the more he aggrandizes his helper, the more dependent he will be on him. The result is that the weak person easily becomes doubly endangered: first by his weakness and, second, by his dependence on a protector who may choose to harm him.[11]

If client-dependency fosters susceptibility to medical aggression, then we must consider other factors which promote the dependent relationship. For in medicine, certain external forces induce the patient to place his trust in a physician. Prescriptions, for example, may serve a useful function in preventing indiscriminate and dangerous self-treatment; but by restricting access to drugs, they close off part of the medical market and give licensed practitioners a monopoly in this realm of therapeutics. The patient is therefore led to accept his doctor's opinion in drug-related matters without question. And licensing itself, ostensibly brought in to raise standards of practice and protect the public, gave doctors at the same time a state-legitimized monopoly of competence. The monopoly of competence, held by a small elite of licensed physicians, magnified the gradient of expertise between expert-doctor and client-patient, thereby furthering the possibilities for profitable professional paternalism. But the belief that doctor, like father, knows best was—as we have seen—somewhat naive.

Here, in essence, is one of the paradoxes or "inherent contradictions" of a market society. In a "free market" for medical services, a certain amount of self-sufficiency went together with a cynical attitude towards the professional healers. But two problems arose: first, the healers banded together in collectives designed to corner the market, thereby undermining "free trade," and secondly, governments intervened in the market for twin motives—not only was it disturbing on humanitarian grounds to think of the sick being exploited by quacks and charlatans, but also there was the waste of "human resources" to be considered. hence the market was closed off by a congruence of professional and political interests.

Client dependency was inevitable once the doctors under state aegis became the ultimate authorities on all matters medical. As for various forms of medical aggression, in a monopoly situation, the profession had control over the definition of illness and its proper treatment. Therefore aggression could be re-defined into accepted practice. If one doctor poisoned his patients, it was malpractice; if all doctors poisoned their patients, it was textbook medicine. So it was that if enough doctors radiated the thymus gland, it was by-the-way that thyroid cancer developed in their patients years later. The professional—read *ideological*—consensus saved the day.

Lastly we come to the impact of Medicare. State-sponsored health insurance was designed to ensure that no one who needed medical care was denied it for want of funds. It offered protection from the financial burden of medical care but not from the dangers of unwarranted investigation and treatment. Indeed, Canadian Medicare, by maintaining the fee-for-service structure, fuelled the interventionist ethic. If the patient could afford it, the doctor would bill him more than the fee agreed upon between the medical association and the provincial government. And if the patient was unable to pay, the doctor was still guaranteed his minimum tariff. Either way, the combination of fee-for-service and a government-supported platform for payment proved a potent reinforcer for the philosophy of aggressive medical investigation and treatment.

That philosophy is perfectly embodied in the old surgeons' maxim: "When in doubt, cut it out"; or in the oft declaimed medical school aphorism that most errors in medicine are errors of omission, not commission. All in all, the cards are stacked for action, for doing something *to* the patient if not *for* the patient. The problem now is how to reshuffle the deck.

Global schemes for reform of the medical profession abound; the most ambitious of these see medical reform as merely part of a general reordering of society. At one pole, libertarians have advocated removal of licensing and prescriptions because these are barriers to greater freedom and responsibility on the part of the health services consumer. They also argue that health insurance sponsored by the state is regrettable: those who need financial assistance to afford health care would be better off receiving a lump sum and using the medical market as they saw fit. But while this stance of nineteenth-century liberalism has its appeal, it goes hand-in-hand with nineteenth-century economics and its latter-day reincarnation in Friedmanite cretinism. We are all to be free consumers in the marketplace jungle—free to exploit and free to be exploited. Particularly in the health field, the libertarian philosophy seems an unwholesome atavism. And an attitude of aggressive consumerism in a reopened medical services market is, first, not likely to be to everyone's taste or within their emotional capabilities in the face of serious illness, and second, in and of itself only a partial protection against medical aggression which would become more rapacious than ever before.

At the other pole is the Marxist-Fabian solution. The terms of social reconstruction obviously vary depending upon whether the ideology is avowedly communist or democratic socialist, and a certain amount of violence is done both camps by discussing them together. However, in the health field, these ideologies have basic features in common: the current curative fixation of medicine is seen as neither efficient nor genuinely compassionate and caring. Preventive services should be emphasized, particularly since under conditions of greater state control over industry, better nutrition and less pollution might be possible with a concomitant decrease in many of the commonest diseases. An improved workplace would also decrease stress and alienation, and the burden of psychosomatic diseases would therefore fall off. "De-professionalised" paramedics would be substituted for physicians in many instances and the power of the medical profession diffused. Ideally, the bourgeois entrepreneurialism of the professional would be lost as the classless or more nearly classless society spelled an end to such forms of "false consciousness."

There can be little doubt that most of the causes of medical aggression would be rooted out by the socialist state apparatus. There can also be little doubt that anyone who bates his breath in anticipation of the Canadian revolution is ignoring our centrist politics to the detriment of his oxygen supply. Accordingly, pragmatism dictates that we stay within the current social democratic tradition in seeking ways to curtail medical aggression.

A first and vitally important step would be removal of the fee-for-service payment mode. As George Bernard Shaw observed in his 1911 Preface to *The Doctor's Dilemma*, "That any sane nation, having observed that you could provide for the supply of bread by giving bakers a pecuniary interest in baking for you, should go on to give a surgeon a pecuniary interest in cutting off your leg is enough to make one despair of political humanity." Fee-for-service makes no real allowance for experience and expertise, and yet it is the old guard of the CMA—precisely those who might be rewarded by a salaried scheme—who have clung to fee-for-service with such tenacity. Clearly this form of remuneration has become a symbol of an entrepreneurial form of medical practice in which the practitioner is able to construe himself a small businessman, and the entrepreneurial mentality goes together with the interventionist ethic.

One sometimes hears that physicians will "work harder" under a fee-for-service set-up. But if the physician is, as the medical ideologues tell us, truly devoted to his patients, then piece-work payment should not be necessary to persuade him to see to their best interests. And if, as I have contended, the physician often puts his own interest ahead of his patient's, then financial incentives to aggressive investigation and treatment are foolhardy. Hysterectomy, tonsillectomy and cholecystectomy figures support the latter viewpoint. Another argument against capitation or salaried payment is the possibility that it might encourage unnecessary referrals and worsen the specialist-to-specialist hand-off. However, referral rates are actually lower in many other nations with a variety of payment schemes than they are in Canada. In fact, R.G. Evans found that between 1957 and 1971, with fee-for-service continually in effect, physicians and surgeons did not work longer hours or see more patients as hospital and medical care insurance schemes became universal: the doctors reorganized their practice patterns so that there was *more* specialist care. An increase in the number of investigative and therapeutic interventions in the hospital sector also was observed.[12]

To sum up, what is clearly needed is a switch to an alternative remuneration format—be it capitation or salary or some combination thereof. When that arrives, we can expect not only better judgment on the part of surgeons in particular, but also a general reordering of the priorities in all areas of medical practice with a concomitant decrease in medical aggression. And although CMA opposition to salaried or capitation schemes has been strong, the increasing number of women in medicine bodes well for the implementation of such plans. Female physicians prefer salaried situations; they also stress face-to-face relationships with patients and down play economic aspects of medical practice in comparison to their male colleagues.[13] Only some 15 percent of Canada's 43,000 doctors are female, but this percentage will be rising in years to come with more than one-third of the classes now in training belonging to the gender with less proclivity for entrepreneurial practice.

Change in the finances of the profession is by no means a complete answer for some of the most aggressive medicine is practiced in teaching hospitals where the staff is salaried. Dr. R.S. Mendelsohn, whose *Confessions of a Medical Heretic* provides an eye-opening indictment of American medicine's excesses, has suggested that a Department of Iatrogenic Disease should be a cornerstone of the new medical school he is seeking to found in Illinois: "In this Department all medical disciplines and specialities will be required to demonstrate how their methods can produce disease and disability. Doctors and professors will be paid to find out how medical care does more harm than good, and how proposed new treatments might prove harmful."[14] Such a department should be established in every Canadian medical school now in operation. It would serve as a valuable balance wheel to the dogmatic interventionism that is so prevalent today. In fact, I would urge that every teaching hospital should have weekly Iatrogenesis Rounds where the daily tragedies attributable to medical aggression could be brought to light on a regular basis. And Death Rounds should not simply be a pathological discussion period: they should be times when the many medical errors of *commission* are illustrated—the first being the death of anyone in hospital away from his or her family.

Other reforms in Canadian medical education might prove helpful. The multiple-choice examinations so commonly used in medical schools effectively condition the student to a mindless and simplistic approach to the patient, who comes to be viewed mechanistically as a biological entity to be experimented with or a pathophysiological problem to be solved. The whole notion of giving out a doctorate for four years of trade school and apprentice work is an academic fraud that debases the other doctoral degrees granted by modern universities. Perhaps awarding students bachelors' degrees in medicine—as is done in the United Kingdom—might deflate the famed medical ego which is so integrally tied to therapeutic paternalism and aggressivity. Note too that certain Canadian medical schools do not offer mandatory courses in ethical and political issues in medicine, with the result that the fledgling physician, who has often studied only sciences in his pre-medical program, has scant appreciation for the human side of his work. Instead, he graduates as a much glorified and exceedingly well-paid technician—a technician moreover with frightening powers and privileges for one so narrowly focused.

It is probably true, however, that no matter what medical reforms are undertaken, the best protection the public has from medical aggression is scepticism and self-sufficiency. Only in the last decade has the press begun to give less prominence in its pages to the stories of heartwarming "medical miracles," and admixed discussion of medicine's drawbacks. But the slow rise of anti-doctor feeling has spurred a new interest in different healing methods. As previously, a cautionary note must be sounded: the holistic practitioner, whatever his claims to altruism, is operating in a market society and is as much a merchant as his mainstream rivals are under the fee-for-service system. On the other hand, organizations such as women's health collectives offer an example of an alternative to the libertarian model: greater freedom and greater responsibility in a cooperative as opposed to individualistic setting. Health collectives, increased public interest in nutrition and stress control, not to mention the growing concern for physical fitness through exercise programs—all of these herald an era in which the body will be rediscovered, enjoyed and treated with less abuse. And it is inconceivable that these developments will not bring about a greater self-sufficiency predicated both on broader dissemination of relevant information and on a desire to participate in discussions concerning the disposition of one's own body. Hence despite the medical profession's reluctance to modify its outlook, the doctor-patient relationship will undergo some striking changes in the next twenty years.

In the meantime, as we watch the ongoing squabbles between the CMA's provincial divisions and their respective governments, and hear threats of medical "unionization" and office closures, some consolation may be found in international experience.

In 1976, when doctors provided only a skeleton emergency service in Bogata, Columbia, the death rate went down 35 percent. During a similar walkout the same year in Los Angeles County, the death rate fell 18 percent. And in Israel, a one month strike by doctors in 1973 dropped the death rate by 50 percent to a lower level than at any time since the previous doctors' strike 20 years before.[15] So that if the CMA curtails its services for political purposes, the resulting decrease in medical aggression is something we might all look forward to eagerly.

Endnotes

1. Gifford-Jones, W: *The Doctor Game*. McClelland and Stewart, Toronto, 1975: p. 36.1.

2. Illich, I: *Medical Nemesis: The Expropriation of Health*. Random House, New York, 1976: p. 93.

3. Cited in Swartz, Donald: "The Politics of Reform," pp. 311-343 in *The Canadian State: Political Economy and Political Power*, (ed. L. Panitch). University of Toronto Press, 1979.

4. Gifford-Jones, op. cit., p. 37.

5. Ibid. p. 60.

6. Mendelsohn, RS: *Confessions of a Medical Heretic*, Warner Books, New York, 1979: p. 27.

7. Gagnier, LA: Droits et Devoirs de la Medecine et des Medecins Canadiens-francais. Imprime au "Devoir," Montreal, 1926: pp. 28-29.

8. Heagerty, JJ: *Four Centuries of Medical History in Canada*. Macmillan, Toronto, 1928: Volume 1, pp. 141-151.

9. Ontario Medical Association: *The Canadian Medical Week* (May 27-June 1, 1918), Hamilton: p. 260.

10. Grant, George: *Technology and Empire*. Anansi, Toronto, 1969: p. 27.

11.   Szasz, TS: *The Theology of Medicine.* Louisiana State University Press, Baton Rouge, 1977: p. 2.

12.   Cited in Swartz, op. cit., cf. pp. 333 and 342.

13.   Gray C: "How will the new wave of women graduates change the medical profession?" *Canadian Medical Assoc. Journal*, Oct. 18, 1980, pp. 798-804.

14.   Mendelsohn, op. cit., p. 290.

15.   Ibid. p. 186.

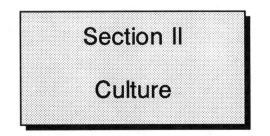

Section II

Culture

Sharing the Continent

Northrop Frye

The underlying premise of this article is that a culture is the consequence of a people's history and an encounter with their geography. Canadians are curiously indifferent to their own history, and, as such, their culture remains continually invisible to them. In this essay Northrop Frye develops the idea of "Canadian identity" and some of the artistic, economic, political and geographic forces which have shaped and continue to shape it. Part of the particular character of Canada is the result of having to "share the continent" with the United States. Canada's continual comparison with, and increasing resemblance to, the U.S. raises the question of what is worth preserving and whether we have the means or collective will to do it.

Practically all Canadians have friends or relatives in the United States, and have spent a good deal of time there. Hence it is generally assumed, in both countries, that English-speaking Canadians, at least, cannot be told apart from Americans. This was a view that I held myself until I spent a couple of years in England as a student. Then I realized that there was a difference, but I found it hard to put the difference into words, and because our civilization is tied up in words, we are apt to think that whatever we can't verbalize is unreal. After that, I began an academic career, and have taught briefly at several American universities. My American students often ask me if I notice much difference between teaching them and teaching Canadians in Toronto. They usually expect the answer to be no, but my answer is yes. Here is, perhaps, something that it is possible to put into words. American students have been conditioned from infancy to think of themselves as citizens of one of the world's great powers. Canadians are conditioned from infancy to think of themselves as citizens of a country of uncertain identity, a confusing past, and a hazardous future. Nine-tenths of the time the responses of my American students are identical with those of Canadian students, but the tenth time I know that I'm in a foreign country and have no idea what the next move is. The sensation must be rather similar to that of a Dane in Germany or a Finn in Russia; or, on a smaller scale, of a Welshman in England. What I should like to try to do here is to define the areas of likeness and of difference a little more precisely. The history and the geography of the two countries have been so different that the cultural response to them has to be different too.

I begin with the geographical differences. Some years ago I first saw Herbert Marcuse's *One Dimensional Man* in a bookshop, and what came into my mind was a quite irrelevant reflection: "I wonder what he'd say if he had to live in a one-dimensional country?" For Canada, through most of its history, has been a strip of territory as narrow as Chile, besides being longer and more broken up. In the United States, the general historical pattern has been based on a north-south axis with a western frontier that moved gradually across mountains and rivers and prairies to the Pacific. In Canada there is a single gigantic east-west thrust down the St. Lawrence, up the Great Lakes, and across the prairies, then through whatever holes a surveyor could find in the Rockies to the west coast. Consider the emotional difference between coming to the United States by ship from England and coming to Canada. The United States presents a fairly symmetrical coastline, with relatively few islands, apart from a minor group in the mouth of the Hudson, and one is reminded of the old remark about Columbus' discovering America: "How could he have missed it?" One enters Canada through the Strait of Belle Isle in the Gulf of St. Lawrence, where five Canadian provinces surround us, with enormous islands and glimpses of a mysterious mainland in the distance, but in the foreground only sea and sky. Then we go down to waterway of the St. Lawrence, which in itself is only the end of a chain of rivers and lakes that starts in the Rockies. The United States confronts the European visitor; Canada surrounds and engulfs him, or did until the coming of the airplane.

In the United States, the frontier has been, imaginatively; an open-ended horizon in the west; in Canada, wherever one is, the frontier is a circumference. Every part of Canada is shut off by its geography, British Columbia from the prairies by the Rockies, the prairies from the Canadas by the immense hinterland of northern Ontario, Quebec from the Maritimes by the upthrust of Maine, the Maritimes from Newfoundland by the sea. A generation ago, Hugh MacLennan took a phrase from Rilke, "two solitudes," as the title for a novel about the mutual isolation of English and French in Montreal. But everywhere in Canada we find solitudes touching other solitudes: every part of Canada has strong separatist feelings, because every part of it is in fact a separation. And behind all these separations lies the silent north, full of vast rivers, lakes and islands that, even yet, very few Canadians have ever seen. The Mississippi, running north to south through the middle of the country, is a symbol of the American frontier and its steady advance into the sunset. The largest river in Canada, the Mackenzie, pouring slightly into the Arctic Ocean at what seems the end of the earth, is a symbol of the terra incognita in Canadian consciousness, or what Rupert Brooke called the "unseizable virginity" of the Canadian landscape. Or, as another British visitor, Wyndham Lewis, remarked: "This monstrous, empty habitat must continue to dominate this nation psychologically, and so culturally."

In looking at two countries as closely related as Canada and the United States, no difference is unique or exclusive: we can point to nothing in Canada that does not have a counterpart, or many counterparts, south of its border. What is different is a matter of emphasis and of degree. In the United States exploration and the building of railways have naturally been of central importance in the imagination of the country. In Canada they have been obsessive. The Confederation of 1867 depended on the building of a railway from one ocean to the other: the political necessity to keep the CPR entirely within Canada meant that the railway had to be built in the face of almost unimaginable natural obstacles. The CPR remained a private corporation, but the great difficulty of establishing communication in Canada meant that Canada became accustomed very soon to nationalized railways, broadcasting corporations, film boards, air lines, and similar efforts of deficit financing. Canadian culture has reflected the same preoccupations. The first wave of exploration was mainly religious and economic, carried on by missionaries and voyageurs and fur-traders, along with the explorers who worked in their interests. The second wave was technological and scientific, an age of railway building and geological surveys. The third wave was cultural, and was spearheaded by painters, from the earliest travelling and military artists of the nineteenth century, Krieghoff, Paul Kane, Thomas Davies, to the Group of Seven and their contemporaries a generation ago.

A strong documentary interest in painting, in films, even in literature, is an obvious and distinctive feature of Canadian culture, and it follows the tradition of the early explorers and missionaries, of the Jesuit Relations and the reports of the Hudson's Bay Company. But it is painting in particular that expresses this interest: painting, the art that began in the deep caves of palaeolithic times, has always had something of an unborn world about it, the projecting on nature of colours in the dark, this last phrase being the title of a Canadian play by James Reaney. Painting is in the front line of imaginative efforts to humanize a non-human world, to fight back, in a sparsely-settled country, against a silent otherness that refuses to assimilate to anything human.

A fascination with landscape is the dominant feature of Canadian painting down to about 1930. Even in later and more abstract painters, Riopelle, for example, it seems to me that there is a strong basis of landscape in the underlying vision. The exploring and pioneering aspect of this is clearest in Tom Thomson, Emily Carr, and the Group of Seven, where we are still very largely in the Canada of the blazed trail and the canoe. The painter keeps shifting our eye from the foreground into the opening in the woods, the bend of the river, the break through the distant hills. The use of expressionist and fauve techniques, with powerful colour-contrasts exploding against one another, suggests a natural world that is unconscious of man and is absorbed in an internecine battle of titans. In historical perspective another element emerges which is much more sinister than simply the unblinking stare of a stark "solemn land," as H.E.H MacDonald called one of his best known paintings. Just as, in a crowded country like Great Britain, the practice of archaeology is a matter of keeping one jump ahead of the bulldozer, so these precious records of nature in her "unspoiled" loveliness of snow and rock and red sumach and

maple seem to be hastily jotted notes of a hunted refugee, set down before
civilization arrives and turns the scene into one more garbage dump.

Literature during this period did not fare so well as painting, because this
long-range perspective in literature is very apt to turn rhetorical, in a rather
bad sense. Thus Charles G.D. Roberts:

> Awake, my country, the hour is great with change!
> Under this gloom which yet obscures the land,
> From ice-blue strait and stern Laurentian range
> To where giant peaks our western bounds command,
> A deep voice stirs...

("An Ode for the Canadian Confederacy").

I quote this because it is typical of what made so much Canadian poetry of a
century ago immature and colonial. The poet is not expressing his feelings but
talking about the feelings he thinks he ought to have, and the clue to his poetic
insincerity is the remote surveying vision that is really focused on nothing but
a map. In other contexts this kind of rhetoric turns didactic, as in Bliss
Carman's rather forced praises of the strenuous life. No poets of this period
gave us the sense of an inward struggling nature that Thomson and Emily Carr
do, except for some brilliant flashes in one writer, Isabella Crawford, who died
unknown at 37. English-Canadian poetry had to wait for E.J. Pratt to convey
the real sense of this centrifugal and linear rhythm in Canadian life. His themes
are those that are most closely connected with this rhythm; the martyrdom of
the Jesuit missionaries, the building of the CPR, the stories of whale hunts and
shipwrecks that bring out the sense of a beleaguered and surrounded garrison.

I have been speaking of one direction in the Canadian imagination; the
direction that followed the east-west Laurentian movement and responded
emotionally to the national motto *a mari usque ad mare*. This was both a
romantic and a conservative movement: romantic because it sought the new
and the unknown, conservative because its original impetus was in Europe. The
Confederation that took shape around a transcontinental railway was part of
a global chain of communication that started in London and linked together all
the pieces of an empire on which the sun never set. But as settlement to the
country advanced, a more longitudinal and north-south consciousness
developed. This perspective focused on the American connection rather than
the British Empire, and tended to see the country as a series of northern spurs
of the United States. When I was growing up in the Maritime Provinces during
the nineteen-twenties, there was a strong political loyalty to Confederation, but
an even stronger sense that Boston was our real capital, and that the Maritimes
formed the periphery of New England, or what was often called "the Boston
states." In the nineteenth century, at least, the Liberal party reflected the north-

south North American outlook, as the Conservative party reflected the Laurentian one.

Once again it is painting that gives us the clearest sense of the contrast. If we turn from the Group of Seven to the Quebec landscape painters, to Maurice Cullen, Suzor-Côté, Clarence Gagnon and the very little of Morrice that was done in Canada, we are in a world of softer and gentler outlines where the sense of being lived in shows through. The painter's eye is more restricted and at the same time more precise. The landscape is receding from a human eye, not absorbed in itself. Quebec is the only part of Canada which has been settled long enough for a sense of imaginative digestion, so to speak, to emerge. When E.J. Pratt spoke of a kind of poetry he disapproved of, a poetry that avoided social issues and cultivated an easy self-indulgence, he described it in the pictorial metaphor of "still life." In his use of this phrase there is, perhaps, something of that odd fear of catching nature's eye that is very characteristic of that stage in Canadian development. It is significant, first, that the best still-life painter in the earlier period, Ozias Leduc, lived and died in Quebec, and, second, that the still-life perspective, where the imagination has completely surrounded the subject, begins to emerge rather later than the Group of Seven, with David Milne, and further west, Lemoine Fitzgerald.

What has been gradually revealed in this development is the fact that cultural movements are different in direction and rhythm from political and economic ones. Politically and economically, the current of history is toward greater unity, and unity in this context includes uniformity. Technology is the most dramatic aspect of this development: one cannot take off in a jet plane and expect a radically different way of life in the place where the plane lands. But culture has something vegetable about it, something that increasingly needs to grow from roots, something that demands a small region and a restricted locale. The fifty states of the Union are not, in themselves, a cultural entity: they are a political and economic entity that provides a social background for a great variety of cultural developments. We speak for convenience of American literature, but its real cultural context usually turns out to be something more like Mississippi or New England or Chicago or an expatriate group in Paris. Even in the much smaller Great Britain we have Thomas Hardy largely confined to "Wessex," Dylan Thomas to South Wales, D.H. Lawrence to the Midlands. Similarly in Canada: as the country has matured, more and more of its local areas have come to life imaginatively.

This fact has given French Canadian writers, in particular, one considerable advantage. The French Canadian poet or novelist knows that he is contributing to the articulateness of a beleaguered language, hence he need have no doubt about his social function or the importance of being a writer in such a situation. He has no competitors closer than European France, and they live in a very different social context. The English Canadian writer has not had this advantage, and the tedium of a permanent identity crisis has afflicted English Canada for a century. Soon after the Second World War, French Canada entered what has been called the quiet revolution, an awareness of belonging both to itself and to the modern world, which shook off most of the isolating features that had been previously restricting its cultural life. I think it was partly a response to the French act of self-definition that made for a sudden and dramatic emergence of English Canadian culture after about 1960. Since then there has been a tremendous cultural explosion, in literature and painting particularly, which has produced a mood that is often called cultural nationalism.

This is a most misleading phrase, and for two reasons. First nationalism suggests something aggressive, like a nineteenth-century jingoist waiting for the next war to start, or a twentieth-century third-world revolutionary. But culture in itself seeks only its own identity, not an enemy: hostility only confuses it. Second, contemporary Canadian culture, being a culture, is not a national development but a series of regional ones, what is happening in British Columbia being very different from what is happening in New Brunswick or Ontario. Even there we find an increasing decentralization: one reason why Montreal has been so lively a cultural centre is that there are a good many Montreals, each one with its own complexities and inner conflicts. Then again, while a certain amount of protection may be needed for Canadian writers and artists, cultural products are export products. If we look at, say, the literature that has come out of Ireland during the last century, we can see that culture, like a grain or wine crop, is produced in a local area but is not necessarily consumed there.

Politically, economically and technologically, the world is uniting; Canada is in the American orbit and will remain so for the foreseeable future. Canadians could not resist that even if they wanted to, and not many of them do want to. Culturally, both nations should run their own show, and the way to run a cultural show is to let a thousand flowers bloom, in Mao's phrase. Things go wrong when cultural developments are hitched on to economic or technological ones. That gives us, on this continent, a sub-culture dominated by advertising and distributed through the mass media. The influence of this in our lives is often spoken of, both inside and outside the United States, as an Americanizing influence. Ten years ago, during the centenary of Confederation, a sour little joke was circulating in Canada to the effect that what had been aimed at in Canada was a combination of British political institutions, American economic buoyancy and French culture, and that what we had, after a century, was French politics, British economic buoyancy, and American culture. However, the growth of an anonymous, mass-produced, mindless sub-culture is American only to the extent that the United States is the world's most highly industrialized society. Its effect on genuine American culture is quite as lethal as its effect everywhere else, and its main features are as Japanese or German or Russian as they are American.

Things go wrong in the opposite direction when economic or political developments are hitched on to cultural ones, as has happened in the Quebec separatist movement. It is a part of M. Levesque's sales pitch to speak of separation as inevitable, and to compare it with the American Revolution. It seems to me a retrograde and counter-historical movement, both in its neocolonial attitude to France and in its arrogant attitude to French Canadians outside Quebec. As for the American analogy, what was of permanent importance there was not the separation from Britain but the principle of *e pluribus unum*: politically and economically, the colonies had to unite, though culturally there was no reason why Massachusetts and Virginia should not be quite different. Separatism in Quebec is an intellectuals' movement, a *trahison des clercs*: it has dominated the communications media for some years, and by-passes economic issues with a simple emotional construct in which Confederation equals bondage and separation freedom. As an intellectuals' movement, even a revolutionary one, it may settle for a purely symbolic separation: if it goes beyond that, whatever is distinctive in the culture of Quebec will be its first casualty.

My reasons for thinking so take me into the second group of conditioning differences from the United States, the historical ones. The pattern of Canadian history has been almost the opposite of the pattern of American history. The United States had a War of Independence against a European power in the eighteenth century, and a civil war on its own soil a century later. Canada had a civil war of European powers on its own soil in the eighteenth century, and a movement of independence against its American partner in the nineteenth. This started with the invasion of 1775 and continued in the war of 1812, which had very little point as a war with Britain, but was in many respects a war of independence for Canada. I discover that Americans, while they know about the bombardment of Washington and the battle of New Orleans, are often hardly aware that this war involved Canada at all, much less that the bombardment of Washington was a reprisal for the burning of what is now Toronto. All through the nineteenth century, up to and beyond Confederation, there continued to be a certain edginess about the aggressive expansion of America, as it came through in Fenian raids and boundary disputes, and Confederation itself completed what the American invasions had begun, the sense that there was an identity on the north side of the border that could be brought into being only by some kind of political unity.

Another historical contrast is even more important. The United States reached its peak of articulateness in the latter part of the eighteenth century, the age when it became a nation, the age of Washington, Adams, Jefferson, and Franklin. The United States is today the oldest country in the world: that is, no other nation has lasted so long with so relatively little social change. The party now in power is the world's oldest political party, and the American flag is one of the world's oldest flags. Canada, by contrast, had no eighteenth century. It started with the expansion of French Canada in the seventeenth century, and started again with the influx of defeated Tories into Ontario and the Maritimes after the Revolution, going directly from Baroque to Romantic expansion, but never achieving the moment of self-definition that the United States achieved.

It would be a great mistake to exaggerate the strength of the British connexion in Canada, even in the nineteenth century. There was a great deal of superficial loyalty, or at least a good many expressions of it, but there was also much resentment, and a feeling that colonials would have been treated with more respect in London if, like Americans, they had represented an independent nation. Some years ago a book appeared in Quebec called *White Niggers of America*, meaning the French Canadians, an expression of strong separatist feelings in Quebec, but the same metaphor had been used over a century earlier by the deeply conservative Haliburton of Nova Scotia, who makes his Sam Slick remark that a colonial and a freed black slave differed in nothing but colour: they had theoretical rights but no power to enforce them.

It would, I think, make for a clearer sense of Canada if we thought of it, not as British North America, but as a country that grew out of a Tory opposition to the Whig victory in the American Revolution, thus forming, in a sense, something complementary to the United States itself. This may sound like a very English-based view of Canadian history, but I am not sure that it is. Not long after the British conquest came the French Revolution with its strongly anti-clerical bias. The clergy remained the ideologically dominant group in Quebec down to a generation ago, and the clergy wanted no part of the French Revolution or anything it stood for. Quebec still flies the pre-revolutionary flag of lilies. Nor, from that clergy's point of view, was the American Revolution really so different from the French one. But apart from the clerical influence, French Canada had excellent and foresighted reasons for accepting a conservative modus vivendi which, from the Quebec Act in the eighteenth century to Confederation in the nineteenth, had as its central idea the uniting of a French and an English community on a basis that guaranteed some cultural integrity for both.

Historically, the Tories stood for the supremacy of the crown and the established church, and for a society closely connected with the land. Conservatives in both Britain and Canada are called Tories, but the real Tories were pre-Conservative: they revolved around a domestic economy and a personal relationship to the working class that was destroyed by the Industrial Revolution. Expressions of Canadian opposition to American ideology, all through the nineteenth century, attack from the left quite as often as from the right. One writer, in 1841, spoke of "the United States, where from the great mixture of races, British feelings and British connexion have given way before a flood of undefinable notions about liberty and equality, mixed with aristocratic wealth, slavery, and bigotry in religion." I quote this not because it is profound but because it is commonplace; and we notice that what the writer dislikes is not only American democracy but American oligarchy, the inequalities of wealth and opportunity. It is not surprising, then, that so many of Canada's intellectuals, both English and French, should be one form or another of Tory radical. One of these, and also one of the ablest commentators on the Canadian scene, George Grant, writes near the end of his *Lament for a Nation*:

> The impossibility of conservatism in our era is the impossibility of Canada. As Canadians we attempted a ridiculous task in trying to build a conservative nation in the age of progress, on a continent we share with the most dynamic nation on earth. The current of modern history was against us.

Yet before we write off Canada as an abortive and quixotic culture that has failed to break through the heavy snow-crust of a technological world, it might be worth asking what there is, in this Tory devotion to crown and church and land, that can be translated into terms of the nineteen-seventies. Human ideas have an extraordinary power of metamorphosis, and many things that are outdated or absurd in their original context may reappear later in a very different aspect. For instance, no church has ever been established in Canada, but there has been a much closer connexion between church and state, especially in education, which has given Canadian culture a distinctive colouring. Again, there may be advantages in having the personal symbol of the Queen instead of the impersonal one of the flag, which Canada did not have until recently, and would hardly miss if it still did not. But I think something rather different is involved here, which I shall illustrate by an example. When I first came to Toronto, in 1929, it was a homogeneous Scotch-Irish town, dominated by the Orange Order, and greatly derided by the rest of Canada for its smugness, its snobbery, and its sterility. The public food in restaurants and hotels was of very indifferent quality, as it is in all right-thinking Anglo-Saxon communities. After the war, Toronto took in immigrants to the extent of nearly a quarter of its population, and large Greek, Italian, Portuguese, Central European, West Indian communities grew up within it. The public food improved dramatically. More important, these communities all seemed to find their own place in the larger community with a minimum of violence and tension, preserving much of their own cultures and yet taking part in the total one. It has always seemed to me that this very relaxed absorption of minorities, where there is no concerted effort at a "melting pot," has something to do with what the Queen symbolizes, the separation of the head of state from the head of government. Because Canada was founded by two peoples, nobody could ever know what a hundred percent Canadian was, and hence the decentralizing rhythm that is so essential to culture had room to expand.

Still more important is the Canadian sense of the close relation of the people to the land. Everywhere we turn in Canadian literature and painting, we are haunted by the natural world, and even the most sophisticated Canadian artists can hardly keep something very primitive and archaic out of their imaginations. This sense is not that of the possession of the land, but precisely the absence of possession, a feeling that here is a nature that man has polluted and imprisoned and violated but has never really lived with.

Canada does not have quite so heavy a burden of guilt toward red and black peoples as the United States, and the French record with the Indians was rather better than the British or Spanish record. Even so there is little to be proud of: in Newfoundland, for instance, a gentle and inoffensive people, the Beothuks, were exterminated as casually as though they were mosquitoes. But still the main focus of guilt in Canada seems to fall on the rape of nature. The deaths of animals seems to have an extraordinary resonance in Canadian literature, as though the screams of all the trapped and tortured creatures who built up the Canadian fur trade were still echoing in our minds. One of the silliest of Tory fetishes, the preserving of game, seems to be taking a very different role in the Canadian imagination.

The seventeenth-century invaders of both countries brought with them the Cartesian ego, the sense of man as a perceiving subject, totally different from everything else in nature by virtue of his consciousness. It was a long time before the philosophers got around to realizing that egocentric consciousness is primarily a consciousness of death, but the poets had always known that: even the nineteenth-century rhetorical poets I spoke of wrote their best poetry in elegiac or nostalgic or other moods that were close to the sense of death. The narrative poets gave us stories of death in log jams, on glaciers, in hunting expeditions where the hunter seems to identify with his victim. This was not of course confined to Canada: one thinks of Whitman, who also wrote his best poetry about death and his worst rhetoric about democracy. But it was so strong in Canada as to give most of its serious literature, especially its poetry, a very sombre cast.

In 1948 a group of Quebec artists, headed by Paul-Emile Borduas, produced a surrealist manifesto called *Refus Global*, which seems to me a most important break-through in Canadian culture, not because of what it said, which was naive and confused enough, but because it was a sign that the old antithesis between a conscious mind and an unconscious nature was breaking down. For Borduas, the human mind contained an It as well as an I or ego, and this It was what he felt needed expression. In more recent painting, in the quasi-realism of Alex Colville and Christopher Pratt, in the ghostly figures of Jean-Paul Lemieux, there is often a feeling of loneliness and emptiness, as though the conscious mind were deliberately draining itself of its contents, and waiting for something else to move in. Meanwhile an interest in Indian and Eskimo art, with all their nature-spirits, has grown into a fascination, and many of our younger poets—Susan Musgrave, John Newlove, Gwendolyn MacEwen—write as though Indians and Eskimos were our direct cultural ancestors whose traditions continue in them and in us. In fiction, there are some curious stories, such as Margaret Atwood's *Surfacing* and Marian Engel's *Bear*, of heroines turning away from their civilized heritage toward an identity with nature. It seems clear that for Canadian culture the old imperialist phrase "going native" has come home to roost. We are no longer an army of occupation, and the natives are ourselves.

The first half of the twentieth century saw a bitter dispute between democratic and Marxist conceptions of the best way to minimize the exploitation of man by man. Nobody seemed to notice that both sides were exploiting nature with equal recklessness. It seems to me that the capitalist-socialist controversy is out of date, and that a detente with an outraged nature is what is important now. Canada is still a place of considerable natural resources, but it is no longer simply a place to be looted, either by Canadians or by non-Canadians. It is of immense importance to the United States itself that there should be other views of the human occupation of this continent, rooted in different ideologies and different historical traditions. And it is of immense importance to the world that a country which used to be at the edge of the earth and is now a kind of global Switzerland, surrounded by all the world's great powers, should have achieved the repatriating of its culture. For this is essentially what has happened in the last twenty years, in all parts of Canada: and what was an inarticulate space on a map is now responding to the world with the tongues and eyes of a matured and disciplined imagination.

Body Ritual Among the Nacirema

Horace Miner

In this article Miner takes a satirical look at the 'Nacirema,' a people whose culture is riddled with magic, and whose everyday lives are based in superstition and the supernatural. Miner subtly sensitizes the reader to his or her own ethnocentricity, and presses the reader to recognize that the primitive and the magical are less a matter of specific practices than the assumptions that we draw upon to interpret those practices.

The anthropologist has become so familiar with the diversity of ways in which different peoples behave in similar situations that he is not apt to be surprised by even the most exotic customs. In fact, if all of the logically possible combinations of behaviour have not been found somewhere in the world, he is apt to suspect that they must be present in some yet undescribed tribe. This point has, in fact, been expressed with respect to clan organization by Murdock (1949: 71). In this light, the magical beliefs and practices of the Nacirema present such unusual aspects that it seems desirable to describe them as an example of the extremes to which human behaviour can go.

Professor Linton first brought the ritual of the Nacirema to the attention of anthropologists twenty years ago (1936: 326), but the culture of this people is still very poorly understood. They are a North American group living in the territory between the Canadian Cree, the Yaqui and Tarahumare of Mexico, and the Carib and Arawak of the Antilles. Little is known of their origin, although tradition states that they came from the east. According to Nacirema mythology, their nation was originated by a culture hero, Notgnihsaw, who is otherwise known for two great feats of strength—the throwing of a piece of wampum across the river Pa-To-Mac and the chopping down of a cherry tree in which the Spirit of Truth resided.

Nacirema culture is characterized by a highly developed market economy which has evolved in a rich natural habitat. While much of the people's time is devoted to economic pursuits, a large part of the fruits of these labours and a considerable portion of the day are spent in ritual activity. The focus of this activity is the human body, the appearance and health of which loom as a dominant concern in the ethos of the people. While such a concern is certainly not unusual, its ceremonial aspects and associated philosophy are unique.

The fundamental belief underlying the whole system appears to be that the human body is ugly and that its natural tendency is to debility and disease. Incarcerated in such a body, man's only hope is to avert these characteristics through the use of the powerful influences of ritual and ceremony. Every household has one or more shrines devoted to this purpose. The more powerful individuals in the society have several shrines in their houses and, in fact, the opulence of a house is often referred to in terms of the number of such ritual centres it possesses. Most houses are of wattle and daub construction, but the shrine rooms of the more wealthy are walled with stone. Poorer families imitate the rich by applying pottery plaques to their shrine walls.

While each family has at least one such shrine, the rituals associated with it are not family ceremonies but are private and secret. The rites are normally only discussed with children, and then only during the period when they are being initiated into these mysteries. I was able, however, to establish sufficient rapport with the natives to examine these shrines and to have the rituals described to me.

The focal point of the shrine is a box or chest which is built into the wall. In this chest are kept the many charms and magical potions without which no native believes he could live. These preparations are secured from a variety of specialized practitioners. The most powerful of these are the medicine men, whose assistance must be rewarded with substantial gifts. However, the medicine men do not provide the curative potions for their clients, but decide what the ingredients should be and then write them down in an ancient and secret language. This writing is understood only by the medicine men and by the herbalists who, for another gift, provide the required charm.

The charm is not disposed of after it has served its purpose, but is placed in the charm-box of the household shrine. As these magical materials are specific for certain ills, and the real or imagined maladies of the people are many, the charm-box is usually full to overflowing. The magical packets are so numerous that people forget what their purposes were and fear to use them again. While the natives are very vague on this point, we can only assume that the idea in retaining all the old magical materials is that their presence in the charm-box, before which the body rituals are conducted, will in some way protect the worshipper.

Beneath the charm-box is a small font. Each day every member of the family, in succession, enters the shrine room, bows his head before the charm-box, mingles different sorts of holy water in the font, and proceeds with a brief rite of ablution. The holy waters are secured from the Water Temple of the community, where the priests conduct elaborate ceremonies to make the liquid ritually pure.

In the hierarchy of magical practitioners, and below the medicine men in prestige, are specialists whose designation is best translated "holy-mouth-men." The Nacirema have an almost pathological horror of and fascination with the mouth, the condition of which is believed to have a supernatural influence on all social relationships. Were it not for the rituals of the mouth, they believe that their teeth would fall out, their gums bleed, their jaws shrink, their friends desert them, and their lovers reject them. They also believe that a strong relationship exists between oral and moral characteristics. For example, there is a ritual ablution of the mouth for children which is supposed to improve their moral fibre.

The daily body ritual performed by everyone includes a mouth-rite. Despite the fact that these people are so punctilious about care of the mouth, this rite involves a practice which strikes the uninitiated stranger as revolting. It was reported to me that the ritual consists of inserting a small bundle of hog hairs into the mouth, along with certain magical powders, and them moving the bundle in a highly formalized series of gestures.

In addition to the private mouth-rite, the people seek out a holy-mouth-man once or twice a year. These practitioners have an impressive set of paraphernalia, consisting of a variety of augers, awls, probes, and prods. The use of these objects in the exorcism of the evils of the mouth involves almost unbelievable ritual torture of the client. The holy-mouth-man opens the client's mouth and, using the above mentioned tools, enlarges any holes which decay may have created in the teeth. Magical materials are put into these holes. If there are no naturally occurring holes in the teeth, large sections of one or more teeth are gouged out so that the supernatural substance can be applied. In the client's view, the purpose of these ministrations is to arrest decay and to draw new friends. The extremely sacred and traditional character of the rite is evident in the fact that the natives return to the holy-mouth-men year after year, despite the fact that their teeth continue to decay.

It is to be hoped that, when a thorough study of the Nacirema is made, there will be careful inquiry into the personality structure of these people. One has but to watch the gleam in the eye of a holy-mouth-man, as he jabs an awl into an exposed nerve, to suspect that a certain amount of sadism is involved. If this can be established, a very interesting pattern emerges, for most of the population shows definite masochistic tendencies. It was to these that Professor Linton referred in discussing a distinctive part of the daily body ritual which is performed only by men. This part of the rite involves scraping and lacerating the surface of the face with a sharp instrument. Special women's rites are performed only four times during each lunar month, but what they lack in frequency is made up in barbarity. As part of this ceremony, women bake their heads in small ovens for about an hour. The theoretically interesting point is that what seems to be a preponderantly masochistic people have developed sadistic specialties.

The medicine men have an imposing temple, or *latipso*, in every community of any size. The more elaborate ceremonies required to treat very sick patients can only be performed at this temple. These ceremonies involve not only the thaumaturge but a permanent group of vestal maidens who move sedately about the temple chambers in distinctive costume and headdress.

The *latipso* ceremonies are so harsh that it is phenomenal that a fair proportion of the really sick natives who enter the temple ever recover. Small children whose indoctrination is still incomplete have been known to resist attempts to take them to the temple because "that is where you go to die." Despite this fact, sick adults are not only willing but eager to undergo the protracted ritual purification, if they can afford to do so. No matter how ill the supplicant or how grave the emergency, the guardians of many temples will not admit a client if he cannot give a rich gift to the custodian. Even after one has gained admission and survived the ceremonies, the guardians will not permit the neophyte to leave until he makes another gift.

The supplicant entering the temple is first stripped of all his or her clothes. In every-day life the Nacirema avoids exposure of his body and its natural functions. Bathing and excretory acts are performed only in the secrecy of the household shrine, where they are ritualized as part of the body-rites. Psychological shock results from the fact that body secrecy is suddenly lost upon entry into the *latipso*. A man, whose own wife has never seen him in an excretory act, suddenly finds himself naked and assisted by a vestal maiden while he performs his natural functions into a sacred vessel. This sort of ceremonial treatment is necessitated by the fact that the excreta are used by a diviner to ascertain the course and nature of the client's sickness. Female clients, on the other hand, find their naked bodies are subjected to the scrutiny, manipulation and prodding of the medicine men.

Few supplicants in the temple are well enough to do anything but lie on their hard beds. The daily ceremonies, like the rites of the holy-mouth-men, involve discomfort and torture. With ritual precision, the vestals awaken their miserable charges each dawn and roll them about on their beds of pain while performing ablutions, in the formal movements of which the maidens are highly trained. At other times they insert magic wands in the supplicant's mouth or force him to eat substances which are supposed to be healing. From time to time the medicine men come to their clients and jab magically treated needles into their flesh. The fact that these temple ceremonies may not cure, and may even kill the neophyte, in no way decreases the people's faith in the medicine men.

There remains one other kind of practitioner, known as a "listener." This witch-doctor has the power to exorcise the devils that lodge in the heads of people who have been bewitched. The Nacirema believe that parents bewitch their own children. Mothers are particularly suspected of putting a curse on children while teaching them the secret body rituals. The counter-magic of the witch-doctor is unusual in its lack of ritual. The patient simply tells the "listener" all his troubles and fears, beginning with the earliest difficulties he can remember. The memory displayed by the Nacirema in these exorcism sessions is truly remarkable. It is not uncommon for the patient to bemoan the rejection he felt upon being weaned as a babe, and a few individuals even see their troubles as going back to the traumatic effects of their own birth.

In conclusion, mention must be made of certain practices which have their base in native aesthetics but which depend upon the pervasive aversion to the natural body and its functions. There are ritual fasts to make fat people thin and ceremonial feasts to make thin people fat. Still other rites are used to make women's breasts larger if they are small, and smaller if they are large. General dissatisfaction with breast shape is symbolized in the fact that the ideal form is virtually outside the range of human variation. A few women afflicted with almost inhuman hypermammary development are so idolized that they make a handsome living simply going from village to village and permitting the natives to stare at them for a fee.

Reference has already been made to the fact that excretory functions are ritualized, routinized, and relegated to secrecy. Natural reproductive functions are similarly distorted. Intercourse is a taboo as a topic and scheduled as an act. Efforts are made to avoid pregnancy by the use of magical materials or by limiting intercourse to certain phases of the moon. Conception is actually very infrequent. When pregnant, women dress so as to hide their condition. Parturition takes place in secret, without friends or relatives to assist, and the majority of women do not nurse their infants.

Our review of the ritual life of the Nacirema has certainly shown them to be a magic-ridden people. It is hard to understand how they have managed to exist so long under the burdens which they have imposed upon themselves. But even such exotic customs as these take on real meaning when they are viewed with the insight provided by Malinowski when he wrote (1948: 70):

> Looking from far and above, from our high places of safety in the developed civilization, it is easy to see all the crudity and irrelevance of magic. But without its power and guidance early man could not have mastered his practical difficulties as he has done, nor could man have advanced to the higher stages of civilization.

References

Linton, Ralph. (1936). *The Study of Man*. New York, D. Appleton-Century Co.
Malinowski, Bronislaw. (1948). *Magic, Science, and Religion*. Glencoe, The Free Press.
Murdock, George P. (1949). *Social Structure*. New York, The Macmillan Co.

The Rise of the New Puritanism

John Allemang

How does one begin to rectify historical injustice or resist the dominant culture? In this article John Allemang outlines some of the newsworthy challenges which have been mounted against the established order. He raises concerns about the intended and unintended consequences of these challenges.

On the first birthday I celebrated in this strange, sanctimonious decade I was given a box of candy. It called itself Rainforest Crunch. It was really nut brittle, and very tasty nut brittle at that. But it was also an inspirational goody cooked up to save us from ourselves. Rainforest Crunch, as its manufacturers earnestly proclaim, is more than a passing pleasure. It uses cashews and Brazil nuts to make an argument for social justice. "Community Products Inc." said a notice on the package "is helping to demonstrate that rainforests are more profitable when preserved for sustainable harvests. The profits from the nuts we buy are used to develop small Brazil nut processing factories that are cooperatively owned and operated by forest peoples, providing them with three to 10 times the normal income from their labour."

Phew! The champagne truffles of the Eighties could never have made such claims. As Rainforest Crunch pried the fillings from my molars, I read that a desire for short-term profits is turning rain forests into wastelands and that, if this destruction isn't halted, all accessible rain forests will be lost by the year 2000. I read on, and gave my sense of guilt free rein. "Start recycling!" it ordered. "Start with this package"—it was made of recycled paper, of course—"Paper, aluminum and tin products often come from the rainforests. Buy more non-packaged items."

This was not a fund-raising letter from Friends of the Earth or the latest warning from David Suzuki. It was nut brittle, and it was lecturing me. Not just lecturing me but telling me to change my life, and change the world. Now.

With candy acting as an agent of social change, the final escape hatch is closed. The Nineties are upon us with a vengeance. Self-important, guilt-tripping, holier-than-thou and unforgiving, this decade is the best revenge on the materialistic spree of the self-centred Eighties.

It's payback time. The puritans whose tsk-tsking went unheard over the last few years are getting ready to exact some penance. As the threats of global warming look more and more ominous, and the recession gives a bad name to the free market, as our elected representatives make a hash of Meech, and Oka softens our ancestral guilt, a new orthodoxy is preparing to take charge. It comes with a sense of urgency and frustration that allows no room for compromise.

Descended from the protest movements and alternative cultures of the Sixties, the new puritanism defines itself in opposition to the status quo and asserts a negativity writ large. Capitalism is bad and leads to the wasteful and destructive exploitation of the planet. Western culture is bad. It oppresses those who aren't straight white males and elevates the ideal of individual liberty. Individual liberty is bad because it leads to people saying what they think and doing as they please. And isn't that what got us into this mess in the first place? "Our future," insist Anita Gordon and David Suzuki in *It's a Matter of Survival,* "lies in group survival and group success, not individual achievement."

No little detail, no part of life, no pleasure, however harmless (and what pleasure really is harmless?) can escape the scrutiny of the new puritans. Feel like a nice glass of Chardonnay? Read the fine print first: "Consumption of alcoholic beverages impairs your ability to drive a car or operate heavy machinery and may cause health problems," says a warning imposed by the neo-temperance movement in California. Want to go for a Sunday drive? Just try not to think about the Greenpeace ad with the picture of the Exxon Valdez skipper and the guilt-ridden caption, "It wasn't his driving that caused the oil spill, it was yours." Think it's okay to stand around and watch the world go by. What decade are you living in? "When women walk down the street," says a poster pasted up in Toronto's Yorkville area, "they are on their way to the store or to work or to visit family and friends or are on a errand. We are not there for your entertainment."

It's enough to make you close the curtains, turn out the lights and gorge on nut brittle. But there is no escape.

And maybe we don't really want to escape. Alcohol abuse, a short-sighted dependency on oil, sexual harassment—no one pretends that these and a thousand other problems don't exist. If the free-spending, self-indulgent Eighties couldn't or wouldn't deal with them, then perhaps it is time for a more radical solution.

When people lose faith in the dreary give-and-take of traditional politics, it is easier for radical proposals to get a hearing. And clearly there is a vacuum waiting to be filled. Polls conducted by Decima Research over the last decade show a growing contempt for Canadian politicians. In the early Eighties, they were described as hard-working and principled by two-thirds of those interviewed. By March 1990, according to data analysed by Allan Gregg and Michael Posner in The Big Picture, 57 percent of Decima's respondents said that politicians were unprincipled, 65 percent said they were incompetent and 81 percent thought they were more interested in making money than helping people.

Principles, competence, helping people. It's nice to think that the new order may be about such things. But the evidence so far for a fundamental shift in values and beliefs is not encouraging. In the name of global survival, the new puritans indulge in relentless moralizing. Preaching tolerance of diversity, they foster intolerance and conformity.

A means to an end, the Sixties radicals would have said. But what kind of paradise, what kind of Eden will be created by this small-minded bullying? Consider the Nineties style of activism displayed by a group called Canadians Against Fur. Just before Christmas, they took to the streets of Toronto and heckled anyone wearing fur. "Productive guilt," CAF founder Tony Smith called these tactics. "Cruelty is everybody's business," he said. "I don't just have a right to speak out against fur. I have an obligation."

The uncompromising tone of moral certainty is clear. Social justice becomes rough justice. An ugly incident in Vancouver last September demonstrated the Nineties' approach to consensus-building. When a 50-year-old Portuguese cafe owner named Joe Antunes complained about women hugging each other in his cafe, his gay and lesbian customers fought right back. They took over the cappuccino bar and held a kiss-in, then moved outside, drove away business, and shouted "We're here, we're queer, we don't want your coffee." A conflict of cultural values? "I don't think bigotry is cultural," said one protester, with conviction. But activists who champion their own differences should not be surprised to discover that there is more than one kind of diversity.

Diversity is a key concept for understanding the zealotry of the Nineties. The happy image it conveys of multicultural harmony is the stuff of government propaganda. What diversity has come to mean is more like: you've kicked us around, now it's our turn to kick you. And given the prevailing climate of white, middle-class guilt, what this comes to mean in turn is: our ancestors kicked you, now it's our turn to kick ourselves. The year 1992 will see a huge outpouring of anger as native peoples, churches and human rights groups line up to denounce the 500th anniversary of Christopher Columbus' arrival in America. The Association of Indian Cultures has given warning in Madrid that it will sabotage the quincentenary. Fidel Castro has cast away his Hispanic heritage and announced that he is now an Indian. In the United States, the National Council of Churches passed a resolution that has nothing good to say about the European contribution to the New World: "For the descendants of the survivors of the subsequent invasion genocide, slavery, 'ecocide,' and exploitation of the wealth of the land, a celebration is not an appropriate observance of the anniversary." The Canadian Council of Churches, meanwhile, is keeping its peace and waiting for the first peoples to show the way. "If there is any demand from the native peoples of Canada," said CCC spokesman Tad Mitsui, "then we will join them in denouncing 500 years of genocide."

Well yes, history is a nightmare, and Columbus is not the ideal candidate for Eurocentric hoopla. But five centuries of unrelenting genocide? Are we all conquistadors? Or is this just further proof of the modern need to find spiritual strength through self-flagellation? What should we answer, that the sins of the past should not be visited on the present, that slavery and violence had a place among the imperialistic Incas, that wallowing in generic shame just isn't very helpful? But it is probably safer to point out, in this climate of ethnic diversity, that any criticism of Columbus is a racist attack on Hispanic culture.

Still, not all racism is created equal. It is permissible, and in some circles laudable, to trash what is euphemistically called the dominant culture. The challenge to an established order is not in itself a bad thing—elites can be stuffy, xenophobic, inbred—but at times it becomes hard to tell the oppressors from the oppressed. Any debate about racism in this decade is bound to end in frustration for all sides, because there is no way to bring together the liberal notions of free speech and toleration with the outraged sensitivities of the anti-racists.

All doubts on that score disappeared during the long and uncomfortable run of a show called Into the Heart of Africa. This was an Eighties kind of art exhibition—ironical, allusive, detached—that had the misfortune to be mounted at the Royal Ontario Museum on the eve of a new decade. The show assembled a random collection of African souvenirs brought home by Victorian and Edwardian missionaries and soldiers. By connecting the artifacts with their collectors, the curator, Jeanne Cannizzo, tried to give some sense to the dusty bygones from the ROM's basement.

But British imperialism has not worn well, if you will pardon my ironic understatement. By showing the missionaries and soldiers as they saw themselves, by describing this chapter of African history as if it was Canadian history (which it also was), Ms. Cannizzo offended people. Not all: some black people thought it was good to relive the humiliations of history because they had happened and been overcome. And some members of the dominant culture, in the guilt-ridden spirit of the Nineties, welcomed the exhibit's description of the white missionaries as culturally arrogant. But many people thought the show glorified the imperialists and perpetuated their stereotypes. Some of the images accompanying the exhibition, such as Lord Beresford impaling a Zulu warrior, were indeed violent. Some were paternalistic, such as Mrs. Thomas Titcombe offering a lesson to Nigerian women on how to wash clothes. That was the point, according to Ms. Cannizzo, who said that the show would help Canadians "to understand the historical roots of racism."

But a quiet *nostra culpa* was not enough for her opponents. "This exhibit promotes racism and race hatred" said a group called The Coalition for the Truth About Africa that organized demonstrations against the exhibition. The show went on at the ROM, but after the clamour in Toronto, no other museum on the continent would touch it and a planned tour was cancelled.

That's not quite the end of the story. Ms. Cannizzo's house was picketed by demonstrators. She was harassed at the University of Toronto, where she taught, and eventually was encouraged to take a leave of absence. Somehow the alleged perpetrator of racism ended up being the victim. "Whether or not she is a racist is a matter of interpretation," said a student politician at the university. "The fact is students don't want this instructor." A matter of interpretation, but convicted all the same. Because when there is no room for debate, there is no need to interpret.

An ironic footnote. In a recent issue of the University of Toronto *Bulletin*, three articles were neatly juxtaposed. A task force on ethnocultural groups and visible minorities called for the university "to create a climate in which diversity can flourish." A brief item announced that students who disrupted the class of Professor Jeanne Cannizzo would not be disciplined by the university because laying charges "would serve no useful purpose." And the registrar of the education faculty, a black woman originally from Guyana, gave her considered thoughts on racism. "When there's a problem, it should be remedied," Claire Alleyne told an interviewer, "but in seeking to do so, I hope the institution won't suffer fools gladly, regardless of their colour. I don't want the university to wallow in ancestral guilt."

But members of the University of Toronto, in their role as the country's intellectual leaders, seem quite prepared to wallow and compromise their institution's liberal principles. Asked to deal with the problem of sexual harassment on campus, a special committee of staff and students defined harassment in part (and please pardon the legalistic language of Nineties conflict-resolution) as behaviour "which emphasized the sex or sexual orientation of one or more individuals in a manner which the actor knows, or ought reasonable to know, creates, or could reasonably be expected to create, an intimidating, hostile or offensive environment for persons of that sex or sexual orientation and/or for persons present at that occurrence."

From this well-intended waffle, it's easy to imagine a situation where the harasser does not know he's harassing and the harassee does not know or care that she has been harassed. It comes as no comfort to learn that the committee is urging a lower, civil standard of proof, that the panel hearing a case on sexual harassment must be biased against its commission, but that there is no agreement, particularly between men and women, on what sexual harassment really is. No matter, says the special committee; this policy aims "to move the community standard of behaviour further along a continuum of understanding." As if "know" and "don't know" were part of the same continuum. The committee says, without apparent irony, that the goals of the policy are "heavily educational."

So what's that to me, you well might say. I don't enjoy the privileges of a university environment, intimidating or otherwise. I don't sip cappuccino at the politically correct cafe of the moment and I feel no connection with 500-year-old discoveries.

But you don't have to be in the forefront of this particular brand of looniness to be affected by it. We're on a continuum of understanding, as they say at the University of Toronto, and any tug from the extreme is going to pull the unresisting right along. And why resist, if it means being denounced as racist, or sexist, or ablest or materialist or just plain fascist? Even in the high-minded Nineties, hypocrisy is still in style.

There is no escaping the Nineties. Do you wince when your lunch-date slathers butter on a slice of bread? There's that Nineties' fear of pleasure again. Are you tempted to watch TV with your children so you can categorize acts of violence? Do you find you're afraid to speak because you might use the wrong words about an oppressed minority? Were you tempted to buy a Beaver Canoe Trees Are for Loving T-shirt because it just might help the planet? Do you listen politely when someone spots your Styrofoam coffee cup and says, "That's bad for our environment, you know. I carry my own mug, which helps reduce the number of cups used in the world, the waste material that has to be gathered, and the problems with the ozone layer caused by the chlorofluorocarbons given off when the Styrofoam decomposes." In other words, welcome to paradise.

Like every dream of perfection, the utopia of the Nineties is filled with nags and scolds and busybodies and prudes who expect and demand compliance. Human failings frustrate them. By seeking an absolute purity in all things, by worshipping pristine nature and untainted native peoples, they are trying to give our muddled species a new model and a fresh start. But the all-too-human qualities of envy, intolerance, impatience, vengeance and self-interest are poisoning this heaven on earth.

Social reformers always face the same problem: some people aren't ready to be reformed. But the new puritans, like the old ones, don't care. Their aim is to wear down, not win over. It is so much easier to rage, when faced with human imperfection, than to persuade or understand or just plain ignore. But you can't claim the higher moral ground by suppressing arguments, rewriting history and legislating away behaviour. Refusing to allow what you don't want to hear is moral cowardice. And that is a rotten foundation for a brave new decade.

Anti-Semite and Jew

Jean Paul Sartre

What is racism? How does it develop and what sustains it? In this excerpt Jean-Paul Sartre attempts to answer this question by examining the anti-Semite as one particular expression of racism.

If a man attributes all or part of his own misfortunes and those of his country to the presence of Jewish elements in the community, if he proposes to remedy this state of affairs by depriving the Jews of certain of their rights, by keeping them out of certain economic and social activities, by expelling them from the country, by exterminating all of them, we say that he has anti-Semitic *opinions.*

This word *opinion* makes us stop and think. It is the word a hostess uses to bring to an end a discussion that threatens to become acrimonious. It suggests that all points of view are equal; it reassures us, for it gives an inoffensive appearance to ideas by reducing them to the level of tastes. All tastes are natural; all opinions are permitted. Tastes, colours, and opinions are not open to discussion. In the name of democratic institutions, in the name of freedom of opinion, the anti-Semite asserts the right to preach the anti-Jewish crusade everywhere.

But I refuse to characterize as opinion a doctrine that is aimed directly at particular persons and that seeks to suppress their rights or to exterminate them. The Jew whom the anti-Semite wishes to lay hands upon is not a schematic being defined solely by his function, as under administrative law; or by his status or his acts, as under the Code. He is a Jew, the son of Jews, recognizable by his physique, by the colour of his hair, by his clothing perhaps, and, so they say, by his character. Anti-Semitism does not fall within the category of ideas protected by the right of free opinion.

Indeed, it is something quite other than an idea. It is first of all a *passion.* No doubt it can be set forth in the form of a theoretical proposition. The "moderate" anti-Semite is a courteous man who will tell you quietly: "Personally, I do not detest the Jews. I simply find it preferable, for various reasons, that they should play a lesser part in the activity of the nation." But a moment later, if you have gained his confidence, he will add with more abandon: "You see, there must be *something* about the Jews; they upset me physically."

This argument, which I have heard a hundred times, is worth examining. First of all, it derives from the logic of passion. For, really now, can we imagine anyone's saying seriously: "There must be something about tomatoes, for I have a horror of eating them?"

Some men are suddenly struck with impotence if they learn from the woman with whom they are making love that she is a Jewess. There is a disgust for the Jew, just as there is a disgust for the Chinese or the Negro among certain people. Thus it is not from the body that the sense of repulsion arises, since one may love a Jewess very well if one does not know what her race is; rather it is something that enters the body from the mind. It is an involvement of the mind, but one so deep-seated and complete that it extends to the physiological realm, as happens in cases of hysteria.

This involvement is not caused by experience. I have questioned a hundred people on the reasons for their anti-Semitism. Most of them have confined themselves to enumerating the defects with which tradition has endowed the Jews. "I detest them because they are selfish, intriguing, persistent, oily, tactless, etc."—"But, at any rate, you associate with some of them?"—"Not if I can help it!" A painter said to me: "I am hostile to the Jews because, with their critical habits, they encourage our servants to insubordination." Here are examples a little more precise. A young actor without talent insisted that the Jews had kept him from a successful career in the theatre by confining him to subordinate roles. A young woman said to me: "I have had the most horrible experiences with furriers; they robbed me, they burned the fur I entrusted to them. Well, they were all Jews." But why did she choose to hate Jews rather than furriers? Why Jews or furriers rather than such and such a Jew or such and such a furrier? Because she had in her a predisposition toward anti-Semitism.

People speak to us also of "social facts," but if we look at this more closely we shall find the same vicious circle. There are too many Jewish lawyers, someone says. But is there any complaint that there are too many Norman lawyers? Even if all the Bretons were doctors would we say anything more than that "Brittany provides doctors for the whole of France?" Oh, someone will answer, it is not at all the same thing. No doubt, but that is precisely because we consider Normans as Normans and Jews as *Jews.* Thus wherever we turn it is the *idea of the Jew* which seems to be the essential thing.

It has become evident that no external factor can induce anti-Semitism in the anti-Semite. Anti-Semitism is a free and total choice of oneself, a comprehensive attitude that one adopts not only toward Jews but toward men in general, toward history and society; it is at one and the same time a passion and a conception of the world. No doubt in the case of a given anti-Semite certain characteristics will be more marked than in another. But they are always all present at the same time, and they influence each other. It is this syncretic totality which we must now attempt to describe.

I noted earlier that anti-Semitism is a passion. Everybody understands that emotions of hate or anger are involved. Bur ordinarily hate and anger have a *provocation:* I hate someone who has made me suffer, someone who condemns or insults me. We have just seen that anti-Semitic passion could not have such a character. It precedes the facts that are supposed to call it forth; it seeks them out to nourish itself upon them; it must even interpret them in a special way so that they may become truly offensive. Indeed, if you so much as mention a Jew to an anti-Semite, he will show all the signs of a lively irritation. If we recall that we must always *consent* to anger before it can manifest itself and that, as is indicated so accurately by the French idiom, we "put ourselves" into anger, we shall have to agree that the anti-Semite has *chosen* to live on the plane of passion. It is not unusual for people to elect to live a life of passion rather than one of reason. But ordinarily they love the objects of passion: women, glory, power, money. Since the anti-Semite has chosen hate, we are forced to conclude that it is the state of passion that he loves. Ordinarily this type of emotion is not very pleasant: a man who passionately desires a woman is impassioned because of the woman and in spite of his passion. We are wary of reasoning based on passion, seeking to support by all possible means opinions which love or jealousy or hate have dictated. We are wary of the aberrations of passion and of what is called monoideism. But that is just what the anti-Semite chooses right off.

How can one choose to reason falsely? It is because of a longing for impenetrability. The rational man groans as he gropes for the truth; he knows that his reasoning is no more than tentative, that other considerations may supervene to cast doubt on it. He never sees clearly where he is going; he is "open;" he may even appear to be hesitant. But there are people who are attracted by the durability of a stone. They wish to be massive and impenetrable; they wish not to change. Where, indeed, would change take them? We have here a basic fear of oneself and of truth. What frightens them is not the content of truth, that thing of indefinite approximation. It is as if their own existence were in continual suspension. But they wish to exist all at once and right away. They do not want any acquired opinions; they want them to be innate. Since they are afraid of reasoning, they wish to lead the kind of life wherein reasoning and research play only a subordinate role, wherein one seeks only what he has already found, wherein one becomes only what he already was. This is nothing but passion. Only a strong emotional bias can give a lightning-like certainty; it alone can hold reason in leash; it alone can remain impervious to experience and last for whole lifetime.

The anti-Semite has chosen hate because hate is a faith; at the outset he has chosen to devaluate words and reasons. How entirely at ease he feels as a result. How futile and frivolous discussions about the rights of the Jew appear to him. He has placed himself on other ground from the beginning. If out of courtesy he consents for a moment to defend his point of view, he lends himself but does not give himself. He tries simply to project his intuitive certainty onto the plane of discourse. I mentioned awhile back some remarks by anti-Semites, all of them absurd: "I hate Jews because they make servants insubordinate, because a Jewish furrier robbed me, etc." Never believe that anti-Semites are completely unaware of the absurdity of their replies. They know that their remarks are frivolous, open to challenge. But they are amusing themselves, for it is their adversary who is obliged to use words responsibly, since he believes in words. The anti-Semites have the *right* to play. They even like to play with discourse for, by giving ridiculous reasons, they discredit the seriousness of their interlocutors. They delight in acting in bad faith, since they seek not to persuade by sound argument but to intimidate and disconcert. If you press them too closely, they will abruptly fall silent, loftily indicating by some phrase that the time for argument is past. It is not that they are afraid of being convinced. They fear only to appear ridiculous or to prejudice by their embarrassment their hope of winning over some third person to their side.

If then, as we have been able to observer, the anti-Semite is impervious to reason and to experience, it is not because his conviction is strong. Rather his conviction is strong because he has chosen first of all to be impervious.

He has chosen also to be terrifying. People are afraid of irritating him. No one knows to what lengths the aberrations of his passion will carry him—but he knows, for this passion is not provoked by something external. He has it well in hand; it is obedient to his will: now he lets go the reins and now he pulls back on them. He is not afraid of himself, but he sees in the eyes of others a disquieting image—his own—and he makes his words and gestures conform to it. Having this external model, he is under no necessity to look for his personality within himself. He has chosen to find his being entirely outside himself, never to look within, to be nothing save the fear he inspires in others. What he flees even more than Reason is his intimate awareness of himself. But someone will object: What if he is like that only with regard to the Jews? What if he otherwise conducts himself with good sense? I reply that that is impossible. There is the case of a fishmonger who, in 1942, annoyed by the competition of two Jewish fishmongers who were concealing their race, one fine day took pen in hand and denounced them. I have been assured that this fishmonger was in other aspects a mild and jovial man, the best of sons. But I don't believe it. A man who finds it entirely natural to denounce other men cannot have our conception of humanity; he does not see even those whom he aids in the same light as we do. His generosity, his kindness are not like our kindness, our generosity. You cannot confine passion to one sphere.

The anti-Semite readily admits that the Jew is intelligent and hard-working; he will even confess himself inferior in these respects. This concession costs him nothing, for he has, as it were, put those qualities in parentheses. Or rather they derive their value from the one who possesses them: the more virtues the Jew has the more dangerous he will be. The anti-Semite has no illusions about what he is. He considers himself an average man, modestly average, basically mediocre. There is no example of an anti-Semite's claiming individual superiority over the Jews. But you must not think that he is ashamed of his mediocrity; he takes pleasure in it; I will even assert that he has chosen it. This man fears every kind of solitariness, that of the genius as much as that of the murderer; he is the man of the crowd. However small his stature, he takes every precaution to make it smaller, lest he stand out from the herd and find himself face to face with himself. He has made himself an anti-Semite because that is something one cannot be alone. The phrase, "I hate the Jews," is one that is uttered in chorus; in pronouncing it, one attaches himself to a tradition and to a community—the tradition and community of the mediocre.

We must remember that a man is not necessarily humble or even modest because he has consented to mediocrity. On the contrary, there is a passionate pride among the mediocre, and anti-Semitism is an attempt to give value to mediocrity as such, to create an elite of the ordinary. To the anti-Semite, intelligence is Jewish; he can thus disdain it in all tranquillity, like all the other virtues which the Jew possesses. They are so many ersatz attributes that the Jew cultivates in place of that balanced mediocrity which he will never have. The true Frenchman, rooted in his province, in his country, borne along by a tradition twenty centuries old, benefiting from ancestral wisdom, guided by tried customs, does not *need* intelligence. His virtue depends upon the assimilation of the qualities which the work of a hundred generations has lent to the objects which surround him; it depends on property. It goes without saying that this is a matter of inherited property, not property one buys. The anti-Semite has a fundamental incomprehension of the various forms of modern property: money, securities, etc. These are abstractions, entities of reason related to the abstract intelligence of the Semite. A security belongs to no one because it can belong to everyone; moreover, it is a sign of wealth, not a concrete possession. The anti-Semite can conceive only of a type of primitive ownership of land based on a veritable magical rapport, in which the thing possessed and its possessor are united by a bond of mystical participation; he is the poet of real property. It transfigures the proprietor and endows him with a special and concrete sensibility. To be sure, this sensibility ignores eternal truths or universal values: the universal is Jewish, since it is an object of intelligence. What his subtle sense seizes upon is precisely that which the intelligence cannot perceive. To put it another way, the principle underlying anti-Semitism is that the concrete possession of a particular object gives as if by magic the meaning of that object. Maurras said the same thing when he declared a Jew to be forever incapable of understanding this line of Racine:

Dans l'Orient desert, quel devint mon ennui.

But the way is open to me, mediocre me, to understand what the most subtle, the most cultivated intelligence has been unable to grasp. Why? Because I possess Racine-Racine and my country and my soil. Perhaps the Jew speaks a purer French than I do, perhaps he knows syntax and grammar better, perhaps he is even a writer. No matter; he has spoken this language for only twenty years, and I for a thousand years. The correctness of his style is abstract, acquired; my faults of French are in conformity with the genius of the language. We recognize here the reasoning that Barres used against the holders of scholarships. There is no occasion for surprise. Don't the Jews have all the scholarships? All that intelligence, all that money can acquire one leaves to them, but it is as empty as the wind. The only things that count are irrational values, and it is just these things which are denied the Jews forever. Thus the anti-Semite takes his stand from the start on the ground of irrationalism. He is opposed to the Jew, just as sentiment is to intelligence, the particular to the universal, the past to the present, the concrete to the abstract, the owner of real property to the possessor of negotiable securities.

Besides this, many anti-Semites—the majority, perhaps—belong to the lower middle class of the towns; they are functionaries, office workers, small businessmen, who possess nothing. It is in opposing themselves to the Jew that they suddenly become conscious of being proprietors: in representing the Jew as a robber, they put themselves in the enviable position of people who could be robbed. Since the Jew wishes to take France from them, it follows that France must belong to them. Thus they have chosen anti-Semitism as a means of establishing their status as possessors. The Jew has more money than they? So much the better: money is Jewish, and they can despise it as they despise intelligence.

We begin to perceive the meaning of the anti-Semite's choice of himself. He chooses the irremediable out of fear of being free; he chooses mediocrity out of fear of being alone, and out of pride he makes of this irremediable mediocrity a rigid aristocracy. To this end he finds the existence of the Jew absolutely necessary. Otherwise to whom would he be superior? Indeed, it is vis-à-vis the Jew and the Jew alone that the anti-Semite realizes that he has rights. If by some miracle all the Jews were exterminated as he wishes, he would find himself nothing but a concierge or a shopkeeper in a strongly hierarchical society in which the quality of "true Frenchman" would be at a low valuation, because everyone would possess it. He would lose his sense of rights over the country because no one would any longer contest them, and that profound equality which brings him close to the nobleman and the man of wealth would disappear all of a sudden, for it is primarily negative. His frustrations, which he has attributed to the disloyal competition of the Jew, would have to be imputed to some other cause, lest he be forced to look within himself. He would run the risk of falling into bitterness, into a melancholy hatred of the privileged classes. Thus the anti-Semite is in the unhappy position of having a vital need for the very enemy he wishes to destroy.

The equalitarianism that the anti-Semite seeks with so much ardor has nothing in common with that equality inscribed in the creed of the democracies.

The latter is to be realized in a society that is economically hierarchical, and is to remain compatible with a diversity of functions. But it is in protest *against* the hierarchy of functions that the anti-Semite asserts the equality of Aryans. He does not understand anything about the division of labour and doesn't care about it. From his point of view each citizen can claim the title of Frenchman, not because he co-operates, in his place or in his occupation, with others in the economic, social, and cultural life of the nation, but because he has, in the same way as everybody else, an imprescriptible and inborn right to the indivisible totality of the country. Thus the society that the anti-Semite conceives of is a society of juxtaposition, as one can very well imagine, since his ideal of property is that of real and basic property. Since, in point of fact, anti-Semites are numerous, each of them does his part in constituting a community based on mechanical solidarity in the heart of organized society.

Any anti-Semite is therefore, in varying degree, the enemy of constituted authority. He wishes to be the disciplined member of an undisciplined group; he adores order, but a social order. We might say that he wishes to provoke political disorder in order to restore social order, the social order in his eyes being a society that, by virtue of juxtaposition, is egalitarian and primitive, one with a heightened temperature, one from which Jews are excluded. These principles enable him to enjoy a strange sort of independence, which I shall call an inverted liberty. Authentic liberty assumes responsibilities, and the liberty of the anti-Semite comes from the fact that he escapes all of his. Floating between an authoritarian society which has not yet come into existence and an official and tolerant society which he disavows, he can do anything he pleases without appearing to be an anarchist, which would horrify him. The profound seriousness of his aims—which no word, no statement, no act can express—permits him a certain frivolity. He is a hooligan, he beats people up, he purges, he robs; it is all in a good cause. If the government is strong, anti-Semitism withers, unless it be a part of the program of the government itself, in which case it changes its nature. Enemy of the Jews, the anti-Semite has need of them. Anti-democratic, he is a natural product of democracies and can only manifest himself within the framework of the Republic.

We begin to understand that anti-Semitism is more than a mere "opinion" about the Jews and that it involves the entire personality of the anti-Semite. But we have not yet finished with him, for he does not confine himself to furnishing moral and political directives: he has a method of thought and a conception of the world all his own. In fact, we cannot state what he affirms without implicit reference to certain intellectual principles.

The Jew, he says, is completely bad, completely a Jew. His virtues, if he has any, turn to vices by reason of the fact that they are his; work coming from his hands necessarily bears his stigma. If he builds a bridge, that bridge, being Jewish, is bad from the first to the last span. The same action carried out by a Jew and by a Christian does not have the same meaning in the two cases, for the Jew contaminates all that he touches with an I-know-not-what execrable quality. The first thing the Germans did was to forbid Jews access to swimming pools; it seemed to them that if the body of an Israelite were to plunge into that confined body of water, the water would be completely befouled. Strictly speaking, the Jew contaminates even the air he breathes.

If we attempt to formulate in abstract terms the principles to which the anti-Semite appeals, it would come to this: A whole is more and other than the sum of its parts; a whole determines the meaning and underlying parts; a whole determines the meaning and underlying character of the parts that make it up. There is not one virtue of courage which enters indifferently into a Jewish character or a Christian character in the way that oxygen indifferently combines with nitrogen and argon to form air and with hydrogen to form water. Each person is an indivisible totality that has its own courage, its own generosity, its own way of thinking, laughing, drinking, and eating. What is there to say except that the anti-Semite has chosen to fall back on the spirit of synthesis in order to understand the world. It is the spirit of synthesis which permits him to conceive of himself as forming an indissoluble unity with all France. It is in the name of this spirit that he denounces the purely analytical and critical intelligence of the Jews. But we must be more precise. For some time, on the Right and on the Left, among the traditionalists and among the socialists, it has been the fashion to make appeal to synthetic principles as against the spirit of analysis which presided over the foundation of bourgeois democracy.

We are now in a position to understand the anti-Semite. He is a man who is afraid. Not of the Jews, to be sure, but of himself, of his own consciousness, of his liberty, of his instincts, of his responsibilities, of solitariness, of change, of society, and of the world—of everything except the Jews. He is a coward who does not want to admit his cowardice to himself; a murderer who represses and censures his tendency to murder without being able to hold it back, yet who dares to kill only in effigy or protected by the anonymity of the mob; a malcontent who dares not revolt from fear of the consequences of his rebellion. In espousing anti-Semitism, he does not simply adopt an opinion, he chooses himself as a person. He chooses the permanence and impenetrability of stone, the total irresponsibility of the warrior who obeys his leaders—and he has no leader. He chooses to acquire nothing, to deserve nothing; he assumes that everything is given him as his birthright—and he is not noble. He chooses finally a Good that is fixed once and for all, beyond question, out of reach; he dares not examine it for fear of being led to challenge it and having to seek it in another form. The Jew only serves him as a pretext; elsewhere his counterpart will make use of the negro or the man of yellow skin. The existence of the Jew merely permits the anti-Semite to stifle his anxieties at their inception by persuading himself that his place in the world has been marked out in advance, that is awaits him, and that tradition gives him the right to occupy it. Anti-Semitism, in short, is fear of the human condition. The anti-Semite is a man who wishes to be pitiless stone, a furious torrent, a devastating thunderbolt—anything except a man.

Sex and Symbol in Fashion Advertising

Arthur A. Berger

In this article culture is treated as a collection of learned "codes" that provide us with meaning. Through an examination of fashion advertising the author introduces us to semiology—the science of signs—and some techniques for breaking these codes. How does an advertisement work? What must a viewer know in order for it to achieve its intended effect? Do advertisements reflect or actively shape society?

While reading an issue of *Vogue* recently, I noticed that I was, somehow, taken by a number of the advertisements for fashions and cosmetics. Many of these advertisements contained striking photographs and suggestive (and in some cases rather overt) copy. I found myself absorbed by the advertisements. They had a remarkable power over me—to seize my attention and to stimulate, if only for a moment, fantasies of an erotic nature. It was not only the physical characteristics of the models that affected me; rather it was a kind of gestalt effect. There was the element of graphic design, of colour, of light, and a host of other matters that "conspired" to excite me.

"What's going on?" I asked myself. That question led me to consider how magazine advertising works to stimulate desire and sell clothes, cosmetics, and everything else that is connected with beauty (in this case) or any product.

In analysing an advertisement there are a number of factors that we must consider, such as: the ambience, the design, the use of white space, the significant images and symbols, the use of language, the type faces used, and the item itself (and its role and function in society). We can also consider how the advertisement attempts to "sell" us and what roles it offers us to imitate, as well as examine how social phenomena might be reflected, indirectly. (Here I'm thinking about such things as alienation, boredom, conformism, generational conflict, and so on.) We can use whatever concepts we have at our command from history, psychology, sociology, anthropology, and any other disciplines to help us "dissect" the advertisement. In applying all of the above it is important to keep one cardinal principle in mind: The creators of any advertisement are trying to generate some kind of an effect or emotional response. So we must start with the effect and work backwards. What is the fantasy? And how is it induced?

Selling Magic

I will answer these questions by examining some of the advertisements in the April 1978 issue of *Vogue* magazine. I've selected advertisements that, for some

reason, caught my attention for a moment and that I think are interesting and
worth examining closely.

Let me start with a double-page advertisement by Revlon for its Formula
2 cleanser and moisturizer. The left-hand page of the advertisement is devoted
to an extreme close-up of a woman's face, but the face is rendered by using
quarter-inch squares of various colours. We are, in fact, given an optical
illusion. If we squint, or place the magazine fifteen feet away from us, the
squares merge together and form a face. But at arm's length, the face is
somewhat distorted and out of focus. It is also larger than life in size. From
there we move over to the right-hand page, which has a great deal of white
space and is formally designed, approximating axial balance. Generally
speaking, large amounts of white space and axial balance (and formality) are
associated with quality and "class" in most people's minds.

The copy of the ad stresses science and technology as opposed to nature.
We find the following suggestive words and phrases in the advertisement:

Revlon Research Group
skin care system
natural electricity
formula
skin care that's simple, scientific
precision tip
beauty technology
hygiene
principle

All of these terms are signifiers for science and technology; we are led to think
of scientists in laboratories discovering remarkable things that lead to "the
New-Face Hygiene" and "beautiful life for your skin." A smaller photograph
on this page shows two medicinal-looking bottles, in which the future-age
Formula 2 cleanser and moisturizer are packaged.

Though this is something of a generalization, there seems to be a polar
opposition in the public's mind that posits a world divided between culture (and
with it science and technology) and nature. Thus the people who created the
Revlon advertisement had two possibilities: to stress nature and all that is
suggested by it, or to stress culture, in this case, science and technology. They

chose the latter course and offered their readers a minicourse in science and technology: *This* principle leads to *those* results.

Ultimately what is being sold here—and what is being sold in most cosmetics ads—is magic, and that is where the large rendering of the woman's face comes in. It is an optical illusion that has two functions: First, it catches our attention because when we look at the face we see that it is really only a huge patchwork of squares. At first glance it seems out of focus and strange. But, if we squint or stare at it, magically it becomes a face, just the same way that Revlon Formula 2's "beauty technology of the future" gives you the gift of "life" (for your skin). Just as the law of closure forces us to complete that which is unfinished, we find ourselves obliged to make sense of the picture, and we visualize the woman's face even more completely than we find it. This act of visualization is what is asked of patrons or purchasers of the product. From the bits and pieces of their old faces they are asked (almost forced) to envision the new faces they will have with Formula 2.

Now that the face is taken care of, let us "finish off" the job (the law of closure once again) and take care of the entire body. For this we can use Benandré, which says it "will do for your body what a facial does for your face." This single-page advertisement has, like the Revlon advertisement, axial balance and a considerable amount of white space. It shows a woman in a glass bathtub bathing herself in "Mediterranean blue" water. A bit of greenery signifies the Mediterranean here. The woman's face is clearly shown, in profile, but her body is not. We see only a diffused figure in blue-green water. Benandré promises that its special form of collagen (a protein contained in the connective tissues and bones, which yields gelatin on boiling) helps the body retain moisture and helps it to restore moisture it loses during the day.

This matter of keeping the skin (and body) moist is interesting. A great deal of cosmetic advertising stresses wetness, moisture, and related concepts, as if the body were in danger of becoming an arid desert, devoid of life, dry, uninteresting, and infertile. These ads suggest that women fear, or should fear, losing their body fluids, which becomes the equivalent of losing their capacity to reproduce. This, in turn, is connected with sexuality and desirability. Anxiety over the body as a kind of wasteland is implicit in appeals in advertisements about retaining and restoring moisture. Dehydration is a metaphor for loss of sexual attractiveness and capacity, that is, desexualization.

Dry skin becomes, then, a sign of a woman who is all dried up and who is not sexually responsive—and who may also be sterile. This is because water is connected, in our psyches, with birth. It is also tied to purity, as in baptismal rites when sin is cleansed from a person. All of this suggests that words and images that picture a body of a woman as being dehydrated and losing water have great resonance.

In *Man and His Symbols*, Carl Jung (1968: 29) writes:

> Every concept in our conscious mind, in short, has its own psychic
> associations. While such associations may vary in intensity...they
> are capable of changing the "normal" character of that concept.
> It may even become something quite different as it drifts below
> the level of consciousness. These subliminal aspects of everything
> that happens to us may seem to play very little part in our daily
> lives. But in dream analysis, where the psychologist is dealing with
> expressions of the unconscious, they are very relevant, for they
> are the almost invisible roots of our conscious thoughts. That is
> why commonplace objects or ideas can assume such powerful
> psychic significance in a dream.

If we substitute "advertisements" for "dreams" in the above quotation, we can
understand why and how we are affected so profoundly by images and words.

The copy in the Benandré ad is full of purple prose indicating power and
luxury. Some of the more interesting words and phrases appear below:

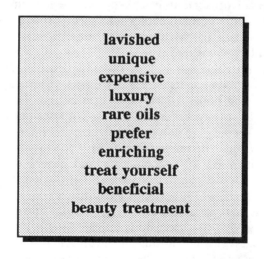

lavished
unique
expensive
luxury
rare oils
prefer
enriching
treat yourself
beneficial
beauty treatment

This product is sold as a kind of indulgence for women. The copy hits at sex
("You'll make the skin of your body as nice to touch as the skin on your face.
Just ask the one who touches you most."), which is always a strong selling point
for beauty aids. But the pictorial element is connected with symbols of
innocence—baptism, cleanliness, and so on. And the towel in the lower right-
hand corner of the ad is a chaste white. From a psychoanalytic perspective,

there is also something regressive about all this. It is almost as if the woman emerges with the skin of a baby. She also is quite undefined sexually; we are certain we are seeing a woman, but her sexuality has been subdued a great deal, which is in keeping with "class" as we have been taught to think of it.

Next let us move on to some clothes for our moist and soft-skinned beauty: Danskins. The advertisement for Danskins shows three female bodies lying down on a blue-green piece of fabric that may also be water—it is hard to say. What is interesting is the arrangement of the bodies, all horizontal and jammed together. Two of the models are lying with their heads on the left and the third is between them with her head to the right side of the picture. Although they touch one another, each seems unaware of any of the others—they all stare off into space in separate directions.

The Danskin ad is extremely simple and formal. It has three elements: a headline, the photograph of the three women, and an element containing six lines of copy, all in capitals. The product advertised is a "freestyle" leotard/swimsuit that comes in various "sensuous styles and colours." The large element of white space contrasts with the crowding in the photograph, a crowding that a Marxist would say reflects a diffuse alienation among the women, who are touching one another but do not seem to be aware of each other. They are all, we must assume, pursuing their private fantasies.

Finally, let us move on to an ad depicting a fully dressed woman in Calvin Klein separates. Here we find a model with her right hand on her hip, her left hand behind her head, and her left knee bent (in the "bashful knee pose") and prominently displayed. The background is grey and there is hardly any text. The shirt the model wears has a plunging neckline, but there is no cleavage showing, and there is a slit in the skirt, which enables her to display her knee.

We are given little textual information: the designer, Calvin Klein; the store where the outfit can be purchased, I. Magnin; and the fabric manufacturer, the Ideacomo group.

The model has long, curly hair. She has a rather cold look on her face, a look that is commonly seen in high-fashion advertising. And she is posed in a way that emphasizes her arms and legs rather than her breasts and hips. Thus attention is focused on her appendages, which are sexually undifferentiated. Yet there is something of a sexually alluring quality about this pose, which shows a lot of upper leg. It may have something to do with the tilt of the hips, the twist of the torso, and the neckline. Perhaps the unnaturalness of the pose is important, also.

Breaking the Advertising Code

The codes of simplicity, white space and formality, appear in the Calvin Klein advertisement just as they did in all the other advertisements discussed to this point. These "couture" codes are learned by people, who are taught, by advertisers, to associate simplicity, spaciousness, and formal structure with "class." In the same manner, we are taught the "meanings" of various typefaces and kinds of images. Soft focus signifies dream-like states, formal structure or design implies "classic" (whatever that means), and so on. All of these associations are carried around in our heads, so that all the advertiser has to do is "activate" us by striking the appropriate responsive chord. As Tony Schwartz (1974: 24-25) writes in *The Responsive Chord*:

> The critical task is to design our package of stimuli so that it resonates with information already stored with the individual and thereby induces the desired learning or behavioural effect. Resonance takes place when the stimuli put into our communication evoke *meaning* in a listener or viewer. That which we put into the communication has no meaning in itself. The meaning of our communication is what a listener or viewer *gets out* of his experience with the communicator's stimulus.

Culture, and "couture," which is part of culture, is a collection of codes we learn that provide us with meaning in the world. But how, specifically, do these codes work, and how do we find meaning in advertisements (as well as other forms of communication)?

In a magazine (or other form of print) advertisement there are two ways that information is communicated—through the text and through pictorial and design elements. We can examine the text to determine what appeals are being pressed forward and what means are used to lead the reader/viewer to desire the product. Anxiety may be provoked. There may be inducements to self-gratifications of varying natures. Snobbery may be invoked. Any number of techniques of persuasion can be used here. And in the pictorial material there is also a "language" that may be employed to generate the desired feelings and fantasies. I have mentioned some of these techniques: design, size, colour, grain, focus, and so on. And I have suggested that we learn to associate certain kinds of advertisements with certain kinds of fashions.

Can we take matters a step further? Can we explain how these associates are made and how the various signs and symbols generate the meanings they do? In some cases, yes. To do so we must expand our vocabulary of analysis. I would like to reintroduce some terms from semiology at this point:

metaphor:	relationship by analogy (example: my love is a red rose)
metonymy:	relationship by association (example: rich people and mansions)
icon:	relationship by resemblance (example: photograph of an object)
index:	relationship by implication (example: smoke implies fire)
symbol:	relationship by convention (example: Star of David and Jews)

There is a problem in differentiating between metonymy and symbol that I find hard to solve. Neither are motivated or natural, but relationships by association seem to be stronger than relationships by convention. Anything can be a symbol once people learn to accept it as such. But the association between wealth and large mansions seems quite logical. Wealthy people, people with "class," tend to live in large houses, have a great deal of land and space for themselves, and are powerful. Thus spaciality becomes associated with wealth and class indirectly, through the matter of living space found in large homes.

In metonymy, then, the relationships are stronger than in symbols. One important form of metonymy is synecdoche, in which a part stands for a whole or vice versa. Monaco (1977: 135) in *How to Read a Film* suggests that in film "close shots of marching feet to represent an army" is synecdochic and "falling calendar pages" to indicate the passing of time are metonymic, and that it is through metonymy and synecdoche that Hollywood and films in general are able to communicate with people so quickly and powerfully. Thus, for example, sweat is an index of body heat (or nervous anxiety) that functions metonymically since "associated details invoke an abstract idea."

Magazine advertisements function in much the same way, using whatever devices they can to signify "abstract ideas"—what we call signifieds—such as passion, love, romance, and so on. Because these advertisements can use language, they can use metaphor, but more often they also wish to imply or suggest things (fantasies of exotic love, hopes for beauty) through pictorial elements that make use of the devices described above in various combinations.

With these terms we can do more than simply say that signs and symbols work on the basis of associations that people learn and that become codes by which they interpret the world and function in it. For example, let us consider our first advertisement, the one for Revlon's Formula 2 cleanser and moisturizer. Although there are many things going on in this advertisement it seems to me that the most important thing in the ad is the way it forces the reader to turn the optical illusion into a face, which suggests, perhaps subliminally, *magic*. Most cosmetic advertisements involve a belief in magic, but usually the appeals are verbal. In this advertisement, however, we are forced to do a great deal of work, work that "convinces" us that it is logical to believe in magic. Why not? We've just done something magical. We've seen that magic works, with our own eyes.

I see this process as indexical. The Revlon products promise beauty by magic just the way the square patches hold the promise of a face, once we learn how to see the patches correctly. The implication is that Revlon is magic and it will work for you the way your eyes work to figure out the optical illusion. There may also be an element of suggesting that beauty is an illusion and is attainable by all who can employ the correct magic. The picture of the woman in the ad is indexical, but the bottles are symbolic and rely upon the conventional look of medicinal products for their power. The stylishness of the advertisement, with its use of white space and simplicity, is also symbolic. There is nothing natural or logical about our associating white space and simplicity with "class." It is historical, part of our culture, and something that most of us learn.

In the Revlon advertisement and in all advertisements we find a kind of chain reaction taking place. The verbal and pictorial elements in the advertisement function as signifiers that generate feelings and beliefs or signifieds for those who look at and read the advertisement. These feelings and beliefs (and, we might add, hopes, fantasies, and the like) are based on codes (structured belief systems), which, in turn, operate via metaphor metonymy, icon, index, and symbols in various combinations. Thus, in order to determine how advertisements and other forms of visual-verbal communication generate meaning, we can move beyond the notion of codes and see how the codes themselves function.

It is a fascinating business taking advertisements apart to see how they function and determining what they reflect about society. It is also a perilous business, for there is always the possibility that we are not examining society's fantasies, or those of the creators of the advertisements, but our own.

In *The Strategy of Desire*, Ernest Dichter (1960: 11), one of the founding fathers of motivation research, writes:

> Human desire is the raw material we are working with. The strategy of desire is the tool of shaping the human factor, the most important aspect of our worldly arsenal. Human progress is a conquest of the animal within us. No conquest is possible without strategy.

Whether or not advertising and other tools of persuasion are leading us to higher levels of development is questionable. One thing seems quite evident—knowing the strategies used by the people who work at creating and shaping our desire is important, for then we can make more rational decisions and avoid manipulation. The person who is a slave to fashion is often also a slave to his or her own emotions—emotions that can be manipulated by the fashion advertising industry. But escape is possible.

References

Dichter, Ernest. 1960. *The Strategy of Desire*. London: Boardman.
Jung, Carl. 1968. *Man and His Symbols*. New York: Dell.
Monaco, J. 1977. *How to Read a Film*. New York: Oxford.
Schwartz, Tony. 1974. *The Responsive Chord*. Garden City, New York: Doubleday.

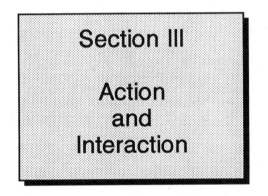

Section III

Action
and
Interaction

The Nature of Symbolic Interactionism

Herbert Blumer

Symbolic interactionism constitutes one of the basic theoretical approaches to the study of social life. In contrast to functionalism's emphasis on order and group cohesion, or conflict theory's image of society as a dynamic struggle among competing interest groups, symbolic interactionism investigates how individuals are continually creating and recreating society "from the ground up" as they go about their everyday affairs. In this article Blumer draws on Max Weber's definition of action as "behaviour that is subjectively meaningful to the acting individual," and discusses the three principal assumptions of this theoretic approach.

The term *symbolic interactionism* has come into use as a label for a relatively distinctive approach to the study of human group life and human conduct.[1]

Symbolic interactionism rests in the last analysis on three simple premises. The first premise is that human beings act toward things on the basis of the meanings that the things have for them. Such things include everything that the human being may note in his world—physical objects, such as trees or chairs; other human beings, such as a mother or a store clerk; categories of human beings, such as friends or enemies; institutions, as a school or a government; guiding ideals, such as individual independence or honesty; activities of others, such as their commands or requests; and such situations as an individual encounters in his daily life. The second premise is that the meaning of such things is derived from, or arises out of, the social interaction that one has with one's fellows. The third premise is that these meanings are handled in, and modified through, an interpretative process used by the person in dealing with the things he encounters. I wish to discuss briefly each of these three fundamental premises.

It would seem that few scholars would see anything wrong with the first premise—that human beings act toward things on the basis of the meanings which these things have for them. Yet, oddly enough, this simple view is ignored or played down in practically all of the thought and work in contemporary social science and psychological science. Meaning is either taken for granted and thus pushed aside as unimportant or it is regarded as a mere neutral link between the factors responsible for human behaviour and this behaviour as the product of such factors. We can see this clearly in the predominant posture of psychological and social science today. Common to both of these fields is the tendency to treat human behaviour as the product of various factors that play upon human beings; concern is with the behaviour and with the factors regarded as producing them. Thus psychologists turn to such factors as stimuli, attitudes, conscious or unconscious motives, various kinds of psychological inputs, perception and cognition, and various features of personal organization to account for given forms or instances of human conduct. In a similar fashion sociologists rely on such factors as social position, status demands, social roles, cultural prescriptions, norms and values, social pressures, and group affiliation to provide such explanations. In both such typical psychological and sociological explanations the meanings of things for the human beings who are acting are either bypassed or swallowed up in the factors used to account for their behaviour. If one declares that the given kinds of behaviour are the result of the particular factors regarded as producing them, there is no need to concern oneself with the meaning of the things toward which human beings act; one merely identifies the initiating factors and the resulting behaviour. Or one may, if pressed, seek to accommodate the element of meaning by lodging it in the initiating factors or by regarding it as a neutral link intervening between the initiating factors and the behaviour they are alleged to produce. In the first of these latter cases the meaning disappears by being merged into the initiating or causative factors: in the second case meaning becomes a mere transmission link that can be ignored in favour of the initiating factors.

The position of symbolic interactionism, in contrast, is that the meanings that things have for human beings are central in their own right. To ignore the meaning of the things toward which people act is seen as falsifying the behaviour under study. To bypass the meaning in face of factors alleged to produce the behaviour is seen as a grievous neglect of the role of meaning in the formation of behaviour.

The simple premise that human beings act toward things on the basis of the meaning of such things is much too simple in itself to differentiate symbolic interactionism—there are several other approaches that share this premise. A major line of difference between them and symbolic interactionism is set by the second premise, which refers to the source of meaning. There are two well-known traditional ways of accounting for the origin of meaning. One of them is to regard meaning as being intrinsic to the thing that has it, as being a natural part of the objective make-up of the thing. Thus, a chair is clearly a chair in itself, a cow a cow, a cloud a cloud, a rebellion a rebellion, and so forth. Being inherent in the thing that has it, meaning needs merely to be disengaged by observing the objective thing that has the meaning. The meaning emanates, so to speak, from the thing and as such there is no process involved in its formation; all that is necessary is to recognize the meaning that is there in the thing. It should be immediately apparent that this view reflects the traditional position of "realism" in philosophy—a position that is widely held and deeply entrenched in the social and psychological sciences. The other major traditional view regards "meaning" as a psychical accretion brought to the thing by the person for whom the thing has meaning. This psychical accretion is treated as being an expression of constituent elements of the person's psyche, mind, or psychological organization. The constituent elements are such things as sensations, feelings, ideas, memories, motives, and attitudes. The meaning of a thing is but the expression of the given psychological elements that are brought into play in connection with the perception of the thing; thus one seeks to explain the meaning of a thing by isolating the particular psychological elements that produce the meaning. One sees this in the somewhat ancient and classical psychological practice of analysing the meaning of an object by identifying the sensations that enter into perception of that object; or in the contemporary practice of tracing the meaning of a thing, such as let us say prostitution, to the attitude of the person who views it. This lodging of the meaning of things in psychological elements limits the processes of the formation of meaning to whatever processes are involved in arousing and bringing together the given psychological elements that produce the meaning. Such processes are psychological in nature, and include perception, cognition, repression, transfer of feelings, and association of ideas.

Symbolic interactionism views meaning as having a different source than those held by the two dominant views just considered. It does not regard meaning as emanating from the intrinsic makeup of the thing that has meaning, nor does it see meaning as arising through a coalescence of psychological elements in the person. Instead, it sees meaning as arising in the process of interaction between people. The meaning of a thing for a person grows out of the ways in which other persons act toward the person with regard to the thing. Their actions operate to define the thing for the person. Thus symbolic interactionism sees meanings as social products, as creations that are formed in and through the defining activities of people as they interact. This point of view gives symbolic interactionism a very distinctive position, with profound implications.

The third premise mentioned above further differentiates symbolic interactionism. While the meaning of things is formed in the context of social interaction and is derived by the person from that interaction, it is a mistake to think that the use of meaning by a person is but an application of the meaning so derived. This mistake seriously mars the work of many scholars who otherwise follow the symbolic interactionist approach. They fail to see that the use of meanings by a person in his action involves an interpretative process. In this respect they are similar to the adherents of the two dominant views spoken of above—to those who lodge meaning in the objective makeup of the thing that has it and those who regard it as an expression of psychological elements. All three are alike in viewing the use of meaning by the human being in his action as being no more than an arousing and application of already established meanings. As such, all three fail to see that the use of meaning by the actor occurs through *a process of interpretation*. This process has two distinct steps.

First, the actor indicates to himself the things toward which he is acting; he has to point out to himself the things that have meaning. The making of such indications is an internalized social process in that the actor is interacting with himself. This interaction with himself is something other than an interplay of psychological elements; it is an instance of the person engaging in a process of communication with himself. Second, by virtue of this process of communicating with himself, interpretation becomes a matter of handling meanings. The actor selects, checks, suspends, regroups, and transforms the meanings in the light of the situation in which he is placed and the direction of his action. Accordingly, interpretation should not be regarded as a mere automatic application of established meanings but as a formative process in which meanings are used and revised as instruments for the guidance and formation of action. It is necessary to see that meanings play their part in action through a process of self-interaction.

Endnotes

1.   The term *symbolic interactionism* is a somewhat barbaric neologism that
        I coined in an off-handed way in an article written in *Man and Society*,
        Emerson P. Schmidt, ed. (New York: Prentice Hall, 1937). The term
        somehow caught on and is now in general use.

Goffman: Rituals of Interaction

Saul Geiser

Erving Goffman's studies of everyday life develop the idea of social action as performance. Here Geiser highlights many of the key concepts in Goffman's research, and emphasizes how both the self and the continuity of social life are simultaneously at risk in an individual's encounters with others.

The Episodic Nature of the Micro-Order

The micro-order may be conceived of as made up of millions of minute and transient episodes of social life. Even where people have long-standing relationships over many years, the actual time they are in communication consists of relatively brief encounters and occasions. In this sense "society" is not an abstraction—it is made up of very specific activities and communications, many of which are fleeting and precarious. To some degree, society as it is really lived is continuously coming into being and passing out of existence.

> A sociology of occasions is here advocated. Social organization is the central theme, but what is organized is the co-mingling of persons and the temporary interactional enterprises that can arise therefrom. A normatively stabilized structure is at issue, a 'social gathering,' but this is a shifting entity, necessarily evanescent, created by arrivals and killed by departures (1967: 2).

Being episodic, the micro-order must be created anew at each successive encounter. Re-creation is accomplished through an exchange of cues and gestures by which the participants indicate to each other their own intended roles in the situation as well as what they expect the others' roles to be. This working consensus will differ from one interaction setting to another.

> Thus, between two friends at lunch, a reciprocal show of affection, respect, and concern for the other is maintained. In service occupations, on the other hand, the specialist often maintains an image of disinterested involvement in the problem of the client, while the client responds with a show of respect for the competence and integrity of the specialist (1959: 10).

Interaction as Theatre

In an important sense, therefore, social interaction is much like theatre. There is an expressive, dramatized element designed to project a definition of reality as much as to carry out practical tasks. Shakespeare's metaphor "all the world's a stage" can be developed into a dramaturgical model of the micro-order, showing how everyday life is pervaded by features of a theatrical performance. Thus, many social establishments are divided into "front-stage" and "backstage" regions. In front-stage areas, such as living rooms and food counters, an idealized display of decorum and cleanliness is affected whenever outsiders are present; backstage, in bedrooms and kitchens, performers can relax in guarded secrecy. Social performances are often staged by teams, such as the husband and wife hosting a dinner party or the doctor and nurse showing spotless clinical efficiency in the presence of patients.

The Management of Impressions

If interaction is like theatre, then individuals must be like actors. The individual as effective "actor" in social encounters must be skilled in the art of "impression management"—controlling his or her image in the eyes of others so as to create a favourable definition of the situation. "For example, in American society we find that eight-year-old children claim lack of interest in the television programs that are directed to five- and six-year-olds, but sometimes surreptitiously watch them. We also find that middle-class housewives may leave *The Saturday Evening Post* on their living room end table but keep a copy of *True Romance* ('It's something the cleaning woman must have left around') concealed in their bedroom...."

> In their capacity as performers, individuals will be concerned with maintaining the impression that they are living up to the many standards by which they and their products are judged. But qua performers, individuals are concerned not with the moral issue of realizing these standards, but with the amoral issue of engineering a convincing impression that these standards are being realized (1959: 42, 251).

The Hazards of Impression Management

Once the individual has projected an impression of himself or herself to others, the others will expect this impression to be maintained throughout the remainder of the encounter as well as in any subsequent encounters.

> The expressive coherence that is required in performances points out a crucial discrepancy between our all-too-human selves and our socialized selves. As human beings we are presumably creatures of variable impulse with moods and energies that change from one moment to the next. As characters put on for an audience, however, we must not be subject to ups and downs. A certain bureaucratization of the spirit is expected so that we can be relied upon to give a perfectly homogeneous performance at every appointed time (1959: 56).

However, such expressive coherence is often difficult to sustain. The individual may make *faux pas* and boners that give away the act; the audience may come into possession of past information about the individual which is inconsistent with the character presently portrayed; outsiders may accidentally enter backstage regions, catching a team in the midst of activity at odds with their front-stage image. A fundamental theme that runs through Goffman's work is the ever-present danger that someone will see through, contradict, or otherwise disrupt a performance.

> When these disruptive events occur, the interaction itself may come to a confused and embarrassed halt. At such moments the individual whose presentation has been discredited may feel ashamed while the others present may feel hostile, and all the participants may come to feel ill at ease, non-plussed, out of countenance, embarrassed, experiencing the kind of anomy that is generated when the minute social system of face-to-face interaction breaks down.
> While the likelihood of disruption will vary widely from interaction to interaction.... There is no interaction in which the participants do not take an appreciable chance of being slightly embarrassed or a slight chance of being deeply humiliated. Life may not be much of a gamble, but interaction is (1959: 12, 243).

The Special Intensity of Face-to-Face Interaction

Face-to-face interaction has a kind of multiplier effect, serving to raise both the emotional intensity as well as the hazards of social interaction. By being in the physical presence of others, the individual gives off information not only by verbal expressions but by clothing, gestures, and physical demeanour; as a result, face-to-face interaction is potentially more threatening to projected definitions of self than interaction mediated by telephone or writing, since more information about the individual is available to the observer.

> Each individual can *see* that he is being experienced in some way, and he will guide at least some of his conduct according to the perceived identity and initial response of his audience. Further, he can be seen to be seeing this, and can see that he has been seen seeing this. Ordinarily, then, to use our naked senses is to use them nakedly and to be made naked by their use. Copresence renders persons uniquely accessible, available, and subject to one another (1963: 16, 22).

Interpersonal Rituals

The main foundation of social order lies in the minute interpersonal rituals—hellos, goodbyes, courtesies, compliments, apologies, and handshakes—that punctuate everyday interaction. "The gestures which we sometimes call empty are perhaps in fact the fullest things of all" (1967: 91).

In the context of religion, "ritual" denotes standardized conduct through which an individual shows respect and regard to an object of ultimate value (usually a supernatural being) or to its stand-in (for example, an idol or a priest). In other words, rituals have mostly ceremonial, but little practical value. Nevertheless, as Durkheim—to whom Goffman owes a theoretical debt—pointed out, ritual and ceremony play an essential role in holding society together; through ritual worship of a common totem, members of primitive tribes reaffirmed their mutual commitment and collective solidarity.

Religious rituals have declined in importance in modern, secular societies, but despite their passing, many kinds of interpersonal rituals remain in force and perform the same function.

There are several types of interpersonal rituals. *Presentation* rituals include such acts as salutations, invitations, and compliments, by which the actor depicts appreciation of the recipient.

> When members of the [hospital] ward passed by each other, salutations would ordinarily by exchanged, the length of the salutation depending upon the period that had elapsed since the last salutation and the period that seemed likely before the next. At table, when eyes met, a brief smile of recognition would be

> exchanged; when someone left for the weekend, a farewell
> involving a pause in on-going activity and a brief exchange of
> words would be involved. In any case, there was the
> understanding that when members of the ward were in a physical
> position to enter into eye-to-eye contact of some kind, this
> contact would be effected. It seemed that anything less would not
> have shown proper respect for the state of relatedness that
> existed among members of the ward (1956/1967: 71).

Avoidance rituals, on the other hand, are practices in which the actors respect
the privacy of others by such distancing behaviours as limiting eye contact
between persons who do not know each other.

> In performing this courtesy the eyes of the looker may pass over
> the eyes of the other, but no "recognition" is typically allowed.
> Where the courtesy is performed between two persons passing on
> the street, civil inattention may take the special form of eyeing
> the other up to eight feet, during which the sides of the street are
> apportioned by gesture, and then casting the eyes down as the
> other passes—a kind of dimming of the lights. In any case, we
> have here what is perhaps the slightest of interpersonal rituals,
> yet one that constantly regulates the social intercourse of persons
> in our society (1963: 84).

Maintenance rituals reaffirm the well-being of a relationship, for example,
where persons with a long-standing relationship who have not seen one another
for a time arrange an encounter: "It is as if the strength of a bond slowly
deteriorates if nothing is done to celebrate it, and so at least occasionally a little
invigoration is called for" (1971: 73).

Ratification rituals, such as congratulations at marriage and commiserations
at divorce, mark the passage of an individual from one status to another:

> Ratificatory rituals express that the performer is alive to the
> situation of the one who has sustained change, that he will
> continue his relationship to him, that support will be maintained,
> that in fact things are what they were in spite of the
> acknowledged change (1971: 67)

Access rituals, such as greetings and farewells, are commonly employed to mark
the transition of persons to and from a state of increased access to one
another:

The enthusiasm of greetings compensates for the weakening of the relationship caused by the absence just terminated, while the enthusiasm of farewells compensates the relationship for the harm that is about to be done to it by separation (1955/1967: 41).

Functions of Interpersonal Rituals

Different rituals serve different specific functions, but all have one essential feature in common: They are a conventionalized means by which the actor portrays ceremonial respect and regard for the self of another. Interpersonal rituals are important for three main reasons: First, they may be likened to traffic signs that serve to keep the flow of interaction moving smoothly and direct it away from areas that could prove dangerous. Like "do not enter" signs, avoidance rituals prevent us from being conversationally accosted in public places and so leave us free to go about our business. Like a green light, invitations and greetings tell us when our interaction is welcome and appropriate. Without the conversational rituals of speaking and listening in turn, social interaction would degenerate into chaotic babble.

A second basic function of interpersonal ritual is to ensure that one's self will escape relatively unscathed when one enters interactional traffic. Each new interactional episode poses a potential threat to the self-image the individual attempts to project; and the self is therefore a "ritually delicate object," ever alert to offences and slights that would reflect unfavourably upon it. Even having one's remarks ignored in conversation can be taken as a sign that one's self is somehow deficient; conversational etiquette requires that one's remarks, however trivial, be acknowledged.

Third, the principle of reciprocity is built into the very structure of interpersonal ritual. It has a "dialogistic" character; that is, it typically involves a standardized exchange of moves and countermoves, or dialogue, between two or more actors: "Hi, how are you?" "Fine, thanks. And you?" Together these moves make up a little ceremony in which both selves receive ritual support; it is like holding hands in a circle, in which one gets back in the left hand what he or she gives with the right. Because such ritual exchanges occur so often in everyday interaction, they provide repeated opportunities for actors mutually to ratify their projected identities and thereby to sustain a workable, if idealized, definition of the situation. Interpersonal ritual thus involves a tacit teamwork, allowing each individual room in which to construct and uphold his or her own chosen identity. It is a curious twist. Though individuals are selfishly concerned to sustain a favourable impression of themselves, their efforts must be ritually expressed as altruistic regard for the identities of others: "His aim is to save face; his effect is to save the situation" (1955/1967: 39).

The Conservative Nature of the Micro-Order

Because of its episodic and fleeting character, the micro-order may seem to be rather flimsy and unstable, lacking a consistent influence on behaviour. In some senses this is true. Since the ritual order depends primarily on informal sanctions to effect conformity, anyone with enough self-assurance can override attempted sanctions simply by not allowing himself or herself to be emotionally affected. Ethnomethodologists profess to see the seeds of a "revolutionary" viewpoint in this analysis: The micro-order exists only because people *believe* it exists; social order is really quite precarious.

Yet Goffman's work has a conservative ring. He is at pains to show how interaction constrains people and why such constraints are necessary if people are to create a shared and consistent definition of reality:

> By entering a situation in which he is given a face to maintain, a person takes on the responsibility of standing guard over the flow of events as they pass before him. He must ensure that a particular *expressive order* is sustained—an order that regulated the flow of events, large or small, so that anything that appears to be expressed by them will be consistent with his face.... While his social face can be his most personal possession and the centre of his security and pleasure, it is only on loan to him from society; it will be withdrawn unless he conducts himself in a way that is worthy of it. Approved attributes and their relation to face make of every man his own jailer; this is a fundamental social constraint even though each man may like his cell (1955/1967: 9-10).

Perhaps the most conservative element in Goffman's account of the micro-order is his emphasis on shared values as the social glue by which society is held together. Unlike theorists of a more radical persuasion who see society as marked by continual conflict and held together by force, he locates the basis of social order in the values people hold in common. Ritual is important insofar as it is a means of ceremonially reaffirming these values. Yet unlike earlier conservative theorists such as Durkheim, who emphasized abstractly shared values and ritual, Goffman shows how ritual performances are a pervasive feature of everyday life:

> To the degree that a performance highlights the common official values of the society in which it occurs, we may look upon it...as a ceremony—as an expressive...reaffirmation of the moral values of the community. Furthermore, insofar as the expressive bias of

performances comes to be accepted as reality, then that which is accepted at the moment as reality will have some of the characteristics of a celebration. To stay in one's room away from the place where the party is given, or away from where the practitioner attends his client, is to stay away from where reality is being performed. The world, in truth, is a wedding (1959: 35-36).

References

A summary and interpretation of works on the micro-order by Erving Goffman. His analyses appear in the following volumes: *The Presentation of Self in Everyday Life* (Garden City, NY: Doubleday Anchor Books, 1959); *Encounters: Two Studies in the Sociology of Interaction* (Indianapolis: Bobbs-Merrill, 1961), *Behaviour in Public Places: Notes on the Social Organization of Gatherings* (New York: The Free Press of Glencoe, 1963); *Interaction Ritual: Essays on Face-to-Face Behaviour* (Garden City, NY: Doubleday Anchor Books, 1967); *Relations in Public: Microstudies of the Public Order* (New York: Harper Colophon Books, 1971). Quoted material, some of which is abridged, is used by permission of the author and copyright holder. This adaptation was prepared by Saul Geiser.

The Ritual Drama of Mutual Pretence

Barney G. Glaser and Anselm L. Strauss

Eight out of ten North Americans will die in hospitals. In this excerpt the authors discuss some of the "implicit mutual understandings" and interaction strategies that have emerged between dying patients and hospital staff.

When patient and staff both know that the patient is dying but pretend otherwise—when both agree to act as if he were going to live—then a context of mutual pretence exists. Either party can initiate his share of the context; it ends when one side cannot, or will not, sustain the pretence any longer.

The mutual-pretence awareness context is perhaps less visible, even to its participants...because the interaction involved tends to be more subtle. On some hospital services, however, it is the predominant context. One nurse who worked on an intensive care unit remarked about an unusual patient who had announced he was going to die: "I haven't had to cope with this very often. I may know they are going to die, and the patient knows it, but (usually) he's just not going to let you know that he knows."

Once we visited a small Catholic hospital where medical and nursing care for the many dying patients was efficiently organized. The staff members were supported in their difficult work by a powerful philosophy—that they were doing everything possible for the patient's comfort—but generally did not talk with patients about death. This setting brought about frequent mutual pretence. This awareness context is also predominant in such settings as county hospitals, where elderly patients of low socioeconomic status are sent to die; patient and staff are well aware of imminent death but each tends to go silently about his own business[1]. Yet, as we shall see, sometimes the mutual pretence context is neither silent nor unnegotiated.

The same kind of ritual pretence is enacted in many situations apart from illness. A charming example occurs when a child announces that he is now a storekeeper, and that his mother should buy something at his store. To carry out his fiction, delicately cooperative action is required. The mother must play seriously, and when the episode has run its natural course, the child will often close it himself with a rounding-off gesture, or it may be concluded by an intruding outside event or by the mother. Quick analysis of this little game of pretence suggests that either player can begin; that the other must then play properly; that realistic (nonfictional) action will destroy the illusion and end the game; that the specific action of the game must develop during interaction; and that eventually the make-believe ends or is ended. Little familial games or dramas of this kind tend to be continual, though each episode may be brief.

For contrast, here is another example that pertains to both children and adults. At the circus, when a clown appears, all but the youngest children know that the clown is not real. But both he and his audience must participate, if only symbolically, in the pretence that he is a clown. The onlookers need do no more than appreciate the clown's act, but if they remove themselves too far, by examining the clown's technique too closely, let's say, then the illusion will be shattered. The clown must also do his best to sustain the illusion by clever acting, by not playing too far "out of character." Ordinarily nobody addresses him as if he were other than the character he is pretending to be. That is, everybody takes him seriously, at face value. And unless particular members return to see the circus again, the clown's performance occurs only once, beginning and ending according to a prearranged schedule.

Our two simple examples of pretence suggest some important features of the particular awareness context to which we shall devote this [discussion]. The make-believe in which patient and hospital staff engage resembles the child's game much more than the clown's act. It has no institutionalized beginning and ending comparable to the entry and departure of the clown; either the patient or the staff must signal the beginning of their joint pretence. Both parties must act properly if the pretence is to be maintained, because, as in the child's game, the illusion created is fragile, and easily shattered by incongruous "realistic" acts. But if either party slips slightly, the other may pretend to ignore the slip.[2] Each episode between the patient and a staff member tends to be brief, but the mutual pretence is done with terrible seriousness, for the stakes are very high.[3]

Initiating the Pretence

This particular awareness context cannot exist, of course, unless both the patient and staff are aware that he is dying. Therefore all the structural conditions which contribute to the existence of open awareness (and which are absent in closed and suspicion awareness) contribute also to the existence of mutual pretence. In addition, at least one interactant must indicate a desire to pretend that the patient is not dying and the other must agree to the pretence, acting accordingly.

A prime structural condition in the existence and maintenance of mutual pretence is that unless the patient initiates conversation about his impending death, no staff member is required to talk about it with him. As typical Americans, they are unlikely to initiate such conversation; and as professionals they have no rules commanding them to talk about death with the patient, unless he desires it. In turn, he may wish to initiate such conversation, but surely neither hospital rules nor common convention urges it upon him. Consequently, unless either the aware patient or the staff members break the silence by words or gestures, a mutual pretence rather than an open awareness context will exist; as, for example, when the physician does not care to talk about death, and the patient does not press the issue though he clearly does recognize his terminality.

The patient, of course, is more likely than the staff members to refer openly to his death, thereby inviting them, explicitly or implicitly, to respond in kind. If they seem unwilling, he may decide they do not wish to confront openly the fact of his death, and then he may, out of tact or genuine empathy for their embarrassment or distress, keep his silence. He may misinterpret their responses, of course, but...he probably has correctly read their reluctance to refer openly to his impending death.

Staff members, in turn, may give him opportunities to speak of his death, if they deem it wise, without their directly or obviously referring to the topic. But if he does not care to act or talk as if he were dying, then they will support his pretence. In doing so, they have, in effect, accepted a complementary assignment of status—they will act with pretence toward his pretence. (If they have misinterpreted his reluctance to act openly, then they have assigned, rather than accepted, a complementary status.)

Two related professional rationales permit them to engage in the pretence. One is that if the patient wishes to pretend, it may well be best for his health, and if and when the pretence finally fails him, all concerned can act more realistically. A secondary rationale is that perhaps they can give him better medical and nursing care if they do not have to face him so openly. In addition, as noted earlier, they can rely on common tact to justify their part in the pretence. Ordinarily, Americans believe that any individual may live—and die—as he chooses, so long as he does not interfere with others' activities, or, in this case, so long as proper care can be given him.

To illustrate the way these silent bargains are initiated and maintained, we quote from an interview with a special nurse. She had been assigned to a patient before he became terminal, and she was more apt than most personnel to encourage his talking openly, because as a graduate student in a nursing class that emphasized psychological care, she had more time to spend with her patient than a regular floor nurse. Here is the exchange between interviewer and nurse:

Interviewer: Did he talk about his cancer or his dying?
Nurse: Well, I got that impression, yes.... It wasn't really openly, but I think the day that his roommate said he should get up and start walking, I felt that he was a little bit antagonistic. He said what his condition was, that he felt very, very ill that moment.
Interviewer: He never talked about leaving the hospital?

Nurse: Never.
Interviewer: Did he talk about his future at all?
Nurse: Not a thing. I never heard a word....
Interviewer: You said yesterday that he was more or less isolated,
              because the nurses felt that he was hostile. But they have
              dealt with patients like this many, many times. You said
              they stayed away from him?
Nurse: Well, I think at the very end. You see, this is what I meant
              by isolation...we don't communicate with them. I didn't,
              except when I did things for him. I think you expect
              somebody to respond to, and if they're very ill we don't....
              I talked it over with my instructor, mentioning things that
              I could probably have done; for instance, this isolation, I
              should have communicated with him....
Interviewer: You think that since you knew he was going to die, and
              you half suspected that he knew it too, or more than half;
              do you think that this understanding grew between you in
              any way?
Nurse: I believe so.... I think it's kind of hard to say but when I
              came in the room, even when he was very ill, he'd rather
              look at me and try to give me a smile, and gave me the
              impression that he accepted.... I think this is one reason
              why I feel I should have communicated with him...and this
              is why I feel he was rather isolated....

From the nurse's account, it is difficult to tell whether the patient wished to talk openly about his death, but was rebuffed; or whether he initiated the pretence and the nurse accepted his decision. But it is remarkable how a patient can flash cues to the staff about his own dread knowledge; inviting the staff to talk about his destiny, while the nurses and physicians decide that it is better not to talk too openly with him about his condition lest he "go to pieces." The patient, as remarked earlier, picks up these signals of unwillingness, and the mutual pretence context has been initiated. A specific and obvious instance is this: an elderly patient, who had lived a full and satisfying life, wished to round it off by talking about his impending death. The nurses retreated before this prospect, as did his wife, reproving him, saying he should not think or talk about morbid matters. A hospital chaplain finally intervened, first by listening to the patient himself, then by inducing the nurses and the wife to do likewise, or at least to acknowledge more openly that the man was dying. He was not successful with all the nurses.

The staff members are more likely to sanction a patient's pretence than his family's. The implicit rule is that though the patient need not be forced to speak of his dying, or to act as if he were dying, his kin should face facts. After all, they will have to live with the facts after his death. Besides, staff members usually find it less difficult to talk about dying with the family. Family members are not inevitably drawn into open discussion, but the likelihood is high, particularly since they themselves are likely to initiate discussion or at least to make gestures of awareness.

Sometimes, however, pretence protects the family member temporarily against too much grief, and the staff members against too immediate a scene. This may occur when a relative has just learned about the impending death and the nurse controls the ensuing scene by initiating temporary pretence. The reverse situation also occurs: a newly arrived nurse discovers the patient's terminality, and the relative smooths over the nurse's distress by temporary pretence.

The Pretence Interaction

An intern whom we observed during our field work suspected that the patient he was examining had cancer, but he could not discover where it was located. The patient previously had been told that she probably had cancer, and she was now at this teaching hospital for that reason. The intern's examination went on for some time. Yet neither he nor she spoke about what he was searching for, nor in any way suggested that she might be dying. We mention this episode to contrast it with the more extended interactions with which this [selection] is concerned. These have an episodic quality—personnel enter and leave the patient's room, or he occasionally emerges and encounters them—but their extended duration means that special effort is required to prevent their breaking down, and that the interactants must work hard to construct and maintain their mutual pretence. By contrast, in a formally staged play, although the actors have to construct and maintain a performance, making it credible to their audience, they are not required to write the script themselves. The situation that involves a terminal patient is much more like a masquerade party, where one masked actor plays carefully to another as long as they are together, and the total drama actually emerges from their joint creative effort.

A masquerade, however, has more extensive resources to sustain it than those the hospital situation provides. Masqueraders wear masks, hiding their facial expressions; even if they "break up" with silent laughter (as a staff member may "break down" with sympathy), this fact is concealed. Also, according to the rules ordinarily governing masquerades, each actor chooses his own status, his "character," and this makes his role in the constructed drama somewhat easier to play. He may even have played similar parts before. But terminal patients usually have had no previous experience with their pretended status, and not all personnel have had much experience. In a masquerade, when the drama fails it can be broken off, each actor moving along to another partner; but in the hospital the pretenders (especially the patient) have few comparable opportunities.

Both situations share one feature—the extensive use of props for sustaining the crucial illusion. In the masquerade, the props include not only masks but clothes and other costuming, as well as the setting where the masquerade takes place. In the hospital interaction, props also abound. Patients dress for the part of not-dying patient, including careful attention to grooming, and to hair and makeup by female patients. The terminal patient may also fix up his room so that it looks and feels "just like home," an activity that supports his enactment of normalcy. Nurses may respond to these props with explicit appreciation—"how lovely your hair looks this morning"—even help to establish them, as by doing the patient's hair. We remember one elaborate pretence ritual involving a husband and wife who had won the nurses' sympathy. The husband simply would not recognize that his already comatose wife was approaching death, so each morning the nurses carefully prepared her for his visit, dressing her for the occasion and making certain that she looked as beautiful as possible.

The staff, of course, has its own props to support its ritual prediction that the patient is going to get well: thermometers, baths, fresh sheets, and meals on time! Each party utilizes these props as he sees fit, thereby helping to create the pretence anew. But when a patient wishes to demonstrate that he is finished with life, he may drive the nurses wild by refusing to cooperate in the daily routines of hospital life—that is, he refuses to allow the nurses to use their props. Conversely, when the personnel wish to indicate how things are with him, they may begin to omit some of those routines.

During the pretence episodes, both sides play according to the rules implicit in the interaction. Although neither the staff nor patient may recognize these rules as such, certain tactics are fashioned around them, and the action is partly constrained by them. One rule is that dangerous topics should generally be avoided. The most obviously dangerous topic is the patient's death; another is events that will happen afterwards. Of course, both parties to the pretence are supposed to follow the avoidance rule.

There is, however, a qualifying rule: Talk about dangerous topics is permissible as long as neither party breaks down. Thus, a patient refers to the distant future, as if it were his to talk about. He talks about his plans for his family, as if he would be there to share their consummation. He and the nurses discuss today's events—such as his treatments—as if they had implications for a real future, when he will have recovered form his illness. And some of his brave or foolhardy activities may signify a brave show of pretence, as when he bathes himself or insists on tottering to the toilet by himself. The staff in turn permits his activity. (Two days before he returned to the hospital to die, one patient insisted that his wife allow him to travel downtown to keep a speaking engagement, and to the last he kept up a lively conversation with a close friend about a book they were planning to write together.)

A third rule, complementing the first two, is that each actor should focus determinedly on appropriately safe topics. It is customary to talk about the daily routines—eating (the food was especially good or bad), and sleeping (whether one slept well or poorly last night). Complaints and their management help pass the time. So do minor personal confidences, and chatter about events on the ward. Talk about physical symptoms is safe enough if confined to the symptoms themselves, with no implied references to death. A terminal patient and a staff member may safely talk, and at length, about his disease so long as they skirt its fatal significance. And there are many genuinely safe topics having to do with movies and movie stars, politics, fashions—with everything, in short, that signifies that life is going on "as usual."

A fourth interactional rule is that when something happens, or is said, that tends to expose the fiction that both parties are attempting to sustain, then each must pretend that nothing has gone awry. Just as each has carefully avoided calling attention to the true situation, each now must avert his gaze from the unfortunate intrusion. Thus, a nurse may take special pains to announce herself before entering a patient's room so as not to surprise him at his crying. If she finds him crying she may ignore it or convert it into an innocuous event with a skilful comment or gesture—much like the tactful gentleman who, having stumbled upon a woman in his bathtub, is said to have casually closed the bathroom door, murmuring "Pardon me, sir." The mutuality of the pretence is illustrated by the way a patient who cannot control a sudden expression of great pain will verbally discount its significance, while the nurse in turn goes along with his pretence. Or she may brush aside or totally ignore a major error in his portrayal, as when he refers spontaneously to his death. If he is tempted to admit impulsively his terminality, she may, again, ignore his impulsive remarks or obviously misinterpret them. Thus, pretence is piled upon pretence to conceal or minimize interactional slips.

Clearly then, each party to the ritual pretence shares responsibility for maintaining it. The major responsibility may be transferred back and forth, but each party must support the other's temporary dominance in his own action. This is true even when conversation is absolutely minimal, as in some hospitals where patients take no particular pains to signal awareness of their terminality, and the staff makes no special gestures to convey its own awareness. The pretence interaction in this case is greatly simplified, but it is still discernible. Whenever a staff member is so indelicate, or so straightforward, as to act openly as if a terminal patient were dying, or if the patient does so himself, then the pretence vanishes. If neither wishes to destroy the fiction, however, then each must strive to keep the situation "normal."[4]

The Transition to Open Awareness

A mutual pretence context that is not sustained can only change to an open awareness context. (Either party, however, may again initiate the pretence context and sometimes get cooperation from the other.) The change can be sudden, when either patient or staff distinctly conveys that he has permanently abandoned the pretence. Or the change to the open context can be gradual: nurses, and relatives, too, are familiar with patients who admit to terminality more openly on some days than they do on other days, when pretence is dominant, until finally pretence vanishes altogether. Sometimes the physician skilfully paces his interaction with a patient, leading the patient finally to refer openly to his terminality and to leave behind the earlier phase of pretence.

Pretence generally collapses when certain conditions make its maintenance increasingly difficult. These conditions have been foreshadowed in our previous discussion. Thus, when the patient cannot keep from expressing his increasing pain, or his suffering grows to the point that he is kept under heavy sedation then the enactment of pretence becomes more difficult, especially for him.

Again, neither patient nor staff may be able to avoid bringing impending death into the open if radical physical deterioration sets in, the staff because it has a tough job to do, and the patient for other reasons, including fright and panic. Sometimes a patient breaks his pretence for psychological reasons, as when he discovers that he cannot face death alone, or when a chaplain convinces him that it is better to bring things out into the open than to remain silent. (Sometimes, however, a patient may find such a sympathetic listener in the chaplain that he can continue his pretence with other personnel.) Sometimes he breaks the pretence when it no longer makes sense in light of obvious physical deterioration.

Here is a poignant episode during which a patient dying with great pain and obvious bodily deterioration finally abandoned her pretence with a nurse:

> There was a long silence. Then the patient asked, "After I get home from the nursing home will you visit me?" I asked if she wanted me to. "Yes, Mary, you know we could go on long drives together...." She had a faraway look in her eyes as if daydreaming about all the places she would visit and all the things we could do together. This continued for some time. Then I asked, "Do you think you will be able to drive your car again?" She looked at me, "Mary, I know I am daydreaming; I know I am

> going to die." Then she cried, and said, "This is terrible, I never
> thought I would be this way."

In short, when a patient finds it increasingly difficult to hand onto a semblance
of his former healthy self and begins to become a person who is visibly dying,
both he and the staff are increasingly prone to say so openly, whether by word
or gesture. Sometimes, however, a race occurs between a patient's persistent
pretence and his becoming comatose or his actual death—a few more days of
sentience or life, and either he or the staff would have dropped the pretence.

Yet, a contest may ensue when only one side wishes to keep up the
pretence. When a patient openly displays his awareness but shows it
unacceptably, as by apathetically "giving up," the staff or family may try to
reinstate the pretence. Usually the patient then insists on open recognition of
his own impending death, but sometimes he is persuaded to return to the
pretence. For instance, one patient finally wished to talk openly about death,
but her husband argued against its probability, although he knew better; so
after several attempts to talk openly, the patient obligingly gave up the contest.
The reverse situation may also occur: the nurses begin to give the patient every
opportunity to die with a maximum of comfort—as by cutting down on normal
routines—thus signalling that he should no longer pretend, but the patient
insists on putting up a brave show and so the nurses capitulate.

We would complicate our analysis unduly if we did more than suggest that,
under such conditions, the pretence ritual sometimes resembles Ptolemy's
cumbersomely patched astronomical system, with interactants pretending to
pretend to pretend! We shall only add that when nurses attempt to change the
pretence context into an open context, they generally do this "on their own"
and not because of any calculated ward standards or specific orders from an
attending physician. And the tactics they use to get the patient to refer openly
to his terminality are less tried and true than the more customary tactics for
forcing him to pretend.

Consequences of Mutual Pretence

For the patient, the pretence context can yield a measure of dignity and
considerable privacy, though it may deny him the closer relationships with staff
members and family members that sometimes occur when he allows them to
participate in his open acceptance of death. And if they initiate and he accepts
the pretence, he may have nobody with whom to talk although he might profit
greatly from talk. (One terminal patient told a close friend, who told us, that
when her family and husband insisted on pretending that she would recover,
she suffered from the isolation, feeling as if she were trapped in cotton batting.)

For the family—especially more distant kin—the pretence context can minimize embarrassment and other interactional strains; but for closer kin, franker concourse may have many advantages.... Oscillation between contexts of open awareness and mutual pretence can also cause interactional strains. We once observed a man persuading his mother to abandon her apathy—she had permanently closed her eyes, to the staff's great distress—and "try hard to live." She agreed finally to resume the pretence, but later relapsed into apathy. The series of episodes caused some anguish to both family and patient, as well as to the nurses. When the patient initiates the mutual pretence, staff members are likely to feel relieved. Yet the consequent stress of either maintaining the pretence or changing it to open awareness sometimes may be considerable. Again, both the relief and the stress affect nurses more than medical personnel, principally because the latter spend less time with patients.

But whether staff or patient initiates the ritual of pretence, maintaining it creates a characteristic ward mood of cautious serenity. A nurse once told us of a cancer hospital where each patient understood that everyone there had cancer, including himself, but the rules of tact, buttressed by staff silence, were so strong that few patients talked openly about anyone's condition. The consequent atmosphere was probably less serene than when only a few patients are engaged in mutual pretence, but even one such patient can affect the organizational mood, especially if the personnel become "involved" with him.

A persistent context of mutual pretence profoundly affects the more permanent aspects of hospital organization as well. (This often occurs at county and city hospitals.) Imagine what a hospital service would be like if all terminal patients were unacquainted with their terminality, or if all were perfectly open about their awareness—whether they accepted or rebelled against their fate.[5] When closed awareness generally prevails the personnel must guard against disclosure, but they need not organize themselves as a team to handle continued pretence and its sometimes stressful breakdown. Also, a chief organizational consequence of the mutual pretence context is that it eliminates any possibility that staff members might "work with" patients psychologically, on a self-conscious professional basis. This consequence was strikingly evident at the small Catholic hospital referred to a few pages ago. It is also entirely possible that a ward mood of tension can be set when (as a former patient once told us) a number of elderly dying patients continually communicate to each other their willingness to die, but the staff members persistently insist on the pretence that the patients are going to recover. On the other hand, the prevailing ward mood accompanying mutual pretence tends to be more serene—or at least less obviously tense—than when open suspicion awareness is dominant.

Endnotes

1. Robert Kastenbaum has reported that at Cushing Hospital, "a Public Medical Institute for the care and custody of the elderly" in Framingham, Massachusetts, "patient and staff members frequently have an implicit mutual understanding with regard to death...institutional dynamics tend to operate against making death 'visible' and a subject of open communication.... Elderly patients often behave as though they appreciated the unspoken feelings of the staff members and were attempting to make their demise as acceptable and unthreatening as possible." This observation is noted in Robert Kastenbaum, "The Interpersonal Context of Death in a Geriatric Institution," abstract of paper presented at the Seventeenth Annual Scientific Meeting, Gerontological Society (Minneapolis: October 29-31, 1964).

2. I. Bensman and I. Garver, "Crime and Punishment in the Factor," in A. Gouldner and H. Gouldner (eds.). 1963. *Modern Society*. New York: Harcourt, Brace and World, pp. 593-96.

3. A German communist, Alexander Weissberg, accused of spying during the great period of Soviet spy trails, has written a fascinating account of how he and many other accused persons collaborated with the Soviet government in an elaborate pretence, carried on for the benefit of the outside world. The stakes were high for the accused (their lives) as well as for the Soviet. Weissberg's narrative also illustrated how uninitiated interactants must be coached into their roles and how they must be cued into the existence of the pretence context where they do not recognize it. See Alexander Weissberg. 1951. *The Accused*. New York: Simon and Schuster.

4. A close reading of John Gunther's poignant account of his young son's last months shows that the boy maintained a sustained and delicately balanced mutual pretence with his parents, physicians and nurses. John Gunther. 1949. *Death Be Not Proud* New York: Harper and Bros. Also see Bensman and Garver, *op. cit.*

5. For a description of a research hospital where open awareness prevails, with far-reaching effects on hospital social structure, see Renée Fox. *Experiment Perilous*. 1959. New York: Free Press of Glencoe.

Interaction: The Work Women Do

Pamela M. Fishman

Who usually asks more questions, men or women? What is the significance of asking more questions? In this research study Fishman analyses conversations between men and women in their homes, and discusses how asking questions connects to the issue of power between the genders.

The oppression of women in society is an issue of growing concern, both in academic fields and in everyday life. Despite research on the historical and economic bases of women's position, we know little about how hierarchy is routinely established and maintained in daily experience. This essay analyses conversations between women and men in their homes, demonstrating how verbal interaction helps to construct and maintain the hierarchical relations between men and women.

Weber (1969: 152) provided the classic conception of power as the ability of one actor in a social relationship to impose their will on another. Recently, Berger and Luckmann (1967: 109) have discussed power from a perspective which specifies an important way of "imposing one's will" on others. They define power as a question of potentially conflicting definitions of reality; that of the most powerful will be "made to stick." Imposing one's will can be much more than forcing someone else to do something. Power may also involve the ability to impose one's definition of what is possible, what is right, what is rational, what is real. Power is a product of human activities, just as the activities are themselves products of the power relations in the socioeconomic world.

Power usually is analysed macrosociologically; it cannot be solely a result of what people do within the immediate situation in which it occurs. What people do in specific interactions expresses and reflects historical and social structural forces beyond the boundaries of their encounters. Power relations between men and women are the outcome of the social organization of their activities in the home and in the economy. Power can, however, be analysed micro-sociologically, which is the purpose of this paper. Power and hierarchical relations are not abstract forces operating on people. Power must be a human accomplishment, situated in everyday interaction. Both structural forces and interactional activities are vital to the maintenance and construction of social reality, including hierarchies.

Recent work on gender and the English language shows that the male-female hierarchy is inherent in the words we use to perceive and name our world; the use of the generic "man" to refer to the human species (Stanley, 1977); the addition of suffixes ("authoress," "actress," "stewardess") when referring to female practitioners (Miller & Swift, 1976); the asymmetrical use of first and last names (women are more often called by their first, men by their last, even when they are of equal rank) (see McConnell-Ginet, 1978, for a full discussion). These and other studies document the male-dominated reality expressed through our language.

Much less attention has been directed toward how male-female power relations are expressed through the dynamics of conversation.[1] To complement other language and gender studies, we need more analyses of the interactional production of a particular reality through people's talk.

Conversational activity is significant for intimates. Berger and Kellner (1970) have argued that at present, with the increasing separation of public and private spheres of life, intimate relationships are among the most important reality-maintaining settings. They apply this argument specifically to marriage. The process of daily interaction in the marital relationship is ideally

> ...one in which reality is crystallized, narrowed and stabilized.
> Ambivalences are converted into certainties. Typifications of self
> and other become settled. Most generally, possibilities become
> facticities (1970: 64).

In these relationships, in these mundane interactions, much of the essential work of sustaining the reality of the world goes on. Intimates often reconstruct their separate experiences, past and present, with one another. Specifically, the couple sustain and produce the reality of their own relationship, and more generally, of the world.

Although Berger and Kellner have analysed marriage as a reality-producing setting, they have not analysed the interaction of marriage partners nor the differences and inequalities which may be involved in the reality-construction process. I shall focus here on the interactional activities that constitute the everyday work done by intimates and the different activities of the partners which emerge. It is through this work that people produce their relationship to one another, their relationship to the world, and those patterns normally referred to as social structure.

Work In Interaction[2]

Sometimes we think of interaction as work. At a party or meeting where silence lies heavy, we recognize the burden of interaction and respond to it as work. The many books written on "the art of conversation" call attention to the tasks involved in interaction. It is not simply an analogy to think of interaction as work. Rather, it is an intuitive recognition of what must be accomplished for interaction to occur.

Interaction requires at least two people. Conversation is produced not simply by their presence, but also by the display of their continuing agreement to pay attention to one another. That is, all interactions are potentially problematic and occur only through the continual, turn-by-turn, efforts of the participants.

Sacks and his followers (Sacks et al. 1974; Schegloff & Sacks, 1974; Schegloff, 1972) have sought to specify how conversationalists accomplish such things as beginnings and endings. They have ignored, however, the interaction between intimates. Schegloff and Sacks (1974: 262) characterize intimates in home situations as "in continuing states of incipient talk." Thus, they contend that their analysis of the activities involved in opening and closing conversations, and in keeping conversation going, do not apply to intimate conversations. But this perspective disregards the many conversations that do not begin with greetings nor end with good-byes. If one sees a movie with friends, conversation afterwards does not begin anew with greetings. In social gatherings lulls occur and conversation must begin again. In any setting in which conversation is possible, attempts at beginning, sustaining, and stopping talk still must be made. And these attempts must be recognized and oriented by both parties for them to move between states of "incipient" and "actual" conversation.

In a sense, every remark or turn at speaking should be seen as an *attempt* to interact. It may be an attempt to open or close a conversation. It may be a bid to continue interaction, to respond to what went before, and elicit a further remark from one's partner. Some attempts succeed; others fail. For an attempt to succeed, the other party must be willing to do further interactional work. That other person has the power to turn an attempt into a conversation or to stop it dead.

Data

The data for this study come from fifty-two hours of tape-recorded conversation between intimates in their homes. Three heterosexual couples agreed to place tape recorders in their apartments. They had the right to censor the material before I heard it. The apartments were small, so that the recorders picked up all conversation from the kitchen and living room as well as the louder portions of talk from the bedroom and bath. The tapes could run for a four-hour period without interruption. Though I had timers to switch the tapes on and off automatically, all three couples insisted on doing the switching manually. The segments of uninterrupted recording vary from one to four hours.

The three couples had been together for various amounts of time—three months, six months, and two years. All were white and professionally oriented, between the ages of twenty-five and thirty-five. One woman was a social worker and the other five people were in graduate school. Two of the women were avowed feminists and all three men as well as the other woman described themselves as sympathetic to the women's movement.

The tape recorders were present in the apartments from four to fourteen days. I am satisfied that the material represents natural conversation and that there was no undue awareness of the recorder. The tapes sounded natural to me, like conversations between my husband and myself. Others who read the transcripts agree. All six people reported that they soon began to ignore the tape recorder, they were apologetic about the material, calling it trivial and uninteresting, just the ordinary affairs of everyday life. Furthermore, one couple forgot the recorder sufficiently to begin making love in the living room while the recorder was on. That segment and two others were the only ones the participants deleted before handing the tapes over to me.

Method

I began the research in order to explore the ways in which power was reflected and maintained in daily interactions. I had some ideas of what to look for, but generally my categories and concepts developed out of the conversations on the tapes. For example, I did not start the analysis with the conception of interactional work, but as I noticed the frequency of questions on the tapes and began to think about how they functioned conversationally, I came to the notion of work.

The frequency counts reported in the body of the paper are from twelve and a half hours of transcribed tapes. Five hours of the transcripts were the first ones I did and these were selected for two reasons. First, when I started the research I was looking for examples of decision making and references to Garfinkel's (1967) "essential features" of conversation. I transcribed segments which showed either of these. Second, I also had the sense while listening to the tapes that some of the conversations were "good" ones and others were "bad." I transcribed some of each in hope that I could find what was going on conversationally that led me to those vague evaluations. The identification of conversational strategies and the conception of conversational work came out of my analysis of these first five hours.

The remaining seven and a half hours were transcribed with no motive but that of transferring more of the tapes to paper. They represent all the talk on one side of tape from each of the three couples.[3] I then used these to double-check the frequency counts of the strategies I had by then specified (the variation has not been significant). The analysis of topic initiations which comes later in this paper was based on all the transcripts.

Preliminary Evidence

Some evidence of the power relations between couples appeared while I was still in the process of collecting the tapes. During casual conversations with the participants after the taping, I learned that in all three couples the men usually set up the tape recorders and turned them on and off. More significantly, some of the times that the men turned the recorders on, they did so without the women's knowledge. The reverse never occurred.

To control conversation is not merely to choose the topic. It is a matter of having control over the definition of the situation in general, which includes not only what will be talked about, but whether there will be a conversation at all and under what terms it will occur. Control over specific details of the situation can be important. The addition of a tape recorder in the home is an example of a change in a routine situation. The men clearly had and actively maintained unilateral control over this new feature in the situation.

This research also raised the issue of a typically private interaction becoming available to a third party, the researcher. The men more often played back the tapes for possible censoring, and they made the only two attempts to exert control over the presentation of the data to me. One case involved the "clicks" that are normally recorded when the recorder is turned off. Since more than one time segment was often on the same side of a tape, I relied on the clicks, as well as my sense of the conversations, to know when a new time segment began. One man carefully erased nearly all the clicks on the tapes, making it difficult to separate out recordings at different time periods. (He said he wanted to make the recording sound smoother.)

The second instance was a more explicit illustration of male censorship. Early on, I made the error of asking a couple to help transcribe a segment of their tape. The error was doubly instructive. First, I saw that the participants could rarely hear or understand the problem areas any better than I even though they had been "on the spot" and were hearing their own voices. Second, the man kept wanting to know why I was interested in the segment, repeatedly guessing what I was looking for. At the time, I only knew that it was an example of decision making and did not know specifically what I wanted. He never accepted this explanation. He became irritated at my continued attempt at literal transcription and kept insisting that he could give me the sense of what occurred and that the exact words were unimportant. He continued the attempt to determine the meaning of the interaction retrospectively, with constant references to his motives for saying this or that. It took hours to withdraw from the situation, as he insisted on giving me the help that I had requested.

The preliminary data suggest that the men are more likely than the women to control conversation. The men ensured that they knew when the tape recorder was on and, thus, when their interaction was available to a third party. They were unconcerned, however, whether the women also knew. Further, in at least two cases they attempted to control my interpretation of the tapes.

Findings: Interactional Strategies

Textual analysis revealed how interactants do the work of conversation. There are a variety of strategies to ensure, encourage, and subvert conversation. The differential use of these strategies by women and men suggests that there is inequality in talk between the sexes. Conversation is more problematic for women, who work harder to make it happen. Talk seems less problematic for men, who exert control over when and how it will occur. As these findings indicate, there are specific ways to see this inequality in action.

While there are problems with generalizing from three couples to male-female conversations overall, I do so for a number of reasons. First, this work suggests many areas for further study: Will other researchers find the same patterns among other heterosexual couples? Do these patterns appear in other hierarchial relations, like bosses and workers, teachers and students? Are there male-female conversational differences in larger groups and are the patterns similar or different? What will we find in video-taped interactions? Second, while the findings are based on the conversations of three couples, they have been confirmed many times by my own informal observations and by reports from other people of their experience. Finally, the findings are helpful. Since the strategies are quite concrete, they can be noticed in conversation. They are cues by which people, and particularly women, can figure out what is happening in their own interactions.

Asking Questions

There is an overwhelming difference between female and male use of questions as a resource in interaction. At times I felt that all women did was ask questions. In the transcripts the women asked two and a half times the questions that the men did.

Other research (Lakoff, 1975) suggests that women ask more questions than men. Lakoff has interpreted women's question-making as an indication of their insecurity, a linguistic signal of an internal psychological state resulting from the oppression of women. But a psychological analysis is unnecessary to explain why women ask more questions than men. Since questions are produced in conversations, we should look first to how questions function there.

Questions are interactionally powerful utterances. They are among a class of utterances, like greetings, treated as standing in a paired relation; that is, they demand a next utterance. Questions are paired with answers (Sacks, 1972). They "deserve" answers. The absence of a response is noticeable and may be complained about. A question does work in conversation by opening a two-part (Q-A) sequence. It is a way to insure a minimal interaction—at least one utterance by each of the two participants. By asking questions, women strengthen the possibility of a response to what they have to say.

Once I had noted the phenomenon of questions on the tapes, I attended to my own speech and discovered the same pattern. I tried, and still do try, to break myself of the "habit" and found it very difficult. Remarks kept coming out as questions before I could rephrase them. When I did succeed in making a remark as a statement, I usually did not get a response. It became clear that I asked questions not merely out of habit nor from insecurity but because it was likely that my attempt at interaction would fail if I did not.

Asking "D'ya Know"

In line with the assumption that children have restricted rights to speak in the presence of adults, Harvey Sacks (1972) describes a type of question used extensively by children as conversational opening: "D'ya know what?" As with other questions, it provides for a next utterance. The next utterance it engenders is itself a question, which provides for yet another utterance. The archetype is, "D'ya know what?" "What?" "Blahblah (answer)." Sometimes, of course, the adult answers with an expectant look or a statement like, "Tell me what." Whatever the exact form of the first response, initial questions like "D'ya know what?" set off a three-part sequence, Q-Q-A, rather than a simple Q-A sequence.

Sacks points out that the children's use of this device is a clever solution to their problem of ensuring rights to speak (at the same time, their use of this strategy acknowledges those restricted rights). In response to the "What?" the children may say what they wanted to say in the first place. Finding such three part "D'ya know" sequences in interaction informs us both about the work of guaranteeing interaction and the differential rights of the participants. This device was used twice as often by the women.

Attention Beginnings

The phrase, "this is interesting," or a variation thereof, occurs throughout the tapes. Ideally, the work of establishing that a remark is interesting is accomplished by both interactants. The first person makes a remark; the second person orients to and responds to the remark, thus establishing its status as something worthy of joint interest or importance. All this occurs without the question of its interest ever becoming explicit.[4] The use of "This is really interesting" as an introduction shows that the user cannot assume that the remark itself will be seen as worthy of attention. At the same time, the user tries single-handedly to establish the interest of their remarks. The user is saying, "Pay attention to what I have to say, I can't assume that you will." The women used twice as many attention beginnings as the men.

There are also many instances of "y'know" interspersed throughout the transcripts. While this phrase does not compel the attention of one's partner as forcefully as "this is interesting" does, it is an attempt to command the other person's attention. The women said "you know" five times as often as the men (for further analysis of this phrase, see Fishman, 1980).

Minimal Response

Another interaction strategy is the use of the minimal response, when the speaker takes a turn by saying "yeah," "umm," "huh," and only that. Women and men both do this, but they tend to use minimal response in quite different ways. The male usages of the minimal response displayed lack of interest. The monosyllabic response merely filled a turn at a point when it need to be filled. For example, a woman would make a lengthy remark, after which the man responded with "yeah," doing nothing to encourage her, nor to elaborate. Such minimal responses operate to discourage interaction.

The women also made this type of minimal response at times, but their most frequent use of the minimal response was as "support work." Throughout the tapes, when the men are talking, the women are particularly skilled at inserting "mm's," "yeah's," "oh's," and other such comments throughout streams of talk rather than at the end. These are signs from the inserter that she is constantly attending to what is said, that she is demonstrating her participation, her interest in the interaction and the speaker. How well the women do this is also striking—seldom do they mistime their insertions and cause even slight overlaps. These minimal responses occur between the breaths of a speaker, and there is nothing in tone or structure to suggest they are attempting to take over the talk.

Making Statements

Finally, I would like to consider statements, utterances that do nothing to ensure their own success or the success of the interaction. Of course, a statement does some interactional work: it fills a turn and provides for a response. However, such statements display an assumption on the part of the speaker that the attempt will be successful as is; it will be understood, the statement is of interest, there will be a response. It is as if speakers can assume that everything is working well; success is naturally theirs.

In the transcribed material, the men produced over twice as many statements as the women, and they almost always got a response, which was not true for the women. For example: many times one or both people were reading, then read a passage aloud or commented on it. The man's comments often engendered a lengthy exchange, the woman's seldom did. In a discussion of their respective vitas, the man literally ignored both long and short comments from the woman on her vita, returning the conversation after each remark of hers back to his own. Each time, she turned her attention back to his vita "as directed."

Topic Initiation

Women use many of these strategies so frequently because conversations are generally more problematic for them than for men. This can be seen by looking at what happens to the topics women and men introduce into conversation.[5]

I considered an utterance to be a topic initiation if it addressed itself to a different subject from the utterance preceding it, or if it reinitiated a topic after an outside interruption, like a phone call, or after a very lengthy silence. In the latter case, I relied on a sense from the tapes that the topic had been dropped and the next mention of it was thus a reintroduction.

Using this method on the transcripts, I found that there were seventy-six topics raised. The women initiated forty-seven of them, the men twenty-nine. That is, the women raised between one and half and two times more topics than did the men.

However, raising a topic does not ensure that it gets talked about. Introducing a topic is an attempt to get a conversation going, not a guarantee that it will occur. In order for the topic to be successful, to turn into an actual conversation, both participants must work to make it happen. They both must orient to the topic and to one another. Not only must one person raise the topic, the other person must respond, and at least some of those responses must contribute to the topic's elaboration. At minimum, the two people need to take turns speaking, thus displaying their mutual orientation to each other and to the topic at hand.

Table 1 shows what happened to the topics raised by women and men. Of the forty-seven topics initiated by the women, seventeen succeeded, while twenty-eight of the twenty-nine topics raised by the mean succeeded. Thus, while the women made 62% of all attempts to introduce topics, they only raised 38% of the topics which evolved into conversation.

Table 1 — Topic Success and Failure

	Success	Failure	Uncertain	Total
M	28	0	1	29
F	17	28	2	47
Total	45	28	3	76

Clearly, the women had much more trouble getting conversations going than the men did. We cannot explain the women's failures on the basis of the content of the topics, since what the women and men wanted to talk about was quite similar—an article in the paper, something that happened during the day, friends, dinner, work. Topics introduced by the women failed because the men did not respond with the attention necessary to keep the conversation going.

In contrast, the men's topics succeeded not because they were inherently more interesting but because the women upheld their part of the conversations. The women responded regularly and in non-minimal ways; they displayed orientation by taking conversational turns. Topics men initiated succeeded because both parties worked to turn the initial attempt into an actual conversation.

Topics fail not only through the extreme case of non-response of the other party. Many topics continue to be pushed by the raiser over some period of time, yet the topic fails conversationally because there is no joint development of it. The increasing use of conversational devices like question-asking and attention beginnings is one sign that a topic is in trouble. Similarly, we can trace topic failure by noting the use of minimal responses (see above) which do nothing to develop the topic or to express interest.

The structure of pause in the conversation is another indication of the failure of a topic. In a developing conversation, the pauses between one person's utterance and the other person's response are often a second or less, and seldom more than three seconds. (There are exceptions to this, such as when a person's pause displays appreciation of a poem or thinking about what has been said. Such displays are normally clear in the utterance following the pause.) Long pauses between turns at speaking usually indicate minimal attention and interest on the part of the responder. It is as if the responder is thinking, "Oh, yeah. I have to say something here." Minimal responses, which are good ways of saying something without saying anything particular, often follow long pauses.

Another indication that the topic is in trouble occurs when a person pauses in the midst of an utterance. Internal pauses often increase when the speaker's utterances have been continually met by minimal responses or long pauses from the other party. The number of "you know's" also increases in these circumstances, and one often finds internal pausing and "you know" together.[6]

Conclusions

There is an unequal distribution of work in conversation. We can see from the differential use of strategies that the women are more actively engaged in ensuring interaction than the men. They ask more questions and use more attention beginnings. Women do support work while the men are talking and it is the women who generally do active maintenance and continuation work in conversations. The men, on the other hand, do much less active work when they begin or participate in interactions. They rely on statements, which they assume will get responses. They much more often discourage interactions initiated by women than vice versa.

These data suggest several general patterns of female-male interactional work. Compared with the men, the women tried more often and succeeded less often in getting conversations going, whereas the men tried less often and seldom failed in their attempts. Both men and women regarded topics introduced by women as tentative; many of these were quickly dropped. In contrast, topics produced by the men were treated as topics to be pursued; they were seldom rejected. The women worked harder than the men in conversation because they had less certainty of success with the topics they raised. The women did much of the necessary work of interaction, starting conversations and then working to maintain them.

The failure of the women's attempts at interaction is not due to anything inherent in their talk, but to the failure of the men to respond, to do interactional work. The success of the men's attempts is due to the women doing interactional work in response to remarks by the men. Thus, the definition of what is appropriate or inappropriate conversation becomes the man's choice. What part of the world the interactants orient to, construct, and maintain the reality of, is his choice, not hers. Yet the women labour hardest in making interactions go.

As with work in its usual sense, there appears to be a division of labour in conversation. The people who do the routine maintenance work, the women, are not the same people who either control or benefit from the process. Women are the "shitworkers" of routine interaction, and the "goods" being made are not only interactions, but, through them, realities.

This analysis of the detailed activity in everyday conversation suggests other dimensions of power and work. Two interrelated aspects concern women's availability and the maintenance of gender. While women have difficulty generating interactions, they are almost always available to do the conversational work required by men and which is necessary for interactions. Appearances may differ by case: sometimes women are required to sit and "be a good listener" because they are not otherwise needed. At other times women are required to fill silences and keep conversation moving, to talk a lot. Sometimes they are expected to develop others' topics, and at other times they are required to present and develop topics of their own.

Women are required to do their work in a very strong sense. Sometimes they are required in ways that can be seen in interaction, as when men use interactional strategies such as attention beginnings and questions, to which the women fully respond. There are also times when there is no direct situational evidence of "requirement" from the man, and the woman does so "naturally." "Naturally" means that it is morally required to do so and a highly sanctionable matter not to. If one does not act "naturally," then one can be seen as crazy and deprived of adult status. We can speculate on the quality of doing it "naturally" by considering what happens to women who are unwilling to be available for the various jobs that the situation requires. Women who successfully control interactions are often derided and doubt is cast on their femininity. They are often considered "abnormal"—terms like "castrating bitch," "domineering," "aggressive," and "witch" may be used to identify them. When they attempt to control conversations temporarily, women often "start" arguments. Etiquette books are filled with instructions to women on how to be available. Women who do not behave are punished by deprivation of full female status. One's identity as either male or female is the most crucial identity one has. It is the most "natural" differentiating characteristic there is.

Whereas sociologists generally treat sex as an "ascribed" rather than as an "achieved" characteristic, Garfinkel's (1967, ch. 5) study of a transsexual describes one's gender as a continual, routine accomplishment. He discussed what the transsexual Agnes has shown him, that one must continually give off the appearance of being female or male in order for your gender to be unproblematic in a given interaction. Agnes has to learn these appearances and her awareness of them was explicit. For "normally sexed" people, it is routine.

To be identified as female, women are required to look and act in particular ways. Talking is part of this complex behaviour. Women must talk like a female talks; they must be available to do what needs to be done in conversation, to do the shitwork and not complain. But all the activities involved in displaying femaleness are usually defined as part of what being a woman *is*, so the idea that it is work is obscured. The work is not seen as what women do, but as part of what they are. Because this work is obscured, because it is too often seen as an aspect of gender identity rather than of gender activity, the maintenance and expression of male-female power relations in our everyday conversations are hidden as well. When we orient instead to the activities involved in maintaining gender, we are able to discern the reality of hierarchy in our daily lives.

The purpose of this study has been to begin an exploration of the details of concrete conversational activity of couples in their homes from the perspective of the socially structured power relationship between males and females. From such detailed analysis we see that women do the work necessary for interaction to occur smoothly, but men control what will be produced as reality by the interaction. They already have, and they continually establish and enforce, their rights to define what the interaction, and reality, will be about.

Endnotes

1.   A notable exception is the work on interruptions in conversation by West (1979), West and Zimmerman (1977), and Zimmerman and West (1975). Other conversational research can be found in Dubois and Crouch (1976).

2.   Throughout this paper, I use the terms interaction and conversation interchangeably, although I do not mean to suggest that conversation covers all the essential components of interaction.

3.   The discrepancy between the possible twelve hours of tape and the actual seven and a half hours of transcript represents long periods of silence.

4.   The notion that joint expression of interest is a necessary feature of conversation is discussed by Garfinkel (1967: 38-42).

5.   The following is a synopsis of material in Fishman, 1978.

6.   See Fishman, 1980, for a full discussion of pause structures.

References

Berger, Peter & Hansfried Kellner. 1970. Marriage and the construction of reality. In Hans Peter Dreitzel (ed.), *Recent sociology, No. 2.* London: Macmillan, 50-72.

Berger, Peter & Thomas Luckmann. 1967. *The social construction of reality.* New York: Anchor Books.

Dubois, Betty Lou & Isabel Crouch (eds.). 1976. *The sociology of the languages of American women.* San Antonio, Texas: Trinity Univ.

Fishman, Pamela M. 1978. What do couples talk about when they're alone? In Douglas Butturff & Edmund L. Epstein (eds.), *Women's language and style.* Akron, Ohio: L & S Books, 11-22.

———— 1980. Conversational insecurity. In Howard Giles, Peter Robinson, & Philip M. Smith (eds.), *Language: social psychological perspectives.* New York: Pergamon Press, 127-32.

Garfinkel, Harold. 1967. *Studies in ethnomethodology.* Englewood Cliffs, N.J.: Prentice-Hall.

Lakoff, Robin. 1975. *Language and woman's place.* New York: Harper & Row.

McConnell-Ginet, Sally. 1978. Address forms in sexual politics. In Douglas Butturff & Edmund L. Epstein (eds.), *Women's language and style.* Akron, Ohio: L & S Books, 23-35.

Miller, Casey & Kate Swift. 1976. *Words and women.* New York: Anchor Press.

Sacks, Harvey. 1972. On the analysability of stories by children. In John Grumperz & Dell Hymes (eds.), *Directions in sociolinguistics: The ethnography of communication.* New York: Holt, Rinehart and Winston, 325-45.

Sacks, Harvey, Emanuel Schegloff, & Gail Jefferson. 1974. A simplest systematics for the organization of turn-taking for conversation. *Language,* 50, 696-735.

Schegloff, Emanuel. 1972. Sequencing in conversational openings. In John Gumperz & Dell Hymes (eds), *Directions in sociolinguistics: The ethnography of communication.* New York: Holt, Rinehart and Winston, 346-80.

Schegloff, Emanuel, & Harvey Sacks. 1974. Opening up closings. In Roy Turner (ed.), *Ethnomethodology.* Middlesex, England: Penguin Education, 197-215.

Stanley, Julia. 1977. Gender-marking in America English: Usage and reference. In Aileen Pace Nilsen, Haig Bosmajian, H. Lee Gershuny, & Julia Stanley (eds.), *Sexism and language.* Urbana, Ill.: National Council of Teachers of English, 43-74.

Weber, Max. 1969. *The theory of social and economic organization.* New York: The Free Press.

West, Candace. 1979. Against our will: Male interruptions of females in cross-sex conversation. In Judith Orsanu, Mariam K. Slater, & Leonore Loeb Adler (eds.), *Language, sex and gender* (Annals of the New York Academy of Sciences, Vol. 327), 81-97.

West, Candace & Don H. Zimmerman. 1977. Women's place in everyday talk: Reflections on parent-child interaction. *Social problems*, 24, 521-29.

Zimmerman, Don & Candace West. 1975. Sex roles, interruptions and silences in conversation. In Barrie Thorne & Nancy Henley (eds.), *Language and sex: Difference and dominance*. Rowley, Mass.: Newbury House, 105-29.

Section IV

Socialization

Mead: Mind, Self, and Society

Leonard Broom and Philip Selznick

In this excerpt the authors present five characteristic and fundamental concerns of the social psychologist George Herbert Mead. Mead was exercised by the question of which came first, the individual or society, and much of his work on socialization can be understood as an attempt to flesh out this dynamic and reflexive relationship.

Preverbal Interaction

Social interaction precedes language, mind, and self-consciousness. Among many animal species, sexual union and care of the young make necessary at least some continuing interaction among individuals; thus, rudimentary family life exists among species lower than man. In most cases common cooperation is made necessary by biological differences in capacity or function, of which sexual and age differentiation are the most striking examples.

Among ants and bees, some individuals are biologically specialized to perform a single function, such as reproduction or food getting. The survival of both individual and species depends upon the interaction of highly specific biological roles in a complex pattern of cooperative acts. In this way ant and bee societies arise. But their organization is, strictly speaking, a biological one, and interaction is based on physical and chemical cures.

Non-verbal communication must precede language. Interaction, even on the biological level, is a kind of communication; otherwise, common acts could not occur. A dancing male bird does not deliberately intend to communicate a readiness to mate; yet communication occurs because it is more or less guaranteed by the nervous system of the species. As a rule, the dance arouses an appropriate response in a female, much as if she understood the meaning of the male's behaviour.

The dance communicates because it stands for something else. It is not an isolated, meaningless bit of behaviour. It is a natural sign, a product and manifestation of a state of organic tension, of a physiological readiness to mate. The tensions behind the mating dance require for their relief appropriate behaviour on the part of the female. Thus, because the dance is a natural sign directed toward another, it can be viewed as gesture, that is, as non-verbal communicative behaviour.

If human beings could not first participate in a non-verbal "conversation" of gestures, they could never communicate by means of language. Before language can convey meaning *to* the child, the mother's behaviour must have meaning *for* the child. Children could never understand the meaning of *angry* or *hungry* unless they first understood angry or nurturing gestures. Nor would the mother's gesture have meaning for the child unless both were participants in a joint activity. The emergence of language depends upon the existence of already established social interaction.

The Importance of Language

Language creates mind and selves. Despite interaction and communication, neither mind nor self-consciousness need be present in these primitive social acts; indeed, without language they cannot be. Language alone makes possible ideas and communication by ideas.

The males bird's mating dance has meaning for the female when it prompts an answering response from her, but it cannot be said to have meaning for the dancing male. He is simply behaving. He is not telling the female he is ready to mate; if anything tells the other, it is the dance and not the dancing bird. The bird's behaviour communicates, but not the bird.

Language makes it possible to replace behaviour with ideas. The mother can teach her child the meaning of "I am angry" only by behaving in appropriate ways, but once the child learns the words, the mother need not behave in an angry fashion in order to communicate displeasure. Because mother and child now share an idea, the child can respond to what the mother says as well as to what she does. It is the mother (not merely her behaviour) who now communicates.

Furthermore, having the idea of anger, the child can think about his mother's anger; it can have meaning even when she is absent or not angry. Thus as the child acquires language he acquires mind. He also becomes self-conscious as he reflects not only about his mother's anger but about himself and his own behaviour. Thus he acquires a self. As he matures, the child no longer adjusts merely to immediate expressions of approval and disapproval. He *takes the attitudes of others* into himself as enduring guides and standards, as part of his own personality.

The Social Self

Mind and self are social. Much of language is factual, simply identifying objects about which people communicate. But through language children also learn the attitudes of caution may go along with *dog* and *fire*. Others are more distinctively social. Factually, *cow* means the same to a Hindu as to an American, but to the Hindu child the meaning of *cow* also includes attitudes of religious reverence and respect. Thus, in learning language, children are initiated into a world of social meanings; they share the meanings objects have for their social group.

Just as the child learns to take the same attitudes toward objects in the environment that others take toward them, so he learns to take the same attitudes toward himself that others take toward him. When the mother tells the child that he has done something good or bad, right or wrong, she is not trying to teach him merely what the words mean. She treats the child as an object toward which she takes a certain attitude and tries to induce the child to do the same. He is encouraged *to take himself as an object*. He evaluates and controls himself in the same way that he evaluates and controls other objects, and he does so from the standpoint of someone else. He is taught, in short, to make appropriate or prescribed responses to his own behaviour just as he has been taught to make appropriate or prescribed responses to other objects in his environment.

Because this control occurs through taking the attitudes of others toward oneself, because it is control from the standpoint of someone else, it is distinctively social in nature. This is how society gets into the individual. No other animal is able to exercise self-criticism; and all self-criticism is social criticism insofar as the principles that guide it are the result of internalizing the attitudes of others toward oneself.

Before he can use the attitudes of others to think about himself, the young child is not *self*-conscious. As an animal, the human child is conscious. He has sensations, feelings, and perceptions of which he is aware. It is by thinking about himself in the light of the attitudes of others toward him that the individual becomes *self*-conscious and begins to acquire a social self.

Maturation and Response to the Other

As the individual matures he develops the capacity to respond to significant others and to a generalized other. All higher forms of communication depend upon the capacity of each to put himself in the place of the other, that is, to control his own responses in terms of an understanding of what the other's responses are likely to be. As he learns to control his behaviour in the light of another individual's attitudes either toward that behaviour or toward the environment, the individual learns *to take the role of the other*. He responds to himself and to the world as he anticipates the other would respond. The capacity to put oneself in the place of the other emerges only with maturity and in the process of social interaction and communication.

The child first internalizes the attitudes of particular individuals, primarily his parents, toward himself. At this stage he does not have the capacity to participate in organized group life or to engage in complex, cooperative games governed by impersonal rules. Social interaction is limited to interaction with specific individuals, and behaviour is largely determined by the child's experience with those who are not merely others but *significant others* for him. At this stage of development, play consists largely of simple role taking. The child plays at being a mother, father, doctor, or postman, re-enacting the behaviour and attitudes of others as individuals.

Gradually the child learns a less personalized, more complex form of role taking as expressed in his developing ability to participate in organized games. In baseball, for example, the acting out of a highly specific individual role is not required. The player adjusts from moment to moment and does so in the light of what a number of others are doing and of the rules and purposes of the game. In performing this role, the child as player responds to a *generalized other.*

Mead used this term to designate "the organized community or social group which gives to the individual his unity of self" (1934: 154). One who takes the standpoint of the generalized other knows what is required to keep the group to its distinctive aims and rules. The individual sees not only his own role, not only the roles of particular others, but the ways roles are related in determining the outcome of group activity. Gradually the individual becomes capable of taking on the point of view of the community as a whole.

The "I" and the "Me"

The social self has a creative, spontaneous aspect. To stress the essentially social nature of the self may seem to imply that the self is completely determined by the internalized attitudes of others. This is not so. To be sure, the internalized attitudes of others represent what the individual takes into account when he acts; they are the demands that group life actually or supposedly makes upon him. Nevertheless, human behaviour has a large element of freedom and spontaneity. The demands of the social situation pose a problem to the acting individual, but there is considerable leeway in what his response in a given situation will be. The baseball player wants to play good ball; in this sense behaviour is determined by accepting the demands and standards of the group. But whether he will make a brilliant play or an error neither he nor anyone else knows beforehand.

Mead called the acting self the 'I.' The 'me,' on the other hand, is that part of the self that is an organization of the internalized attitudes of others. The 'I' responds to the 'me' and takes it into account, but it is not identical with it.

There may be varying amounts of 'I' and 'me' in behaviour. In impulsive behaviour, the 'me' is absent; in Freudian language, the 'I' is not being censored by the 'me.' Social control is present to the extent that the 'I' is controlled by the 'me.' The oversocialized individual is overdetermined by his 'me.' In more normal circumstances, the individual responds to a situation in its social aspects but does so with some regard for his own unique capacities and needs. The most gratifying experiences are those in which the demands of the 'me'—or of the social situation—permit the expression and realize the potentialities of the 'I.'

The enlargement of the self is dependent upon and in turn supports the breadth of community values. What the self is and how it develops depends upon the nature of the community whose attitudes the individual has internalized. Membership in a community is more than physical presence in it; the small child belongs to a play group, not to the city in which he lives; "...until one can respond to himself as a community responds to him, he does not genuinely belong to the community" (1934: 265).

The self will be isolated and alienated from other selves if it is a member of a socially isolated group or one with narrow or provincial values. The self becomes enlarged to the extent that it belongs to a group engaged in activities that bring it into contact with other groups. Nationalism, which seems to be and often is a constraining and limiting influence, has nevertheless played its part in creating broader human communities. Similarly the self becomes enlarged to the extent that it belongs to a community that subscribes to universal values, such as the objective standards of science or a religious belief in human brotherhood.

Behavioural Study of Obedience

Stanley Milgram

In this social psychological study Milgram set out to discover why, and under what circumstances, people obey authority. Are some people naturally inclined to obey or is it a matter of socialization? Under what conditions will an individual act in ways that he or she finds morally reprehensible?

Obedience is as basic an element in the structure of social life as one can point to. Some system of authority is a requirement of all communal living, and it is only the man dwelling in isolation who is not forced to respond, through defiance or submission, to the commands of others. Obedience, as a determinant of behaviour, is of particular relevance to our time. It has been reliably established that from 1933-45 millions of innocent persons were systematically slaughtered on command. Gas chambers were built, death camps were guarded, daily quotas of corpses were produced with the same efficiency as the manufacture of appliances. These inhumane policies may have originated in the mind of a single person, but they could only be carried out on a massive scale if a very large number of persons obeyed orders.

Obedience is the psychological mechanism that links individual action to political purpose. It is the dispositional cement that binds men to systems of authority. Facts of recent history and observation in daily life suggest that for many persons obedience may be a deeply ingrained behaviour tendency, indeed, a prepotent impulse overriding training in ethics, sympathy, and moral conduct. C.P. Snow (1961) points to its importance when he writes:

> When you think of the long and gloom history of man, you will find more hideous crimes have been committed in the name of obedience than have ever been committed in the name of rebellion. If you doubt that, read William Shirer's *Rise and Fall of the Third Reich*. The German Officer Corps were brought up in the most rigorous code of obedience...in the name of obedience they were party to, and assisted in, the most wicked large scale actions in the history of the world (p.24).

While the particular form of obedience dealt with in the present study has its antecedents in these episodes, it must not be thought all obedience entails acts of aggression against others. Obedience serves numerous productive functions. Indeed, the very life of society is predicated on its existence. Obedience may be ennobling and educative and refer to acts of charity and kindness, as well as to destruction.

General Procedure

A procedure was devised which seems useful as a tool for studying obedience (Milgram, 1961). It consists of ordering a naive subject to administer electric shock to a victim. A simulated shock generator is used, with 30 clearly marked voltage levels that range from 15 to 450 volts. The instrument bears verbal designations that range from Slight Shock to Danger: Severe Shock. The responses of the victim, who is a trained confederate of the experimenter, are standardized. The orders to administer shocks are given to the naive subject in the context of a "learning experiment" ostensibly set up to study the effects of punishment on memory. As the experiment proceeds the naive subject is commanded to administer increasingly more intense shocks to the victim, even to the point of reaching the level marked Danger: Severe Shock. Internal resistances become stronger, and at a certain point the subject refuses to go on with the experiment. Behaviour prior to this rupture is considered "obedience," in that the subject complies with the commands of the experimenter. The point of rupture is the act of disobedience. A quantitative value is assigned to the subject's performance based on the maximum intensity shock he is willing to administer before he refuses to participate further. Thus for any particular subject and for any particular experimental condition the degree of obedience may be specified with a numerical value. The crux of the study is to systematically vary the factors believed to alter the degree of obedience to the experimental commands.

The technique allows important variables to be manipulated at several points in the experiment. One may vary aspects of the source of command, content and form of command, instrumentalities for its execution, target object, general social setting, etc. The problem, therefore, is not one of designing increasingly more numerous experimental conditions, but of selecting those that best illuminate the process of obedience from the socio-psychological standpoint.

Related Studies

The inquiry bears an important relation to philosophic analysis of obedience and authority (Arendt, 1958; Friedrich, 1958; Weber, 1947), an early experimental study of obedience by Frank (1944), studies in "authoritarianism" (Adorno, Frenkel-Brunswik, Levinson and Sanford, 1950; Rokeach, 1961), and a recent series of analytic and empirical studies in social power (Cartwright, 1959). It owes much to the long concern with suggestion in social psychology, both in its normal forms (e.g., Binet, 1900) and in its clinical manifestations

(Carcot, 1881). But it derives, in the first instance, from direct observation of a social fact; the individual who is commanded by a legitimate authority ordinarily obeys. Obedience comes easily and often. It is a ubiquitous and indispensable feature of social life.

Method

Subjects

The subjects were 40 males between the ages of 20 and 50, drawn from New Haven and the surrounding communities. Subjects were obtained by a newspaper advertisement and direct mail solicitation. Those who responded to the appeal believed they were to participate in a study of memory and learning at Yale University. A wide range of occupations is represented in the sample. Typical subjects were postal clerks, high school teachers, salesmen, engineers, and labourers. Subjects ranged in educational level from one who had not finished elementary school, to those who had doctorate and other professional degrees. They were paid $4.50 for their participation in the experiment. However, subjects were told that payment was simply for coming to the laboratory, and that the money was theirs no matter what happened after they arrived. Table 1 shows the proportion of age and occupation types assigned to the experimental condition.

**Table 1 — Distribution of Age and Occupational Types
in the Experiment**

Occupations	20-29 years n	30-39 years n	40-45 years n	Percentage of total occupations
Workers, skilled and unskilled	4	5	6	37.5
Sales, business, and white-collar	3	6	7	40.0
Professional	1	5	3	22.5
Percentage of total (Age)	20	40	40	

Note: Total N = 40.

Personnel and Locale

The experiment was conducted on the grounds of Yale University in the elegant interaction laboratory. (This detail is relevant to the perceived legitimacy of the experiment. In further variations, the experiment was dissociated from the university, with consequences for performance.) The role of experimenter was played by a 31-year-old high school teacher of biology. His manner was impassive, and his appearance somewhat stern throughout the experiment. He was dressed in a grey technician's coat. The victim was played by a 47-year-old accountant, trained for the role; he was of Irish-American stock, whom most observers found mild-mannered and likable.

Procedure

One naive subject and one victim (an accomplice) performed in each experiment. A pretext had to be devised that would justify the administration of electric shock by the naive subject. This was effectively accomplished by the cover story. After a general introduction on the presumed relation between punishment and learning, subjects were told:

> But actually, we know very little about the effect of punishment on learning, because almost no truly scientific studies have been made of it in human beings.
> For instance, we don't know how much punishment is best for learning—and we don't know how much difference it makes as to who is giving the punishment, whether an adult learns best from a younger or an older person than himself—or many things of the sort.
> So, in this study we are bringing together a number of adults of different occupations and ages. And we're asking some of them to be teachers and some of them to be learners.
> We want to find out just what effect different people have on each other as teachers and learners, and also what effect punishment will have on learning in this situation.
> Therefore, I'm going to ask one of you to be the teacher here tonight and the other one to be the learner.
> Does either of you have a preference?

Subjects then drew slips of paper from a hat to determine who would be the teacher and who would be the learner in the experiment. The drawing was rigged so that the naive subject was always the teacher and the accomplice always the learner. (Both slips contained the word "Teacher." Immediately after the drawing, the teacher and learner were taken to an adjacent room and the learner was strapped into an "electric chair" apparatus.

The experimenter explained that the straps were to prevent excessive movement while the learner was being shocked. The effect was to make it impossible for him to escape from the situation. An electrode was attached to the learner's wrist, and electrode paste was applied "to avoid blisters and burns." Subjects were told that the electrode was attached to the shock generator in the adjoining room.

In order to improve credibility the experimenter declared, in response to a question by the learner: "Although the shocks can be extremely painful, they cause no permanent tissue damage."

Learning task.

The lesson administered by the subject was a paired-associate learning task. The subject read a series of word pairs to the learner, and then read the first word of the pair along with four terms. The learner was to indicate which of the four terms had originally been paired with the first word. He communicated his answer by pressing one of four switches in front of him, which in turn lit up one of four numbered quadrants in an answer-box located atop the shock generator.

Shock Generator.

The instrument panel consists of 30 lever switches set in a horizontal line. Each switch is clearly labelled with a voltage designation that ranges from 15 to 450 volts. There is a 15-volt increment from one switch to the next going from left to right. In addition, the following verbal designations are clearly indicated for groups of four switches going from left to right: Slight Shock, Moderate Shock, Extreme Intensity Shock, Danger: Severe Shock. (Two switches after this last designation are simply marked xxx.)

Upon depressing a switch: a pilot light corresponding to each switch is illuminated in bright red; an electric buzzing is heard; an electric blue light, labelled "voltage energizer," flashes; the dial on the voltage meter swings to the right; various relay clicks are sounded.

The upper left-hand corner of the generator is labelled Shock Generator, Type ZLB, Dyson Instrument Company, Waltham, Mass. Output 15 Volts - 450 Volts.

Details of the instrument were carefully handled to ensure an appearance of authenticity. The panel was engraved by precision industrial engravers, and all components were of high quality. No subject in the experiment suspected that the instrument was merely a simulated shock generator.[1]

Sample Shock.

Each naive subject is given a sample shock on the shock generator, prior to beginning his run as teacher. This shock is always 45 volts, and is applied by pressing the third switch of the generator. This shock is applied to the wrist of the naive subject, and has its source in a 45-volt battery wired into the generator. This further convinces the subject of the authenticity of the generator.

Shock Instruction.

The subject is told to administer a shock to the learner each time he gives a wrong response. Moreover—and this is the key command—the subject is instructed to "move one level higher on the shock generator each time the learner flashes a wrong answer." He is also instructed to announce the voltage level before administering a shock. This serves to continually remind subjects of the increasing intensity of shock administered to the learner.

Preliminary and Regular Run.

Pretests revealed that the procedure of reading words and administering shocks requires some practice before it can be handled smoothly. Therefore, immediately preceding the regular run, the teacher is given a preliminary series of 10 words to read to the learner. There are 3 neutral words in the practice series (i.e., words that the learner answers correctly), so that shocks are administered for 7 of the words, with the maximum shock at 105 volts (moderate shock). Almost all subjects master the procedure by the time the preliminary run is over.

Subjects are then presented with a second list, and are told that the procedure is the same as for the first list; the experimenter adds, however:

> When you get to the bottom of the list, repeat it over again, and continue giving shocks, until the learner has learned all the pairs correctly.

The instructor instructs the subject to start from 15 volts and increase the shock level one step each time the learner gives a wrong answer.

Feedback from the Victim.

In all conditions the learner gives a predetermined set of responses to the word pair test, based on a schedule of approximately three wrong answers to one correct answer. In the present experimental condition no vocal response or other sign of protest is heard from the learner until Shock Level 300 is reached. When the 300-volt shock is administered, the learner pounds on the wall of the room in which he is bound to the electric chair. The pounding can be heard by the subject. From this point on, the learner's answers no longer appear on the four-way panel.

At this juncture, subjects ordinarily turn to the experimenter for guidance. The experimenter instructs the subject to treat the absence of a response as a wrong answer, and to shock the subject according to the usual schedule. He advises the subjects to allow 5-10 seconds before considering no response as a wrong answer, and to increase the shock level one step each time the learner fails to respond correctly. The learner's pounding is repeated after the 325-volt shock is administered; afterwards he is not heard from, nor do his answers reappear on the four-way signal box.

Experimenter Feedback.
At various points in the experiment the subject may turn to the experimenter for advice on whether he should continue to administer shocks. Or he may indicate that he does not wish to go on. It was important to standardize the experimenter's response to these inquiries and reactions.

If the subject indicated his unwillingness to go on, the experimenter responded with a sequence of "prods," using as many as necessary to bring the subject into line.

> Prod 1:   Please continue *or* Please go on.
> Prod 2:   The experiment requires that you continue.
> Prod 3:   It is absolutely essential that you continue.
> Prod.4:   You have no other choice, you *must* go on.

The prods were always made in a sequence: Only if Prod 1 had been unsuccessful, could Prod 2 be used. If the subject refused to obey the experimenter after Prod 4, the experiment was terminated. The experimenter's tone of voice was at all times firm, but not impolite. The sequence was begun anew on each occasion that the subject balked or showed reluctance to follow orders.

Special Prods.
If the subject asked if the learner was liable to suffer permanent physical injury, the experimenter said:

> Although the shocks may be painful, there is no permanent tissue damage, so please go on. [Followed by Prods 2, 3, and 4 if necessary.]

If the subject said that the learner did not want to go on, the experimenter replied:

Whether the learner likes it or not, you must go on until he has learned all the word pairs correctly. So please go on. [Followed by Prods 2, 3, and 4 if necessary.]

Dependent Measures

The primary dependent measure for any subject is the maximum shock he administers before he refuses to go any further. In principle this may vary from 0 (for subject who refuses to administer even the first shock) to 30 (for a subject who administers the highest shock on the generator). A subject who breaks off the experiment at any point prior to administering the thirtieth shock level is termed a *defiant* subject. One who complies with experimental commands fully, and proceeds to administer all shock levels commanded, is termed an *obedient* subject.

Further Records.
With few exceptions, experimental sessions were recorded on magnetic tape. Occasional photographs were taken through one-way mirrors. Notes were kept on any unusual behaviour occurring during the course of the experiments. On occasion, additional observers were directed to write objective descriptions of the subjects' behaviour. The latency and duration of shocks were measured by accurate timing devices.

Interview and Dehoax.
Following the experiment, subjects were interviewed; open-ended questions, projective measures, and attitude scales were employed. After the interview, procedures were undertaken to assure that the subject would leave the laboratory in a state of well being. A friendly reconciliation was arranged between the subject and the victim, and an effort was made to reduce any tensions that arose as a result of the experiment.

Results

Preliminary Notions.
Before giving an account of the experimental results, it is instructive to consider how persons predict others will perform when commanded to administer powerful shocks to another person. Fourteen Yale seniors, all psychology majors, were provided with a detailed description of the experimental situation. They were asked to reflect carefully on it, and to predict the behaviour of 100 hypothetical subjects. More specifically, they were instructed to plot the

distribution of obedience of "100 Americans of diverse occupations, and ranging in age from 20 to 50 years," who were placed in the experimental situation.

There was considerable agreement among the respondents on the expected behaviour of hypothetical subjects. All respondents predicted that only an insignificant minority would go through to the end of the shock series. (The estimates ranged from 0 to 3%; i.e., the most "pessimistic" member of the class predicted that of 100 persons, 3 would continue through to the most potent shock available on the shock generator—450 volts.) The class mean was 1.2%. The question was also posed informally to colleagues of the author, and the most general feeling was that few if any subjects would go beyond the designation Very Strong Shock.

Result of Experiment 1

Subjects Accept Situation.
With few exceptions subjects were convinced of the reality of the experimental situation, that they were administering shocks to another person, and the most potent shocks were extremely painful. In the post-experimental interview subjects were asked: "How painful to the learner were the last few shocks that you administered to him?" Subjects were instructed to indicate their answers on a printed 14-point scale ranging form "Not at all painful" to "Extremely painful." The modal response was 14 (Extremely painful) with the mean at 13.42.

Signs of Extreme Tension.
Many subjects showed signs of nervousness in the experimental situation, and especially upon administering the more powerful shocks. In a large number of cases the degree of tension reached extremes that are rarely seen in socio-psychological laboratory studies. Subjects were observed to sweat, tremble, stutter, bite their lips, groan, and dig their fingernails into their flesh. These were characteristic rather than exceptional responses to the experiment.

One sign of tension was the regular occurrence of nervous laughing fits. Fourteen of the 40 subjects showed definite signs of nervous laughter and smiling. The laughter seemed entirely out of place, even bizarre. Full-blown, uncontrollable seizures were observed for 3 subjects. On one occasion we observed seizure so violently convulsive that it was necessary to call a halt to the experiment. The subject, a 46-year-old encyclopedia salesman, was seriously embarrassed by his untoward and uncontrollable behaviour. In the post-experimental interviews, subjects took pains to point out that they were not sadistic types, and that the laughter did not mean they enjoyed shocking the victim.

Distribution of Scores.

It had been conjectured that persons would not, in general, agree to administer shocks beyond the level designated as Very Strong Shock. The distribution of maximum shocks for this experiment is shown in Table 2. The obtained distribution of scores deviates radically from the prediction.

Upon command of the experimenter, each of the 40 subjects went beyond the expected break-off point. No subject stopped prior to administering Shock Level 20. (At this level—300 volts—the victim kicks on the wall and no longer provides answers to the teacher's multiple-choice questions.

Of the 40 subjects, 5 refused to obey the experimental commands beyond the 300-volt level. Four more subjects administered one further shock, and then refused to go on. Two broke off at the 330-volt level, and 1 each at 345, 360, and 375 volts. Thus a total of 14 subjects defied the experimenter. It is instructive to reprint their remarks at the point of defiance, as transcribed from the tape recordings:

> [0124]   I think he's trying to communicate, he's knocking.... Well it's not fair to shock the guy...these are terrific volts. I don't think this is very humane.... Oh, I can't go on with this; no, this isn't right. It's a hell of an experiment. The guy is suffering in there. No, I don't want to go on. This is crazy. [Subject refused to administer more shocks.]

> [0123]   He's banging in there. I'm gonna chicken out. I'd like to continue, but I can't do that to a man...I'm sorry I can't do that to a man. I'll hurt his heart. You take your check.... No really, I couldn't do it.

These subjects were frequently in a highly agitated and even angered state. Sometimes, verbal protest was at a minimum, and the subject simply got up from his chair in front of the shock generator, and indicated that he wished to leave the laboratory.

Of the 40 subjects, 26 obeyed the orders of the experimenter to the end, proceeding to punish the victim until they reached the most potent shock available on the shock generator. At that point, their experimenter called a halt to the session. (The maximum shock is labelled 450 volts, and is two steps beyond the designation: Danger: Severe Shock.) Although obedient subjects continued to administer shocks, they often did so under extreme stress. Some expressed reluctance to administer shocks beyond the 300-volt level, and displayed fears similar to those who defied the experimenter; yet they obeyed.

After the maximum shocks had been delivered, and the experimenter called a halt to the proceedings, many obedient subjects heaved sighs of relief, mopped their brows, rubbed their fingers over their eyes, or nervously fumbled cigarettes. Some shook their heads, apparently in regret. Some subjects had remained calm throughout the experiment, and displayed only minimal signs of tension from beginning to end.

Discussion

The experiment yielded two findings that were surprising. The first finding concerns the sheer strength of obedient tendencies manifested in this situation. Subjects have learned from childhood that it is a fundamental breach of moral conduct to hurt another person against his will. Yet, 26 subjects abandoned this tenet in following the instructions of an authority who has no special powers to enforce his commands. To disobey would bring no material loss to the subject; no punishment would ensue. It is clear from the remarks and outward behaviour of many participants that in punishing the victim they are often acting against their own values. Subjects often expressed deep disapproval of shocking a man in the face of his objections, and others denounced it as stupid and senseless. Yet the majority complied with the experimental commands. This outcome was surprising from two perspectives: first, from the standpoint of predictions made in the questionnaire described earlier. (Here, however, it is possible that the remoteness of the respondents from the actual situation, and the difficulty of conveying to them the concrete details of the experiment, could account for the serious underestimation of obedience.) But the results were also unexpected to persons who observed the experiment in progress, through one-way mirrors. Observers often uttered expressions of disbelief upon seeing a subject administer more powerful shocks to the victim. These persons had a full acquaintance with the details of the situation, and yet systematically underestimated the amount of obedience that subjects would display.

The second unanticipated effect was the extraordinary tension generated by the procedures. One might suppose that a subject would simply break off or continue as his conscience dictated. Yet, this is very far from what happened. There were striking reactions of tension and emotional strain. One observer related:

> I observed a mature and initially poised businessman enter the laboratory smiling and confident. Within 20 minutes he was reduced to a twitching, stuttering wreck, who was rapidly

Table 2 — Distribution of Breakoff Points

Verbal designation and voltage indication	Number of subjects for whom this was maximum shock
Slight Shock 15	0
30	0
45	0
60	0
Moderate Shock 75	0
90	0
105	0
120	0
Strong Shock 135	0
150	0
165	0
180	0
Very Strong Shock	
195	0
210	0
225	0
240	0
Intense Shock 255	0
270	0
285	0
300	5
Extreme Intensity Shock	
315	4
330	2
345	1
360	1
Danger: Severe Shock	
375	1
390	0
405	0
420	0
XXX 435	0
450	26

approaching a point of nervous collapse. He constantly pulled on his earlobe, and twisted his hands. At one point he pushed his fist into his forehead and muttered: "Oh God, let's stop it." And yet

he continued to respond to every word of the experimenter, and
obeyed to the end.

Any understanding of the phenomenon of obedience must rest on an analysis
of the particular conditions in which it occurs. The following features of the
experiment go some distance in explaining the high amount of obedience
observed in the situation.

1.   The experiment is sponsored by and takes place on the grounds
of an institution of unimpeachable reputation, Yale University. It
may be reasonably presumed that the personnel are competent
and reputable. The importance of this background authority is
now being studied by conducting a series of experiments outside
of New Haven, and without any visible ties to the university.

2.   The experiment is, on the face of it, designed to attain a worthy
purpose—advancement of knowledge about learning and
memory. Obedience occurs not as an end in itself, but as an
instrumental element in a situation that the subject construes as
significant and meaningful. He may not be able to see its full
significance, but he may properly assume that the experimenter
does.

3.   The subject perceives that the victim has voluntarily submitted to
the authority system of the experimenter. He is not (at first) an
unwilling captive impressed for involuntary service. He has taken
the trouble to come to the laboratory presumable to aid the
experimental research. That he later becomes an involuntary
subject does not alter the fact that, initially, he consented to
participate without qualification. Thus he has in some degree
incurred an obligation toward the experimenter.

4.   The subject, too, has entered the experiment voluntarily, and
perceives himself under obligation to aid the experimenter. He
has made a commitment, and to disrupt the experiment is a
repudiation of this initial promise of aid.

5.   Certain features of the procedure strengthen the subject's sense
of obligation to the experimenter. For one, he has been paid for
coming to the laboratory. In part this is cancelled out by the
experimenter's statement that:
Of course, as in all experiments, the money is yours simply for
coming to the laboratory. From this point on, no matter what
happens, the money is yours.[2]

6.   From the subject's standpoint, the fact that he is the teacher and
the other man the learner is purely a chance consequence (it is

determined by drawing lots) and he, the subject, ran the same risk as the other man in being assigned the role of learner. Since the assignment of positions in the experiment was achieved by fair means, the learner is deprived of any basis of complaint on this count. (A similar situation obtains in Army units, in which—in the absence of volunteers—a particularly dangerous mission may be assigned by drawing lots, and the unlucky soldier is expected to bear his misfortune with sportsmanship.)

7.   There is, at best, ambiguity with regard to the prerogatives of a psychologist and the corresponding rights of his subject. There is a vagueness of expectation concerning what a psychologist may require of his subject, and when he is overstepping acceptable limits. Moreover, the experiment occurs in a closed setting, and thus provides no opportunity for the subject to remove these ambiguities by discussion with others. There are few standards that seem directly applicable to the situation, which is a novel one for most subjects.

8.   The subjects are assured that the shocks administered to the subject are "painful but not dangerous." Thus they assume that the discomfort caused the victim is momentary, while the scientific gains resulting from the experiment are enduring.

9.   Through Shock Level 20 the victim continues to provide answers on the signal box. The subject may construe this as a sign that the victim is still willing to "play the game." It is only after Shock Level 20 that the victim repudiates the rules completely, refusing to answer further.

These features help to explain the high amount of obedience obtained in this experiment. Many of the arguments raised need not remain matters of speculation, but can be reduced to testable proportions to be confirmed or disproved by further experiments.[3]

The following features of the experiment concern the nature of the conflict which the subject faces.

10.   The subject is placed in a position in which he must respond to the competing demands of two persons: the experimenter and the victim. The conflict must be resolved by meeting the demands of one or the other; satisfaction of the victim and the experimenter are mutually exclusive. Moreover, the resolution must take the form of a highly visible action, that of continuing to shock the victim or breaking off the experiment. Thus the subject is forced

into a public conflict that does not permit any completely satisfactory solution.

11.   While the demands of the experimenter carry the weight of scientific authority, the demands of the victim spring from his personal experience of pain and suffering. The two claims need not be regarded as equally pressing and legitimate. The experimenter seeks an abstract scientific datum; the victim cries out for relief from physical suffering caused by the subject's actions.

12.   The experiment gives the subject little time for reflection. The conflict comes on rapidly. It is only minutes after the subject has been seated before the shock generator that the victim begins his protests. Moreover, the subject perceives that he has gone through but two-thirds of the shock levels at the time the subject's first protests are heard. Thus he understands that the conflict will have a persistent aspect to it, and may well become more intense as increasingly more powerful shocks are required. The rapidity with which the conflict descends on the subject, and his realization that it is predictably recurrent may well be sources of tension to him.

13.   At a more general level, the conflict stems from the opposition of two deeply ingrained behaviour dispositions: first, the disposition not to harm other people, and second, the tendency to obey those whom we perceive to be legitimate authorities.

Endnotes

1.   A related technique, making use of a shock generator, was reported by Buss (1961) for the study of aggression in the laboratory. Despite the considerable similarity of technical detail in the experimental procedures, both investigators proceeded in ignorance of the other's work. Milgram provided plans and photographs of his shock generator, experimental procedure, and first results in a report to the National Science Foundation in January 1961. This report received only limited circulation. Buss reported his procedure 6 months later, but to a wider audience. Subsequently, technical information and reports were exchanged.

2.   Forty-three subjects, undergraduates at Yale University, were run in the experiment without payment. The results are very similar to those obtained with paid subjects.

3.   A series of recently completed experiments employing the obedience
       paradigm is reported in Milgram (1964).

References

Adorno, T.W., Frenkel-Brunswik, E., Levinson, D., and Sanford, R.N. (1950).
    The authoritarian personality. New York: Harper. [35], [RI-35].
Arendt, H. (1958). "What was authority?" In C.J. Friedrich (ed.), *Authority* (pp.
    81-112). Cambridge, MA: Harvard University Press.
Binet, A. (1900). *La suggestibilité.* Paris: Schleicher.
Cartwright, S. (ed.), (1959). *Studies in social power.* Ann Arbor: University of
    Michigan Institute for Social Research.
Milgram, S. (1961, Jan. 25). *Dynamics of obedience.* Washington: National
    Science Foundation.
Milgram, S. (1964). Some conditions of obedience and disobedience to
    authority. *Human Relations,* 18, 57-76.
Rokeach, M. (1961). "Authority, authoritarianism, and Conformity." In I.A.
    Berg and D.M. Dass (eds.), *Conformity and deviation* (pp. 230-237). New
    York: Harper.
Snow, C.P. (1961, Feb.) *Either or Progressive.* 24.
Weber, M. (1947). *The Theory of Social and Economic Organization.* Oxford:
    Oxford University Press.

Socialization to Competence Among Medical Students

Jack Haas and William Shaffir

Socialization does not cease after childhood or adolescence, but is a lifelong process. In this paper the socialization of adults is examined within the context of a formal organization, namely medical school. The specific focus is on the process through which medical students become "competent." This competence is found to reside less in a technical mastery of scientific methods or knowledge of "objective" facts, than in an ability to appear competent by demonstrating an understanding of what is expected.

Introduction

This paper[1] describes the adoption of a cloak of competence as a critical part of the professionalizing process. We observed medical students in an innovative three-year program attempting to come to grips with the problem of meeting exaggerated expectations.[2] The profound anxiety they feel about learning medicine and becoming competent is complicated by the pressing practical demands of the situation, particularly faculty, staff and institutional expectations.

As students move through the program they are converted to the new culture and gradually adopt those symbols which represent the profession and its generally accepted truths. These symbols (language, tools, clothing, and demeanour) establish, identify and separate the bearer from outsiders, particularly client and paraprofessional audiences. Professionalization, as we observed it, involves the adoption and manipulation of symbols and symbolic behaviour to create an imagery of competence and the separation and elevation of the profession from those they serve....

The Expectations of Competence

Medicine is a distinctively powerful and unique profession. Freidson outlines the characteristics of this occupation that set it apart from others. These are:

1. A general public belief in the consulting occupation's competence, in the value of its professed knowledge and skill.
2. The occupational group...must be the prime source of the criteria that qualify a man to work in an acceptable fashion.

3. The occupation has gained command of the exclusive competence to determine the proper content and effective method of performing some tasks (1970a: 10-11).

Medicine's position, Freidson notes, is equivalent to that of a state religion: "it has an officially approved monopoly of the right to define health and illness and to treat illness" (1970a: 5)....

Becoming Professional

From the outset, students are impressed by the tremendous responsibility of the physician. During their examination of various "psychosocial" problems, in Phase I,[3] students recognize that the physician's role is very broad. They learn that the medical profession not only deals with medical problems *per se*, but also with many apparently non-medical problems. The small group tutorial sessions, which form the major vehicle for learning at this stage of medical school, help shape students' enlarging conception of medicine and its practice. While early sessions are intended essentially to introduce students to the school's philosophy—the educational rationale underlying the distinctive structure and organization of the medical curriculum—they also serve to teach students the duties and responsibilities of the medical profession. An excerpt from the Phase I manual for incoming students illustrates this point:

> You are also becoming health professionals—members of an historic community concerned with the alleviation of human illness, the maintenance of health and the understanding of disease. You will begin to realize the special nature of the 'doctor-patient relationship.' Some of you will have initial difficulty with some of the physical things—blood, operations, injury, autopsies. Other experiences are more difficult to incorporate into your growth as a health professional—deformity, chronic illness, death, pain. You will see that physicians and other health professionals are ordinary human beings—with tempers, insensitivities and varied motivations (Phase I Manual, 1974: 25).

The physicians' influence on the way students learn about and define medical situations is critical to the professionalizing process. From the earliest stages of their medical training, and as they advance through the program, students continually watch doctors' working habits, listen to their philosophies of medical practice, take note of their competencies and incompetencies, and reflect upon the nature of their own present and future relationships with patients....

A dramatic shift in the professionalization process occurs when the students are given greater responsibility for patient health care and management. This occurs during the clerkship phase. Students become more integral members of a health care team, are delegated some tasks requiring personal responsibility, and become accountable in ways almost entirely new to them. As they assume increased responsibilities and make medical judgments for which they must account to a variety of professionals, they develop an increasingly sympathetic outlook towards their future profession....

As students observe and experience the problems of medical care and practice, they develop an understanding and identification with the profession and the ways its members confront their problems. Students are less quick to voice criticisms of what they see, as they come to take the role, directly or indirectly, of those they will soon follow....

The Symbols of Professionalism

The professionalization of medical students is facilitated by symbols the neophytes take on which serve to announce to insiders and outsiders how they are to be identified. During the first weeks of their studies students begin wearing white lab jackets with plastic name tags identifying them as medical students. In addition, since clinical skill sessions are included in the curriculum from the beginning, students participate in a variety of settings with the tools of the doctoring trade carried on their person. This attire clearly identifies students to participants and visitors of the hospital/school setting. Along with their newly acquired identity kit, students begin to learn and express themselves in the medical vernacular....

The significance of these symbols to the professionalization process is critical. The symbols serve, on the one hand, to identify and unite the bearers as members of a community of shared interests, purposes and identification (Roth, 1957). Simultaneously, the symbols distinguish and separate their possessors from lay people, making their role seem more mysterious, shrouded, and priest-like (Bramson, 1973). The early possession of these symbols serves to hasten their identification and commitment to the profession, while, at the same time, facilitating their separation from the lay world.

At this point, their very selection of medicine as a career has produced a set of reactions by friends, family and others which reinforce in the students' minds the idea that they are becoming very special people. Immediately upon acceptance into medical school, students perceive themselves being related to, in typified fashion, as medical students and future physicians. This reaction of others intensifies as students enter training and immerse themselves in it. At the same time, students see that they must devote more and more time and energy to their studies, and less time to past relationships and interests....

One of the first difficult tasks that faces students is to begin to learn and communicate in the symbolic system that defines medical work and workers. Immediately in tutorials, readings, demonstrations and rounds, students are inundated with a language they know they are expected to become facile in. Their task is even more difficult because this exotic language is used to describe very complex processes and understandings. Students are taken aback at the difficulty of learning to communicate in their new language. They begin carrying medical dictionaries to help them translate and define terms and phrases....

The separation between "we" and "they" becomes clearer to students as they are absorbed into the medical culture. As they move through the culture, they learn how the symbols are used to communicate and enforce certain definitions of the situation. Students learn how practising physicians use these symbols of the profession to shape and control the definition of the situation....

Turning Off Your Feelings

Previous research on medical students has shown that a major effect of medical education is to make the medical student more cynical and less idealistic. Our data also suggest that as students move through school and develop a professional self-image, and thus begin to take on the identity of a doctor, their views on medicine become transformed from what they describe as an idealistic phase to what they believe is a more realistic one. Accounting for this transition, one student claims:

> ...first of all, the exposure to what really goes on. You sort of keep your eyes open and you really get an idea of the real world of medicine.... The other part of it is when you're allowed responsibility...and you really become involved with patients.

Students become less vocal in their questioning and criticisms of the medical profession. They attribute many of their earlier concerns to naivete, and argue for a more sympathetic view of doctors and the profession as a whole.

> I think I went through a phase, as I went from knowing very little about medicine to a little bit.... You go through a sort of stage of disillusion in which you sort of expect doctors to be perfect, and the medical profession and treatment and everything else to be perfect. And you find out that it's not. So you sort of react to that. I think now, after about two years, I'm starting to get to the

> phase now where I'm quite pleased with it really. Part of it is
> getting into arguments about other professions and this brings out
> things that you've thought about but not really verbalized.... A
> particular friend of mine is in law and he was talking about
> malpractice suits and it really makes you think that knowing
> doctors the way you do, and I've seen them operate, if other
> professions were as self-critical as doctors were and had a good
> sense of responsibility to duty, then I think a lot of the
> professions would be a lot better off....

Though not entirely pleased by the outcome of this transformation, students
know that their views of medicine are being altered. They describe these
changes as part of their personal and professional growth. They argue that they
are becoming more mature personally and developing a clearer and sharper
understanding of the world of medicine. Most importantly, they admit a
willingness to accept the situation as a small price for becoming more
competent. With only minor exceptions they accept the present sacrifice of
their ideals as a necessary condition of medical training, and hope to recapture
their idealism at a later time....

The hope and belief that they will be in a more opportune position to
express and act upon their initial idealism after graduation is coupled, for many,
with a more sombre realization that matters are unlikely to change. On the
basis of their observations and deliberations many students become resigned to
their behaviour as physicians always coming under close scrutiny and control
from their colleagues. Most students do not have high hopes of being able to
change medicine.

Although they are often initially dismayed by how physicians and other
hospital staff treat patients, they come to accept that the objectification of
patients is a routine feature of doctor-patient relationships. It is the
"professional" way to deal with medical situations.[4] In time they accept the
view that patients must be objectified and depersonalized or the doctor will be
unable to maintain clinical objectivity (Coombs and Powers 1975; Emerson,
1970). While initially bothered, even offended, by this detachment, they come
to see it as part of the professional situation over which they have little
control....

Striving for competence is the primary student rationale to explain avoiding
or shutting off emotional reactions. As they progress through the program
students come to express the belief that their relationship with the patient
should be governed strictly by the patient's medical problem; emotional feelings
are a hindrance. They believe that they do not have time for both learning and
caring, and learn to stifle their feelings because of the higher value they and
others place on competence.

Students also believe that they are being trained for busy lives. Accepting the hectic pace as inevitable, they recognize that it is not temporary, but will continue throughout their medical career. Their work in the hospitals impresses on them the long hours that physicians devote to their work:

> If you look around at people who are teaching you, they often have a pretty rough life as far as time commitment and work. The work doesn't end when you get out of medical school and you can see somebody who is forty-five or fifty and married and has a couple of kids, in on Saturday afternoons working away, and being on call in the evenings.

Students recognize that many physicians work long and irregular hours. As they embark upon the clerkship phase of the program, they discover that the hospital routine they must fit demands that their everyday lives be organized around medicine....

The dominant concern with learning medicine leads students to maintain their learning efficiency and productivity. Students come to believe that they have no time for the frills of emotional involvement and quickly learn to close off feelings that interfere with their work (Lief and Fox, 1963). The following statement by a student emphasizes the idea of productivity:

> You can't function if you think about things like that [death and dying]. Everything you see sort of gets in there and turns about in your mind and you aren't productive. The reason you have to shut it off is because you won't be productive.... I think that my prime objective is to learn the pathology and just to know it and then, understanding that, I can go back to these other things and worry about the personal part of it.

During the first ten weeks of the curriculum the students are introduced to, among other things, the psychosocial component of health care. As many students are interested in working with and helping people, and are aware that medical problems have many different causes, the emphasis on the psychosocial issues gives them an opportunity to express their views concerning social, economic, political and moral aspects of medicine. However, even before Phase I is completed, they are eager to start what they consider to be their "real" medical studies. Reflecting the views of others in the class, a student says:

> [In Phase I] you really concentrate on a lot of psychosocial issues. But it becomes really obvious before the ten weeks are up that

> you are getting tired of talking about that kind of stuff, and you
> want to get on with it.

The students' concern for the psychosocial aspects of medicine are not entirely ignored when they enter Phase II of their program. As they are gradually introduced to the content and "core" of medicine, they begin to realize that there is too much to know and little time in which to learn it all. Like the religious or political convert who becomes fanatically observant and committed, students devote themselves to the task of learning medicine. Time becomes a commodity that must be spent wisely. They become very concerned about not misusing or wasting their time studying certain topics deemed unproductive. In this context, the psychosocial component becomes less important.

> One thing you have to do at medical school is pick up all the
> pathophysiology and to pick up all of the anatomy and pick up
> the clinical histories, the presentations, the clinical skills and so
> on. So psychosocial time is really a luxury, it can't really be
> afforded sometimes....

Although they put them aside, students continue to recognize that psychosocial matters are important. They believe this area must be neglected, however, in the interest of acquiring as much medical knowledge and competence as possible. They believe that if they feel for their patients and become involved with them they will not become professionally competent....

Most students move to the view that personal concerns for the patient should not intrude on the physician's professional responsibility....

Student concerns about learning medicine, making the most efficient use of time, and establishing some bases of certainty and security in their work are all reflected in the selected interest they take in patients with unusual pathology (Becker *et al.*, 1961). Discussing the kind of patients that he looked forward to seeing, a student claims:

> A patient who has physical findings. Gees, I don't care what the
> findings are. It's a fantastic experience to see that physical finding.
> They may only have two or even one.... In order to do a physical
> exam you've got to have something there to feel. Someone can
> tell you this is the way to feel for a lump in the stomach, but if
> there is no lump there you are not going to lean how to feel it....
> I thing that's what I get the most out of, getting exposure to the
> pathology, feeling things that I may not feel.

The high point for students is making a correct diagnosis by sleuthing out relevant material, and knowing with some assurance the diagnosis is valid and the treatment competent....

Students alter their understanding of how medicine should be practiced. Unable to feel as deeply concerned about the patient's total condition as they believe they should, they discover an approach that justifies concentrating only on the person's medical problem. As a student remarks:

> Somebody will say "Listen to Mrs. Jones' heart. It's just a little thing flubbing on the table." And you forget about the rest of her. Part of that is the objectivity and it helps in learning in the sense that you can go in to a patient, put your stethoscope on the heart, listen to it and walk out.... The advantage is that you can go in a short time and see a patient, get the important things out of the patient and leave.

As students learn to objectify patients they lose their sensitivity for them. When they can concentrate on the interesting pathology of the patient's condition, students' feelings for the patient's total situation are eroded.... The students do not lose their idealism and assume a professional mask without a struggle. But even when they see and feel the worst, students recognize that they do not have the time to crusade. That would interfere with the learning of medicine and impede their efforts to become competent....

Acting the Professional Role

Students believe they are expected to act as if they are in the know, not in ways which might put their developing competence into question. The pressure to be seen as competent by faculty, fellow students, hospital personnel and patients narrows the range of alternative roles students can assume. Students recognize their low status in the hospital hierarchy and on hospital rotations. They realize that the extent of their medical knowledge can easily be called into question by fellow students, tutors, interns, residents and faculty. To reduce the possibility of embarrassment and humiliation which, at this stage in their medical career, is easily their fate, students attempt to reduce the unpredictability of their situation by manipulating an impression of themselves as enthusiastic, interested, and eager to learn. At the same time, students seize opportunities which allow them to impress others, particularly faculty and fellow students, with their growing competence and confidence....

Although a basic objective of the school's philosophy is to encourage learning through problem-solving and a questioning attitude throughout the medical career, the philosophy does not help students' overriding problem of appearing competent. A perspective shared by students to manage an appearance of competence is to limit their initiatives to those situations which will be convincing demonstrations of their competence. Some students decide, for example, to ask questions in areas with which they are already familiar, to cultivate an impression of competence.

> The best way of impressing others with your competence is asking questions you know the answers to. Because if they ever put it back on you: "Well what do you think?" then you tell them what you think and you'd give a very intelligent answer because you know it. You didn't ask it to find out information. You ask it to impress people.

The general strategy that the students adopt is to mask their uncertainty and anxiety with an image of self-confidence. Image making becomes recognized as being as important as technical competence. As one student remarks: "We have to be good actors, put across the image of self-confidence, that you know it all...." The pressure to conform is perhaps even more extreme at this school than at other medical schools because its evaluation system is much more pervasive and a large part of it is generated by students. Students observe each other, seeking to establish a base of comparison....

The students are acutely aware of the relationship between impression management and successful evaluation. While the evaluation ought to consist of an objective assessment of the students' abilities to conduct a diagnosis and prescribe a course of treatment, the outcome is, in fact, shaped by the students' abilities to behave as if they are able to accomplish these tasks....

Conclusion

Our findings should be analogous to other professions and their socialization processes. The process of making some expert and more competent separates professionals from those they are presumed to help and serves to create a situation where the exaggerated expectations of competence are managed by symbolically defining and controlling the situation to display the imagery of competence. Impression management is basic and fundamental in those occupations and professions which profess competence in matters seriously affecting others.

Edgerton (1967) believes that the central and shared commonality of the mentally retarded released from institutions was for them to develop themselves in a cloak of competence to deny the discomforting reality of their stigma. The development of a cloak of competence is, perhaps, most apparent for those who must meet exaggerated expectations. The problem of meeting other's enlarged expectations is magnified for those uncertain about their ability to manage a convincing performance. Moreover, the performer faces the personal problem of reconciling his private self-awareness and uncertainty with his publicly displayed image. For those required to perform beyond their capacities, in order to be successful, there is the constant threat of breakdown or exposure. For both retardates and professionals the problem and, ironically, the solution, are similar. Expectations of competence are dealt with by strategies of impression management, specifically, manipulation and concealment. Interactional competencies depend on convincing presentations and much of professionalism requires the masking of insecurity and incompetence with a symbolic-interactional cloak of competence.

Endnotes

1.   This paper is based on data that were collected largely during the first two years of a three-year study we are conducting on the socialization of medical students at a medical school in Ontario, Canada. The data were collected by means of participant observation and interviews. We have observed students during the full range of their educational and informal activities and to date have interviewed fifty-five of the eighty students in the class. We are presently completing the fieldwork phase of the study as students approach their licensing examination and graduation. We will be writing a monograph, based on the research, in the coming year.

2.   Unlike most medical schools, the school we are studying has a three-year program where long summer vacations are eliminated. Admission is not restricted to individuals with strong pre-medical or science backgrounds. The school de-emphasizes lectures and has no formal tests or grades. Students are introduced to clinical settings from the very beginning of their studies. Learning revolves around a "problem-solving" approach as students meet in six-person tutorial groups. An analysis of the consequences of such innovations will be described in subsequent writings.

3.   The program is divided into five Phases: Phase I lasts ten weeks; Phase II twelve weeks; Phase III forty weeks; Phase IV, essentially the last half of the three-year program, is the clinical clerkship. Student electives,

vacations and a review phase—Phase V—make up the remainder of the
M.D. program.

4.   The core of the professional attitude toward the patient is to be found
      in what Parsons (1951) has termed "affective neutrality." As Bloom and
      Wilson have written: "This orientation is the vital distancing mechanism
      which prevents the practitioner from becoming the patient's colleague
      in illness.... Affective neutrality constitutes the physician's prime
      safeguard against the antitherapeutic dangers of countertransference"
      (1972: 321). The management of closeness and detachment in
      professional-client relations is discussed in Joan Emerson (1970), and in
      Charles Kadushin (1962). For a discussion of the socialization of medical
      students toward a detached attitude, see Morris J. Daniels (1960). For
      an insightful analysis of how student-physicians come to manage the
      clinical role pertaining to death and dying, and learn to retain
      composure, no matter how dramatic the death scene, see Coombs and
      Powers (1975).

References

Becker, Ernest, *Escape from Evil*. New York: The Free Press, 1975.

Becker, Howard S. and Blanche Geer, Everett C. Hughes and Anselm Strauss.
Boys in White: Student Culture in Medical School. Chicago: University of
Chicago Press, 1961.

Bloom, Samuel W. and Robert N. Wilson. "Patient-Practitioner Relationships,"
pp. 315-39 in H.E. Freeman, S. Levine and L.G. Reeder (eds.), *Handbook
of Medical Sociology*. Englewood Cliffs, N.J.: Prentice-Hall, 1972.

Bramson, Roy. "The Secularization of American Medicine," *Hastings Center
Studies*, (1973), pp. 17-28.

Coombs, Robert H. and Pauline S. Powers. "Socialization for Death: The
Physician's Role," *Urban Life*, Vol. 4 (1975), pp. 250-71.

Daniels, Morris J. "Affect and Its Control in the Medical Intern," *American
Journal of Sociology*, Vol. 66 (1960), pp. 259-67.

Davis, Fred. "Professional Socialization as Subjective Experience: The Process
of Doctrinal Conversion among Student Nurses," pp. 235-51 in Howard S.
Becker *et al.* (eds.), *Institutions and The Person*. Chicago: Aldine Publishing
Company, 1968.

Edgerton, Robert B. *The Cloak of Competence: Stigma In The Lives Of the
Mentally Retarded*. Berkeley: University of California Press, 1967.

Emerson, Joan P. "Behaviour in Private Places: Sustaining Definitions of
Reality in Gynecological Examinations," pp. 73-97 in Hans Peter Dreitzel
(ed.), *Recent Sociology*. New York: The Macmillan Company, 1970.

Eron, Leonard D. "Effect of Medical Education on Medical Students," *Journal of Medical Education*, Vol. 10. (1955), pp. 559-66.

Fox, Renée. "Training for Uncertainty," pp. 207-41 in Robert K. Merton, George G. Reader and Patricia L. Kendall (eds.), *The Student Physician*. Cambridge, Mass.: Harvard University Press, 1957.

Freidson, Eliot, *Profession of Medicine*. New York: Dodds Mead and Co., 1970a.

————. *Professional Dominance*, New York: Atherton, 1970b.

Geer, Blanche (ed.). *Leaning to Work*. Beverly Hills: Sage Publications, Inc., 1972.

Goffman, Erving. *The Presentation of Self in Everyday Life*. New York: Doubleday Anchor Books, 1959.

Hass, Jack. "Binging: Educational Control Among High Steel Ironworkers," *American Behavioural Scientist*, Vol. 16 (1972), pp. 27-34.

————. "The Stages of the High Steel Ironworker Apprentice Career," *The Sociological Quarterly*, Vol. 15 (1974), pp. 93-108.

————. "Learning Real Feelings: A Study of High Steel Ironworkers' Reactions to Fear and Danger," *Sociology of Work and Occupations*, Vol. 4 (1977), pp. 147-70.

Haas, Jack, Victor Marshall and William Shaffir. "Anxiety and Changing Conceptions of Self: A Study of First-year Medical Students," Paper presented at the Canadian Sociological and Anthropological Association, May, 1975.

Hughes, Everett C. "The Sociological Study of Work: An Editorial Forward," *American Journal of Sociology*, Vol. 57 (1952), pp. 423-26.

————. *Men and Their Work*. Glencoe: The Free Press, 1958.

Kadushin, Charles. "Social Distance between Client and Professional," *American Journal of Sociology*, Vol. 67 (1962), pp. 517-31.

Lief, Harold I. and Renée Fox. "Training for 'Detached Concern' in Medical Students," pp. 12-35 in Lief, H.I., V. Lief and N.R. Lief (eds.), *The Psychological Basis of Medical Practice*. New York: Harper and Row, 1963.

Mayer, John E. and Aaron Rosenblatt. "Encounters with Danger: Social Workers in the Ghetto," *Sociology of Work and Occupations*, Vol. 2 (1975), pp. 227-45.

Olsen, Virginia L. and Elvi W. Whittaker. *The Silent Dialogue*. San Francisco: Jossey-Bass Inc., 1968.

Parsons, Talcott. *The Social System*. London: Routledge and Kegan Paul, 1951.

————. "Research with Human Subjects and the Professional Complex," *Daedalus*, Vol. 98 (1969), pp. 325-60.

Phase 1 Manual, 1974.

Quint, Jeanne C. "Institutionalized Practices of Information Control," *Psychiatry*, Vol. 28 (1956), pp. 119-32.

Ross, Ailen D. *Becoming a Nurse*. Toronto: The Macmillan Company of Canada Ltd., 1961.

Roth Julius A. "Ritual and Magic in the Control of Contagion," *American Sociological Review*, Vol. 22 (1957), pp. 310-14.

Schanck, Richard L. "A study of a Community and Its Groups and Institutions Conceived of as Behaviours of Individuals," *Psychological Monographs*, Vol. 43, No. 2 (1932).

Siegler, Miriam and Humphry Osmond. "Aesculapian Authority," *Hastings Center Studies*, Vol. 1 (1973), pp. 41-52.

Equality to Benefit from Schooling: The Issue of Educational Opportunity

Stephen Richer

As a primary site and instrument of socialization our education system purportedly provides an equal opportunity for all members of society to fulfil their potential. But is this actually the case? In this excerpt Richer argues that the pedagogy and the curriculum content, particularly at an elementary level, effectively reproduce inequalities persistent in the social order. The uniformity of structure and content across schools, classrooms and teachers masks a "hidden curriculum" which, says Richer, contributes to the reproduction of the inequality between men and women and the lower and middle classes.

...Do we therefore dismiss the notion of the school as reproducer of the social order? The answer is no, but in order to analyse the role of the school in this regard we must be sensitive to the dynamics of *classroom interaction*, particularly at the early elementary level. My contention is that it is precisely the *lack* of interschool and intraschool variation in pedagogical structure and curriculum content, particularly at the elementary level, which is partially responsible for the data alluded to above on inequality of returns to education. I shall argue that *it is the uniformity of schooling juxtaposed against the variability in children which is salient*. I shall take the position that there is an inequality to benefit from the schooling experience due to the exposure of different children to the *same* educational experience.[1] The reason for focusing on early elementary schooling arises out of the increasing conviction of many researchers in education that it is in these initial years that basic processes are set in motion which to a large extent determine educational and perhaps even occupational mobility. It is at this level that children are the most malleable and hence most vulnerable to the school as an agent of socialization.

Cultural Capital and the Hidden Curriculum

Given this desired focus, how can we begin to investigate equality to benefit from education in elementary schools? Two useful concepts are those of cultural capital and the notion of the hidden curriculum. The former, most fully developed by Bourdieu (1964, 1966, 1970) connotes the idea of a differential distribution in society of cultural trappings which are essential for success. Kennett (1973), in summarizing the thrust of Bourdieu's work, explicates five postulates underlying it:

1. Society is essentially a repressive system.
2. There is diffused within society a cultural capital "transmitted by inheritance and invested in order to be cultivated."
3. The education system functions to "discriminate in favour of those who are the inheritors of this cultural capital."
4. The notion of school failure as due to lack of talents, or of groups lacking certain characteristics which makes them unfit for success, is "a mystification, an ideology of the dominant group."
5. Culture has a political function.

There are thus two sides of the cultural capital coin:

1. People vary with respect to their possession of cultural capital.
2. Schools operate within the assumptions underlying this cultural capital.

The latter point leads us to the so-called hidden curriculum, the name given to the bundle of values and norms implicitly transmitted in the schools. To quote Giroux and Penna (1977), the concept refers to "...those unstated norms, values and beliefs that are transmitted to students through the underlying structure of classrooms, as opposed to formally recognized and sanctioned dimensions of classroom experience."

I am convinced that in order for students to be successful in school they would be better to master the hidden rather than the formal curriculum. The point is, of course, that certain students (those already imbued with the cultural capital underlying the hidden curriculum) have a greater capacity to learn its subtleties than other children. In the rest of this paper I shall do two things:

1. Outline the content of the hidden curriculum.
2. Develop links between school success and certain types of children based on compatibility with the demands of the hidden curriculum.

I rely heavily for our discussion on my longitudinal study of Ontario kindergarten children.

Content of the Hidden Curriculum

The study just alluded to was carried out in Ottawa and involved four years of observation in six kindergarten classrooms. With the aid of video tapes and a team of observers, it was possible to collect detailed data on the organization and daily workings of such classrooms. A thematic analysis of the tapes and

Table 1 — A Typical Kindergarten Schedule (Ottawa School, 1978)

Activity	Space	Time
Good Morning Time (Series of songs, e.g., Good Morning, If You're Happy & You Know It)	Piano area	9:00 — 9:10 a.m.
Demonstration by teacher of how to cut and paste a fire engine	Piano area	9:10 — 9:20 a.m.
Coordination exercises	Piano area	9:20 — 9:25 a.m.
Game (Simon Says)	Area in front of doll's house	9:25 — 9:35 a.m.
Walking across hall to French	Hall	9:35 — 9:38 a.m.
French	French Teacher's room across the hall	9:38 — 9:50 a.m.
1/2 class—construction of fire engine	Work-table area	9:50 — 10:15 a.m.
Others—Free Play	Doll's house area, Jungle Gym, Block area	
Rotation of above		10:15 — 10:40 a.m.
Snack	Piano area	10:40 — 10:55 a.m.
Show and Tell (children speak a little about materials brought from home)	Piano area	10:55 — 11:00 a.m.
Story (read by teacher)	Piano area	11:00 — 11:15 a.m.
Prepare for going home	Counter area	11:15 a.m.

researchers' diaries led to the following description of what has been termed the "hidden curriculum." Basically, we identified two major aspects of the hidden curriculum: the cognitive (i.e., the way in which school knowledge is organized), and the social, which we discuss at two levels—the societal level and the level of schooling as an institution.

Cognitive Dimensions of the Hidden Curriculum

To understand the way knowledge is organized in our society, it is helpful to begin with a typical kindergarten activity schedule.

Table 1 presents such a schedule for one particular class (although it is very similar to that of other classes observed).[2] The important implicit aspect of this curriculum structure is the relatively clear demarcation which exists among subjects, even at this very early level of schooling. As Table 1 indicates, the day is divided into clearly defined time-space-activity blocks which have virtually no linkages or connections among them. That is, "knowledge" is presented to the child as a set of relatively discrete, self-contained subjects. In Bernstein's words, this exemplified a strong "classification" type of knowledge organization. Classification refers to "the nature of the differentiation" among curriculum contents—"where classification is strong, contents are well insulated from each other by strong boundaries. Where classification is weak, there is reduced insulation between contents for the boundaries between contents are weak and blurred." (Bernstein, 1971: 49) Such a knowledge code clearly reflects wider trends in industrial societies towards increased specialization in the division of labour (see also Esland, 1971; Young 1971).

The point is that children have to learn in a way that forces them to think in terms of relatively fragmented units of information, as opposed to thinking styles which preserve the gestalt or interconnectedness of the social and/or physical world. We shall return to this issue at a later point.

Social Dimensions of the Hidden Curriculum

This aspect of the hidden curriculum consists, I suggest, of two major levels of information—information about the society the children will eventually be entering, and information about public schooling as an institution.

The Societal Level
Talcott Parsons, writing about the school class as a social system, delineated the function played by formal schooling in preparing children for life in an industrial society. Utilizing his set of pattern variables as basic value and role configurations, he argues convincingly, albeit rather abstractly, that the school weans the child away from the particularism and affectivity characteristic of

family life, gradually replacing these with the values of universalism and affective neutrality. The school experience is thus the child's first encounter with the kind of roles he or she will have to engage in when out in the work world (Parsons, 1959). My own study of several kindergarten classes found Parsons' arguments still relevant. Underlying the various classroom activities, even at this initial stage of schooling, can be discerned a set of general values characteristic of the wider society. The major themes involve:

1. the ethic of interindividual competition;
2. an emphasis on materialism;
3. the primacy of work over play; and
4. the submission of self.

First, the child from the first day of formal schooling finds himself competing with other children. Differentiation of the children in terms of success or failure is evident in the games played, early printing exercises, proper school comportment and achieving attention from the teacher. Some children do better than others in motor coordination events and are rewarded accordingly. Games such as Simon Says and Cross the River produced a winner—the first, the best in attentiveness and reflex, and the second, the best jumper in the class. By the middle of the second month in the classes observed, stars were allotted for especially neat printing, usually accompanied by verbal praise. Show and Tell, a period where children talked briefly about items brought from home, became a period where they sought to impress the teacher with their favourite doll, toy soldier or truck, this inevitably at the expense of their peers. At a more covert level, the children were placed in the position of competing throughout the day for both teacher approval and attention. Regarding the former, children adhering to the teacher's conception of proper school behaviour were clearly treated differently from those behaving otherwise. While there were children in the class who rejected this competition for a while and refused to participate, by the end of the first two months of school all the children were actively seeking the teacher's approval. This was accomplished by the teacher through various types of rewards and punishments. Regarding competition for teacher attention, Jackson has given a good description of the competition that constantly exists for this commodity. Given the situation of 30 or so children in a teacher-centred communication structure, "delay, denial and interruption" are no doubt inevitable and frequent occurrences (Jackson, 1968).

The institution of Show and Tell, we argue, became a competition along the axis of material possessions. This period, which occurred every day in the classes studied (and in virtually all elementary classes I have observed), was ostensibly established in schools to provide children the opportunity to speak before their peers about an object or objects familiar to them. Confidence in front of others and verbal skills are assumedly enhanced in the process. While these certainly may occur, an unanticipated consequence of Show and Tell would appear to reinforce interindividual competition and simultaneously to inculcate the values of materialism and private property. In a typical session, a child stands before the group exhibiting a toy or watch, or perhaps a new article of clothing. The teacher usually comments positively on its "niceness" and asks various questions about the object; for example, "Where did you get this?" "Who gave it to you?" "What is it supposed to do?" and "Does anyone else here have something like this?" For the child who has many toys and games at home, this activity becomes an exciting one. He or she proudly produces possessions day after day. Rewarded for bringing them by teacher as well as peer attention, he or she cannot help but see the value of material possessions.

The activities for which tangible rewards are allotted provide a clue as to which types of activities are valued in a group. In kindergarten, rewards such as paper stars, animal picture stamps or coloured check marks were distributed only for "3 R" type activities; that is, letter and number printing and various puzzle worksheets. Play activities, including games and songs, produced occasional praise if well done but no further recognition. In short, those we would term school work activities were associated with tangible rewards, while play activities were not. This, along with the physical centrality of the teacher's desk, the blackboard, and the children's work area, served, I would argue, to convey to the child the primacy of work over play, a primacy to be reinforced from that point on in his/her life.

Perhaps the least "hidden" aspect of the hidden curriculum is the transmission of what we would call submission of self. The theme of "man" as essentially wild, self-interested and aggressive in the pursuit of his interests appears in the writings of many philosophers and social scientists. Parsons, for example, in *The Structure of Social Action* wrestles with the contradiction between these attributes of man and the existence of order, eventually coming to his solution of the internalization of norms regulating social action (Parsons, 1939). The kindergarten classroom, although at first glance an unlikely arena for the acting out of the Parsonian solution, nevertheless evoked for me time and again the struggle between individual voluntarism and societal constraint. What the child learns here, sometimes painfully, is that the collectivity has precedence over his or her own desires and wishes.

In Parsons' terms, there is a move from a self to a collectivistic orientation (Parsons, 1951). The child learns that he/she must put aside his or her own wishes in favour of the wishes of a recognized authority figure in adult society, in this case the teacher. He/she is to accept as natural and right that people above him/her in a status hierarchy can dictate his or her own behaviour, an acceptance that is to be generalized to other organizations he or she will encounter.

From the first day of school, the teachers observed made this their primary task. Convinced, as are the large majority of teachers I have observed, that "You cannot teach them a thing if you can't control them," a great deal of effort was expended on achieving classroom order. Through an elaborate set of rewards and punishments, orderly behaviour was reinforced and its opposite punished. The concern of the teachers with their initial inability to effect control was also evident in the teacher interviews conducted regularly after each observation session. Two standard questions were asked during these interviews: "What were your impressions today?" and "Which children stood out today?" The questions were purposely phrased very generally so that teachers could raise anything they wished. Nevertheless, in the first several weeks, both questions were answered with regard to the presence or absence of control on that particular day:

> The class is too big to handle. They don't know enough to sit in groups. We have to have some conformity. While some are sitting at the piano others are wandering around. (September 5)

> It was better today, there was a little more control over the children. They didn't abuse the free playtime. The end of the day is a very disappointing time. I just can't control them any more. You cannot teach them a thing if you can't control them. In all, they are responding to me better as a person of authority and resource. (September 6)

> Monday mornings always seem to be good. It's a good teaching day. I'm refreshed from the weekend and the children are too. It gets worse up to the end of the week and by Friday they're right up there. (September 10)

The question "Which children stood out today?" might theoretically have resulted in discussions of particularly "bright" children, of conspicuous articles of clothing, or of children with various physical attributes. Instead, the children who "stood out" for the teacher were those she perceived as behaviour problems: "There are three problem boys, John, Mark, Phillip." (September 5) or "Billy—I can't get through to him." (September 6) or "Robert K I can't figure him out. I can't reason with him." (September 7) or "Billy needs constant discipline. I believe things would be better with a smaller class." (September 12)[3]

The relationships between the teacher and six or seven of the children observed in the first month or so thus consisted largely of a contest of wills. The following exchanges, one from September 5 and another from September 8, provide vivid illustrations:

(September 5)
Teacher: "Billy, join the group please."
Billy: "I don't feel like coming."
Teacher: "Yes, you do."
Billy: "No, I don't. You might think I do, but I don't."

(September 8)
Teacher: "You're not doing what everyone else is doing."
Robert: "I know, I don't want to."
Teacher: "But I want you to. Come on."

It is clear, then, that for the child there is no alternative but to eventually submit. In terms of resources, the contest is inherently unequal, the teacher possessing greater age and physical size, not to mention legitimate authority. The latter is manifested both in the support of fellow professionals as well as in the tacit backing of the larger community who, in effect, grant a mandate to teachers to socialize their sons and daughters.

The outcome, then, undoubtedly functional from a societal perspective, is that the children learn to accept external authority and concomitantly to repress their own egocentric interest, a requisite for later participation in large-scale bureaucratic organizations.

The Institution of Public Schooling
From the first day of kindergarten, the child is presented with a set of values about appropriate school behaviour which he/she will encounter time and again throughout his/her formal education. These are in large part school-specific counterparts of the societal level values alluded to above. School is presented as a place where children compete with one another along the work axis for various rewards which are meted out by an adult to whom they are expected continually to defer. This last aspect, the submission of self, is expressed in schools in terms of a set of normative expectations clustered into the role of student. These expectations are transmitted by the teacher and involve attentiveness, ways of receiving attention and ways of overall comportment.

First, children are expected to listen when the teacher speaks. One of the teachers, for example, experimented with two major techniques of obtaining attention. In the first week, she told the children that when she called "All hands up," they were to stop whatever they were doing, raise their hands and "close their mouths." This signified her desire to address the class. This was abandoned, however, as it proved unsuccessful after the third or fourth attempt. The second technique, eventually adopted, was to require certain types of behaviour in particular parts of the classroom. We refer here to the association between spatial area and appropriate activity, exemplified in Table 1. The most relevant area was the piano area. When the children were gathered here, the teacher expected the exhibition of "piano manners." These entailed being quiet, sitting up straight, and listening when others were talking. An excerpt from October 29, is a typical illustration of the way in which the teacher sought to bring about the acceptance of the manners idea:

Teacher:	"Can we have piano manners? (pause) What are piano manners?"
Two or three children:	"Sitting up straight and listening."
Teacher:	"That is right. If I have people who don't give me piano manners, they'll put their hands on top of their heads."

By the end of the first week in November, piano manners were virtually automatically displayed by the children in this area of the room, and the teacher was able to drop explanatory repetitions of the kind quoted above.

Children were thus expected to give attention on demand to the teacher. They were also expected to conform to a set of rules concerning the *seeking* of attention. As early as September 5, in all the classes the children were told to raise their hands if they wished to speak and not to interrupt when someone else was speaking. It should be pointed out that most of the children were quite familiar with the hand-raising phenomenon before the teacher held forth on it, which implies some anticipatory socialization in the home *vis-à-vis* student behaviour.

As for general comportment, the children were to learn that school was a place where one behaves differently than one does away from school. This difference is expressed in one teacher's distinction between "inside" and "outside" voices—school is a place for the former; that is, quiet talk, hushed voices. A set of expected behaviours called "hall manners" by the same teacher are also a good illustration. When the children left the classroom to go to French or Gym, or to a school assembly, they were expected to line up in single file, place their two hands on their head, and walk directly to the appropriate area. In short, as a student is attentive to the teacher, one seeks recognition through appropriate channels, and one generally behaves docilely.

Student Cultural Capital and the Hidden Curriculum

The argument to be made here is that certain children, because of the cultural capital which they carry, are more compatible than others with the above aspects of schooling. Specifically, it is my contention that middle-class children and females are better "matched" to the demands of schooling than their lower-class and male counterparts. This accounts to a large extent, I suggest, for their differential success in the schools.

There has been much work done in the U.S. on cultural differences among the social classes (classic works are Hyman, 1954; Kohn, 1963, 1969; Kluckhohn and Strodbeck, 1961; Reissman, 1962). Despite some inconsistencies among studies, there is general agreement in this literature that one can differentiate the American lower and middle classes along four lines; attitudes towards achievement; future versus present orientation; extent to which competition versus cooperation characterizes life style; and extent to which materialism is a salient value. With some caution, one can produce a fair amount of evidence consistent with the following: members of the lower as opposed to the middle class are less motivated to achieve, more likely to stress the present as opposed to the future as the major source of rewards, more inclined to value cooperation as opposed to competition, more inclined to respond to material as opposed to symbolic rewards and, related to this latter point, more inclined to settle disputes through physical rather than verbal means.

The relevant research in Canada, although less abundant than that in the U.S., is nevertheless consistent with these typifications. (For general summaries see Elkin and Handel, 1972; Elkin, 1964; Pike and Zureik, 1975; Jones and Selby, 1972.)

By way of summarizing the above social class discussion, I am suggesting that certain middle-class characteristics, notably the tendency to defer gratification, the greater concern with interindividual competition, the tendency towards an analytical-goal orientation, the greater reliance on verbal rather than physical skills, and the greater likelihood of responding to non-material rewards, ensure a rather distinct advantage from the first days of formal schooling.

Endnotes

1.   Clearly, at the secondary level one finds greater differentiation of schools by curriculum content and perhaps teaching style. As I shall be arguing, however, it is the focus on elementary schooling (particularly the early grades which is most salient.

2.   Much of the data reported in this paper came from one classroom, the central one in our study. The findings, however, hold without exception for all the classes observed.

3.   Observations made in other classes as well as the literature on classroom research (Jackson, 1968) indicate that the concern with order is by no means unique to this study. Indeed, it seems to pervade the atmosphere in most, if not all, traditional schools.

References

Bernstein, B. 1971. "On the Classification and Framing of Educational Knowledge." In M.F.D. Young, ed., *Knowledge and Control*. London: Collier-Macmillan.

Bourdieu, P. 1966. "L'Ecole conservatrice: Les inegalities devant l'ecole et devant la culture," *Review Francaise de Sociologie*, 7:325-347.

Bourdieu, P. 1970. *La Reproduction*. Paris: Editions de Minuit.

Bourdieu, P. and J.C. Passeron. 1964. *Les Heritiers*. Paris: Editions de Minuit.

Elkin, F. 1964. *The Family in Canada*. Ottawa: Canadian Conference on the Family.

Elkin, F. and G. Handel. 1972. *The Child and Society: The Process of Socialization*. New York: Random House.

Esland, G.M. 1971. "Teaching and Learning as the Organization of Knowledge." In Michael Young, ed., *Knowledge and Control*.

Giroux, H. and A. Penna. 1977 "Social Relations in the Classroom: the Dialectic of the Hidden Curriculum," *Edcentric*. 40-41: 39-46.

Hyman, H.H. 1954. "The Value-System of Different Classes." In R. Bendix and S. Lipset, eds., *Class Status and Power*. London: Routledge and Kegan Paul.

Jackson, P.W. 1968. *Life in the Classroom New York: Holt, Rinehart and Winston*.

Jones, F. and J. Selby. 1973. "School Performance and Social Class." In T.J. Ryan, *Poverty and the Child*. Toronto: McGraw-Hill Ryerson.

Kennett, J. 1973. "The Sociology of Pierre Bourdieu," *Educational Review*, 25.

Kluckholn, F.R. and F. L. Strodtbeck. 1961. *Variations in Value Orientations*. Chicago: Row Peterson.

Kohn, M. 1963. "Social Class and Parent-Child Relationships: An Interpretation," *American Journal of Sociology*, 68: 471-480.

Kohn, M. 1969. *Class and Conformity*. Homewood: Dorsey Press.

Parsons, T. 1939. *The Structure of Social Action*. Glencoe: The Free Press.

Parsons, T. 1951. *The Social System*. Glencoe. The Free Press.

Parsons, T. 1959. "The School Class as a Social System," *Harvard Educational Review*, 29: 297-318.

Pike, R.M. and E. Zureik, eds. 1975. *Socialization and Values in Canadian Society*, Vol. 2. Toronto: McClelland and Stewart.

Riessman, F. 1962. *The Culturally Deprived child*. New York: Harper and Row.

Young, M. 1971. "Curricula, Teaching and Learning as the Organization of Knowledge." In M. Young, ed., *Knowledge and Control*. London: Collier-Macmillan.

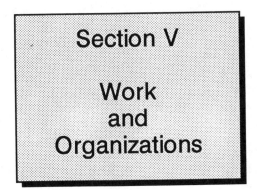

Section V

Work
and
Organizations

Alienated Labour

James W. Rinehart

"The worker becomes poorer the more wealth he produces, the more his production increases in power and extent. The worker becomes a cheaper commodity the more commodities he produces.... The more the worker exerts himself, the more powerful becomes the alien objective world he fashions against himself, the poorer he and his inner world become, the less there is that belongs to him." There are few statements that capture the lived experience of a problem with such analytic force as Karl Marx's characterization of alienated labour, published in 1844 and partly quoted above. In the following excerpt, Rinehart discusses Marx's ideas in the context of the contemporary workplace, and considers some possible solutions to the problem of alienation.

According to Marx, there are four aspects of alienated labour. First, this condition entails an estrangement of working people from the products of their labour. The product—the purpose for which it is created, how it is disposed of, its content, quality, and quantity—is not determined by those whose labour is responsible for its manufacture. Under industrial capitalism, workers are obliged to surrender their power to determine the product of labour via a wage contract which in effect gives this power over to employers, that is, the capitalist class....

Because the products of labour are determined by employers rather than by workers, it is employers who reap most of the benefits of productive activity. Even when working people experience absolute gains in their standard of living, their position, relative to that of capitalists, deteriorates. Marx wrote: "It follows therefore that in proportion as capital accumulates, the lot of the labourer, be *his payments high or low*, must grow worse."[1] Because products are under the control of owners of the means of production, increases in labour output such as those resulting from scientific advances, technological innovations, and refinements in the social organization of the workplace, accrue to the benefit of the propertied class. "The increase in the quantity of objects," Marx observed, "is accompanied by an *extension* of the realm of alien powers to which man is subjected."[2] Intensified productivity, then, extends and deepens the alienated position of workers in the system of production; it simultaneously stretches out the class system by increasing the political and economic gulf which separates workers and capitalists.[3]

If working people are estranged from the products of labour, they must also be alienated from the work process itself, that is, from their own labour activity. As Marx wrote, "the external character of labour for the workers appears in the fact that it is not his own but someone else's, that it does not belong to him, but to another."[4] Just as workers must give up their power to control the product of their toil, they also cede their ability to determine the intensity and duration of work, to define the manner in which work is organized, divided, and allocated, and to determine the tools and machines used in the production process. Furthermore, it is the employer who decides whether or not work will be performed at all.

From the fact that working people are estranged from the process and product of labour, Marx deduced two more aspects of alienation. The first one, self-estrangement, is tied to his conception of the meaning and purpose of work, which he viewed as *the* medium for self-expression and self-development. Work, Marx said, was the activity in which people can most clearly manifest their unique qualities as human beings. Properly organized, work brings out and reflects distinctively human attributes, that is, those which differentiate humans from all other species. It is through labour that humans should be able to shape themselves and the society in which they live in accordance with their own needs, interest, and values. Under alienating circumstances, however, work becomes not an endeavour which embodies and personifies life, not a source of personal and social gratification, but simply a means for physical survival. Marx argues that working people come to feel most contented in those activities that they share with all other living species—in procreating, drinking, and eating—in a word, in the satisfaction of physiological needs, while their peculiarly human activity—work—people feel debased. Accordingly, work takes on an instrumental meaning: it is regarded simply as a means to an end. Individuals, then, are estranged from themselves; they are alienated from their own humanity.

The final type of alienation deals with the relationship of individuals to one another. Marx believed that people who occupy dominant and subordinate positions at the workplace are alienated from each other. Their relationship is an antagonistic one and is based purely on pecuniary considerations. This asymmetry of workplace relationships creates the foundation for a class structure that entails sharp differences in power, privilege, and life chance, and that inhibits social intercourse across class lines. Marcuse argues that "the system of capitalism relates men to each other through the commodities they exchange. The social standing of individuals, their standard of living, the satisfaction of their needs, their freedom, and their power are all determined by the value of their commodities."[5] Alienation obviously characterizes the relationship between classes, but it also penetrates the interaction of people in the same class. Capitalists are compelled to drive out their competitors, and workers must competitively sell their labour power—their skills, talents, and energies—in order to survive.[6] This necessity leads to or exacerbates divisions within the working class, most notably along the lines of sex, age, and ethnicity....

Since Marx's time, the concept of alienation has been broadened to apply to a bewildering array of disadvantaged groups, deviant behaviours, and aberrant mental states. After examining the literature on the subject one writer concluded that the term "has been used in such a variety of ways that it comes close to being a shorthand expression for all the socially based psychological maladies of modern man."[7] Despite this melange, there are two ideas that are common to most usages of the concept. Alienation always entails a notion of human estrangement—from persons, objects, values, or from oneself. Second, the source of alienation is seen as residing in the social structure rather than in individual personalities; its causes are social rather than psychological. Our usage of alienation retains the notions of estrangement and social causation. At the same time, we follow Marx in viewing alienation as characteristic of a certain kind of organization of work, one whose source lies primarily in the special set of socio-economic circumstances that accompanied the development of industrial capitalism.

When we speak of alienation in this book we are referring to a condition in which individuals have little or no control over (a) the purposes and products of the labour process, (b) the overall organization of the workplace, and (c) the immediate work process itself.[8] Defined this way, alienation is objective or structural in the sense that it is built into human relationships at the workplace and exists independent of how individuals perceive and evaluate their jobs. Alienation, then, can be viewed broadly as a condition of objective powerlessness....[9]

Structural alienation means that work is not organized in accordance with the needs and interest, talents and abilities of working people. However, a complex set of psychological, cultural, and social forces influence the degree to which individuals *recognize* the sources of alienation, *adapt* to alienating work, and *express*—verbally and behaviourally—their disenchantment with work. Obviously, not all working people are conscious of their alienated position in work organizations in the sense that they are able to locate and articulate the socio-economic factors responsible for it. But all workers in objectively powerless circumstances do possess an *alienated consciousness* in that they directly experience and are acutely aware of the *effects* of structural alienation, such as repetitive and insecure jobs, insufficient wages, and arbitrary work rules. The test of the existence of alienated mental states is to be found not so much in the ability of individuals to articulate the causes of alienation, but primarily in their verbal and behaviourial reactions to work....

Sources of Alienation

We can single out three major sources of alienated labour—concentration of the means of production in the hands of a small but dominant class, markets in land, labour, and commodities, and an elaborate division of labour.... A brief explanation of each is required at this point.

The alienating impact of elite ownership of the means of production is direct and obvious. If relatively few individuals control the productive apparatus, they will operate it to their own advantage. The majority of people, who will be obliged to work for the few, will be excluded from determining the products and the labour process.[10] The relationship between wage labour and capital is also an *exploitative* one, insofar as employers extract unpaid labour from working people. A major source of business profits is the appropriation by employers of surplus value, which is the difference between the value of commodities and services produced or provided by workers and the wage cost of maintaining these workers. Workers are required to remain at work beyond the point when they have produced an amount equal to their wages. During these unpaid hours a surplus (surplus value) is produced. Employers appropriate this surplus and reinvest a portion of it in the business in order to further expand their profits. This relationship of alienation and exploitation establishes the basis for permanent antagonisms between wage labour and capital. In their drive to generate profits and expand capital, employers strive to keep wages low, introduce labour-replacing machinery, and speed up, routinize, and control work. For their part, workers seek job security, adequate wages, the reduction of work time, and control over the labour process.[11]

The term "market" refers to an economic arrangement in which the distribution and use of land, the production of goods and services, and the income and security of individuals are regulated by money and prices, operating through supply and demand and subject to the relative power of buyers and sellers, employers and employees, and creditors and debtors.[12] A market society places land, labour, and commodity production under the domain of prices. Prices and profits become the ultimate determinants of the means and ends of production, and people are compelled to make decisions based on calculations of pecuniary gain. Business firms must take whatever steps are necessary to accumulate capital or to simply stay afloat. Consequently, human considerations are secondary to those of profitability. From the point of view of the employer workers represent merely another cost of production and are evaluated as commodities like any other object that is bought and sold.

The division of labour also exerts an alienating impact on work. While there are a number of different types of the division of labour, the most important ones are specialization and the separation of mental and manual labour or, more accurately stated, the separation of the conception of work from its performance. Specialization is a twofold process which entails a fragmentation of work into minute tasks and the permanent assignment of these tasks to specific individuals. Performed under such conditions, work becomes repetitive and mindless and narrowly circumscribes the development of human capacities. Although the separation of the conception and performance of work is only one type of specialization, we discuss it separately because it is the most salient form of labour division in terms of its consequences for alienation. In this case, certain individuals are responsible for the organization, conceptualization, and design of work, while others are assigned to the role of carrying out the tasks.

The structure and consequences of the three sources of alienation can be analysed separately, but what must be stressed is their interdependence. With the rise of industrial capitalism each one stimulated the development of the other two. While markets and the division of labour antedated the industrial revolution, industrial capitalists intensified the fragmentation of work and stimulated the expansion of domestic and international markets. In turn, the greater productivity and profits made it possible by the extended division of labour and the growth of consumer demand, in conjunction with mergers and the bankruptcy of non-competitive firms, contributed to the concentration of the means of production in fewer and fewer hands.

Technology and Industrialism

All too often the three factors discussed above are ignored, and alienated labour in modern society, if recognized at all, is regarded either as a permanent feature of the human condition or as the inevitable price we pay for the benefits of industrial technology. One way of evaluating the first thesis—that the alienation transcends socio-historical boundaries—is to review the anthropological materials on the subject of work. Even a cursory perusal of these data reveals situations that are completely different from our own. In peasant and primitive societies work is an integral and not unpleasant aspect of existence. Work is fused with the totality of activities carried out by the community; it is embedded in and permeated by family and community relationships and obligations. Instead of being viewed as an onerous necessity by those who perform it, work is often regarded as indistinguishable from play, sociability, and leisure.[13]

It may come as a surprise to some readers that technology, mechanization, or industrialism have not been included among the causes of alienated labour. Many scholars who acknowledge the presence of serious discontents with work in modern societies attribute the problem to sophisticated technology, which allegedly requires centralization of knowledge and authority and a detailed division of labour.... This position of technological determinism cannot be sustained. At a given level of technological development, wide variations in alienation still exist in relation to the different ways in which production is socially organized. Alienation is *created* not by the existing state of technology and productive capacity, but, as Edwards and his associates realize, by "the power relations in society which, for example, dictate the ends of productive effort, the use to which technology is to be put, and the very criteria by which some technologies are methodically developed and others left dormant and undeveloped."[14] The primary causes of alienation, then, reside in the social relations of production and particularly in relations of domination and subordination which give to the few the ability to direct and shape production to their own ends.[15]

Under capitalism, the development and selection of technology are guided not only by the goals of productivity and profitability, but also by employers' and managers' determination to minimize workers' control over the labour process.[16] Braverman states: "The capacity of humans to control the labour process through machinery is seized upon by management from the beginning of capitalism as the *prime means whereby production may be controlled not by the direct producer but by the owners and representatives of capital.* Thus, in addition to its technical function of increasing the productivity of labour—which would be a mark of machinery under any social system—machinery also has in the capitalist system the function of divesting the mass of workers of their control over their own labour."[17]

That the social relations of production are a primary cause of alienation does not mean that technology has no effect on workers. Some forms of technology are certainly more onerous to workers than others. The point we wish to stress is that technology's role in contributing to alienated labour is a derivative and secondary one....

Possible Solutions

A number of possible solutions to alienated labour were considered. Leisure is no answer because work dominates our waking hours and affects the way in which we spend our time away from the job. Advanced technology provides no solution because its character and uses are decided by individuals and organizations interested in profitability and the perpetuation of class relationships. The net result of development in automated technology is to shift employment toward the least desirable end of the occupational spectrum. Moreover, the monitoring capabilities of new electronic equipment enable managers to tighten their control over the labour process. Workplace reforms introduced by practitioners of classical human relations and its contemporary QWL versions have the appearance of striking at the core of alienation.

Ostensibly, these programs democratize the workplace and provide more challenging jobs. Once the progressive rhetoric is penetrated, however, these measures are exposed as schemes implemented to achieve management's purposes. Similarly, job redesign is undertaken not to create challenging jobs but to enhance profits by rationalizing the labour process. Both the human relations approach and its more sophisticated contemporary variant-participative management—are used to promote collaborative relationships between bosses and workers and to erode and ultimately destroy the collective power of workers and unions. Unions have improved workplace conditions and the terms on which employees are obliged to dispose of their labour powers. At the same time, unions represent an institutionalization rather than a resolution of conflict; collective bargaining and the contract stabilize labour-management relations. Since unions operate within rather than challenging the essential boundaries of capitalist power, they are able to deal with some of the effects but not the causes of alienated labour.

We are left with one answer—workers' control. Recall that alienation in the first instance is a structural condition in which workers are detached from control of their labour and its products. The antitheses of alienated labour is workers' control—not just over their immediate jobs but over the entire work process and its objectives. Workers' control strikes at the fundamental sources of alienation; it would entail a transfer of power from elites to working people. Decisions about the purposes of work could thus be aligned with the interest, values, and needs of workers and their communities. Technology would be designed and deployed not to enhance profits and class power but to fulfil the needs of workers and the broader community. The specialization of labour could be attacked and jobs rotated and enlarged in accordance with the needs and dispositions of individuals. The gulf separating manual and intellectual labour could be bridged, in part by the act of conceptualizing and planning, which workers in control must do, and in part by mass education, which would arm ordinary working people with a knowledge of the processes of production and distribution. These goals cannot be reached through the medium of worker-owned enterprises operating in capitalist economies dominated by gain corporations. While worker-owned enterprises obviously relieve alienation, opportunities for beginning and successfully running such undertakings are limited. Moreover, the transforming potential of such enterprises is constrained by market forces and the necessity to generate profits. The only genuine solution to alienation involves a total restructuring of the workplace, the economy, and the state; that is, the establishing of a truly collective mode of production—a democratically planned economy and worker-managed enterprises. No less than such a radical change can overcome alienation. The most intransigent source of alienation is the market, which transcends national boundaries and exerts its centripetal pull over even the most reluctant nations.

But the market is nothing more than a term which summarizes a very complicated set of human relationships. As such it is not a mysterious force and is amenable to change and to the degree that the social relationships underlying it are transformed....

Endnotes

1. Karl Marx, *Capital*, Vol. I, London: Lawrence and Wishard, 1974, p. 604. (Italics added.)

2. Cited in Istvan Mészáros, *Marx's Theory of Alienation*, New York: Harper Torchbooks, 1972, p. 156.

3. The magnitude of the disparity in wealth and power of working people and capitalists in staggering. A rough estimate of the discrepancy could be obtained by comparing the net holdings of the working class with those of the capitalist class, which in the case of the latter must include not only their personal net worth but the factories, utilities, financial institutions, military establishments, etc., that they control and that are used to further their interests. *Cf.* Martin Nicolaus, "The Unknown Marx," in Carl Oglesby, ed., *The New Left Reader*, New York: Grove Press, 1969, pp. 84-110.

4. *Economic ad Philosophic Manuscripts of 1844, op. cit.*, pp. 72-73.

5. Herbert Marcuse, *Reason and Revolution,* Boston: Beacon Press, 1968, p. 279.

6. "Labour power" refers to the human capacity for labour and consists of the mental and physical capabilities we exercise in the production of useful goods and services. The term "labour process," which appears throughout...is defined as the process "by which raw materials are transformed by human labour, acting on the objects with tools and machinery: first into products for use and, under capitalism, into commodities to be exchanged on the market." See Paul Thompson, *The Nature of Work: An Introduction to Debates on the Labour Process*, London: Macmillan, 1983, p. xv.

7. William A. Faunce, *Problems of an Industrial Society*, Second Edition, New York: McGraw Hill, 1981, p. 134.

8. Alienation from the purposes and products of labour involves the question of whether the basic aim of production is profit or satisfaction of human needs, and as a related question, what will be produced and for whom. Alienation from the organization of production entails issues like the allocation of jobs, employment policy, work rules, organization of the flow of work, the purchase of machinery, etc. The referent of the final dimension is the worker's specific job. Relevant considerations here are the pace of work, freedom of movement about the workplace, the choice of work techniques, etc.

9. While unequal power is at the root of alienation, for the most part power is neither sought nor maintained for its own sake. Under capitalism, for example, power enables those who hold it to extract economic surpluses from workers and to monopolize wealth and privilege.

10. In Western societies the basis of elite control of the means of production is private property, which confers on owners the legal right to use property as they see fit. In the Soviet Union and Eastern Europe, the means and ends of production are controlled by the upper echelons of the Communist Party, *Cf.* Milovan Djilas, *The New Class*, New York: Frederick A. Praeger, 1957.

11. Karl Marx, *Capital, op. cit.*, pp. 173-221.

12. As Karl Polanyi notes, markets were never more than incidental to the economics of pre-capitalist societies. See his *The Great Transformation,* Boston: Beacon Press, 1957.

13. *Cf.* George Dalton, ed., *Tribal and Peasant Economies*, Garden City: The Natural History Press, 1967; Marshall Sahlins, *Stone Age Economics*, New York: Aldine-Atherton, 1972.

14. Richard C. Edwards, Michael Reich, and Thomas E. Weisskopf, eds., *The Capitalist System*, Englewood Cliffs: Prentice-Hall, 1972, p. 3. One illustration of the independence of alienated labour and technology is the transformation of Canadian Eskimo carving. In traditional Inuit society objects were carved for decoration, use in games, religious purposes, or self-amusement. However, over a long period of time the nature and functions of Eskimo carving were transformed through contact with white society. The change was accelerated around 1949 when the Canadian government began to encourage the development of

a "carving industry" in order to provide a new income source for the Inuit. The result was a form of art which differed markedly from that which had prevailed in the remote past. The size, media, motif, and style of the carvings were shaped by government representatives so that the objects would appeal to the standards of taste of white society. From the point of view of our discussion of technology and alienation it is instructive to find out what happened to the modern Eskimo carver. In one study, 20 Inuit artists were interviewed. "With the exception of a seventeen-year-old boy who had made only three things in his life, and didn't mind at all, all the others stated that they didn't like it, or that they hated carving. They went ahead at it in the realization that if they wanted money this was one of the few methods at hand for earning it. In this sense it happens to be a necessary occupation, but to the majority carving had become boring and mechanical." This study as well as a fascinating account of the development of Eskimo carving is contained in Charles A. Martijn, "Canadian Eskimo Carving in Historical Perspective," *Anthropos*, 59, 1964, pp. 546-596. The above quote is taken from page 570 of this article. We are grateful to Don Barr for bringing this case to our attention.

15.   The ideological implications of attributing alienation to technology per se or industrialism should be obvious. This common practice obscures and distorts the role of class relationships in creating and perpetuating alienation. It portrays technology as the villain and humans as helpless prisoners of the machine. Lewis Mumford writes: "It was because of certain traits of private capitalism that the machine—which was a neutral agent—has often served, and in fact has sometimes been, a malicious element in society, careless of human life, indifferent to human interest. The machine has suffered for the sins of capitalism; capitalism has often taken credit for the virtues of the machine." See *Technics and Civilization,* New York: Harcourt, Brace, 1934. P. 27.

16.   *Cf.* David F. Noble, *Forces of Production: A Social History of Industrial Automation,* New York: Alfred A. Knopf, 1984.

17.   Harry Braverman, *Labour and Monopoly Capital: The Degradation of Work in the Twentieth Century*, New York: Monthly Review Press, 1974, p. 193.

Ten Labour Myths

Ed Finn

Over a third of Canada's non-agricultural workers belong to unions, compared to less than a fifth of non-agricultural workers in the United States. Despite the relatively high proportion of unionized workers in Canada, Finn argues there are a number of prevalent, though erroneous, views of unions and union activities held by most Canadian citizens. Why?

Mankind has always been plagued by myth and superstition.
There was a time when most people believed that the Earth was flat, and the Moon made of green cheese. There was a time when "witches" were burned at the stake, and "doctors" used leeches as a cure for every ailment.

We like to think we live in more enlightened times today. But myths still dominate the thinking of many people—and nowhere more pervasively than in the world of labour relations.

Most Canadians are labour illiterates. They accept as truth numerous lies and distortions about unions that have no more factual basis than those superstitions of the past that they now ridicule.

But a belief in labour "bogey-men" is no less ridiculous than a belief in witches or demons. A belief that unions are harmful to our economy is no less preposterous than a belief that the Earth is flat.

The truly intelligent and open-minded citizen will make an effort to find out the truth about unions. This brief examination of the ten most widely accepted labour myths may serve as a learning tool in that re-education process.

1.   *Union-won wage increases are the chief cause of inflation, so controls on wage increases will keep down the cost of living.*

If this myth hasn't been permanently punctured by our experience with wage controls (1975-1978), it never will be. During that period, average wage settlements were reduced to less than one-third their pre-controls level. If wages really are the chief factor in inflation, that should have produced a sharp drop in prices. But it didn't. Prices kept skyrocketing, forcing most workers to take cuts in their real income. The truth is that wage increases do not cause price increases.

Wages go up as a response to rising prices. That has been the finding of every objective, scientific study. Most economists would agree with economic columnist Dian Cohen's statement: "There has not been a shred of evidence...that wages have added anything to the Canadian rate of inflation." Over the past 50 years, total labour income, as a percentage of the Gross National Product, has fluctuated only a few percentage points—proving that

rising wages and salaries have simply maintained their usual share of a growing
GNP.

Wages are continually subject to restraint through the machinery of
collective bargaining, compulsory conciliation, and legal restrictions on the right
to strike. Unlike other forms of income—profits, stock dividends, rents,
professional fees—wage levels must be set through negotiations with employers.

The only fair (and effective) form of wage control is price control. If limits
were enforced on price increases, it would automatically lower workers' need
and expectations, and they would gladly settle for correspondingly lower wage
hikes.

2. *Labour-management conflict can and should be replaced by labour-
    management co-operation.*

As an ideal, this is quite acceptable. But unfortunately we live in a society that
is based on competition, not co-operation: a society in which we are all
supposed to compete with one another for our respective shares of the national
income. That's the underlying principle of private enterprise.

No doubt the jungle, too, would be a much better place if the animals
would stop hunting and killing one another. Given their nature, however, the
suggestion that the lion and lamb lie down together is not very practical.
Particularly not for the lamb.

The world of industry and employment is also a jungle, a world in which the
strong prosper and the weak languish.

Many persons in both unions and companies wish it were otherwise. But
they are trapped in the present system. They know that it will take a complete
reversal of basic beliefs, and the abandonment of our entire economic
philosophy, before a change to labour-management co-operation can take
place.

Conflict is built into the present system, and strikes are simply one of its
manifestations. As long as the relationship between management and labour is
based on their respective power, the extent of that power will occasionally be
tested—if only because so many employers refuse to take workers' requests for
better pay and working conditions seriously unless they are willing to strike for
them.

3. *Unions don't need, and shouldn't be given the right to strike.*

Although it's not generally realized, the right to strike is a fundamental right
no less important than freedom of speech or freedom of the press. Why?
Simply because it is a vital part of the collective bargaining process.

Free collective bargaining is the only instrument that workers have to protect and promote their interests in our economic system. Without that ultimate right to withdraw their labour, they would have no strength to bargain, and would have to accept whatever wage and working condition their employer decided to impose on them.

The only thing workers have to bargain with is their skill or their labour. Denied the right to withhold it as a last resort, they become powerless. The strike is therefore not a breakdown of collective bargaining—it is the indispensable cornerstone of that process.

4.   *The right to strike should be replaced by compulsory arbitration.*

Compulsory arbitration has never worked in any democratic country where it has been tried. It has been a dismal failure in Australia, where the incidence of annual strikes is three to five times the Canadian average. It has flopped in both Britain and the United States as well.

When British Columbia introduced compulsory arbitration of labour disputes in 1968, the number of mandays lost through strikes and lockouts in that province quadrupled in the next two years. The B.C. experiment fizzled out shortly afterward.

The Federal Task Force on Labour Relations ruled out compulsory arbitration as an acceptable alternative to the right to strike. "The inconvenience caused by strikes," said the Commission in its historic report, "is a small price to pay for the maintenance of the present collective bargaining system and the basic human rights on which it is founded."

In any event, a ban on strikes is impossible to enforce in a free society. Only in a police state can workers be forced to work against their will. In a free society, compulsory arbitration doesn't eliminate strikes; it merely makes them illegal.

5.   *Unions are always making "unreasonable" wage demands.*

What is a "reasonable" wage demand?

One that meets the workers' needs? One based on the employers' ability to pay? One that's tied to productivity?

The fact is that nobody has yet devised a workable formula for determining wage increases that would be considered reasonable by the workers, by their employer, by the public, the press and the government.

Besides, most employers—except occasionally when in genuine financial stress—still refuse to open their books to union negotiators.

Unions are thus denied access to the data on profits, productivity and labour costs that they must have in order to formulate "reasonable" demands.

The only alternative in our private enterprise society is to go for as much as they think their members are entitled to get.

6.   *Strikes are the main cause of low productivity and do irreparable harm to the economy.*

The costs of strikes are greatly exaggerated, amounting on average to the loss of only one-half worker-day a year for each employee.

As the Federal Task Force on Labour Relations pointed out, this is only a small fraction of the time lost through illness, accidents and unemployment.

An effective anti-flu vaccine would save far more working time than the most repressive anti-strike law.

Most companies can now completely offset the loss of production during a strike by stockpiling beforehand and using excess capacity and overtime afterwards. Most of the business allegedly lost during strikes is merely deferred. This is borne out by strike studies showing that most business firms affected by strikes have been able to maintain their annual production norms.

There is no reliable standard for assessing the effects of a strike or the damage (if any) it causes. There is a tendency to quote unverified estimates of the daily losses a strike is supposedly inflicting, without taking into account what a struck firm is saving in wages and other operating costs. Isolated cases of hardship are also widely publicized, giving the impression that they are numerous. In this way a strike can be made to appear much more harmful than it actually is.

7.   *Workers in unions are pushed around and often forced to go on strike by power-man "labour bosses."*

The term "labour boss" was coined to portray the typical union leader as the equivalent of the company vice-president he faces across the bargaining table. It implies that a union officer has the same authoritarian control over his members that the company boss exerts over his subordinates.

In fact, the union leader is elected by the union's rank-and-file members at a convention, and is answerable to them for his or her actions. The members dictate to the leader, rather than the other way around.

The Senate Report on Growth, Employment and Price Stability pointed out that "the Canadian Labour movement is, for the most part, as far as any human organization can be from an obedient, boss-directed civilian army.... The typical union leader is much less a 'boss' than a replaceable politician with a difficult and turbulent constituency."

Union always conduct membership votes before taking strike action, and a strike occurs only when approved by a clear majority.

It is inconceivable that workers would walk a picket line, in all kinds of weather, sometimes having confrontations with police and strike-breakers, existing on strike pay that is only a fraction of their normal income, if a majority of them were opposed to the strike. It simply couldn't happen.

Most union leaders measure their success by the extent to which they can avoid strikes, and they do manage to settle 95 out of 100 contract negotiations without a strike. But a .950 batting average evidently doesn't satisfy some of the public and the press. Though tolerant of most other imperfections in an imperfect world, they demand perfection from the collective bargaining process.

8.   Strikes could be eliminated by getting rid of unions.

Sorry, that wouldn't do it. Workers have been going on strike since the dawn of recorded history, in every civilization, and under all kinds of political systems. Whenever workers' discontent rises to an intolerable level, they'll strike, whether they're building the great pyramids of Egypt, working as potters or goldsmiths in the Middle Ages, or sorting mail in the twentieth century. Canada's first recorded strike for better wages—by the fur trade voyageurs at Rainy Lake, in August, 1794—occurred long before the first union was formed in this country.

Modern unions, in fact, through collective bargaining, prevent many more strikes than they initiate. Do away with unions, and the ensuing economic chaos would make current strike disruptions seem trivial by comparison.

9.   The public is not represented in—and is the innocent victim of—strikes by workers in the public sector.

Unions in the public sector have to bargain directly with government officials or their agents. Who are these officials representing if not the public?

The mandatory conciliation process, along with the other legal rituals that must be followed before a legal strike can begin, are all imposed by government in the name of the public.

Public employees are exactly what their label implies. They are the public's employees.

They are our employees, and when they go on strike they do so for the same reason employees in the private sector go on strike because they are dissatisfied with the way we—through our elected representatives—are treating them.

If the services provided by postal workers, by garbage collectors, by hospital workers, by workers in transportation and other key industries are truly essential, why are such workers so often among the lowest paid? If their jobs are so indispensable why are they not treated accordingly?

The public, as an employer, really has no more right to claim immunity from strikes than any other employer who doesn't make an honest effort to treat his workers fairly.

Unions representing public employees have no alternative when governments refuse to bargain in good faith than to exercise their right to strike, when their members vote for this action.

People who may be hurt by such strikes should make an effort to look at both sides of the dispute—to determine if their employees' demands are justified. If this is clearly the case, then public pressure should be directed at governments to offer a fair settlement, rather than to enact strike-breaking laws.

10.   The strike weapon makes unions too big and powerful.

"Big" and "powerful" are relative terms. In actual fact, most Canadian unions are quite small, and together they represent less than 40% of the country's non-farm workers.

Because collective bargaining usually involves only one union local at a time, most strikes that take place are confined to one community or region.

Even the largest unions in terms of size and resources, pale by comparison with multinational corporations such as Inco, Imperial Oil, or Canadian Pacific.

If unions were even one-tenth as powerful as they are thought to be, they would be able to organize the five million Canadian workers still outside unions. They would be winning more of their strikes and increasing their members' wage rates a lot more than they actually are.

Besides, there's no relation between union size and power and the incidence of strikes. In Sweden and West Germany, for example, 80 to 90% of all workers belong to unions, yet these countries have few strikes—mainly because of the more enlightened policies of their governments and employers.

Granted, strikes sometimes hurt or inconvenience innocent people. But so does almost every form of economic activity. When prices go up, that hurts. When profits are taken out of the country and invested abroad, that hurts.

Anti-union spokesmen ignore the fact that workers are people, too. All they want is a fair payment for their labour—a fair share of the economic benefits which they help to produce. And why, when a strike occurs, blame only the workers and their unions, as if they were the only ones involved? It takes two parties to make a quarrel, and, more often than not in industrial disputes, it's management that is mostly to blame.

The Educational Implications of Our "Technological Society"

James Turk

Microelectronics and the shift from a manufacturing to a service-based economy are two of the major developments that are altering the nature and organization of work today. What are the implications of these changes for our secondary and post-secondary schools? In a presentation at a conference on liberal education at Ryerson Polytechnical Institute, Turk challenges conventional views about the direction of these changes and their educational implications.

In this talk, I want to do three things. One is to address a prevalent myth about new technologies and their implications for education. The second is to attempt to clarify some terms that are essential for any meaningful discussion of the issues before us. The third is to focus on the educational implications of new technologies for workers—both production workers and salaried workers.

As you may have already surmised, one difference of a *labour* perspective is that we do not assume a session on "Career Implications in Technology" need focus primarily or solely on management. Workers have "careers" too—jobs which they hope to pursue and do well. And post-secondary institutions like Ryerson have had, and should increasingly have, a role to play in the education of these workers for their "careers." More about that later.

Myth About the New "Technology Society"

The context for this conference is the oft-repeated and commonly held notion that the dramatic outpouring of new and sophisticated micro-electronic technologies means that our educational system needs to be reshaped. Workers will need more sophisticated job skills, and schools, from the primary to the post-secondary levels, must prepare workers for the new high-tech age by giving greater emphasis to science, by making "computer literacy" a priority, and so forth.

The underlying view is that the employment future lies with those able to perform professional and technically sophisticated work.

I want to call into question much of this conventional wisdom. Let me begin with a myth which does not serve us well in our discussions of education and technology, namely, that the new microelectronic technologies will require a more highly skilled, better trained workforce.

Generally, the opposite is the case. The history of the development of the microelectronic technologies, and of their subsequent use, is a history of designing and using machines which deskill work and diminish the role of workers. Insofar as possible, decision making, which formerly was undertaken on the shop or office floor, is removed to the confines of management.

The deskilling is not inherent in new technologies. There is nothing natural or inevitable about deskilling. The new technologies have been consciously designed to deskill work—to allow employers to draw from a larger (and therefore less highly paid) labour pool. Technologies could be designed which enhance and make use of workers' skills, but designers and purchasers of new technologies have little interest in such approaches.[1]

The result is that the design and use of the new technologies is creating a pear-shaped distribution of skills. On the one hand, jobs are being created for a relatively small number of highly skilled people to design, program, and maintain the equipment. On the other hand, the present skills of the great majority of workers are being diminished, and many of their jobs eliminated.

This pattern applies across the board. Let me give you three examples.

In manufacturing operations, machinists have been one of the more highly skilled trades. Roger Tulin, a skilled machinist who has spent his evenings getting a Ph.D. in social sciences, has written on the changing machinist's work with computer-controlled machine tools:

> For many jobs, the new machines are better and more reliable than conventional methods of machining...computer-numerical-controls could allow skilled machinists who can program, set up, and operate these machines to reach new levels of craftsmanship. The most highly skilled metal workers like to make perfect parts. That's the source of their satisfaction. The new technology could allow them to conceive and execute work that was previously beyond anyone's reach.
>
> However, this hasn't been what shop managers have wanted...their interest is to get the work out with the least amount of labour time possible. So the programming and setting up is usually done by a small group of specialists. "Operators," at lower wages and skill levels, run the production cycles. They are given only the bits of information necessary to keep the cycle running. It's the unused capability, the frustration of the human potential for creative work, that makes the reality of work life so dismal for large numbers of NC and CNC operators.
>
> As machine tools have been made more and more fully automatic, the areas of production which require a full set of conventional skills have been cut back further and further. The

"monkey" in the machine shop, who pushes buttons on a task that's broken down to fit so-called monkey intelligence, [this comment is based on a popular ad for CNC equipment which shows a monkey producing "skilled" work] is but a symbol of how management sees the future.[2]

David Noble, in his exceptional work on the history of technology,[3] shows in painstaking detail the history of the development of computer-controlled machine tools and how, at each step in their development and use, the priority was to take skill away from the operator and subject the operator to more direct management control.

One can see the same deskilling in the development and use of office technologies. Evelyn Glenn and Roslyn Feldberg of Boston University have undertaken extensive examinations of the changing character of clerical work. Their conclusions are clear-cut:

> ...narrow, largely manual skills displace complex skills and mental activity...close external control narrows the range of worker discretion...impersonal relationships replace social give and take.[4]

Their study of a number of different organizations adds that "the larger organizations are leading the changes by developing technologies and organizational techniques [for achieving these ends]."[5]

The same pattern of deskilling has also been identified within technical professions. Phillip Kraft, of the State University of New York at Binghamton, has carefully examined the changing nature of programming or software production. His conclusions are remarkably similar to Tulin's, Noble's and Glenn and Feldberg's:

> What is most remarkable about the work programmers do is how quickly it has been transformed. Barely a generation after its inception, programming is no longer the complex work of creative and perhaps even eccentric people. Instead, divided and routinized, it has become mass-production work parcelled out to interchangeable detail workers. Some software specialists still engage in intellectually demanding and rewarding tasks...but they make up a relatively small and diminishing proportion of the total programming workforce. The great and growing mass of people called programmers...do work which is less and less distinguishable from that of clerks or, for that matter, assembly line workers.[6]

The point of these comments is to argue that contrary to the widely held (and widely perpetrated) view that the new technologies are increasing the demand for a more highly skilled workforce, the opposite is the case.

Evidence for this claim comes not only from scholars studying the workplace, but also from organizations like the U.S. Bureau of Labor Statistics which projects job growth over the next decade or so.

Its projections, the most sophisticated in North America, are quite startling for proponents of the high-tech future. Not one technologically sophisticated job appears among their top 15 occupations which are expected to experience the largest job growth.

The category which will contribute the most new jobs through 1995 is janitors—alone accounting for 775,000 new jobs or 3% of all new jobs created in the United States. Following janitors, in order, are cashiers, secretaries, office clerks, sales clerks, nurses, waiters and waitresses, primary school teachers, truck drivers, nursing aides and orderlies.

If you want to go down the list further, the eleventh occupation with the most substantial growth is salespeople, followed by accountants, auto mechanics, supervisors of blue-collar workers, kitchen helpers, guards and doorkeepers, fast food restaurant workers.[7]

In a separate examination of high technology sectors, the Bureau concludes,

> It should be reiterated that even when high tech is very broadly defined...it has provided and is expected to provide a relatively small proportion of employment. Thus, for the foreseeable future the bulk of employment expansion will take place in non-high tech fields.[8]

In short, the persistent deskilling of the majority of existing jobs, and the best forecasts for the nature of future jobs, lead to the same conclusion: a pear, rather than an inverted pyramid, describes the emerging skills distribution in our "technological society."

The Meaning of "Skills"

Before, talking about educational implications, I mentioned that I wanted to say a word about definitions. The key term in much of this discussion is "skills."

Many who would dissent from my argument would point to the fact that workers are (and presumably therefore need to be) better educated now than twenty years or forty years ago. Certainly workers today—from the shop floor to the manager's office—on average, have far more schooling than in the past. But that is no evidence that they are, or need be, more skilled. The lengthening of the average period of schooling has relatively little to do with changing occupational requirements for most workers. Rather the lengthening of years in school has resulted from attempts to decrease unemployment levels (beginning in the 1930s), to use the educational system to absorb some of the returning service personnel after World War II, to changing social expectations about the right to more education, and so forth.

In response to the higher level of average grade attained, employers have introduced higher minimum levels of education as requirements for hiring—whether it be a retail clerk at Eaton's, a machine operator at Canadian General Electric or an entry-level management trainee at General Motors.

But there has been no study which has demonstrated that the higher levels were a result of the changing nature of the jobs rather than an increased supply of people who had spent longer in school.[9]

Moreover, one must recognize that traditional designations of "skill" have only an inexact relation to what we would commonly mean by "skill." To put it differently, the definition of "skill" must be understood politically as well as descriptively. For example, things that are required in jobs done primarily by women tend to be defined less as skill than things required in jobs done traditionally by men.[10]

Similarly, there are often necessary "skills" required in the most "unskilled" work—a point employers often discover when they open a new plant in a low-wage area and find that they cannot get the production they expected initially because the inexperienced workforce does not have the "skills" required by the "unskilled" work.

I mention this only to highlight for you the fact that the definition of "skill" is more problematic than we conventionally take it to be. When I have argued that work is being deskilled, I am not referring to job classifications of skill, nor to educational requirements imposed by employers, but to the mastery of craft, that is the knowledge of processes and materials; the ability to conceptualize the product of one's labour and the technical ability to produce it.

As Braverman notes, most discussions of skill use the term as "a specific dexterity, a limited and repetitive operation, 'speed as skill', etc."[11] He goes on to say that the concept of skill has been degraded to the point that:

> ...today the worker is considered to possess a 'skill' if his or her job requires a few days' or weeks' training, several months of training is regarded as unusually demanding, and the job that calls for a learning period of six months or a year—such as computer programming—inspires a paroxysm of awe. (We may compare this with the traditional craft apprenticeship, which rarely lasted less than four years and which was not uncommonly seven years long.[12]

To this point I have attempted to argue that new technologies in workplaces from a manufacturing plant floor to software production houses to offices are designed and used to deskill the work of the vast majority of workers, and, concomitantly, the definition of skill is also being degraded, giving the impression that the real degradation of skill is not as stark as it is.

What has come to be defined as skills training is a distorted and narrow kind of job training of the sort described many years ago by the Gilbreths in the *Primer* on scientific management:

> Training a worker means merely enabling him to carry out the directions of his work schedule. Once he can do this, his training is over, whatever his age.[13]

Even today, with all the mystifying hype about job enrichment and new forms of work organization, Frank Gilbreth's characterization of training is a perfect description of most so-called "skills training."

Educational Implications

The implications of all this is what concerns us today.

The most obvious and important implication is that there is little foundation to the view that rising skill levels for the labour force as a whole demand the reshaping of school, college and university curricula to provide more emphasis on mathematics, computer science, and technical training.

While some jobs will require a significant amount of this type of education, the great majority (and a growing percentage) will require little of this knowledge in order to fulfil the requirements of the work. If anything, on average, there will be a diminution of the need for this kind of technical education as essential job prerequisite.

The dangers of a misplaced emphasis on more technical knowledge at all levels of the educational system are several.

First, false expectations are being created. Students will be primed with the myth about the skills their future jobs will require, and then, when they get jobs (if they get jobs), they will discover the cruel joke of their skilled training for what they find to be deskilled jobs.

Second, the rush to emphasize computer literacy and a more technical curriculum can force a de-emphasis of more important educational priorities that today's and tomorrow's students will require, not only for their jobs but for greater fulfilment in their lives.

The deskilling of work means that people will have increasingly to find meaning outside their work. The rapidity of technological change means that people will likely shift jobs (regardless of whether they shift employers) more frequently in their working lives. The greater availability of information and the burgeoning quantity of that information will put greater pressures on people who want to be informed and active participants in their society.

All of these factors mean that the priorities for education from kindergarten through university, including technical and vocational programs, must be to provide people with the capabilities to think critically, and to develop their cognitive, expressive and analytical skills to the fullest. It must, as well, provide people with extensive knowledge of their social, cultural, political and economic institutions, and prepare and encourage them to participate actively in the shaping of decisions that affect their lives.

Far from de-emphasizing a solid general education in the humanities, social and natural sciences, the implications of the emerging "technological society" are that we should be stressing this type of education more than ever.

Certainly there is a necessary place for people specializing in technical matters, but that may be no greater a need in the future than it has been in the past. More likely, there will be a lesser need for such specialized education. Given the power of what can be done with the new technologies, even our scientists will need a sound, general education more than ever. It will be essential for them to have a humanistic perspective from which they pursue their scientific achievements. The quality of our everyday lives, even the future of humankind, is dependent on scientists realizing the broader implications of what they are doing.

Our production and office workers will need narrow job training, which should be provided by the employer. Our skilled craftspeople that survive the deskilling mania of technology designers will continue to need proper apprenticeships (which have increasingly disappeared over the past forty years).

But all will need, as well, a tough, critical, informative general education—beginning at the primary level through to the highest levels—if we are to achieve our fullest potential as individuals and as a society.

Endnotes

1. See Noble, David. 1984. *Forces of Production: A Social History of Industrial Automation*. New York: Knopf; and Zimbalist, Andrew (ed.). 1979. *Case Studies on the Labor Process*. New York: Monthly Review Press.

2. Tulin, Roger. 1984. *A Machinist's Semi-Automated Life*. San Pedro, California: Singlejack Books, p. 14.

3. Noble, *op. cit.*

4.   Glenn, Evelyn and Roslyn Feldberg. 1977. "Degraded and Deskilled: the Proletarianization of Clerical Work." *Social Problems* 24: 42.

5.   Ibid., p. 52.

6.   Kraft, Phillip. 1977. *Programmers and Managers: The Routinization of Computer Programming in the United States.* New York: Springer-Verlag, p. 97. See also Greenbaum, Joan. 1979. *In the Name of Efficiency: Management Theory and Shopfloor Practices in Data Processing Work.* Philadelphia: Temple University Press.

7.   U.S. Bureau of Labor Statistics. "Occupational Employment Projections Through 1995." *Monthly Labor Review* (Nov. 1983): 37-49.

8.   U.S. Bureau of Labor Statistics. "High Technology Today and Tomorrow: A Small Slice of the Employment Pie." *Monthly Labor Review* (Nov. 1983): 58.

9.   See Berg, Ivar. 1971. *The Great Training Robbery.* Boston. See also Braverman, Harry. 1974. *Labor and Monopoly Capital.* New York: Monthly Review Press, pp. 424-449.

10.   Gaskell, Jane. 1983. "Conceptions of Skill and the Work of Women: Some Historical and Political Issues." *Atlantis* 8(2): 11 - 25.

11.   Braverman, p. 443-444.

12.   Braverman, p. 444.

13.   Quoted in Braverman, p. 447.

Accounting for Learning/Accounting for Care: Practices for Normalizing the Crisis

Marie L. Campbell

Studies of the relationship between work and how it is organized have a long history within sociology and have often yielded important insights into the problems we face on the job. In this recent ethnographic study of college preparation for the nursing profession, Campbell explores how the content and structuring of the learning process as well as the organization of work activities in the hospital interrelate and unwittingly contribute to the crisis that nurses currently face. Specifically, Campbell shows us that the curriculum, with its emphasis on accountability, prepares nurses to normalize the unreasonable demands being placed upon their profession and the healthcare system in general as part of their learning process.

This paper analyses one aspect of a crisis in nursing to which, it is argued here, the profession is unwittingly contributing. Educational measures taken to help nurses adapt to continuous and rising pressures are also creating a workforce better able to function non-critically in an environment that is not good for either nurses or patients. This paper reports a study of a diploma nursing program in a community college, the registered nurses acquire their basic preparation.[1] Conducted over two years, it includes a nine-month period of intensive ethnography of an Ontario community college nursing program.

It is in the organization of instruction and learning that I see nursing both adapting and contributing to the crisis. The next generation of nurses is being prepared to fit smoothly into the organizational infrastructures created to handle rising demands on the health care system. It is my contention that these nurses will not be able to see the crisis for what it is; thus, they won't question it or engage in struggle around it. This is because their preparation trains them to normalize it.

The instruction in this program asks nurses to work in relation to theories of nursing in ways which direct and thus approach limits nurses' attention to aspects of nursing that exclude its social organization. This paper explicates how "working with theory" is done in nursing instruction and learning. It attempts to show how and to what purpose the approach is used, specifically, that the instructional program employs a managed approach to getting things done efficiently which relies on textually mediated action (Smith, 1984). New nurse graduates are given more integrated training in thinking and acting in relation to systematic frameworks than their predecessors because "accounting" for their learning is now required for getting through their instructional program successfully.

A nice synchronization is achieved between this teaching and new demands in nursing practice. Within nursing practice, increased attention is being given to nursing accountability, how nurses' work is made known and knowable to others, especially through documentary processes. Accountability has been taken up both as a professional concern, and as institutional technology. It has become a matter of standards-setting, record-keeping and training. For instance, "the Nursing Process" is a special mode of thinking about and documenting nursing work which has gained almost universal acceptance within nursing, as a method to both think prospectively about a course of appropriate nursing action and then to *account for* it.[2] The steps of the "nursing process" provide an accountable documentary trail of nursing decision making and action. While record-keeping has always been an accepted part of nursing, until recently nurses have treated it as secondary to the main goals of patient care. Now, as patient treatment records offer health care managers the means to speak authoritatively about resource utilization, they are becoming the basic instrument of cost-control. Implementation in agencies of Quality Assurance mechanisms, productivity reviews, utilization audits and the like has nurses learning a practice of nursing in which the work of accounting for care is becoming a more and more important and time-consuming part. Nurses are now expected to make accounts of their work to satisfy a number of such different 'needs to know,' not just communication with the health care team.

Accounting, as it is being talked about here, has a special meaning, related to doing things with words. Documentary accounts stand in for experience and "say things" on behalf of people who are no longer present. On the one hand, nothing could be more commonplace for nurses and nursing students than making reports of what they do. Nursing instructors now regularly work with the curriculum objectives as unremarkable components of their instructional systems. On the other hand, and forming the central problematic in this paper, is the view that something very different, and not at all commonplace, happens when a textual account is substituted for an experienced actuality. I will be arguing that learning to create textual accounts of nursing, whatever else it does, also plays a part in the crisis in nursing. By creating the smooth appearance of "good nursing" in the documentation, nurses cover up and cover themselves off against the lived processes of constructing those accounts, including where necessary, deficiencies in the health care system that actually interfere with patient care.

Texts, Plans and Accounts of Action

As management practices in health care institutions have made information a key resource in health care work organization, nurses themselves have been active in the same textualizing process. Over the past twenty years, nursing scholars have built a nursing discourse composed of nursing theories and conceptual models of nursing. Nursing research has burgeoned in the same time, investigating the relations between what nurses do and how they think about it. The profession has been building this body of knowledge, uniquely its own, as a basis for professionalizing purposes. Organizing a curriculum around a conceptual model or models of nursing has been a central theme in curriculum development during the past ten years.

Underlying the use of a model of nursing as the basis of instruction is the implicit belief in a "planning model of action" which Suchman (1987) defines as "something located in the actor's head, which directs his or her behaviour" (p. 3). This would appear to describe how instruction in the nursing program I observed proceeds. It follows, therefore, that learning, in this program, is a matter of students internalizing the "something," in this case, the Roy model of nursing[3] and the Nursing Process as interpreted in this curriculum and its instructional tools. The concepts of this model provide a problem-solving schema the application of which to nursing situations is expected to direct students' action.

The planning model of action postulates a causal relation between a course of action to be taken and its representation, first in a plan and then in an account of what was done. Suchman elaborates: "given a desired outcome, the actor is assumed to make a choice among alternative courses of action, based upon the anticipated consequences.... *Accounts of action taken...are (assumed within the planning model of action to be) just a report on the choices made.*" (p. 51, my emphasis)

There are more questions than answers within social science theory about the actual relationship between projected and reconstructed courses of action, that is, plans and accounts, and actions *in situ*.[4] In a telling example, Suchman argues that in paddling a canoe through rapids, rationality may help to anticipate action before the fact and reconstruct it afterwards, but "when it actually comes down to the details of getting your canoe through the rapids, you effectively abandon the plan and fall back on whatever embodied skills are available to you." (p. 52) Citing ethnomethodologists, she argues that it is frequently only acting in a present situation that makes its possibilities become clear, and we often do not know ahead of time, or at least with any specificity what future state we desire to bring about. Only when we encounter it, and identify it as desirable, are we able to say that this is the goal toward which our previous actions, in retrospect were directed "all along." (p. 52)

The paper argues that the accounting mode of instruction requires students in the program studied to learn to act in ways which prospectively and retrospectively "reify" nursing actions based on the curriculum's plan of what nursing is. Students' sense of an interaction with a client is mediated by what must be said/written/done about it to produce it as adequate in an instructor's reading. I conclude that the accounting approach teaches nurses how to subordinate the sense derived from the particulars of the occasion to the (documentary) requirements of the curriculum plan.

In respect to the understanding of "crisis" I am developing, learning sense-making for mediated action has a particular significance. Becoming skilled in mediated action gives nurses the means of "repairing," in records and other documents, nursing conditions that are always inadequate as to time available, material resources, knowledge, etc., and of producing a seamless accountable version of what was done. Because an underlying reality will always remain unaddressed and unreported, accountably "good nursing" can nevertheless fail as patient care. This kind of preparation of nurses to contend with everything and anything that confronts them, and to resolve it into elements of a comprehensive conceptual frame which stands for "good nursing," indeed actually constructing "good nursing" in documents, contributes unwittingly to the crisis in nursing. I will attempt to elaborate and demonstrate this contention throughout the following analysis.

Instruction as an Accountable Process

The nursing program under study is a three-year one, divided into six college semesters. The research focuses on instruction in the final two semesters of the 1989-90 program. In Semester Five, students attend two days of classes at the College and spend three days in supervised clinical practice in local health care agencies. Semester Six consists of a preceptorship, where students (now called pre-graduates) are hospital-based and follow typical work schedules, paired for individual guidance with designated staff nurses.

The curriculum of this program is laid out in Workbooks, one for each of the five college-based semesters. The Workbook offers students (and instructors) a detailed plan of the knowledge to be mastered, consisting of general topics, learning objectives, methods of lesson presentation, references to required and supplementary readings and a quiz reviewing the main points of each curriculum section. Classes in each subject are conducted by instructors who follow closely the workbook lesson outline using audio-visual aids for illustration and emphasis. A particular filmstrip or video presentation often provides the basis for answering the Workbook's specific questions, and for classroom discussion of a lesson's learning objectives.

Labs in which technical nursing skills are demonstrated and practiced follow a similarly designed workbook format. Skills to be learned through lab demonstrations at the third-year level include nursing activities related to blood administration, use of electronic pumps for intravenous infusions, and recording and reporting of nursing work. Students gather in groups of 10-15 to listen to instruction and watch instructors give demonstrations with equipment or materials, sometimes borrowed for the occasion from a medical supply company or a local hospital. A short hands-on practice opportunity is provided right in the classroom. For the "recording and reporting" lab, students practice devising the type of reports that nurses tape at the end of a hospital shift.

Clinical practice is interspersed with classroom instruction throughout the course of studies but takes on increasing importance in the third year of the program. In Semester Five, the focus of the curriculum is on "integration" of knowledge from earlier units of the program especially addressing more complex health problems. So too the aim of Semester Five clinical instruction is to have students learn to nurse patients with complex combinations of health problems. Besides teaching students the knowledge necessary for the nursing judgments they will be required to make and offering them sufficient opportunities to practice nursing skills in the workplace, another major goal of the instructional program is to inculcate in students an approved approach to doing nursing.

The curriculum itself is formulated around a theoretical "model of nursing" which instructors feel provides students with an appropriate and workable approach to learning to nurse. The "Roy Model of Nursing" is the set of ideas about nursing which, along with the "The Nursing Process," is "integrated" into the nursing curriculum of this program.[5] In this curriculum, concepts are translated into a set of instructions for students to follow as they "assess" their patient, that is, conceptualize the relationship between him/her and a proposed course of nursing actions. This curriculum approach has the practical goal of making the nursing knowledge that students are taught generalizable and portable across all nursing workplaces and situations. Students are expected to "use their model" in all their clinical placements, even those where nursing staff use different approaches to thinking and recording nursing are used. The model is supposed to help students make sense of what nurses *not* using this particular model say and do. Students are explicitly coached in making such transitions in lessons focusing on the technical language of other nursing frameworks, and how to "translate" and substitute one for the other.

For students, using the Roy model and Nursing Process means having an empty frame that they fill with content about a patient as they decide what to do and how to sequence actions. "Using the model" means using the language of the model in response to instructors' questions about the patient and the proposed action. It also means doing the nursing action in a way that provides for its recording to facilitate on-going medical and nursing care and, as discussed in more detail below, to leave a documentary trail for various organizational and instructional purposes, including evaluation of students' learning.

The Accounting Approach to Teaching and Learning

Accountability is a topic which is addressed in several ways throughout the nursing instructional program. In the fifth semester Nursing course, "accountability" like "responsibility" is treated as a personal attitude to work which students are required to assume. More explicitly, it appears in lab classes as a set of practices to be rehearsed and mastered. It is not enough that students know what to do for their assigned patients and how to go about it, but they must learn to make an objective demonstration of their knowledge in documents. This is accounting and it plays a special part in contemporary nursing. Documents actually coordinate the activities of instructor, students, hospital staff, etc., through which instruction is delivered accountably.

Documents link instructors into a coordinated course of social action in which statements in the Health Professions Act of Ontario and the Ontario College of Nurses' Standards of Practice are realized in college programs. In its mandate to approve programs, the College, in association with the Ministry of Colleges and Universities, sets standards. These standards determine the general shape of the instructional program, e.g., how many hours of what kinds of experiences are offered to students. Governing of nurses' professional education takes place through the mediation of documents at the program levels; this is how uniformity of the nursing "product" is produced across multiple sites and administratively diverse instructional programs.

Besides accountability to the College of Nurses and the Ministry, instructors' records are part of the internal administration of the nursing program. For instance, documentation about students' achievement in clinical placement informs and legitimates discriminatory decision making about student progress. Instructors are responsible for deciding which students are making satisfactory progress in terms of instructional goals. If a student's progress is unsatisfactory or marginal, the instructor must be able to make that case in the appropriate forum and support it with documentary evidence. College procedures allow for several levels of challenge to instructors' decisions about which students should repeat a course, or a term, or who should be dismissed from the program. Documentary evidence of students' learning is constructed from a variety of sources, in processes examined in this paper. In them, we see instructors and students using subjective experiences as the data for production of objective documents. At issue is the adequacy of these documentary forms of the learning process to satisfy the curricular requirements for learning mediated by nursing plans. The following is an exploration of what indeed may be satisfied and what less satisfied by the documentary processes.

The Performance Evaluation is a good place to begin to investigate the accounting approach to teaching and learning as a social course of textualized action. The Evaluation form lists program objectives and gives examples of "behaviours" which would constitute meeting objectives. Much of the instructor-student and student-client interaction and the accounting of them is orientated by these concepts. Students are required to use the Performance Evaluation Form to evaluate themselves, transposing lived experience into the appropriate categories of the Form, learning to shift and sort, retain and discard bits, finally arriving at an account that will serve its specific purposes. This evaluation form is a key document in establishing the authorized account of students' progress through the program. Students' interpretive work and its meaning as preparation for both their student and nursing careers is central to the argument being made and will be discussed later in the paper. First, the inquiry focuses on instructors' "use" of the form, what place the form takes in instructions activities.

The Evaluation Form guides instructors in choosing patients to assign to students for their weekly clinical instruction sessions, as indicated by the following comment:

> I know the Semester Five Evaluation because I use it. Every time
> that I would select a patient I would be looking at the choice in
> terms of Semester Five Evaluation.... It tells me what the
> students are supposed to be able to do. [Instructor Two, p. 29]

Knowing what they are supposed to be able to do helps the instructor identify patients whose care includes those particular interventions, that level of knowledge, etc. that will fulfil their own teaching and students' learning objectives. She can set students an assignment in which she (the instructor) can check that item off on her Evaluation Form. This does not mean that students are not having other experiences than the targeted ones, but both instructor and student learn to orient their attention to the learning experiences that "meet objectives."

Both instructor and student are required to "make something" documentary of the patient assignment, as a teaching and learning experience. They must eventually interpret it as an instance of "meeting objectives" or not. Working with the Evaluation Form helps instructors construct knowledge of students' learning which becomes the official version. This account establishes what is competent or adequate enough performance by students of their assignments. Instructors talk to students, quiz them, reassure them, and help them. They constantly work along side them, to identify problems and rescue students who are having trouble in difficult situations by giving advice or physically taking over a task. This highly personal interaction becomes grist for the evaluation mill, but only in its documentary or textualized form. Instructors' anecdotal

notes made daily on observations of students at work are way-stations of
accounting in the social construction of official knowledge.

Students' written work is also part of how instructors arrive at a final
version. Written assignments about patient care are the means by which
students must demonstrate that they have incorporated into their thinking and
can use the curriculum plan as a basis for taking action in a particular situation.

> They submit to me a Clinical Data Sheet completed, plus a
> Nursing Care Plan that follows through on this patient. (The
> Clinical Data Sheets) are simply data collection and sorting. It's
> a prompter for them *to use their conceptual frame of reference*. I
> look at their documentation (the completed data collection sheet
> and care plan) to see if they reflect our frame of reference.
> [Instructor Five. p. 20, my emphasis)

Such an assignment teaches the accounting approach to nursing by requiring
students to practice seeing their patients as instances of the concepts of the
model of nursing. The instructor looks at everything they write to find in it the
particular authorized topics, sequences, use of language that appear in the
curricular plan, what she calls "our frame of reference." Instructors expect to
see the elements of the curriculum plan in students' recording in hospital
records, too. Students write up or "chart" what they are doing with patients in
the patient's medical record where it becomes another instance of "adequate
student performance" for instructors to find.

> Different teachers have said...that clinical practice is really very
> hard for them to evaluate because for one thing they are not
> always with us; they don't always know what we're doing.... A lot
> of times, it's finding out what we are doing by what we chart,
> afterwards. [Student One, i., p. 10]

Charting is not just any written version of "what we are doing" as this student
expresses it. It is another occasion on which an account must be constructed in
such a way that instructors can "see," in documentation, students meeting
objectives. The written account comes to stand in for the reality of students'
actions, whatever they were. Learning to produce accounts adequate to the
teaching and learning purpose is a teachable subject and is an integral part of
the instructional program.

> Sometimes I'll give my students a little session. I'll say this is what
> happened and now write it out as if you were going to enter it as

> a 10:00 entry. I'll just go around the table and say "tell me what you wrote." [Instructor Two, i, p. 32]

The skill required and being taught is the ability to sort through the range of experiences one has as a student and decide what happened that can be represented as an instance of the curricular plan being put into action. Students must learn the concepts and language that will meet expectations for this kind of textual construction. They must grasp the interprative frame so that they can build satisfactory versions of their experiences into the account. What satisfies, of course, relates to the courses of action either administrative or instructional, into which the accounts must be inserted. Learning to account—getting the idea of what's being asked and how to do it, makes a difference to student careers.

> Part of the reason for us having the evaluation form is so that we can keep a running track of what we have or haven't been doing...I mean it's not life or death but it's just if you come to the end of the semester and you have...a "not complete" on one objective, they have the option of saying you have to do extra clinical work, or in your next rotation you're going to have to do an extra assignment to try and make up this objective. [Student One, i., interview, p. 12]

For students to "make something" documentary of their patient assignment means learning how to do self-evaluations that actually show themselves to be "meeting objectives." Participation in self-evaluation is training for students to look back at their own practical action, whatever nursing activities they performed during their days in clinical placement, and see it in terms of specific concepts and a specific conceptual organization.

> (Students) are supposed to, especially after the first couple of weeks (of a clinical rotation) we're supposed to go through the evaluation form and see if we have or haven't done anything. (The form) give(s) examples of each of the categories to use as a guideline of what—you know, things that you have done or could do to—in order to achieve the objective. [Student One, i., pp. 10-11]

Students learn how to use the resources of work settings to make accounts that are targeted to the purposes for which they know the report is or will be used. And they learn how to make questionable experiences "count" as compliance with the categories.

> Sometimes, I know, I've looked at a category and thought, you
> know, "uhmm, I haven't really done it" but you sort of stretch
> what you've done to fit the category.... Generally, Personal and
> Professional Growth are the ones that you find you tend to be
> really shovelling it. [Student One, i., pp. 11-12]

As students gain the ability to see their actions in terms of abstract course
objectives they can participate with instructors in determining their progress.

> It allows you to think and pull out stuff that you have done that
> the teacher hasn't seen you do. She hasn't seen you in
> conversation with a patient, she hasn't seen you with members of
> the health team like physiotherapy...it gives you a chance to
> make yourself look good because she reads them. [Student Three,
> i., p. 26]

In the college program, both the instructor and the student contribute to the
account which will be treated as "true" about the instructional process. As long
as the issue is not clear-cut, each is attempting to shape it and gain control of
what it finally will "say." Instructors build an account that represents their
understanding of the student's progress, as they judge it from their observations
and interactions. They also must gain student's acceptance of their evaluation.
The self-evaluation helps to involve the student in the decision process and
accept its outcome. Some students are better than others at the conceptual
work involved in self-evaluation. Those who need help to grasp the
interpretative frame may be given instruction in how to do self-evaluation. One
instructor explains how she asked her students to focus on successive portions
of the evaluation tool and practice explaining how in their work with assigned
patients they "met objectives":

> Now what I have done in the past in terms of the (self)
> evaluation form, I do this about every two weeks, I say to the
> students, "OK, this week I want you to focus on the whole section
> "Knowledge Of The Person Adapting" and I want you to go
> home and think about what you've done this week and give me
> examples of how you personally have met those objectives. So
> that's what they're doing when they're filling their self-evaluations.
> [Instructor Two, i., p. 25]

While students agree that instructors know who is really in trouble before the
evaluation, they recognize that there is room for negotiation and that self-
evaluations are important to negotiating, especially in contested cases.

> Those self-evaluation forms can pass you or fail you on your
> rotation if you get too many U.P.'s (Unsatisfactory progress). Now
> if there are unsatisfactory notations on hers and you feel that you
> have met them, then you have to discuss it. But if you sign it
> without having anything to say, like "I disagree, we have had this
> and I have done that," then you're cooked. You haven't given
> yourself an opportunity to speak... [Student Three, i., p. 26].
> You go in and you have this (form) filled out and she asks you;
> she goes through every page with you and if she has any
> questions about them and you have it filled in, then you can show
> her what you've done. [Student Two, i., p. 22]

Nursing students may be able to do the work but still not be able to do the
accounting of it. Learning to account for one's work in the specific terms of the
curriculum "plan" is a different kind of learning than learning to carry out the
nursing activities themselves. The former requires additional attention from the
instructor:

> Some of the students will say..."I really don't understand this;
> what do you mean?" So, in conference I'll say "This is what this
> objective is focusing on. Can you think of an example of *how you*
> *might have done that* in the last three days?" and I ask them to
> hand them in to me and I look at them. [Instructor Two, i., p. 25
> (emphasis mine)]

Self-evaluation, done this way, is instruction. Students learn abstract thinking
when they learn to see pieces of their everyday activities as instances of the
concepts on their evaluation forms.

> I'll bring it to conference and say..."OK, you worked on the first
> four objectives; now let's share a bit because all of our
> experiences are different and I want you to give me an example
> of how you think you're working towards this objective." And the
> students will all give examples and it's a good experience for them
> because they see that there is not only one way of meeting the
> objective. [Instructor Two, i., p. 26]

This kind of exercise is training for students to abstract out of practical work
experience those events which "fit" the conceptual framework that has been
provided first in the curriculum and then in the self-evaluation form. This
prepares students in the kind of abstract thinking which will make them
competent "accounters" of themselves and their work when they are graduate

nurses in the nursing workforce. In doing self-evaluations, they are taking their experience and "working it over" to find how to present it in the correct conceptual package.

Charting is a special case of accounting; besides providing documentary evidence of students' clinical progress for instructors to find, it concurrently accounts to the health care institution for patient care given by the student. The instructional system and its instruments intersect with the health care system and its own procedures for objectifying knowledge. The clinical instruction of students, then, is simultaneously "teaching nursing" and "giving patient care." The instructor is responsible for seeing that students do the patient care according to the health care agency's treatment plans and standards and that they "chart" it accordingly. This paper can only begin to intimate how important it is to the health care system to have nurses entering the nursing workforce prepared to create objective knowledge of nursing in texts. Official texts speak in the absence of nurses speakers, a feature of hospital documentation that is essential to contemporary organization, and all kinds of medical and administrative activities.[6] When students are prepared to be competent accounters of *learning*, they are already orientated to a documentary practice of nursing that hospitals rely on increasingly, for organizing and coordinating administrative and therapeutic action.

Can Accountable Nursing be Counted On?

Instructors place a great deal of trust in what I am calling "the plan" and "the accounting approach" to instruction. Establishing that students meet objectives establishes the credibility of the instruction as adequate preparation of students to nurse. This is the final test of instruction and one which is not taken lightly by instructors who are themselves professional nurses. The accounting approach reduces instructors' uncertainty in the very difficult, even dangerous, instructional milieu which characterizes the college nursing program. Instructors trust that having students work with a model of nursing provides something of a guarantee about the nursing "product." Practising expressing what they've done in the form of the curriculum objectives immediately after they do the work is expected to make the model central to students' perception of patients, to their choices about the proper course of action *and to their reporting*. An instructor explained:

> I don't think they need to sit down and think about it for two
> hours at home. I want them to be doing it on the spot, so that
> what they're doing at the bedside and this (accounting) are
> synonymous.... Because that shows them that what they're doing

> in the clinical area is learning that is current and *it's directly related to the evaluation.* [Instructor Two, i., p. 25]

Representation of anticipated and reconstructed action when it is seen as "synonymous" with doing it, "realizes" the causal connection between curricular plan and nursing action. This makes instructors see a curriculum based on a conceptual model of nursing, taught with instructions for applying it, a big improvement over trying to teach students "everything that they need to know." Used as a guide to action, it helps students make actionable sense out of any array of problems and possibilities that confront them. That is what instructors value about their curriculum "model of nursing."

> It gives (students) a structure and a way of completing an assessment. So they are not just focusing on a number of things, they are sort of trying to group behaviours together...so you are not just going in to a patient's room and saying "Where do I start?" [Instructor Two, i., p. 41]

The curriculum plan helps teachers organize and convey complex knowledge and its application. "The model" itself can be codified and referred to, on the spot, both to teach and to assess students' progress.

> I'll sit down with them and say "I'd like to talk to you about Mr.————." I want them to give me an assessment,...to go through all the "needs" and "modes" and to tell me what they have observed in these "needs" and "modes." If they don't have their own Indices Card, I have mine there and I'll put it in front of them and say "Take a look at this and tell me what you think." It keeps them on track and helps to direct them. [Instructor Six, i., pp. 15-16].

Mediation of students' action by the plan inherent in the curriculum's model of nursing helps students identify and tie together the otherwise loose ends of observations, demands and responses into a course of relevant action. As a schema of relevance, it helps students decide what to include and exclude, while providing assurance that they are addressing the important features of the nursing situation.

> (The model) is good because it's comprehensive; it's theoretical, so it will fit whatever the practice setting. [Instructor One, i., p. 19]

(Ours) is a nice model because it's holistic. [Instructor Four, i., p. 23]

Having looked at a patient or situation in a mediated way, and identified and performed the called-for actions, the model's "holistic" structure reassures nurses that they have responded adequately. It helps students create the appearance of completion in the nursing action taken, by showing how discrete interventions add up to the model's formulation of nursing. Instructors need this reassurance because they recognize the difficulty of actually teaching students *to nurse* within the constraints of program time and material conditions.

> More and more we have to have a person who can think on their own. You cannot possibly give them everything they need to know.... The volume of scientific knowledge goes up so rapidly, we have trouble keeping up. We move things in and out of our theory components (in the curriculum) based on the prevalence of the health problem, whether it is a good one to draw a lot of the systems and modes and theory together. [Instructor Four, i., p. 23]

Students learn from their experience of accountable instruction that *nursing is* recognizing and categorizing the "data" in their interactions with patients that satisfy the categories of the conceptual model.

> It gives students a way to view their patients, their patient is *something* and it describes *what that patient is*. And it describes what I do when I interact with that particular person. Our particular model is really strong in terms of assessment because it not only tells me—it classifies—it describes the patient in a way that tells me what sort of information I have to collect. [Instructor Five, i., p. 16, my emphasis]

This describes a particular kind of sense-making in which students learn to use a plan to mediate experience and construct an authorized version of reality. Patients are to be confronted as beings in which "the elements of the model" reside. This is the process of objectification, a mental step which establishes the causal connection between plans and action. Alternatively, plans could be treated as simply one resource amongst many available to nurses. However, that use of plans would open up a much wider discretionary field where students might be distracted by all kinds of issues extraneous to the economy of action demanded in the nursing workplace of the 1990s. An instructor puts her finger on the key point.

> Interactions nurses have with patients must be goal-directed. There's no time for social chit-chat...your interactions with the patient must be meaningful. You are either giving information to the patient or you're collecting information from the patient or you're doing a technique. [Instructor Five, i., p. 15]

Besides the smooth appearance of adequate learning which plans help to construct, instructors see this mediated practice of nursing articulating students smoothly into the contemporary practices of managing nursing and hospitals.

> They're able to operationalize that (model) in relationship to patient care in a very succinct, concise manner.... (They can make a) very concise Nursing Care Plan and pass information on to the next people looking after the patient. [Instructor Seven, i., p. 17-18]

Conciseness is a necessary feature of nursing accounting when change occurs rapidly, both patients and personnel move about, in and out of health care agencies at a rapid pace. Reports must be made quickly and only the relevant details included. There is no time for reading through reams of notes. Learning a form of nursing practice mediated by textual accounts helps new generations of nurses adapt to demands for precise accounting that will stand as adequate nursing against legal, professional and other administrative tests.

Instructors in this study are not without concerns about their program's graduates. They mention as problems students' lack of "critical thinking" [Instructor Eight, i., p. 18] or "failure to understand the implications of their actions" [Instructor Two, i., p. 11] or "not realizing what data is significant" or not "being able to prioritize" [Instructor Two, i., p. 13]. Instructor Three worries about rigidity being produced by too prescriptive use of the curriculum model [i., pp. 31-32]. In trying to describe the attitude she finds too prevalent among her students, another instructor notes their main preoccupation:

> Nurses just sort of bustle around and do the I.V.'s and the tests and all the things they need to do to sort of "cover their ass." [Instructor Eight, i., p. 22]

This comment may capture exactly what is productive and, conversely, what is counterproductive about the skills, conceptual and practical, which the accounting approach to nursing instruction is teaching. When students learn to equate "good nursing" with meeting documentary objectives, as graduates they will be skilled in constructing "care" as a documentary reality. They will know how to make nursing interventions that are adequate for all practical purposes and which this instructor calls "covering their ass." The management of contemporary health care agencies recognizes as organizationally adequate just such action. Quality assurance systems, for instance, construct "adequacy," as a documentary reality, from nursing and medical record audits.[7]

The textually mediated practice of nursing has new importance in the information-structured hospital. The health care literature confirms that hospitals are relying ever more heavily on systematically produced information.[8] Information is a key resource for managing finances, personnel and increasingly the health care labour process. To be useful in assessing resource utilization or to account for the cost of providing services, nursing knowledge must be specially constructed to interface with other data. Nurses are doing that as they account for their work in information systems. Being information workers not only absorbs nursing time but this analysis shows how it *directs nurses' attention to elements of patient care and features of the patient themselves that provide the "data" for the required accounting.* There is some discussion in the nursing literature of nurses needing to be the authors of the systems which they use,[9] but this misses the point being made in this paper. Making sense of nursing situations when nurses are responsible for its accounting (i.e., nursing as mediated action) is a different kind of undertaking than making sense of nursing situations in the everyday world of illness, pain, fear, human interaction, medical emergencies, therapies, and so on. Learning to nurse requires that students gain the ability to do both kinds of sense-making. The conclusion reached from the present analysis is that the nursing instructional program being studied subordinates one to the other. It trains adequate account-makers and teaches them how to cover all the documentary bases.

This contributes to the crisis in two ways. First, when nurses' work is aimed at creating the *appearance* of adequacy and holism as it is in mediated action, then nurses are participating in the continuing erosion of the nursing contribution to patient care. By learning to skim the surface, attending to patients as sources of targeted data, getting only what is necessary to cover all documentary bases, etc., nurses are learning how to pick up the pace of nursing, but they are also undermining their own conditions of work and of work satisfaction. To the extent that the health care organization supports only the documented part of nurses' work, this accounting approach to nursing contributes to the ongoing erosion of patient safety and comfort. Regardless of the intent of individual nurses and managers, it undermines and replaces care-centred nursing.

Secondly, the accounting approach to nursing obscures and organizationally obliterates nursing knowledge and nursing action outside or beyond that which is mediated and documented. Nursing sense-making for *situated action* remains a necessary, if undervalued, part of nurses' work and nurses' education, but is not an explicit or high profile part of this nursing curriculum. Yet it is a component of nursing knowledge and skill on which hospitals, doctors and patients continue to rely. My research shows that nursing "on the ground" requires nurses to perform both kinds of reasoning. Any claim to higher value for their work depends on identifying, and getting recognition for the nursing action whose sense arises out of the intensely social situation in which nurses work so skilfully.

Endnotes

1. My research does not compare college against university nursing programs, nor does it evaluate the college program that I studied. Any generalizations that I make from the study are based on whatever consistency is to be found in use of similar instructional practices in nursing programs in Canada and the USA.

2. See Little, Dolores and Doris Carnevali. 1976. *Nursing Care Planning,* 2nd Edition. Philadelphia: Lippincott, Chapter 2, pp. 11-21.

3. The Roy Model is one of a number of so-called "models of nursing" available to curriculum developers. (Roy, C and H. Andrews. 1986. *Essentials of the Roy Adaptation Model.* Norwalk: Appleton-Century-Crofts.)

4. See Suchman's (1984) discussion in her chapters Three and Four, pp. 27-67.

5. "Integrated" is a technical term used by nursing instructors to refer to a particular form of curriculum, as explained here: "Integrated relates to the fact that we are using a nursing model and all the components that go into making a nurse are integrated into that model. So, in other words, we don't teach paediatric nursing or obstetrical nursing, we integrate it, using the model as the organizer." (Instructor Three, i. p. 3-4)

6. See, for example, Campbell, M. "The Structure of Stress in Nurses' Work," Chapter 24, in Bolaria and Dickinson (eds.). 1988. *Sociology of Health Care in Canada.* Toronto: Harcourt Brace Jovanovitch; and

Campbell, M. "Systematization of Nursing and the Promise of
Computers: A New Phase in Nurses' Struggle for Control?" in Dimitz,
E. (ed.) 1990. *Proceedings of the International Conference on Computers
in Hospital Care*. Austrian Academy of Science, Vienna.

7.   See Campbell, M. 1984. *Information Systems and Management of
Hospital Nursing: A Study in Social Organization of Knowledge*.
Unpublished Ph. D. dissertation. University of Toronto (OISE).

8.   E.g., Krawczyk, M. "Is MIS investment the key to solid hospital
management?" *Health Care*, June 1989, pp. 10-11; Meeting, D., G.
Saunders, R. Curcio. "Using DRGs and Standard Costs to Control
Nursing Labour Costs." *Healthcare Financial Management*, September
1988, pp. 62-74.

9.   Kiley, M. et al., *Nursing Management*, 1983, pp. 25-27.

References

Campbell, M., "The Structure of Stress in Nurses' Work," in Bolaria and
Dickinson, eds., *Sociology of Health Care in Canada*, Toronto: Harcourt
Brace Jovanovitch, 1988.
Campbell, M., "Systematization of Nursing and the Promise of Computers: A
New Phase in Nurses' Struggle for Control?" in Dimitz, E., ed., *Proceedings
of the International Conference on Computers in Hospital Care*, Austrian
Academy of Science, Vienna, 1990.
Campbell, M., *Information Systems and Management of Hospital Nursing: A
Study in Social Organization of Knowledge*, unpublished PhD Dissertation,
University of Toronto, (OISE), 1984.
Kiley, Marylou, et al., "Computerized Nursing Information Systems (NIS),"
Nursing Management, Vol. 14, No. 8, pp. 26-19, 1983.
Krawczyk, M., "Is NIS Investment the Key to Solid Hospital Management?,"
Health Care, June, pp. 10-11, 1989.
Little, D. and Carnevali, D., *Nursing Care Planning*, 2nd ed., Philadelphia:
Lippincott, 1976.
Meeting, D., Saunders G., Curcio, R., "Using DRGs and Standard Costs to
Control Nursing Labour Costs," *Healthcare Financial Management*,
September, pp. 62-74, 1988.
Roy, C. and Andrews, H., *Essentials of the Roy Adaptation Model*, Norwalk:
Appleton-Century-Crofts, 1986.

Smith, D.E., "Textually Mediated Social Organization," *International Social Science Journal*, Vol. 36, No. 1, pp. 59-75, 1984.

Suchman, L.A., *Plans and Situated Actions*, New York: Cambridge University Press, 1987.

Section VI

Poverty, Wealth and Stratification

Why Have an Economic System

Gary Rabbior

The kind and degree of poverty, wealth and stratification within a society are intimately tied to the prevailing economic system. The following article outlines basic principles, types, goals and criteria by which major economic systems can be assessed, and examines the particular case of Canada.

To formulate laws and to govern a society establishes a political system. To tend to the injured and sick, a health care system is established, to communicate and exchange information—a communication system, and so on. These systems are complex and vital to our society. Each system has a particular focus addressing societal needs or problems.

Why is there a need for an economic system? Mankind appears to have made the decision quite some time ago to give up total independence. Back in cave-man days, people were quite independent. It was possible to provide your home (cave) and to kill, catch or pick food while at the same time acquiring clothes. All in all, quite self-sufficient but not the greatest life-style.

To improve the "standard of living" or "quality of life" was pretty difficult. Providing your own food, clothing and shelter was time-consuming and allowed little opportunity for developing/creating new methods, styles, sizes, etc. The desire to improve the standard of living prompted a fundamental change from total independence to *interdependence*.

People found that the standard of living could be improved through *specialization*. That is, rather than people attempting to provide everything for themselves, each person concentrates on what he/she does best (e.g., house builder, fisherman, baker). People can then exchange the product of their skill for that of others.

Today, of course, we don't trade goods and services as much as we use money to facilitate the exchange process. Each of us seeks to acquire money (income) in return for particular skills and then uses this money to obtain goods and services produced through the skills of others. Hence, people became interdependent to work together to improve the standard of living in the society. With interdependence came complexity. Trading, exchanging, selecting skills, training, etc. involves organization. A society in which people depend on each other is more complicated to organize than one in which everyone fends for themselves.

There, the need to establish an economic system evolved. Society has to put in place a system which will make decisions and attend to: producing goods and services, managing resources, providing skills, distributing goods and services, developing new technology and so on. Each society has to decide what type of system will be established to organize its economic affairs.

Types of Economic Systems—In Theory

Every economic system will have to address three fundamental economic questions:

1. What to produce.
2. How to produce.
3. How to distribute what is produced.

Types of economies will differ, particularly in how they are organized to make these decisions. Theoretically, there are three types of economic systems, the traditional economy, the market economy and the command economy.

Traditional Economy

How do you celebrate Christmas or other holidays? In many cases, family tradition probably contributes significantly to the decisions.

In an economy, tradition or custom can play a role in how economic decisions are made. An economic system in which decisions are made largely on the basis of tradition and custom is referred to as a *traditional economy*.

An example often used is the native people's society in North America prior to the arrival of the Europeans. Decisions regarding what to produce, how to produce and how to distribute were based largely on the tribe's customs from the past.

Today, third world countries often have large "traditional" components to their economies, especially in rural areas—more so than industrialized countries which have changed their ways and systems significantly from those of the past. In these traditional economies, the three questions of what, how and for whom are often answered as follows—What has always been produced will continue to be produced, using the same methods that have always been used and the products will be allocated as they have historically been distributed.

In Canada, tipping is an example of one carry-over from the past. The process of tipping, when, how much, etc. is largely based on custom. Therefore, although tradition does not usually play a major role in industrialized countries it still has some effect.

Market Economy

What is a market? A market is the term used to refer to the situation where producers (suppliers) of a good or service interact with buyers, and goods and services are exchanged according to a market price. The market price will be determined by factors such as:

- how much buyers are willing to pay
- what quantities buyers are willing to buy at a particular price
- how much sellers are willing to supply at a particular price
- how many producers are supplying a particular good or service

Essentially, a market price will be determined through the independent decisions of buyers and sellers and will change when other factors change.

In a *market-based economy*, individuals can own the factors of production (land, resources and capital). Individual producers decide what to produce and how to produce. An important objective in their decisions is to earn a profit for the business. Decisions regarding what and how to produce usually aim to maximize profit while incorporating other important criteria into the decisions (e.g., desire to have a good reputation, to be a responsible corporate citizen, to stabilize the firm, to achieve growth, etc.)

The decision of what to produce is very much determined by consumers. Producers earn a profit if people buy what they produce. Therefore, what consumers want will be the major determinant for what to produce. This is referred to as *consumer sovereignty*.

The characteristics of a market economy could be summarized as:

- private ownership of the factors of production
- individual producers decide what to produce
- consumers will influence what is produced through their demand for goods and services
- producers decide how to produce
- distribution takes place largely through markets where consumers obtain goods and services if they are willing/able to pay the price

Command Economy

An alternative to the market-based economy is the *command economy*. The term *command* is used because the decisions for the economy are not based on individual decisions but, rather, are made by a central planning committee/authority.

The decision about what to produce, for example, would be determined by such a central planning committee/authority. In theory, the central group is assigned the task of establishing certain goals for the economy and then organizing the economy to achieve these goals.

Because the decisions are made by a central planning committee, it is vital that such an authority (usually the government) owns and controls the factors of production. In this type of system it would be a severe problem if the central planning committee decided resources should be used in one way but the owners decided another. Therefore, in a command economy, there is no private ownership of the factors of production. The factors of production are owned by the state.

As mentioned, the decision regarding what to produce is made by the central planning authority. Whereas profit, company stability, growth, etc. provide the incentive for production in a market-based economy, the incentive in a command economy is less personalized. The economy is planned to achieve certain goals and production decisions will be made by the central authority in keeping with these goals. These centrally-made decisions will, in turn, determine the production activities of individuals. Whereas in the market economy consumers play a key role in determining what will be produced, this is not the case in a command economy. In a centrally-planned economy consumers will select from the goods and services which the central authority decides will be available. Consumers' preferences may exert some influence, but to a much less degree than in a market economy.

In the same way that the central planning authority decides what to produce, the same group will make most of the decisions related to how to produce. And similarly, this group decides how the goods and services will be distributed. Much less emphasis is placed on personal incentive and more emphasis is placed on collective necessity.

The command economy, in summary, is characterized by:

- state-ownership of the factors of production
- a centrally-planned economy
- a central planning authority/committee deciding goals, what to produce, how to produce and how to distribute
- consumers play a minor role, if any, in determining what is produced

Mixed Economy—The Common Reality

As described, a market economy places heavy emphasis on individual decision making. A command economy emphasizes centralized planning and the state government plays a dominant role. In general, government plays a minor role in the economy of a market-based system and a major role in a command system.

Most of the world's economies mix aspects of the two types of systems. In some market economies the government plays a significant role. In some command economies some markets are allowed to operate. In reality, there are more *mixed economies* than there are pure examples of the three theoretical types.

Canada's Economy

Canada has a mixed economy. It is largely a market-based economy but the government plays a prominent role. Private producers decide what to produce but are constrained by government regulations. There are safety standards, health standards, quality standards, environment standards and others which govern how producers produce goods and services.

The government affects how goods and services are distributed by subsidizing prices, increasing incomes (e.g., welfare), providing certain social services (e.g., health care) and so on.

In addition, the government has a significant impact on the economy through its economic policies such as fiscal and monetary policies. The government regulates the money supply, regulates communication systems, etc.

Therefore, although Canada has a largely market-based economy, it is classified as a mixed economy because of the significant role of government. The Canadian political system reflects the debate within Canada as to the role government should play in the economy. Some argue for less government involvement—some argue for more.

The issue of government involvement in the economy is a major one. Questions arise such as:

- should government produce goods and services which are, or could be, produced by private companies? (e.g., Petrocan, Air Canada)
- should government regulate the prices of certain goods or services or allow market forces to determine them? (e.g., the airline industry)
- should government act as a selling agent for certain producers? (e.g., marketing boards)
- should government regulate business activity more or less than it does currently?

These questions, and others, are at the "heart and soul" of many of the major issues in Canada today. Students are encouraged to investigate the Canadian economic system, how it is organized, the roles played by government and private producers and to critically evaluate the current "state of affairs."

The "Isms"

You have probably heard economic systems classified in another way. Specifically, you have probably heard of the following terms:

- capitalism
- socialism
- communism
- fascism

The "isms" tend to take the political system into consideration in conjunction with the economic system. The following provides a brief summary of the general characteristics of each of the "isms":

Capitalism: private ownership of the factors of production, market-based, democratic political system.

Socialism (Democratic Socialism): mix of public and private ownership (major resources usually owned by the state), considerable central planning, some/many markets allowed to operate, democratically-elected government.

Communism (Authoritarian Socialism): state ownership of the factors of production, central planning, few, if any, markets allowed to operate, no democratic elections—single ruling party.

Fascism: private ownership of factors of production, dictatorial political system, considerable central planning, markets allowed to operate under significant political scrutiny.

Determining Economic Goals

The type of economic system which a society establishes will be determined by a number of factors including:

- the priorities of the people in the society
- their philosophies/goals

- their geographical location
- their political system, etc.

Based on these many factors, a society will establish an economic system. A set of goals for the economic system will also be identified. There are many goals which could be identified for the economy. The goals themselves will be different form society to society and the priorities assigned to goals will also vary.

Recognizing that goals differ, and receive different priorities, we can still introduce some of the more common goals. These would include:

Economic Stability: generally stable price levels with high employment.

Economic Growth: the increased production of goods and services.

Appropriate Distribution of Income: income distributed in the society according to the preference of the society.

Viable Balance of Payments: on net, the society in a positive economic relationship with the rest of the world (e.g., more money coming into the country than going out).

Proper Allocation of Resources: the limited resources of the society used efficiently and in a manner consistent with the society's preferences.

Economic Independence: relatively self-sufficient and not overly dependent on others.

Stable Currency: the society's currency maintaining a stable value with respect to the currency of other countries.

These are some of the goals that may be set for an economy, As mentioned, they may differ from economy to economy and differ in priority. From time to time a society may also change its goals or assign them a different priority. Such changes may be gradual/rapid, peaceful/violent, organized/chaotic, etc. As with any aspect of significant change in a society, changing past decisions may take place through a democratic or non-democratic process. Certainly there are many examples in the world today of economic systems which have gone through substantial change either democratically (e.g., U.S. changing from Carternomics to Reaganomics) or non-democratically (e.g., Afghanistan—pre-Soviet invasion and post-Soviet invasion).

The economy of a society plays a significant role in the lives of virtually everyone in that society. It is not uncommon for economic change and political change to be closely linked.

Assessing Economic Performance

Once a country determines goals, criteria will have to be established for evaluating how well a country is doing in terms of achieving its goals. In other words, if one of a country's goals is high employment—what is high employment? For that country, is employment high when unemployment is 0%, 4% or 10%? These criteria must be established.

Furthermore, statistical means to measure performance must be developed. Statistics will provide information indicating the degree of success an economy is having in achieving its objectives.

Some of the more common criteria used to evaluate economic performance would be:

1. Level of Growth—as measured by Real GNP
2. General Level of Prices (rate of inflation)—as measured by some form of price index
3. Level of Employment
4. Level of Productivity—usually measured by output per hour worked
5. Standard of Living—usually measured by income per capita or per household
6. Balance of Trade
7. Balance of Payments
8. Value/Stability of Currency—often measured in terms of U.S. dollars.

Conclusion

Our economy plays a vital role in our lives. Each of us individually, and collectively as a society, is faced with many decisions related to the economy. To help us understand our own economic system, it is important to look at other types of economic systems and how they function.

As was mentioned, it is difficult to find any real world examples which are perfect models of the theory. However, it is hoped that this introduction to economic systems will provide sufficient background information to enable the reader to go forward now into the "real world" with some understanding, appreciation of the facts and ability to evaluate and analyse.

Where to Draw the Line on Poverty

Sean Fine

How many people live in poverty? What is poverty in an affluent nation such as Canada? How precise must we be? In this brief, but compelling, article Fine outlines the disagreements over what constitutes the poverty line in Canada. Why is it so difficult to make such a determination?

Poverty is an imprecise term, Statistics Canada says. But people who consider themselves poor can tell you precisely what it means.

Two years ago, Jacqueline Fletcher was raising four teenagers on $24,000 a year in rural Nova Scotia. Now, just one child lives at home.

> "I feel like a big weight has been lifted off me now because I can make choices," said Ms. Fletcher of Sheet Harbour, an employment outreach worker with the Native Council of Nova Scotia. "I don't have to buy a dozen oranges at 99 cents when they're half dried out, when I can get good oranges now."

But for the country's social policy makers, do dried-out oranges mean Ms. Fletcher had been living in poverty?

This week, (*October 27, 1990*) Statistics Canada, the federal government's statistical agency, and a group of academics, economists and business people will meet privately to discuss what poverty is and how it should be measured.

The outcome will be of more than just academic interest. To define the word is to define the problem. And that is highly political.

For instance, it seems obvious that you are poor if you can't afford to eat. But are you also poor if you can't eat half as well as your neighbour? And are you then deserving of, say, tax breaks or free day care?

> "In one sense, yeah, poverty should be measured very much on a relative basis," said Donald Eastman, a member of the National Statistics Council, an advisory body to Statscan. "And yet I suspect 80 percent of the people alive in this world right now would love to live at Canada's poverty level."

But advocates for the poor have a quick retort for those who compare low-income lines in Canada with more extreme poverty in the Third World. "I would challenge any of them to try living below those (Canadian low-income) levels," said Cheryl Boon, a researcher for the National Anti-Poverty Organization in Ottawa.

Canada has no official poverty line. Instead, it has what Statscan describes as low-income cutoff lines, which vary by community and family size. A family of four in 1990 requires nearly $28,000 in pretax income in a big city and $19,000 in the country.

Canada's Unofficial Poverty Line

Family Size	Community size				
	500,000 +	100,000- 499,999	30,000- 99,999	Less than 30,000	Rural
1	$14,078	12,365	12,079	11,011	9,583
2	19,082	16,762	16,374	14,926	12,991
3	24,255	21,303	20,812	18,972	16,513
4	27,927	24,528	23,961	21,843	19,012
5	30,513	26,799	26,180	23,932	20,547
6	33,120	29,088	28,417	25,905	22,547
7+	35,622	31,287	30,565	27,864	24,251

Note: Based on National Council of Welfare estimates of Statistics Canada's low income cut-offs (1986 base) for 1990

But those lines are under attack from both sides. The poor say they underestimate what it takes to live in dignity. Others say they are too high and lead to an overblown sense of Canadian poverty.

Statscan itself acknowledges that its low-income lines, developed in the late 1960s, need rethinking. "Most people don't understand what it's all about. It's very arbitrary," said Ray Ryan, director-general of the labour and household surveys branch of Statscan.

It insists that the cutoffs do not measure poverty. For example, Statscan does not consider sources of income outside such traditional sources as employment, investment and social assistance. And money is only one measure; death and disease rates, malnutrition, literacy and education levels, housing and neighbourhood conditions are others.

Below the low-income cutoffs, Mr. Ryan said, "we say these people are in straitened circumstances. They're in circumstances where it's difficult to get by. They don't have much left over to do much else."

The low-income cutoffs measure the point at which families or individuals spend more than 58.5 percent of their income on the necessities: food, shelter and clothing.

That figure is based on a 1978 finding that Canadian families spend an average of 38.5 percent of their income on necessities. Twenty percent is added arbitrarily to determine where low-income lines start.

When the system was first begun in 1967, it was based on a 1959 survey that found that the average Canadian household spent 50 percent of its income on necessities. To be considered a low-income household at that time, you had to spend more than 70 percent.

Mr. Eastman, a senior employee of Dofasco Inc. in Hamilton, Ont., said that by changing this unofficial poverty line "we have conveyed an impression that, despite the taxload, we have not been able to accomplish anything on poverty. People say, 'If I'm doing this much and it's not accomplishing anything, why bother?'"

Senior levels of the federal government bureaucracy express the view that Canada's current low-income lines only confuse matters, that the lines are too high and most Canadians do not see them as real poverty so it is hard to build enough political will to fight poverty.

And it becomes harder for government to aim programs at those who really need help, according to this view.

Some social agencies are alarmed by this view. "This is just a political machination to try to push down the level of poverty by attempting to doctor the poverty line," said Andrew Mitchell, program director at Metro Toronto's Social Planning Council, a private agency.

By basing government social programs on too narrow a definition of the poor, he said, "you also destroy the political base" for fighting poverty.

Advocates for the poor say poverty in a relatively wealthy country such as Canada means more than simply the inability to meet basic needs. It also means being denied the chance to take part in community activities—buying hockey equipment for the children, for example.

"Poverty is the level below which you can't live in health and dignity," said Sue Cox, assistant executive director of Toronto's Daily Bread Food Bank. "I think that allows for something a little more than basic needs. It might let you go to a movie."

There is poverty, she said, and there is acute poverty such as is found in food bank lineups, where people generally have incomes of 40 to 60 percent of the Statscan low-income lines.

Pam Fleming, 33, a Vancouver antipoverty worker who lives on $13,000 a year (1,000 less than the Statscan low-income line for a big-city single person), said she had no choice last year but to live in a building where drug addicts slept in communal washrooms and people banged on the walls and threatened to kill one another. "I haven't had a decent dental checkup for a couple of years because that is bloody expensive, and I know I've got cavities."

Brian Curley was a surveyor with Prince Edward Island's Highways Department for 17 years before becoming ill. His family now lives on welfare. His housing costs are paid, and he, his wife and a remaining child at home each receive about $100 a month for food. The amount is based on a diet put together by university nutritionists. "It's enough to give you something to eat, all right," Mr. Curley said, but the official diet "doesn't give you any tea or coffee or dessert."

He has to dip into the food fund to buy newspapers or magazines, or to pay for clothing or transportation.

Statscan has expressed a willingness to begin measuring acute poverty. It is also being urged to record how long people stay poor and to count how many people are just above and just below its arbitrary low-income lines, wherever they might be set.

Some ask, for example, whether Canada has really beaten the problem of poverty among its senior citizens, even though most now live above Statscan's low-income lines.

"It has been suggested that elderly Canadians are simply the richest of the poor," said Robert Glossop, chairman of Statscan's advisory committee on social conditions and a senior employee of the Vanier Institute of the Family in Ottawa.

Mr. Glossop said Canadians are ambivalent about poverty measures: Many will respond that $28,000 seems like a lot of money, but if you ask them what they need to live on, they will come back with a higher figure.

Controlling Interest—Who Owns Canada?

Diane Francis

"The rich get richer and the poor get poorer," is a cliche which has an unfortunate ring of truth about it unless, of course, you are one of the richer. In the Introduction to her book Controlling Interest: Who Owns Canada? *Dianne Francis outlines the economic development of this process in corporate Canada. What happens when power becomes concentrated in the hands of a few? What are the implications for the political, cultural and economic life of Canada, and for promoting the disparity between rich and poor?*

Even businesspeople are beginning to be alarmed about the degree of concentration in Canada. "In a number of years there will be six groups running this country," warns Bernie Ghert, president of Cadillac Fairview Corp., the country's second-largest development company.

"We must grapple with the problems of concentration of substantial economic power in Canada in the hands of a new aristocracy consisting of twenty or thirty powerful families and the Canadian banks," says Henry Knowles, a Toronto lawyer and formerly Canada's top securities watchdog. But bankers like Richard Thomson, chairman of the Toronto-Dominion Bank, are also concerned, from a different viewpoint. "I worry about the political backlash if it is not dealt with. This could lead to socialism."

Concentration is an issue of vital importance to all Canadians and their political leaders. And it is more pervasive and more serious than I thought when I began my research. Unbridled, concentration forces Canadians to overpay for many goods and services, removes job opportunities, hurts small investors, taxes the poor to help the rich, weakens our competitive position as a trading nation, and ultimately threatens our democratic process.

Controlling Interest profiles Canada's thirty-two wealthiest families who, along with five conglomerates, already control about one-third of the country's non-financial assets, nearly double what they controlled just four years before. Combined, their revenues in 1985 were nearly $123 billion, far greater than the federal government's income of around $80 billion. Just one member of this élite group, Bell Canada Enterprises, had a cash flow of $3.2 billion in 1985, greater than that of either the Canada Pension Plan or the *Caisse de dépôt et placement du Québec*. By comparison, in the U.S. the 100 largest firms, few of which are controlled by individuals, own one-third of the non-financial assets.

Canada has become a collection of family dynasties and management fiefdoms, with more billionaire families per capita than the United States. While their actual net worth is unknown, Canada probably has six billionaire families: the Reichmanns, the Irvings, the Eatons, Edgar and Charles

Bronfman, the Westons, and the Thomsons. The rest of the families profiled in this book are each worth not less than $100 million in net terms, and they control enterprises with at least $1 billion in assets and/or sales.

In the U.S., by comparison, there are only a dozen billionaire families in an economy twelve times as large. The wealthiest man in America is Sam Moore Walton, sixty-seven, an Arkansas-based department store entrepreneur worth US $2.8 billion, according to a *Forbes* magazine report in 1985. But all indications are that K.C. Irving and the Reichmanns are also worth that much. Because both empires are private fortunes headed by tight-lipped individuals, we may never know.

The thirty-two profiles in this book are not a definitive list of the country's thirty-two richest families. The McConnells of Montreal, for instance, are wealthier, in net terms, than many profiled here. They control some $400 million, half of which is locked away in a trust fund for the eleven grandchildren of J.B. McConnell, who made his money in publishing, the stock market, and sugar. That money is invested in hundreds of different companies as a form of private pension plan for family members. The family does not hold controlling interest in any corporation. Its remaining $200 million was put by J.B. McConnell into two charitable foundations, the Griffith Foundation and the McConnell Foundation, which collectively contribute more money to charities in Canada than any other single entity, roughly $11 million in 1985.

The McConnell family, like others, is worth more than, say, Conrad Black and his brother, Montegu, but its money is passively invested, not leveraged to gain control over a corporate empire considerably greater in value. Similarly, others with considerable means who have invested their huge sums of money in small or passive ways include the Siebens family, rumoured to be worth some $300 million to $400 million, and families such as the Southams and the Atkinsons, whose empires are large, but divided among dozens of heirs, some of whom take little, or no, interest.

Canada's inordinately high degree of concentration means that all kinds of goods and services—everything from your glass of orange juice in the morning, to the clothes you put on, to the office where you work, to the department store and mall where you shop, to that after-work beer and a night at the ball game—are likely to be produced by these families and conglomerates. Concentration has become so significant that the country is hurtling towards a new form of economic and political feudalism, a twentieth-century version of Upper Canada's Family Compact back in the 1800s, when agrarian Ontario was politically and financially controlled by the few.

Canada has come full circle. What began as an area controlled by the Hudson's Bay Company and the North West Company has ended up as a country that is little more than a collection of financial franchises. Competition among Canadian capitalists rarely breaks out in the absence of any meaningful combines laws within or foreign rivalry from without. This means that instead of a lively, competitive marketplace yielding jobs, innovations, or opportunities for new entrepreneurs, Canada has far too many cash cows controlled by far too few proprietors. The result is that, whether buying beer or tranquillizers, gasoline, eyeglasses, or shopping centre space, Canadian consumers pay too much. Like economic serfs, we are paying private-sector surcharges, levied by a diminishing number of families and faceless conglomerates, on just about everything.

By far the most heated competition in Canada has been to buy the fiefdoms themselves, as conglomerates and families spent most of the 1970s borrowing millions against what they already owned to acquire more. At the last count by federal officials, some 4,685 takeovers had been made between 1974 and 1984, compared with 3,464 significantly smaller takeovers in the ten previous years. The concentration continues, hurtling us towards an even more closely held economic oligarchy than already exists. Tragically, the issues do not have top political priority, even though controlling interest in the entire country is at stake, and so are political freedoms.

Ottawa has never blocked a specific takeover but did ban briefly all takeovers during 1981—for good reason. Some $14 billion left the country in "Canadianizations" in the first eight months, encouraged by the Liberals' ill-fated National Energy Program. "The takeover thing had gone haywire," recalls Rowland Frazee, chairman of the Royal Bank of Canada. "The banking system was running out of capital. I told MacEachen he had to order an end to it."

On July 29 he did just that. Canada teetered that month on the edge of a currency collapse, a banking crisis, and full-scale bankruptcies, thanks to corporate Canada's take-over frenzy and a government that understood little about economics. Not surprisingly, what was a recession in the United States became a depression here, as unemployment soared and the economy virtually ground to a halt. It was the year of the near-miss, but nothing was learned. It was a year that left corporate Canada with an enormous mortgage, but nothing has changed. And we are still paying the price for 1981.

In the absence of rules, ours has been a financial system fashioned after our national sport of hockey, but without referees or penalty boxes. Unchecked, "free-enterprisers" destroy their own system, mopping up all opportunities and pushing political leaders towards socialist alternatives. Unbridled, free enterprise devours its young as surely as an unofficiated hockey game sidelines the most talented players in the game, if they are small.

Calgary entrepreneur Rob Vanderham can tell you what concentration is all about. As president of Peyto Oils Ltd., an oil and gas exploration company, he felt more keenly than most about his job—after all, he had helped found the company in 1970 and had built it, by 1980, into an enterprise with sales of some $10 million and assets of more than $70 million. Then, in January 1980, while sunning himself in the Caribbean, he got a call from the office. Someone was snapping up the stock, trading had been suspended, and he and his company were no longer players. Now they were pucks. Only a few days earlier an Eastern broker had rounded up 38 percent of Peyto's stock from its largest institutional shareholders and peddled them to Westburne International Industries Ltd., a Calgary-based conglomerate, for $31.8 million. Vanderham, a Dutch immigrant with 10 percent of Peyto's stock, recalled, "As soon as that first call came, I knew it was all over. I put the phone down and felt as though somebody had just stolen my baby."

Economists measure two types of concentration: the accumulation of assets in industries that may not be related (by conglomerates or passive holding companies), and the increase of market share within a sector by a few firms. Both types of concentration have relentlessly accelerated in Canada, and both are economically harmful. Only 20 of Canada's 400 largest public corporations are widely held. Some 380 have a shareholder with at least 15 percent of the stock and in 374 of these, controlling interest of at least 25 to 30 percent is held by a family or conglomerate. By comparison, only 75 of the companies in the American Standard & Poor's 500 stock index have a large shareholder.

Of Canada's 100 largest public companies, which represent as much as half of the country's corporate assets, 25 percent of the total sales and assets are family-controlled, 25 percent are in the hands of widely held conglomerates, such as Bell, 25 percent are foreign-controlled, and 25 percent are public enterprises, such as Crown corporations, utilities, or co-ops. But by far the most aggressive acquisitors are the families.

"We don't need to worry about family wealth," says Hal Jackman, a Toronto tycoon with extensive insurance and trust company assets. "For most, it will be shirt-sleeves to shirt-sleeves in three generations." While that is true for some, the new reality is that changes to tax and securities laws brought in during the 1970s permit the creation of dynasties and fiefdoms, able to reign for as long as they wish. This means the country will be run by a royalty of rich families, ensconced for generations if they wish.

Of course, not all concentration is harmful. If a company is going to fight its way into a bigger foreign market for a few years before it gets a first order, it needs to be big. To compete abroad, a company must have long production runs to reduce unit costs, special technology developed by investing millions in research, as well as millions of dollars to finance expansion. Such gearing up for export often means Canadian companies are oversized within Canada's relatively small economy (it is smaller than California's). However large they may loom here at home, these companies are often tiny compared with their foreign rivals. This is why many argue against concentration curbs: they maintain that lessening competition at home will sabotage success abroad.

But only a handful of Canadian companies have used monopoly positions as springboards into the international big leagues: the big five chartered banks, Canadian Pacific, and Northern Telecom, Canada's greatest corporation. What Canada needs, and lacks, is ten Northern Telecoms. Instead, we have ten companies like Argus Corporation, a notably ugly conglomerate that bled Massey-Ferguson for years, steadfastly refusing to give it cash transfusions for research. Argus lent nothing to the company in the way of operations; it was a passive controlling shareholder, extracting dividends and refusing to allow the company to issue more shares because it did not want to invest more or be diluted. Massey eventually borrowed itself into huge debts it could not afford and a government bail-out in 1979. Then Argus chairman Conrad Black, who inherited the mess, sensibly walked away. But just a few years later, in 1985, Black's Argus jettisoned another of its troubled assets, Dominion Stores—selling out when stormy weather hit and patience, expertise, and cash were needed.

Instead of building world-class contenders, corporate Canada is preoccupied with collecting unrelated assets back at home and gobbling up the accomplishments of other players in unrelated fields, through the cunning use of tax avoidance and the games only paper entrepreneurs can play. It is a parasitical game that will not make the economic pie grow. It will shrink, as the pieces change hands and workers are thrown out of jobs because of duplication.

And this acquisitiveness affects every single Canadian. As if they weren't rich enough already, Canadian billionaires drive trucks through tax loopholes, leaving ordinary Canadians to ante up more to pay for government services, or do without.

The profiles of Canada's thirty-two wealthiest families reveal a great deal about Canada's power élite. For a goodly portion of the 1970s, most have been playing Monopoly with the money of average Canadians. Finding that inflation suddenly gave them enormous borrowing power, they borrowed Canadian savings socked away in Canadian banks that behave, at times, like open-ended slush funds for the tycoons sitting on their boards.

Not only can these families and conglomerates raise huge bank loans for takeovers, but they are also able to raise "free" equity money easily. The successful ones have become masters of what could be dubbed Canada's monetary merry-go-round—an economic anomaly created after the Second World War when the government required that at least 90 percent of all Canadian pension, life insurance, and trust funds must be invested in Canada. Up to 10 percent could be invested elsewhere, but it was carefully restricted to certain conservative types of investments. Designed to provide capital to develop the country and increase the nation's wealth, this rule has single-handedly fostered more concentration of power than has anything else.

And it will continue to fuel the merry-go-round until every single one of the country's public companies falls into the hands of a few families or conglomerates, probably by the end of the decade. For instance, the Reichmanns in the spring of 1986 made a successful $3.3-billion take-over bid for the gigantic Hiram Walker distillery and energy conglomerate. To make their bid, they used Gulf Corp., an energy and paper conglomerate in which the family has an 80-percent stake. Gulf's bid resulted in Hiram's common shareholders getting a handsome capital gain, which is why virtually all the shares were sold, mostly those held by "institutional investors" such as pension plans, mutual funds, or life insurance and trust companies.

Eager to take profits, the managers of these massive funds must turn around and find new investments. And that had become even more difficult, for two reasons. They continue to be deluged with cash. In 1985, public pension plans like the *Caisse de dépôt et placement du Québec* as well as private schemes totalled $238 billion—equivalent to Ottawa's entire national debt by 1985 and enough to buy half of all the shares of every company on the Toronto Stock Exchange. Even more dramatic, they were growing by $60 million a day, or $19 billion a year. Indications are that this trend will not slow down. In addition, fund managers are faced with a decreasing number of shares to buy, because of the thousands of takeovers that have occurred.

This is how the resulting merry-go-round works: eventually, perhaps months or even years later, the Reichmanns will pay for the $3.3-billion Hiram takeover by selling shares in Gulf to the very same institutional investors who have just sold their Hiram common shares. These institutional investors will gladly buy such paper instruments, because they are captive in Canada and desperately need new "paper." They will also buy the new Gulf shares because the shares' underlying value will be the same sound, profitable Hiram assets that led them to buy Hiram common shares in the first place.

And so institutional investors have become locked into a system that offers them fewer and fewer investment choices and is rigged to reward the paper entrepreneurs. Used in this way, the hundreds of billions of dollars of Canada savings contribute little to the nation's wealth. In fact, the system results in greatly inflated stock prices in Canada for what little stock is left on exchanges, as more and more pension dollars chase fewer and fewer stocks. This is very harmful because it means foreign investors, bringing fresh capital, are not easily attracted. It also means Canadian savings have been increasingly invested in stocks at inflated prices, which will yield disappointing results for Canadians in their collective old age.

Japan also limits pension investments outside the country, but the big difference is that Japan's captive pool of capital has been wisely utilized, because that country has many more real entrepreneurs, capable of putting the money to good use. The money has been loaned or invested to individuals and companies that have created export empires, creating jobs and new goods and services in order to increase profits and the nation's wealth.

Not all forms of concentration can be curbed, nor should they be. Only big players who cause injuries or prevent other players from getting onto the ice to participate must be disciplined. However, even big players who play by the rules and are hugely successful raise questions. Canada's biggest empire, Bell Canada Enterprises, has a telephone monopoly in Ontario and Quebec and large takes in a number of companies. In 1983, Bell convinced federal regulators to allow it to embark on a "diversification" strategy, and since then it has bought controlling interest in a major corporation every year. Now Bell and its affiliated companies have combined market values that are equivalent to about 9 percent of the entire Toronto Stock Exchange float.

Bell's success is based on three things: it does not have to compete, its management is obviously good at negotiating highly beneficial telephone rates before federal communications regulators, and it shops the takeover market carefully. The question is, given its awesome size, do advantages such as these deserve such enormous rewards, or is it not time to let Bell share its monopoly position, particularly long-distance services, with new, possibly more innovative entrants? Or perhaps Bell should prune its profits, passing along more benefits to phone users rather than to its shareholders and those of companies it takes over.

Another example of questionable success of a big player is the Canadian Pacific empire, which is second only to Bell. The base upon which this huge conglomerate grew is largely the land and sub-surface rights—equivalent in size to Nova Scotia—given by the fledgling government of Canada to the railway's original developers. Little wonder that CP owns Canada's most profitable and successful oil exploration company because it has the choice of so many lands to explore and no royalties to pay, as well as one of its wealthiest real estate development companies, with valuable acreage in the downtowns of most Canadian cities. CP is profitable mostly because of such ancient gifts—combined with a railway that operates mostly like a utility with guaranteed profits. Beginning in the early 1970s, with tax changes paving the way, CP leaped into the takeover game, but it has had problems with most of its acquisitions. CP may be a conglomerate that has become unwieldy, a financial dinosaur roaming too far afield.

Some say conglomerates are beneficial because they provide additional financial muscle when trouble hits one subsidiary or another. Conversely, however, the conglomerate structure also means that when a subsidiary is in trouble, it drags down the other, well-run operations. Conglomerates are only as strong as their weakest links, and they concentrate decision making into fewer and fewer hands. When mistakes are made, the amplification is dramatic.

An example of a conglomerate gone awry is the Dome Petroleum empire, which contributed mightily to Canada's near-miss in 1981. Dome's aggressive managers had built the company with foolishly expensive takeovers, always being bailed out by international oil price hikes. But in 1981, they decided to pay $4 billion for a company they could not afford. Not only did Dome Pete shareholders lose their proverbial shirts as a result, ending up with a negative equity value five years later, but Dome Pete raped the shareholders of its sister company, Dome Mines, in which it had a controlling interest of 40 percent.

By July 1981, Dome Petroleum faced soaring interest rates on its huge debt and plummeting stock values, a disaster in light of the fact that it hoped to swap its stock to buy the other half of Hudson's Bay Oil shares. In a vain attempt to shore up its sagging stock price, Dome Petroleum directors lobbied the board of Dome Mines to borrow up to $125 million and buy Dome Pete stock. The mining company, which already owned 27 percent of the oil giant, actually spent $75 million. "Thank heavens we only took up three million shares," says former Dome Mines president Malcolm Taschereau. "Even that ran up to a cost of $75 million and eventually resulted in Mines having to dispose of other assets."

The stock swap was never accepted by the market, and Dome went to the wall. The new Dome Pete shares held by Dome Mines were worthless, wiping $75 million in value off the company's books. It was a case of a controlling shareholder harvesting a company for its own ends rather than for the good of all shareholders. In 1982, Dome Mines was dragged even further into the mess when it was forced to sign a $225-million loan guarantee to the Toronto-Dominion Bank to support Dome Petroleum. Taschereau became increasingly uncooperative above executing his board's decisions and resigned in mid-1983.

Eventually, Dome was bailed out by its bankers, who stretched out loan repayments to avoid embarrassment and loan loss provisions on their books. But Dome Mines was a sorry lesson that he who lives by the conglomerate dies by the conglomerate. Despite that publicly aired display of disaster management, current examples of potentially dangerous interlocking directorships and financial arrangements exist throughout corporate Canada, particularly in the heavily debt-laden Edper empire of Peter and Edward Bronfman, which is the subject of the lengthiest family profile in this book.

Apologists say that concentration is the natural result of tariffs and foreign ownership restrictions needed to create jobs and buy back the country. Of course, foreign ownership proscriptions have backfired because tariffs and other restrictions also protect foreign-owned outfits already operating inside the country, many of whom enjoy near-monopolistic privileges as a result.

In addition, foreign ownership restrictions in Canada's resource and manufacturing sectors are unnecessary. Resources are already owned by the people, and owners of companies exploiting those companies must pay royalties, regardless of nationality. As for manufacturing, the Auto Pact, a special bilateral treaty, already enshrines job protection in the only significant manufacturing field in Canada.

Throughout our history, concentration, and what to do about it, has been the black hole of Canadian economic policy. Our leaders do not understand the importance of concentration, cannot define it, and have no tools with which to measure it. This is not surprising, given that Canada is a newly industrialized country with its own populist traditions. In the U.S., regulators monitor the biggest players and penalize them when they use bullying tactics. Big is bad, according to American populist tradition. It must be watched.

An example of where all of Canada might be headed can be seen in one province, New Brunswick, where the Irving empire reigns supreme. In fact, the Irving family virtually *is* New Brunswick's private sector, apart from a few notable competitors like the wealthy McCains. Former New Brunswick premier Louis Robichaud recalls that one of K.C. Irving's sons told him, "My father's never lost a New Brunswick election in his life," even though Irving never sought public office. But for years, Irving could make or break politicians, a chilling fact in a country where thirty-two families control an inordinate portion of the economy. Even worse, the extent of family wealth is unknown because disclosure requirements are lax or non-existent in Canada, in contrast to other industrialized countries.

While unassailed and misunderstood in Canada, the concentration issue has nonetheless nagged. Countless royal commissions and regulatory hearings have been held into concentration's various manifestations, most notably in the oil and newspaper businesses. The Royal Commission on Corporate Concentration concluded in 1978 that concentration was a necessity. But the commission listened principally to the business community and failed miserably to fulfil its mandate.

Concentration of power has grown like cancer, spreading rapidly while one federal consumer minister after another wrestles with reforms of the toothless Combines Investigation Act. The Americans, on the other hand, have recognized the importance of having tough anti-trust laws. Their system pits business against business, for small and medium-sized firms can blow the whistle on big market-place bullies when necessary, thus protecting the fastest-growing and most innovative businesses in any economy. Perhaps the Americans are more attuned to this because of their respect for individual freedoms. Restraint of trade and other anti-competitive abuses destroy an individual's right to ply his chosen trade.

Cartels also rob consumers of choices and bargains. The best example of such marketplace abuse occurred in 1986, when Canadian motorists were deprived for months of the benefits of collapsing oil prices, benefits that American motorists enjoyed immediately. Only under the glare of publicity and after Opposition battering did Canadian oil companies begin to reduce gasoline prices. But prices for diesel fuel and home heating oil actually increased in many parts of the country to make up for lower gasoline prices.

In March 1986, following a series of articles I had written in the *Toronto Star*, criticizing these and other pricing practices, Imperial Oil and Petro-Canada spokesmen actually admitted to me that they had sold Canadian gasoline to Americans for up to 7.5 cents a litre less than they were charging Canadians. Petrocan chairman Wilbert Hopper subsequently said this was a slip-up by an "overenthusiastic salesman in Vancouver" that would never happen again. But Imperial's chairman Arden Haynes said plainly, "Why would we sell to the competitors? And if we used it ourselves to reduce prices, we'd end up taking market share away from someone who would drop their prices and get that market share back from us." In other words, Haynes is a perfect example of Canada's cartelists, who live in fear lest competition ever break out.

Industry-wide explanations during the period between December 1985 and March 1986, when oil prices were falling by 60 percent, were no more satisfactory. Canadian oil companies said it took eighty days for crude to be transported and processed for consumption, and because of this delay they could not afford to pass along immediate savings without massive losses. The Americans did not use excuses, but competed almost immediately. Canadian explanations were feeble defences for cartelism, while the Americans competed because their government has understood for years how markets work and how to police them to ensure that they work.

The result is that about 40 percent of U.S. gasoline stations are independents, compared with Canada's paltry 20 percent. The American wholesale and refinery sectors are characterized by literally dozens of independents in many regions, while in Canada five major refiners reign over 86 percent of the country's entire marketplace: Petro-Canada, Imperial, Shell Canada, Texaco Canada, and Irving Oil. Because they dominate refining, they also dominate gasoline stations, because they supply them with products although they also own competing gasoline stations. This is a conflict of interest that should never have been allowed: refiners are at once competitors and suppliers to independents, which allows them to ensure that their competition never enjoys pricing advantages.

The U.S. government jealously guards competition, a cornerstone of capitalism. When Texaco's parent company took over Getty Oil in 1984, the U.S. marketplace watchdog, the Federal Trade Commission, forced Texaco to sell off much of its wholesale and refinery operations in new England, because the takeover had resulted in four firms controlling 70 percent of the market. When Gulf was taken over by Chevron in 1985, the commission ordered Chevron to divest several thousand gasoline stations and several refineries in certain regions because of concentration levels. Whether in oil or in other industries, what is intolerable in the U.S. is the norm in Canada.

Canadians have yet to understand that competition creates jobs and opportunities and enhances a nation's economic well-being, because it imposes economic efficiencies.

It is Canada's misfortune that most Canadian politicians have been concerned with how to hand out money and win votes, rather than with how to create economic wealth. Pierre Trudeau, whose wealth was the result of his father selling a chain of gasoline stations to Imperial Oil, said shortly after becoming prime minister that if he had to choose between the growth of the GNP and an improvement in the quality of life, he would disregard the economics. Unfortunately, he followed through.

Without regulation, Canada's corporate barons have played fast and loose with tax and securities laws, and sometimes their actions have bordered on theft. Canada has not come to grips with securities rules that address the level of concentration that exists. This is due to lack of knowledge on the part of most Canadians. And it is hardly surprising. Nearly one out of three Canadians works for a non-profit enterprise (mostly governments, their agencies, and Crown corporations). That means one-third of all Canadian workers do not live under bottom-line discipline. And Canada's history has not been dogged by the strings of financial scandals that led to consumer movements after America's industrialization. Canadians simply do not have experience dealing with crooks, nor do they have a heritage of fighting for economic rights. So they do not understand these rights. Neither does Parliament or the courts.

Not surprisingly, certain politicians, the churches, and grass-roots organizations have taken the matter into their own hands, fighting concentration on an ad hoc basis. This has given rise to Canada's unique forms of "people's capitalism" such as credit unions and cooperatives. Uniquely Canadian counterweights to the concentration of power in the hands of the banks or grain merchants, they have been joined by 1,000 Crown corporations, aimed at stemming foreign investment or central Canada's industrial and monetary power.

In some cases, public enterprise in Canada has been necessary to fill the vacuum created by a Canadian private sector almost totally populated by paper entrepreneurs, who are uninterested in projects that add to the nation's wealth. But in many other cases, the managers of our public enterprises put politics before economics, creating useless schemes or feather-bedding government services as make-work mega-projects.

Lacking a vibrant, open, and competitive marketplace, Canada has created jobs by spending billions providing top-notch government services, entitlements, schools, hospitals, airports, and roads. But a nation without potholes is a nation of pothole-fillers—and huge mortgages. The tragedy for Canada is that far too large a portion of our economy is run about as efficiently as our post office. And the rest is run for the sake of a handful of wealthy, family-owned mutual funds.

And So They Were Wed

Lillian Breslow Rubin

How do classes persist and perpetuate themselves as classes? Why are class differences and gender differences so difficult to eradicate? In this excerpt Rubin examines the culture of one segment of the working class to begin to develop answers to these questions. On the basis of interviews with relatively young but long-married men and women, she uncovers differences in the ways men and women describe and understand love, courtship and the other sex. Rubin also discusses the socio-cultural and economic environment and pressures within which the meaning of marriage and children take root.

They were young when they met—sometimes just in high school, sometimes just out. They were young when they married for the first time—on the average, 18 for women, 20 for the men; the youngest, 15 and 16 respectively. And they were young when they divorced and remarried. One-fourth of the women and one-fifth of the men were married once before. And although the present marriages average almost nine years, the mean age of the women is only 28; of the men, 31:

How did you decide that this was the person you wanted to marry?

Most people hesitate, not quite sure how to respond to that question. When the answers do come, usually they are the expected ones—those that affirm the romantic ideals of American courtship and marriage. "We fell in love." "We were attracted to each other." "We were having fun." "He was the right one." As the conversation continues, however, the stories they tell about how they met and why they married are inconsistent with those first socially acceptable responses.

Some describe meetings and matings that seemed to happen by chance:

> We met at the show where we all used to go on Friday nights. We started to go together right away. Four months later, I got pregnant so we got married. [Twenty-eight-year-old housewife, mother of four, married 11 years.]

...or marriages that took place almost by accident, without choice or volition:

> I don't know exactly why I married her instead of somebody else.
> I guess everybody always knows they're going to have to get
> married. I mean, everybody has to some time, don't they? What
> else is there to do but get married? [Thirty-four-year-old
> maintenance man, father of five, married 13 years.]

Some—the young divorcees—often married because they were exhausted
from the struggle to support and care for their small children. One such
woman, a 31-year-old mother of four, married eleven years to her second
husband, was divorced at nineteen. With a husband who couldn't have
supported her even if he wanted to, and a family who "would have helped, but
[who] had their own problems," she recalls:

> I really wasn't sure I wanted to get married again. But financially,
> it was terrible. I got no support at all. I think even then I knew
> that I probably would have taken a lot more time about
> remarrying if I didn't have those really awful financial problems.

> I was so tired of working, and I felt like I was giving my kids so
> little. I began to be afraid that they wouldn't even know who their
> mother was. It was to the point where I was picking them up,
> taking them home, giving them a bath, putting them to bed,
> putting up my hair, and going to bed myself. I was too tired for
> anything else—not for them and not for me. On the weekends it
> was just about all I could do to get things straight in the house
> and get ready for the next week. Rest? Who knew about that
> then!

> It finally all caved in on me when I came to pick up my kids after
> work one night, and they didn't want to go home with me. [*Near
> tears*.] Can you believe it? They wanted to stay with the baby-
> sitter. I couldn't even blame them. I sure wasn't any fun to be
> with; and it was getting so they knew her better than me.

> So Johnny was around, and he really was different than my first
> husband. I figured he was a responsible guy, and he cared about
> me and my kids. So we got married. And, you know, now I still
> have to work. [*Then quickly, as if wanting to take the words back*.]
> But it's not as bad; in fact, you can't compare it. I work only part
> time, and we don't have such awful money problems. Besides, I

don't have to do *everything* all by myself. Johnny helps out with
the kids and stuff when I need him to.

How did you decide this was the person you wanted to marry?

Often wives and husbands disagree. For just as Jessie Bernard in her book *The
Future of Marriage* found two marriages—his and hers—for many couples there
are also two courtships—his and hers. A 29-year-old mother of three, married
11 years, recalls:

> We met at the coffee shop where some of us kids used to hang
> out. I guess we knew right away because we began to go steady
> right after. We just fell in love right away.
>
> I thought he was a big man. I was still in high school, and it was
> like—you know, he wasn't just another kid in school. He got out
> the year before, and he was working and making lots of money
> (it seemed like lots then anyway), and we could go out and do
> cool things. Then after a couple of months, he gave me his class
> ring. Boy, I was surprised. It was really big, so I put a tape
> around it so it wouldn't fall off. Then that wasn't comfortable, so
> after a while, I had the ring made smaller, and I figured if he
> didn't say anything—I mean, if he said it was okay to do it—this
> must be a sure thing. And it was! And we got married.

Her 30-year-old husband tells the story differently:

> We met at this place and I kind of liked her. She was cool and
> kind of fun to be with. Before I knew it, we were going steady. I
> don't exactly know how it happened. I had this class ring from
> high school and she kept wanting me to give it to her. So finally
> one night I took it off and did it. And the next thing I knew, she
> took it down and had it made smaller. She made a big thing out
> of it, and so did her family. Don't get me wrong; I like her good
> enough. But I just didn't think about getting married—not then
> anyhow. But then, after we were going together for almost a year,
> it just seemed like the thing to do. So we did.

Over and over such differences in recollections appear, each sex playing out its
stereotypic role—the women more often focusing on the romantic view of the
meeting and the marrying, the men on the "I-don't-know-how-she-caught-me"
view. Typical of these differences is this couple, both 26, married eight years.

The wife:
> We just knew right away that we were in love. We met at a
> school dance, and that was it. I knew who he was before. He was
> real popular; everybody liked him. I was so excited when he
> asked me to dance, I just melted.

The husband:
> She was cute and I liked her, but I didn't have any intention of
> getting married. I went to this school dance and she was there. I
> sort of knew who she was, but I'd never talked to her before.
> Then that night she worked it so that her girlfriend who I knew
> introduced us. I felt kind of funny knowing she wanted me to
> dance with her, so I asked her. That started it.

> Then, I don't know, we just got to seeing each other; she always
> seemed to be there. And like I said, she was cute and fun. By the
> time we graduated, everybody was just expecting us to get
> married. I thought about breaking it off; I even tried, but she
> cried so much I couldn't stand it.

Although both wives and husbands frequently start a discussion about how they
came to choose their mates with a certain defensiveness and a seeming lack of
awareness, the women more often than the men move rather quickly to
demonstrate a sophisticated self-awareness, as this couple, parents of three
children, married 13 years, shows.

The wife:
> I guess the reason we got married was because he was out of a
> job, and he was being kicked out of his boardinghouse.

> *You weren't planning to marry, then?*

> Well, we had never really talked about marriage although maybe
> we both kind of knew it would happen. At the time it all
> happened kind of sudden. I said, "What are you going to do
> about this situation?" He said, "I don't know; maybe we could get
> married." I said, "Okay, let's do it." And we did.

> *But what made you say "okay?" What attracted you most about him?*

> I think the fact that he liked me. I guess that was really important
> to me. I didn't date very much, and then this guy came along, and

he liked me. Also, I guess I felt needed; that's important, especially when you're just a kid. Nothing makes you feel more important [*Pausing reflectively, then adding.*] Now that I look at him, I also see that he reminds me very much of my dad. I suppose that was part of it, too, even though back then I certainly didn't know it.

The husband:

What do you mean, how did we decide? *We* didn't really decide; *she* did mostly, if you know what I mean.

But what made you go along? What attracted you most about her?

I don't know. We were seeing each other every day, and what else was there to do but to get married. [*With a tight, angry laugh.*] She was hard to get, I guess. A lot of girls play that way, you know, because they know it gets to a guy. She sure knew how to get to me.

Undoubtedly, all these explanations speak to some part of the truth. Like women and men in all classes, however, these couples marry for a complex of reasons, many of them only dimly understood, if at all. First among those reasons may be the social-psychological milieu in which we all come to adulthood—the nuclear family which promises (even if it doesn't always deliver) intimacy, and leaves us yearning for more; a society in which almost everyone marries, and where those who don't are viewed as deviant and deficient. So we come together because we need to feel close to someone; because it's what most of us do at a certain stage of life; because it's the accepted and the expected, the thing to do if one is finally to be grown up. Still, there is a quality of urgency among the young people of the working class that is not so evident in a comparable group of middle-class, college-educated men and women—an urgency that is rooted in their class history and family backgrounds.

There are those—women and men—from hard-living families, aching with pain, needing a place in which to feel safe, a place to which they belong:

My mother left us when I was nine. It was bad enough living in the house with just my father, but then when he got married, it was just awful.

He married a real bad woman. They met in a bar. They both drink a lot—too much. And a little while after they met, she

> moved into our house with her two kids. I was so ashamed, I
> could have died—them living together in our house like that.
> After a year or so, they got married and things got even worse.
> She's got a foul mouth and she was really awful to us kids. She'd
> curse us and call us the most awful, terrible names. When she got
> drunk, she'd be even worse. She'd knock us down and kick us
> while she was cursing us out.
>
> It wasn't much of a family before she came, but it was a whole lot
> better. My father tried the best he could. Even though he was
> drunk a lot of the time, he wasn't mean. And we all felt we had
> *somebody*. After she came, there was just nobody, nobody.
>
> I used to dream all the time about a home of my own. I wanted
> so much to have a place where I'd be secure. So when I met
> Barney, I thought, "here's a guy who loves me and needs me."
> And that felt so good so we got married. [Twenty-four-year-old
> sales clerk, mother of two, married seven years.]

It was not only the children of hard-living families who married young, however.
Whether hard-living or settled, most lived in relatively poor neighbourhoods
where parents saw around them many young people whose lives were touched
by the pain and delinquency that often accompanies a life of poverty. In such
an environment, parents tend to be terribly fearful about their children's
future—fearful that they will lose control, that the children will wind up "on the
streets," or worse yet, in jail. Therefore, they try to draw the reins of control
very tight—keeping a close watch, imposing strict rules about manners and
behaviour, strict regulations about time and activities.

But these same parents and children live in a society where respect is
accorded to the financially successful, where the mark of ability is represented
by one's annual income. Such parents, believing that they haven't "made it,"
feel unsure of themselves, their worth, and their wisdom—a perception that
often is shared by their children.

No words are necessary to convey these feelings. Children know. They know
when their teachers are contemptuous of their family background, of the values
they have been taught at home. They know that there are no factory workers,
no truck drivers, no construction workers who are the heroes of the television
shows they watch. They know that their parents are not among those who
"count" in America. And perhaps mot devastating of all, they know that their
parents know these things as well. Why else would they urge their children on
to do "better," to be "more" than they are? Why else would they carry within
them so much generalized and free-floating anger—anger that lashes out

irrationally at home, anger that is displaced from the world outside where its expression is potentially dangerous?

Such children, then, not only are exposed to the values of the larger society which denigrate their parents' accomplishments and way of life, but those values also are taught to them in implicit and explicit ways by their own parents. Under such circumstances, it is difficult, indeed, for working-class parents either to provide acceptable parental role models for their children or to enforce their authority.

The acceptance and transmission of definitions of self-worth that are tied to material accomplishments and acquisitions is one of the unacknowledged and most painful of the "hidden injuries" that this society has visited upon the working class. When the insecurities that derive from these injuries are denied, as they most often are (for who can face the humiliation of being debased in one's own and one's children's eyes), the response is to cling ever more tightly to old and familiar ways, and to shout ever more loudly about their value.

It is of such economic and sociocultural realities that child rearing patterns are born. And it is to those experiences that we must look to explain the origins of child rearing patterns in working-class families that, on the surface, appear rigid and repressive. In that context, the widely accepted theories that their authoritarian personalities are responsible for the observed relations between parents and children become highly questionable. Instead, those theories seem to reflect the inability of their middle-class creators to understand either the context in which the behaviour takes place or its subjective meaning to the actors involved.

These parenthetical comments aside, the fact remains that most working-class parents feel free to relax their vigilance only after children marry. For the young in those families, then, marriage becomes a major route to an independent adult status and the privileges that accompany it.

The fact that life is different for the college-educated, middle-class young needs little documentation; our television screens and newspaper headlines shouted the news to us through the decade of the sixties. The young people of that class find outside of marriage at least some of the independence and adult privileges that are available to the working-class young only within marriage. Thus, the children of the professional middle-class consistently marry later. Among those I met, the average age at marriage was 23 for women, 25 for men.

In other ways, too, the children of these classes have different experiences and are expected to assume different responsibilities within the family. In the working-class home, for example, the family economy generally rests on at least some help from grown or growing sons. Thus, boys are expected to work early and contribute a substantial part of their earnings to the family. And although they may have more freedom from certain kinds of parental surveillance and restraints than their sisters, they, too, generally live at home—in houses that are too small to permit even minimal privacy—until they marry:

> I had to work from the time I was 13 and turn over most of my pay to my mother to help pay the bills. By the time I was 19, I had been working for all those years and I didn't have anything—*not a thing*. I used to think a lot about how when I got married, I would finally get to keep my money for myself. I guess that sounds a little crazy when I think about it now because I have to support the wife and kids. I don't know *what* I was thinking about, but I never thought about that then. But even so, my wife doesn't get it all, you can bet on that. [Thirty-three-year-old automobile painter, father of three, married 13 years.]

For the girls, the culture dictates that "nice" girls remain under the parental roof until a husband comes to take them away. For them, there is no other road to womanhood and independence:

> I was only 17 when I got married the first time. I met him just after I graduated from high school, and we were married six weeks later. I guess that was kind of fast. I don't know, maybe it was rebound. I had been going with a boy in high school for a couple of years, and we had just broken up. Actually, I guess the biggest thing was that there was no other way if I wanted to get away from that house and to be a person in myself instead of just a kid in that family. All three of us girls married when we were very young, and I guess we all did it for the same reason. All three of us got divorced, too, only for my sisters it didn't work out as lucky as for me. They've both had a lot of trouble. [Thirty-year-old housewife, mother of three, married nine years.]

It is true that several couples did speak of living together before marriage, but in all but one instance, the women had been married before and had borne one or more children. One of these women said of that period of her life:

> We met and things just clicked, so we started living together right away. I know that sounds terrible, but that's the way it was. Before I'd ever gotten married, I'd never have thought of doing anything like that. But after all, I'd already been married. And anyway, we only did it for a couple of months; then we got married.

Mostly, however, working-class teenagers chafe under living conditions that are oppressive and parental authority that feels repressive. Marriage often is seen as the only escape—a route they take very early in their lives.

But there are still other components to the urgency to marry. For while parents try desperately to circumscribe and control their children's behaviour, to make them into respectful and respectable adults, the children—especially the boys—often get into youthful trouble and are themselves frightened by those experiences. Thus, there are the men who recall those years as a time when they were facing the choice between a hard-living and a settled-living life, and who saw a "good woman" as the way to the settled-living path:

> I was 17 and hanging around with a loose crowd, and all of us got into a lot of trouble—you know, with the police and all that kind of stuff. I had this girlfriend who was also 17. She quit school when she was about 15, I guess, and she already had a kid (he was about two, I guess) when I knew her. So you can see, I was just asking for it, running around with people like that.
>
> I already had some run-ins with the police, just some juvenile, y'know, kid stuff. And then I got picked up for a heavy rap—robbery. That really scared me. While I was waiting for my trial and wondering what was going to happen to me (I used to have nightmares about going to jail), I met Ann. She was the sweetest, most honest, innocent girl I ever knew. I just knew I needed a girl like her to help me change my ways. She did, too. I beat that rap, and after that Ann would come and pick me up and take me to school every day; then she'd wait for me to take me home.
>
> We both finished high school, and I'm proud of that because nobody else in our families did. Then we got jobs and saved our money; and then we got married. I've never been sorry either, because she still keeps me straight. [Twenty-seven-year-old mechanic, father of two, married eight years.]

Not an exceptional story when one considers that well over one-third of the men and 10 percent of the women told of juvenile records—four boys and two girls being defined by the authorities as incorrigibles by age 12 or 13, the rest held on a variety of charges ranging from petty theft, to breaking and entering, to grand theft, to assault with a deadly weapon. These charges, which sound so serious, often grow out of such activities as breaking into a vacant house, stealing a two-by-four from a construction site, getting into a street fight, or joy-riding in a stolen car. As one young man, telling of his troubles with the police, said:

> You know, they always put those terrible names on it. They always make it sound so much worse than it is.

Not always; it depends on who is getting into trouble. Several men in a comparable group of professional middle-class adults recalled similar activities, yet not one had a juvenile record. Usually, they were not even picked up. On the rare occasion when they were, they were released immediately into the custody of their parents, leading one to assume that the police tend to view such behaviour differently depending upon the class composition of the neighbourhood in which it is found. In working-class neighbourhoods of any colour, these behaviours are called crimes; in middle-class neighbourhoods, they are just boyish pranks.

The rate of juvenile arrests among the working-class people I met suggests a very high level of police activity in white working-class communities—activity about which we hear almost nothing. We are accustomed to the cry of police harassment from black communities whose young people also have a very high rate of arrests. But such high juvenile arrest rates in white communities catch us by surprise since they receive so little publicity. Partly, that may be because whites experience black crime as more dangerous to the society than white crime and, therefore, attend less to the latter. Partly, and not unrelated to this kind of racist consciousness among whites, it may be a matter of what the media consider news. And partly, it may indicate a less troubled relationship between the police and white working-class communities—perhaps because policemen are often white and working class in origin. The last may also be the reason why—in contrast to black youth who tend to see the police as an alien and repressive enemy who harass and victimize them without cause—the whites tend to accept police definitions of themselves an to agree that they "got what was coming." One man, aged 24, recalling his juvenile troubles, says:

> Boy, I always felt like a big man every time I got into trouble. I got mad when I got caught sometimes, but I always knew the cops were right and I was wrong.

Another, aged 39, says flatly:

> I had plenty of run-ins with the police, but I can't say I didn't get what was coming to me. I got what I deserved, being the smart-alecky kid I was.

Finally, there are those—44 percent of the couples to whom I talked—who married because the woman became pregnant, another statistic that seems extraordinarily high but that is so prevalent among working-class youth that it is experienced as commonplace. Speaking of his first marriage, a 31-year-old machinist, now in a seven-year-old second marriage, remembers:

> I had gone with this girl for two years, and I suppose we expected to get married, but not yet. She was 18 and I was 19 when she got pregnant. Once that happened, there was nothing else to do but get married. My one consolation was that I outlasted everybody else. Everybody I knew then was getting married because the girl got pregnant; nobody got married without that. And most of them were getting caught a lot sooner than I did.

"Getting caught"—a phrase that was used over and over again:

> I got caught right away; it really happened quick. A lot of people I know got away with it much longer. [Twenty-two-year-old housewife mother of two children, married six years.]

> We had been fooling around for a few months, then all of a sudden, she got caught. [Thirty-year-old cook's helper, father of three, married nine years.]

> I felt so mad because I got caught when other people were doing the same thing and getting away with it. My sister-in-law and a couple of my girlfriends were doing it, too, and they didn't get caught so they got to have a big wedding, and to be all dressed up like a bride and all that stuff that I wanted so bad and couldn't have because I got caught. [Twenty-four-year-old clerk, mother of one, married six years.]

"Getting caught," with its clear implication of an accident. What does it really mean when 80 percent of these couples engaged in sexual relations before marriage—a figure that accords with the recent literature documenting the increase over earlier generations in the rate of premarital sex. Since class and education breaks differ in these studies, none shows data that are directly comparable to mine. But the best known, Morton Hunt's *Sexual Behaviour in the 1970s*, reports that among his married respondents aged 25-34, 92 percent of the men and 65 percent of the women *at all educational* levels experienced premarital coitus, not necessarily with their present spouse.

But the focus on the *rate* of behaviour or the *change* from earlier generations, while both impressive and sensational, ignores the way in which people *experience* their behaviour. And among the men and women in this study one thing is quite clear: while most people talked relatively openly about their premarital sexual experiences, most of the women, at least, were not free of guilt about them. Indeed, only one woman spontaneously commented positively about the experience of premarital sex with her husband:

> I think it's a hundred percent better to have it. I mean, I don't think you should sleep with just anybody, but I think it's better. If Joe and I had gotten married and had never had anything before, it could've been a disaster. I wouldn't like to marry a man and not know anything about what he needs or how he was; and I'd rather he knew something about me, too. Otherwise, I might be afraid of failing him, or maybe he might fail me. You know, I don't mean to sleep with just everybody and anybody, but if you fall in love.... [Twenty-five-year-old mother of two, married five years.]

A more typical response came from a woman who still speaks with pain of that period in her life:

> I was raised quite a strict Catholic, and I had many guilt feelings about having sex before we were married. Then when I got pregnant, I was so upset I almost died. It took me quite a while to get over those terrible feelings, and I still have problems. [Thirty-year-old mother of three, married 12 years.]

Another woman, aged 26, married seven years, says:

> My sexual adjustment after we were married was very hard. I think I felt guilty about what I had done before. I really felt terrible about it, and I just couldn't enjoy it because I felt so bad. In fact, I still have trouble with it and I worry about what my husband is *really* thinking about me because I let him have me before we were married.

"I let him have me before we were married"—words that suggest the very traditional ways in which so many of these working-class women think about and experience their sexual activities; words that suggest their bodies are something to be given away at the socially mandated moment; words that were not heard from the college-educated middle-class women. In fact, one of the interesting class differences is that the middle-class women—72 percent of whom also engaged in premarital coitus—generally spoke with less guilt about it. Partly, that may be due to class differences in the *expressed* attitudes about such behaviour. Among the working-class women—even though people around them engaged in premarital intercourse; even though they, too, were doing so—there seemed to be a wider gap than in the middle class between the ideal statements of the culture and the reality of the behaviour. Thus, among the working-class women, there was a greater sense that they were doing "wrong," an act to hide in shame from the world around them.

Such fears and the feelings that accompany them are mirrored in the women who resisted premarital intercourse, all of whom showed a decided sense of relief that they had not "given in," partly because it enabled them to feel superior to friends or sisters:

> I wanted so bad to have a white wedding and to not have to say he had to marry me. My sisters, they had to get married, and it was *so* important to me not to have to. I didn't want ever to lose my self-respect like so many girls I knew did. [Twenty-seven-year-old typist, married eight years.]

...and partly because experience has taught them that the women who did often were stigmatized and demeaned in the eyes of their husbands:

> I'm very glad we didn't because I've heard his friends throw it back in their wives' faces now. And when I've heard that, I think, "Boy, am I glad he doesn't have that as a weapon to use on me." [Twenty-eight-year-old housewife, married 10 years.]

These concerns suggest that the "good girl-bad girl" split remains alive for many of these women, and that their fears of being tagged with the "bad girl" label are rooted in social reality and reinforced in interactions with their men who "throw it back in their wives' faces." So deep is this fear, in fact, that it plays a vital part in most of the premarital pregnancies. In this era of The Pill, over three-quarters of the women who became pregnant before marriage pleaded innocent of knowledge about birth-control measures. Some may actually have known nothing. But for most, it turned out that it wasn't that they didn't know, but rather that they had believed that only "bad girls" engage in such advance planning. One woman in her early twenties, married five years, put it this way:

> You know, I was really an innocent. I thought only bad girls went
> out and got birth-control pills. I would never have done anything
> like that.

Another 26-year-old, married eight years, said:

> I was just a dumb kid. I didn't know hardly anything at all. And
> I certainly wasn't the kind of girl who'd go out and get pills or
> something like that.

The implication here is that unmarried sex is forgivable if she is carried away
on the tide of some great, uncontrollable emotion—forgivable, that is, because
she succumbed to a natural force stronger than she; she just couldn't help
herself. In that context, birth-control planning, implying as it does preparation
for the sex act, is incompatible with her definition of self as a "good girl." The
formulation goes something like this: "good girls" do but don't plan; "bad girls"
do and plan.

Viewed from this perspective, few, if any, of these pregnancies could be said
to be accidental. Indeed, if we shift focus from the women to the men, we see
that they, too, were participants in what appears to be an unconscious drama
of getting pregnant and getting married. Both men and women shared the
widespread fantasy that "It couldn't happen to me." Both repeated one version
or another of "A lot of people I know got away with it, at least for a lot longer
than I did;" or, "I just never thought about it happening to me." Not
unexpectedly, however, when pushed about what they *did* think would happen,
the women were more open than the men, more able to own their behaviour,
too quick to take *sole* responsibility for the pregnancy. One woman who
became pregnant at 17 explained how it happened:

> I guess I was really stupid. I wasn't taking precautions; we'd just
> do withdrawal. I guess we'd been sleeping together for about six
> months when one time I just said, "Leave it in; don't take it out."
> And I got caught.

The use of the first-person pronoun is striking. It seems not to have occurred
to her that her partner in the act might share some responsibility for protecting
against an unwanted pregnancy. Small wonder, however, since social attitudes
generally assume that since it is the woman who gets pregnant, it behooves her
to take care—an attitude shared by the man in this family who lamented:

> I felt like I got cornered, and I still get mad at her for that
> sometimes, even now. I never could figure out what she was

thinking about, doing that. I sure wish she'd had enough sense to use some birth control.

What, one wonders, was this young man thinking about when he failed to have "enough sense" to do so? But it occurs to neither wife nor husband to ask him that question about his role in this "accidental" pregnancy.

While we can speculate about the underlying psychological causes of these pregnancies, once again, the sociocultural context in which these young people live gives us more grounded clues. Most come from poor families, live in homes with little or no privacy, feel hemmed in by parental restraints, and yearn for the freedom, independence, and adult status that marriage seems to offer. A young woman, married at 19, says:

I thought finally there's be no one telling me what to do any more.

A young man, married at 20:

I wanted to have something of my own finally. And I wanted to get my old man off my back, to be able to do what I wanted without having to answer to him all the time.

When asked directly to examine the reasons for their premarital pregnancies, however, the women speak more readily than the men, with more awareness of their needs and motivations. No surprise in a culture where women are trained from birth to attend to the emotional side of life, and men, the instrumental side. Exploring the "why's" of her behaviour, one woman who became pregnant at 18 mused:

I think I was ready to move out of the house, and I knew the only way I could do that was to get married. [*Looking down at her hands hesitantly.*] Do you think that had something to do with my getting pregnant? I gotta admit, inside myself I was really thrilled. I wanted to be married, and I wanted a baby. I was scared to death to tell my parents, but I was really very happy. Wow! I hardly ever thought about those things before. I sure never thought I'd dare tell anybody that.

Another, pregnant at 17 and trying to understand that event in her life, said:

I've wondered a lot about why that happened to me. I read somewhere that you psychologists think that everything that happens to us is our fault. I mean, that we sort of do things to ourselves. Maybe that's true sometimes, not all the time, but sometimes. I sure did want to get out of that house, but my father would never stand for us girls going any place without being married. And I just knew I *had* to get away.

But how could you be sure that getting pregnant meant that you'd get married?

She looked puzzled, as if the question made no sense, then replied:

I don't understand. Of course, if you get pregnant, you get married; everybody does. Everybody just expected us to get married when I got pregnant—my parents, his parents, our friends.

Her husband confirmed that perception:

I always figured if I messed around with anybody where it happened, I'd have to marry her. All of us guys did.

There were, of course, some pregnancies among those who did use birth control that may have been genuine accidents—cases in which the women, while never doubting that the men would marry them, vainly sought a way out. But they were defeated by a culture that offers no real options. One 28-year-old mother of three recalls that time:

When I found out I was pregnant, I didn't tell anyone but my girlfriend—not my parents, not my boyfriend, nobody. I thought I would go to some unwed mothers home and have the baby and then come back and say I was on vacation. I suppose that sounds silly now, but I wasn't able to make any other plans.

Did you ever consider abortion?

Never! I could never do that. God, I remember even now how terrified I was. I kept thinking it couldn't be true. I remember even thinking that I would take my mom's car and drive it off a cliff. I knew he'd marry me; I never doubted that. *But I didn't want to get married.* I wanted to *do* things, and to *have* things. I never had any clothes. In fact, it always seemed like I had less money, less everything, than anybody else. I don't mean it was my parents' fault; they gave us what they had. They just didn't have much.

I still remember how much I didn't want to get married. I wanted to get a job and have some things. I was afraid if I got married it would be the end of my chance for a better life. I wasn't wrong about that either.

But my girlfriend kept arguing with me, and finally she told my boyfriend. They both kept saying that I had to get married, and that I couldn't go away. Finally, they told my parents, and then it was all of them against me. So I got married. It never did work; we got divorced less than two years later. But by then I had two children. What a mess!

Some of the men also spoke of their panic on hearing the news:

I just wasn't ready for that. I was too young; I was too irresponsible; I didn't want to settle down. I looked at myself and I thought, "How did you get here?" I just didn't know what to do. And then at the same time, I knew there was nothing else I *could* do. No matter what I thought, I knew I'd have to marry her.

One recalled the wedding grimly:

It's hard to think about it. I don't remember too much of that whole period. Something you don't want to remember, you just don't remember. I do remember that I was very nervous at the wedding. I felt like screaming and running out, but there was just no way out.

Retrospectively, several said that they felt they had been entrapped and might do otherwise if they had it to do over again:

I'm not sure what I'd do if I had to face that again. A guy can't help but feel he got trapped into getting married when a girl gets pregnant like that. I don't know, maybe if I knew what I know now, I wouldn't marry her.

But most would agree with the man who said flatly:

If a girl got pregnant, you married her. There wasn't no choice.
So I married her.

Not one person, woman or man, even considered abortion—generally not
because of religious scruples, but because the idea, they said, was "disgusting,"
"impossible," "not a choice," or because it "just never occurred" to them. Not
one seriously considered *not* getting married. Despite the disclaimers of some
of them, for most of the men as well as the women, marriage appears to have
been the desired outcome. The culture, we know, inhibits men from giving
voice to their needs for nurturance and to their fantasies about marriage and
family, while encouraging women to do so. Women, therefore, find those
dreams, needs and motivations more accessible to their consciousness. But the
men's behaviour suggests that their unspoken, perhaps unconscious, dreams
may not be so different. Thus, marriage comes young; courtships generally are
short—counted in weeks or months, rarely years—even when not terminated
by a pregnancy. For like young people in all classes, in all cultures, these young
working-class men and women strive toward manhood and womanhood. And
while what constitutes those estates differs in many ways, they are alike in one
fundamental aspect. Both are tied closely to marriage and parenthood in the
American culture—values that may be changing, but that still find their clearest
and liveliest expression in the white working class.

Section VII

Gender Relations

The "Facts of Life" as Usually Written Contrasted With a Matriarchal Culture Perspective

Ruth Herschberger

In this succinct comparison Herschberger illustrates differences in the way male-dominated versus female-dominated societies might describe the elementary facts of human reproduction. Herschberger implicitly raises a number of questions, including how value-neutral the objective language of science actually is, and how we decide to treat a speech as factual.

A Patriarchal Society Writes Biology.	*A Matriarchal Society Writes Biology.*
The simple and elementary fact behind human reproduction is that a fertile female egg awaits impregnation in the fallopian tube, and the active male sperm must find this egg and penetrate it.	The simple and elementary fact behind human reproduction is that the active female egg must obtain a male sperm before it can create life.
The female sex apparatus is a depression to receive the sex cells; the male organ is advanced in order to expel the cells.	The male sex apparatus is a tiny factory that continually manufactures sex cells for the female.
When the male becomes sexually excited by internal stimuli, his sexual mechanism is called into play. There is a spontaneous erection of the penis and the passageways from the testicles are thrown open.	When the female becomes sexually excited by internal stimuli, there is a spontaneous erection of the clitoris and a flow of blood into the fine sensitive tissues of the vagina. This causes a similar erection of the region and of the vulva, while the involuntary musculature of the vagina begins rhythmically to contract.
The sperm has a long way to travel through the vas deferens, through the penis, through the vagina and uterus, and finally into the tiny tube where the female egg is waiting.	The sperm is provided with a continuous enclosed passageway—thus making its conveyance as simple as possible. For the female, there is a remarkable gap—which the egg must traverse alone.

A Patriarchal Society Writes Biology.

Nature has provided for this purpose an aggressive and active male cell. Each sperm is composed of rich and highly specialized material and is equipped with a fine wriggling tail that gives it the power of self-locomotion.

No less than 225 million cells are emitted from the man's body with each ejaculation.

When coitus and ejaculation take place, the male sperm—millions in number and each one swimming like a fish—begin their concentrated search for the egg.

The instant one of the sperm penetrates the receptive egg, the creation of a new human being has occurred.

A Matriarchal Society Writes Biology.

Because of the central importance of reproduction, the female egg has been provided with a size much greater than that of the male sperm. The female egg is actually visible to the naked eye and is the largest cell in the body. The male "germ" cells are unbelievably small and must be magnified one hundred times to be visible at all.

The male sperm is produced superfluously since the survival of any one sperm is improbable. The egg, being more resilient and endowed with solidity, toughness, and endurance, can be produced singly and yet affect reproduction.

At the height of orgasm, the uterus contracts, becomes erect, and prolongs its neck downward, dipping into the seminal fluid that draws the semen up to the vicinity of the egg.

Sometimes none of the sperm suits the egg. When an egg does select a male sperm, the sperm is required to shed its wisplike tail. Nature seems to be insisting that the sperm sacrifice its independence for the larger destiny of the female egg. For the future, the new human being wholly depends on the courage and acumen of the egg in establishing a placenta.

A Patriarchal Society Writes Biology.

A Matriarchal Society Writes Biology.

Many women say that they do not experience either pleasure or orgasm.... And from the point of view of function, it may be said that orgasm for women is a luxury, whereas the satisfactory discharge of the male function of orgasm is indispensable foronconception.

If a woman obtains her orgasm before the man obtains his, it is absolutely essential that she sees that he receives one. This is especially true if fertilization is desired...but, also, for the humanitarian reason of reducing the congestion of the penis.

Reaffirming the Obvious

Steven Goldberg

Where do the differences between men and women come from? Is sexual equality possible, or even desirable? Goldberg here argues that the historical tendency toward male rule is due to inherent biological traits. Males' positions of prominence and dominance in political, religious, corporate and other spheres are offered as evidence of this biological "destiny."

That anyone doubted it, was astonishing from the start. All experience and observation seemed to attest to the presence of core-deep differences between men and women, differences of temperament and emotion we call masculinity and femininity. All analyses of such differences were, it seemed obvious, empty or incoherent unless they saw the differences, as related to substrative differences between men and women, differences that gave masculine and feminine direction to the emotions and behaviour of men and women. The question to be answered, it seemed, was how these substrative differences manifest themselves on a social and institutional level—not whether the differences exist.

Yet there it was. A generation of educated people was jettisoning the evidence of both experience and intellect in order to propound a clearly indefensible hypothesis: emotional and behavioural differences between men and women, and the social expectations associated with them, are primarily the result of environmental factors to which physiology is of little relevance. Proponents supported this view with arguments ranging from the confused to the misrepresentative. Individuals who are exceptions were invoked as somehow refuting the possibility of physiological roots of behaviour, a manoeuvre that makes about a much sense as arguing that a six-foot-tall woman somehow demonstrates the social causation of height. Myths about matriarchies were introduced as historical evidence, an approach that would justify a belief in cyclopses. The primary argument supporting this view, an argument accepted even in college textbooks, was the argument that emotional and behavioural differences between men and women were caused primarily by socialization.

The central problem with this approach is that it does not explain anything; it merely begs the question: Why does not one of the thousands of separate societies on which we have evidence reverse male and female expectations? Why does every society from that of the Pygmy to that of the Swede associate dominance and attainment with males? To say that males are more aggressive because they have been socialized that way is like saying that men can grow moustaches because boys have been socialized toward that end. There is no outside experimenter for society, setting up whatever rules seem desirable. Possible social values are limited by observation of reality; if male physiology is such that males have a lower threshold for the elicitation of dominance behaviour, then social expectations denying this cannot develop.

Ten years ago it was not clear to all that there had never been a society reversing the sexual expectations I discuss. Social science texts, out of ignorance or tendentiousness, misrepresented ethnographic studies and asserted the existence of societies that reversed the sexual expectations. Recourse to the original ethnography on every alleged exception demonstrated beyond the possibility of reasonable dispute that not one of the thousands of societies (past and present) on which we have any sort of evidence lacks any of three institutions: patriarchy, male attainment, and male dominance.

All societies that have ever existed have associated political dominance with males and have been ruled by hierarchies overwhelmingly dominated by men. A society may have a titular queen or a powerful queen when no royal male is available; there were more female heads of state in the first two-thirds of the sixteenth century than the first two-thirds of the twentieth. An occasional woman may gain the highest position in a modern state; the other eighteen ministers in Golda Meir's cabinet, and all other Israeli prime ministers, were male. In every society from the most primitive to the most modern—whatever the yardstick—it is the case that political dominance, in particular, is overwhelmingly in the hands of men.

Whatever the non-maternal roles that are given highest status—whichever these are and whatever the reasons they are given high status in any given society—these roles are associated with males. A modern example describes the situation that obtains in every society: if being a medical doctor is given high status (as in the United States), most doctors are male; if being an engineer is given high status and being a doctor relatively low status (as in the Soviet Union), then most engineers are male and most non-hierarchical doctors may be female. There are societies—although modern societies, by their nature, could not be among them—in which women perform objectively far more important economic functions while working harder and longer outside the home than do men. Indeed, save for political and hierarchical leadership, internal and external security, and nurturance of the young, every task is seen as male in some societies and female in others. However, in every society that which is given highest status is associated with men. It is tempting to explain this as a residue of male political dominance, but this view gets things backwards. Male roles do not have high status because they are male; nor do high-status roles have high status because they are male. Many male roles have low status and many low-status roles are male. High-status roles are male because they have (for different reasons in different societies) high status; this high-status motivates males to attain the roles—for psychophysiological reasons—more strongly than it does for females (statistically-speaking). Social expectations conform to limits set by this reality.

The emotions of both males and females of all societies associate dominance with the male in male-female relationships and encounters. The existence of this reality is evidenced by the ethnographies of every society; the observations and statements of the members of every society; the values, songs, and proverbs of every society; and, in our own society, also by feminists who abhor this reality and incorrectly attribute it primarily to social and environmental causes. We might argue that in the family the women of some or all societies have greater power, attributable to either a male abdication or a female psychological acuity that enables women to get around men. But the question relevant to universality is why both the men and women have the emotional expectation of a male dominance that must be gotten around.

The social sciences have discovered precious few non-trivial institutions that are both universal and sufficiently explicable with direct physiological evidence. The three institutions I discuss require explanation and this explanation must be simple. I mention this in anticipation of the inevitable, however wrongheaded, criticism that any physiologically-rooted theory is simplistic, determinist, or reductionist. Were we to attempt to explain variation in the forms of these institutions in physiological terms, an explanation would, in all likelihood, be simplistic. Physiology is in all likelihood irrelevant to differences between, say, American patriarchy and Arabic patriarchy. An explanation sufficient to explain the universal limits within which all variation takes place, if it is to be at all persuasive, requires a single factor common to, and imposing limits on, all societies that have ever existed. Indeed, the very extensiveness of the cross-cultural variation in most institutions emphasizes the need to explain why the institutions we discuss always work in the same direction. No reality is inevitable simply because it is universal, but when an institution is universal we must ask why. If the reason for universality is a physiological factor giving direction to the motivations that make us what we are, then we must entertain the possibility that the institution is an inevitable social resolution of the psychophysiological reality....

Differences between the male and female endocrine/central nervous systems are such that—statistically speaking—males have greater tendency to exhibit whatever behaviour is necessary in any environment to attain dominance in hierarchies and male-female encounters and relationships, and a greater tendency to exhibit whatever behaviour is necessary for attainment of non-maternal status. Using somewhat unrigourous terms, we might say that males are more strongly motivated by the environmental presence of hierarchy, by a member of the other sex, or by status to do what is necessary to attain dominance. It is irrelevant whether we conceptualize this as a lower male threshold for the release of dominance behaviour, a greater male drive for dominance, a greater male need for dominance, or a weaker male ego that needs shoring up by attainment of dominance and status. It is the reality of the male-female difference that matters, not the model used to explain the difference that any model must explain. Likewise, it is irrelevant why our species (and those from which we are descended) evolved the psychophysiological differentiation; all that matters for an explanation of universality is that the differentiation exists....

Physiology does not determine the actual behaviour required for dominance and attainment in any given society: that is socially determined. What physiology accounts for is the male's greater willingness to sacrifice the rewards of other motivations—the desire for affection, health, family life, safety, relaxation, vacation and the like—in order to attain dominance and status. This model makes clear why physiology need not be considered in a casual analysis of the behaviour of a given individual exception. At the same time physiology is necessary for analysis of the existence on a societal level of the universal institutions I discuss. Even the effects of virtually pure physiology expect many exceptions (as the six-foot-tall woman demonstrates). Dominance motivation no doubt has other causes—experiential and familial—in addition to the physiological causes and, for the exception, these may counteract the physiological factors.

When we speak of an entire society, the law of large numbers becomes determinative. The statistical, continuous, and quantitative reality of the male's greater dominance tendency becomes concretized on the social level in absolute, discrete, and qualitative terms. The statistical reality of the male's greater aggression becomes in its pure and exaggerated form: "men are aggressive (or dominant); women are passive (or submissive)." This leads to discrimination, often for the woman who is an exception and occasionally for every woman. Discrimination is possible precisely because the statistical reality makes the exception an exception, exposed to the possibility of discrimination. The six-foot-tall girl who wishes she were short lives in a world of boys who are praised for being six feet tall.

As long as societies have hierarchies, differentiated statuses, and intermixing of men and women, they will possess the only environmental cues necessary to elicit greater dominance and attainment behaviour from males. In utopian fantasy a society lacking hierarchy, status, and male-female relationships may be possible, but in the real world it is not. In the real world, societies have cultures. These cultures will value some things more than others and—particularly in the modern, bureaucratic society—some positions more than others. If male physiology is such that males are willing to sacrifice more for these things and positions, they will learn what is necessary and do what is necessary—whatever that may be in any given society—for dominance and attainment. There are other necessary conditions: it is not only gender that keeps a black woman from ruling the Republic of South Africa. Nevertheless, within any group possessing the other necessary conditions, dominance will go to those most willing to sacrifice for dominance and status (and social values will lead to such expectations)....

The male-female differentiation that I have discussed is the one for which the evidence is by far the most overwhelming. There are other differences that may well be functions of endocrine-central nervous system differentiation. The stereotype that sees logically abstract thinking as "thinking like a man" and psychological perception as "woman's intuition" without question reflects empirical realities; it is only the cause of these realities that is open to question. A score on the SAT mathematics aptitude section that puts a girl in the ninetieth percentile among girls places a boy only the sixty-eighth percentile among boys; among mathematically-precocious students (thirteen years old), a score of 700 is thirteen times more likely to be attained by a boy than a girl (with equal numbers of boys and girls with similar mathematical background taking the test). There also seems to be a linear relationship between the importance of logical abstraction to an area and the percent of those at the highest levels who are men; there has never been a woman at the highest level of mathematics, chess, or composing music (which is not thought of as a macho enterprise), while there have been many women of genius in literature and the performing arts....

Nothing I have written about patriarchy, male attainment, or male dominance implies (or precludes) males' better performing roles once they attain them. Whether the male tendencies increase performance or retard it is another issue (save for the fact that a position must be attained before it can be performed). Similarly, nothing I have written implies the desirability of any particular social or political program. "Is cannot imply ought," and no scientific analysis of how the world works can entail a subjective decision on which of two programs is preferable. We might accept what I have written and see this as demonstrating the need for an equal rights law limiting the male physiological advantage for attainment. Or we might see the same evidence as justifying a socialization system that provides clear role models by emphasizing the sex differences I discuss. Science is silent on such a choice.

Inevitabilities of Prejudice

Cynthia Fuchs Epstein

In this response to the previous article Epstein argues against Goldberg's methods and conclusions, and the sociobiological view of the world more generally. She draws on political and historical changes to suggest that the natural inequity view persists in large part because of people's desire to view the world in terms of sex differences.

Is there any reason to believe that patriarchy is more inevitable than anti-Semitism, child abuse, or any other mode of oppression that has been around for as long as anyone can remember? On the basis of his own experience, Aristotle believed that slavery was inevitable; and although it is still around in some countries, few reasonable people now believe it must be inevitable. Unfortunately, people with credentials for reasonableness, such as a new school of sociobiologists and their popularizers—among them Steven Goldberg—feel comfortable believing that the subordination of women is inevitable, programmed into human nature.

Many forms of oppression seem inevitable because they are so difficult to dislodge. History shows us that. It is easier to maintain oppression than to overthrow it. This is because when a group has a power advantage (which may emerge by chance, or historical accident), even if it is small, it may escalate rapidly if those in power can monopolize not only material resources but the avenues of communication as well. The Nazis did so effectively. Karl Marx cautioned that the owners of production were also the owners of the production of ideas. This means that the values and knowledge of a society usually reflect the views of those who rule, often by convincing those in subordinate statuses that they deserve what they get. The Nazis argued that they belonged to the "master race" and tried to build a science to prove it. They were less subtle than other rulers, but their case is instructive: beware the thesis of any powerful group that claims its power is derived solely from "divine right" or from its genes.

If anything is inevitable, it is change. Change in history is characteristic of human experience and reflects the human capacity to order and reorder it, to understand the processes of its ordering, and to sweep away old superstitions. As Robert K. Merton pointed out in the *American Journal of Sociology* in 1984: "What everyone should know from the history of thought is that what everyone knows turns out not to be so at all."

Some twelve years have passed since Steven Goldberg published his book, *The Inevitability of Patriarchy*, more than a decade which has produced thousands of studies of gender differences and similarities, an extensive re-analysis of the relationship and applicability of primate behaviour to human behaviour, and debate and analysis of sociobiological interpretation. Goldberg has offered us once again, a view of women's subordination as inevitable simply because it has always existed. The thesis, unchanged from his formulation of a decade ago, is uninformed about the rich body of scholarship that has been published—much of it disproving his assumptions about significant differences in men's and women's emotions, cognitive capacities, and situation in the structure of the social hierarchy. In these intervening years, there have also been changes in the statuses and roles of women in the United States and in other parts of the world—these also invalidate Goldberg's perspective on the constancy and universality of his observations about the subordination of women.

Women in the United States, as elsewhere, have been elected and appointed to positions of power. They have joined the ranks of the prestigious and the powerful in the domains of law and medicine, and are entering specialities and practices to which they were denied admission and discouraged from pursuing only a decade ago. Women are now judges at every level of the judiciary in the United States, as well as prosecutors in the courts engaging in adversarial and assertive behaviour, exhibiting what may be termed as "dominant behaviour." There is considerable evidence that women perform well, sometimes even better than do men, in examinations that determine admission to all fields in professional and graduate schools, where women constitute from a third to half of all students. Each year sees an increase in the number of women admitted to schools of engineering and science in spite of men's supposed greater social orientation toward careers in these fields.

Women have also become university professors and researchers and have thus been empowered to challenge many biased views about human nature and to fill gaps left by male scholars who have characteristically had little interest or inclination to do research in this field. Therefore, a revised view of what is "natural" or "inevitable" is part of the contemporary intellectual agenda.

Women are also making inroads in blue-collar technical work, heretofore denied them because of restrictions in apprenticeship programs made yet more difficult because of personal harassment. Women have experienced the same exclusionary mechanisms exercised against all minority groups who have had the audacity to compete with white males for the privileged positions guarded by "covenants" instituted by unions and ethnic clusters. According to a 1985 Rand Corporation research study by Linda Waite and Sue Berryman, *Women in Non-Traditional Occupations: Choice and Turnover*, women behave similarly to men in that they exhibit similar work force commitment and turnover rates once involved in non-traditional jobs such as those of the blue-collar crafts or in the army. These researchers emphasize that policies equalizing work conditions for men and women also equalize commitment to the job.

Increasing convergence of gender role behaviour is also seen in studies of crime. Girls' crime rates show increasing similarity to that of boys. Girls and boys both commit violent crimes and exhibit increasingly similar criminal histories.

Certainly much of the challenge and change is due to the women's movement and the insistence of women on their rights to equality. Sizable numbers of women in every sphere of society have taken an aggressive role in contesting the domination of men in personal, political, and intellectual life. Given the short period of time in which women have been active on their own behalf and in which they have succeeded in engaging the support of sympathetic men, their strides have been great both with regard to social rank and intellectual accomplishment.

This movement has evolved within the historical context still affected by centuries of oppression that have created and perpetuated the sense that women's inequality is natural. Yet no society, no social group, and especially no ruling group, has ever left gender hierarchy (nor any other form of hierarchy) to nature. It has not been women's incompetence or inability to read a legal brief, to perform brain surgery, to predict a bull market, or to make an intonation to the gods that has kept them from interesting and highly paid jobs. The root of discrimination against women, preventing their access to a variety of fields, has been a rule system replete with severe punishments for those who deviate from "traditional" roles. Access is now achieved through political and social action, and not at all through genetic engineering.

Sociobiologists, on the other hand, argue that the division of labour by sex is a biological rather than a social response. If this were so, sex-role assignments would not have to be coercive. Social groups do not actually depend on instinct or physiology to enforce social arrangements because they cannot reliably do so. Societies assign groups to be responsible for such social needs as food, shelter, and child care; nowhere do they depend on nature to meet these requirements. The types of work that men and women perform in each society are stipulated by society, allowing few individuals to make choices outside the prescribed range. The assignments are justified on the basis of ideologies claiming that they are just and reflect popular, cultural opinions that the arrangement is good (or that, if not, little can be done about it).

Such ideologies and popular views suppose that a fit exists between the job and worker—a fit that makes sense. This argument relies on the maintenance of gender differences. Division according to sex is reinforced by requirements that men and women dress differently (whether it is to don the veil or a skirt if female; and trousers or a *doti* if male), learn different skills (women's literacy rates are considerably lower than those of males in the Third World; in the Western world males and females still are "encouraged" to choose "sex-appropriate" subjects) and engage in different forms of activity. Violators are punished for infractions. Sometimes a raised eyebrow will keep a woman in line; in the extreme she may even face being stoned to death or burned alive (as in the recent outbreak of deaths over dowries in India).

The literal binding of women's feet or the constraint of their minds by law and social custom is part of the process by which the gender division of human beings perpetuates a two-class system. The hierarchy is kept in place subtly by the insistence that people behave in the way society's opinion moulders say they should. Thus, "ideal" roles mask real behaviour. If we look at what men and women actually do—or *can* do without the distorting mirror of "ideal" gender roles—there is a fundamental similarity in personalities, behaviour, and competence, given equal opportunity and social conditions. This is what the vast array of scholarship in psychology, sociology, and physiology has revealed in the last decade.

The research has been so extensive that it is impossible to summarize it here, although I shall review it in my forthcoming book, *Deceptive Distinctions*. By now, reviewers have re-analysed thousands of articles on gender differences in every attribution and behaviour imaginable. Despite what everyone believes, the similarities far outweigh the differences, even in considering aggression. As for the differences that census takers count—frequencies of women and men in different jobs and leisure activities—these clearly seem to be a result of social rules and habits....

Sex Hormones

The question relevant to gender in society is the meaning of differences. For Goldberg, there is an unbroken line between "androgen binding sites in the brain, rough and tumble play in infants, and the male domination of state, industry and the nuclear family." E.O. Wilson is more cautious: "we can go against it if we wish, but only at the cost of some efficiency." If the hormone testosterone is supposed to make men aggressive and thus fit for public office, "female" hormones and the cycles attached to them are seen as detrimental to women's participation in public life. Edgar Berman, medical adviser to the late Senator (and Vice-President) Hubert Humphrey, warned against women's participation in public affairs because of their "raging hormones." (Berman later published a book, *The Compleat Chauvinist*, in which he provided "biological evidence" for his views that menopausal women might create havoc if they held public office. Chapter titles from his book are: "The Brain That's Tame Lies Mainly in the Dame," "Testosterone, Hormone of Champions," and "Meno: The Pause that Depresses.") More recently, United Nations Ambassador Jeane Kirkpatrick reported that White House critics resisted her advancement into a higher political post because of the "temperament" she exhibited as a woman. No similar attributions of hormonal barriers to decision making posts have been offered for men, although they have been excused from infidelity that is explained in popular culture by "male menopause," or by the sociobiologists who see it as an evolutionary response of men.

Many sociobiologists of the Wilson school have been committed to a model of inequity as a product of the natural order, arguing that male domination (patriarchy) is the most adaptive form of society, one that has conferred an advantage on individuals who operate according to its precepts. This thesis—put forth by E.O. Wilson, Lionel Tiger, Robin Fox, and Steven Goldberg—maintains that the near universality of male dominance arose because of the long dependence of the human infant and as a result of hunting and gathering, the early modes of obtaining food. Male-based cooperation was expressed through dominance relations. Men guarded the bands and thus ensured survival. There was pressure on men to perfect hunting skills and on women to stay home and mind the children. Each sex would have developed cognitive abilities attached to these activities. A socially imposed hierarchical division of labour between the sexes gradually became genetically fixed....

Man the Hunter; Woman the Gatherer

In recent years, anthropologists have re-evaluated the perspective of "man the hunter," which long served as a model of the origins of human society.... Using this model, primatologists and anthropologists such as Sherwood Washburn and Irven De Vore in *the Social Life of Early Man* and Desmond Morris in *The Naked Ape* had reasoned that hunting, a male activity, was a creative turning point in human evolution—that it required intelligence to plan and to stalk game, and to make hunting and other tools. It also required social bonding of men, the use of language to cooperate in the hunt, and then the distribution of meat and the development of tools for hunting and cutting the meat. According to Washburn and Lancaster in Lee and De Vore's *Man the Hunter*, "In a very real sense our intellect, interests, emotions and basic social life—all are evolutionary products of the success of the hunting adaptation...." The question is, what merit is there to the model and the explanations derived from it?

Among others, Frances Dahlbert in *Woman the Gatherer* suggests the account can only be considered a "just-so story" in the light of new scholarship. Beginning in the 1960s, research on primates, on hunter-gatherer societies, and archaeological and fossil records made this story obsolete. For example, the paleoanthropological myth of man the hunter was deflated when the "killer ape" of Robert Ardrey's *The Hunting Hypothesis*, the presumed australopithecine forebear of humans, turned out to be predominantly vegetarian.... A greater challenge to the man the hunter model came from Sally

Linton in Sue Ellen Jacobs's *Women in Cross-Cultural Perspective*. Linton attacked the validity of theories of evolution that excluded or diminished women's contributions to human culture and society. She noted that women contribute the bulk of the diet in contemporary hunting and gathering societies, that small-game hunting practiced by both sexes preceded large-game hunting practiced by men, and that females as well as males probably devised tools for their hunting and gathering and some sort of carrying sling or net to carry babies. According to this view, the collaboration and cooperation of women was probably as important to the development of culture as that of men....

People persist in wanting to view the world in terms of sex differences. They insist that individuals conform to ideal roles and turn away from their real roles, common interests and goals, and from their mutual fate. These people disregard the obvious truth that most things that most people do most of the time can be performed equally well by either sex. The persistence of the view, as well as the persistence of physical and symbolic sex segregation, is created and maintained for a purpose, which is to maintain the privileges of men who predictably resist claims to the contrary. I suspect that the debates will continue and may do so as long as one group derives advantage from suppressing another. But evidence is mounting that supports equality between the sexes and which no truly reasonable people can continue to deny.

Woman's Place in Man's Life Cycle

Carol Gilligan

In this excerpt from her book In A Different Voice *Carol Gilligan challenges major developmental theorists from psychology with regard to their views on moral development and morality. Drawing on interviews with children and adults, Gilligan identifies differences in male and female worldviews and values, and in the kind of relationships they develop to support these. A guiding question for the reader: what are the differences between the masculine and feminine systems of valuing that emerge from her research?*

In the second act of *The Cherry Orchard*, Lopahin, a young merchant, describes his life of hard work and success. Failing to convince Madame Ranevskaya to cut down the cherry orchard to save her estate, he will go on in the next act to buy it himself. He is the self-made man who, in purchasing the estate where his father and grandfather were slaves, seeks to eradicate the "awkward, unhappy life" of the past, replacing the cherry orchard with summer cottages where coming generations "will see a new life." In elaborating this developmental vision, he reveals the image of man that underlies and supports his activity: "At times when I can't go to sleep, I think: Lord, thou gavest us immense forests, unbounded fields and the widest horizons, and living in the midst of them we should indeed be giants"—at which point, Madame Ranevskaya interrupts him, saying, "You feel the need for giants—They are good only in fairy tales, anywhere else they only frighten us."

Conceptions of the human life cycle represent attempts to order and make coherent the unfolding experiences and perceptions, the changing wishes and realities of everyday life. But the nature of such conceptions depends in part on the position of the observer. The brief excerpt from Chekhov's play suggests that when the observer is a woman, the perspective may be of a different sort. Different judgments of the image of man as giant imply different ideas about human development, different ways of imaging the human condition, different notions of what is of value in life.

At a time when efforts are being made to eradicate discrimination between the sexes in the search for social equality and justice, the differences between the sexes are being rediscovered in the social sciences. This discovery occurs when theories formerly considered to be sexually neutral in their scientific objectivity are found instead to reflect a consistent observational and evaluative bias. Then the presumed neutrality of science, like that of language itself, gives way to the recognition that the categories of knowledge are human constructions. The fascination with point of view that has informed the fiction of the twentieth century and the corresponding recognition of the relativity of judgment infuse our scientific understanding as well when we begin to notice how accustomed we have become to seeing life through men's eyes.

The penchant of developmental theorists to project a masculine image, and one that appears frightening to women, goes back at least to Freud (1905), who built his theory of psychosexual development around the experiences of the male child that culminate in the Oedipus complex. In the 1920s, Freud struggled to resolve the contradictions posed for his theory by the differences in female anatomy and the different configuration of the young girl's early family relationships. After trying to fit women into his masculine conception, seeing them as envying that which they missed, he came instead to acknowledge, in the strength and persistence of women's pre-Oedipal attachments to their mothers, a developmental difference. He considered this difference in women's development to be responsible for what he saw as women's developmental failure.

Having tied the formation of the superego or conscience to castration anxiety, Freud considered women to be deprived by nature of the impetus for a clear-cut Oedipal resolution. Consequently, women's superego—the heir to the Oedipus complex—was compromised: it was never "so inexorable, so impersonal, so independent of its emotional origins as we require it to be in men." From this observation of difference, that "for women the level of what is ethically normal is different from what it is in men," Freud concluded that women "show less sense of justice than men, that they are less ready to submit to the great exigencies of life, that they are more often influenced in their judgments by feelings of affection or hostility" (1925, pp. 257-258).

Thus a problem in theory became cast as a problem in women's development, and the problem in women's development was located in their experience of relationships. Nancy Chodorow (1974), attempting to account for "the reproduction within each generation of certain general and nearly universal differences that characterize masculine and feminine personality and roles," attributes these difference between the sexes not to anatomy but rather to "the fact that women, universally, are largely responsible for early child care." Because this early social environment differs for and is experienced differently by male and female children, basic sex differences recur in personality development. As a result, "in any given society, feminine personality comes to define itself in relation and connection to other people more than masculine personality does" (pp. 43-44).

In her analysis, Chodorow relies primarily on Robert Stoller's studies which indicate that gender identity, the unchanging core of personality formation, is "with rare exception firmly and irreversibly established for both sexes by the time a child is around three." Given that for both sexes the primary caretaker in the first three years of life is typically female, the interpersonal dynamics of gender identity formation are different for boys and girls. Female identity formation takes place in a context of ongoing relationship since "mothers tend to experience their daughters as more like, and continuous with, themselves." Correspondingly, girls, in identifying themselves as female, experience themselves as like their mothers, thus fusing the experience of attachment with the process of identity formation. In contrast, "mothers experience their sons as a male opposite," and boys, in defining themselves as masculine, separate their mothers from themselves, thus curtailing "their primary love and sense of empathic tie." Consequently, male development entails a "more emphatic individuation and a more defensive firming of experienced ego boundaries." For boys, but not girls, "issues of differentiation have become intertwined with sexual issues" (1978, pp. 150, 166-167).

Writing against the masculine bias of psychoanalytic theory, Chodorow argues that the existence of sex differences in the early experiences of individuation and relationship "does not mean that women have 'weaker' ego boundaries than men or are more prone to psychosis." It means instead that "girls emerge from this period with a basis for 'empathy' built into their primary definition of self in a way that boys do not." Chodorow thus replaces Freud's negative and derivative description of female psychology with a positive and direct account of her own: "Girls emerge with a stronger basis for experiencing another's needs or feelings as one's own (or of thinking that one is so experiencing another's needs and feelings). Furthermore, girls do not define themselves in terms of the denial of preoedipal relational modes to the same extent as do boys. Therefore, regression to these modes tends not to feel as much a basic threat to their ego. From very early, then, because they are parented by a person of the same gender...girls come to experience themselves as less differentiated than boys, as more continuous with and related to the external object-world, and as differently oriented to their inner object-world as well" (p. 167).

Consequently, relationships, and particularly issues of dependency, are experienced differently by women and men. For boys and men, separation and individuation are critically tied to gender identity since separation from the mother is essential for the development of masculinity. For girls and women, issues of femininity or feminine identity do not depend on the achievement of separation from the mother or on the progress of individuation. Since masculinity is defined through separation while femininity is defined through attachment, male gender identity is threatened by intimacy while female gender identity is threatened by separation. Thus males tend to have difficulty with relationships, while females tend to have problems with individuation. The quality of embeddedness in social interaction and personal relationships that characterizes women's lives in contrast to men's, however, becomes not only a descriptive difference but also a developmental liability when the milestones of childhood and adolescent development in the psychological literature are

markers of increasing separation. Women's failure to separate then becomes
by definition a failure to develop.

The sex differences in personality formation that Chodorow describes in
early childhood appear during the middle childhood years in studies of
children's games. Children's games are considered by George Herbert Mead
(1934) and Jean Piaget (1932) as the crucible of social development during the
school years. In games, children learn to take the role of the other and come
to see themselves through another's eyes. In games, they learn respect for rules
and come to understand the ways rules can be made and changed.

Janet Lever (1976), considering the peer group to be the agent of
socialization during the elementary school years and play to be a major activity
of socialization at that time, set out to discover whether there are sex
differences in the games that children play. Studying 181 fifth-grade, white,
middle-class children, ages ten and eleven, she observed the organization and
structure of their play-time activities. She watched the children as they played
at school during recess and in physical education class, and in addition kept
diaries of their accounts as to how they spent their out-of-school time. From
this study, Lever reports sex differences: boys play out of doors more often
than girls do; boys play more often in large and age-heterogeneous groups; they
play competitive games more often, and their games last longer than girls'
games. The last is in some ways the most interesting finding. Boys' games
appeared to last longer not only because they required a higher level of skill
and were thus less likely to become boring, but also because, when disputes
arose in the course of a game, boys were able to resolve the disputes more
effectively than girls: "During the course of this study, boys were seen
quarrelling all the time, but not once was a game terminated because of a
quarrel and no game was interrupted for more than seven minutes. In the
gravest debates, the final word was always, to 'repeat the play,' generally
followed by a chorus of 'cheater's proof'" (p. 482). In fact, it seemed that the
boys enjoyed the legal debates as much as they did the game itself, and even
marginal players of lesser size or skill participated equally in these recurrent
squabbles. In contrast, the eruption of disputes among girls tended to end the
game.

Thus Lever extends and corroborates the observations of Piaget in his study
of the rules of the game, where he finds boys becoming through childhood
increasingly fascinated with the legal elaboration of rules and the development
of fair procedures for adjudicating conflicts, a fascination that, he notes, does
not hold for girls. Girls, Piaget observes, have a more "pragmatic" attitude
toward rules, "regarding a rule as good as long as the game repaid it" (p.83).
Girls are more tolerant in their attitudes towards rules, more willing to make
exceptions, and more easily reconciled to innovations. As a result, the legal

sense, which Piaget considers essential to be moral development, "is far lees developed in little girls than in boys" (p.77).

The bias that leads Piaget to equate male development with child development also colours Lever's work. The assumption that shapes her discussion of results is that the male model is the better one since it fits the requirements for modern corporate success. In contrast, the sensitivity and care for the feelings of others that girls develop through their play have little market value and can even impede professional success. Lever implies that, given the realities of adult life, if a girl does not want to be left dependent on men, she will have to learn to play like a boy.

To Piaget's argument that children learn the respect for rules necessary for moral development by playing rule-bound games, Lawrence Kohlberg (1969) adds that these lessons are most effectively learned through the opportunities for role-taking that arise in the course of resolving disputes. Consequently, the moral lessons inherent in girls' play appear to be fewer than in boys'. Traditional girls' games like jump rope and hopscotch are turn-taking games, where competition is indirect since one person's success does not necessarily signify another's failure. Consequently, disputes requiring adjudication are less likely to occur. In fact, most of the girls whom Lever interviewed claimed that when a quarrel broke out, they ended the game. Rather than elaborating a system of rules for resolving disputes, girls subordinated the continuation of the game to the continuation of relationships.

Lever concludes that from the games they play, boys learn both the independence and the organizational skills necessary for coordinating the activities of large and diverse groups of people. By participating in controlled and socially approved competitive situations, they learn to deal with competition in a relatively forthright manner—to play with their enemies and to compete with their friends—all in accordance with the rules of the game. In contrast, girls' play tends to occur in smaller, more intimate groups, often the best-friend dyad, and in private places. This play replicates the social pattern of primary human relationships in that its organization is more cooperative. Thus, it points less, in Mead's terms, toward learning to take the role of "the generalized other," less toward the abstraction of human relationships. But it fosters the development of the empathy and sensitivity necessary for taking the role of "the particular other" and points more toward knowing the other as different from the self.

These observations about sex difference support the conclusion reached by David McClelland (1975) that "sex role turns out to be one of the most important determinants of human behaviour; psychologists have found sex differences in their studies from the moment they started doing empirical research." But since it is difficult to say "different" without saying "better" or "worse," since there is a tendency to construct a single scale of measurement, and since that scale has generally been derived from and standardized on the basis of men's interpretations of research data drawn predominantly or exclusively from studies of males, psychologists "have tended to regard male behaviour as the 'norm' and female behaviour as some kind of deviation from that norm" (p. 81). Thus, when women do not conform to the standards of psychological expectation, the conclusion has generally been that something is wrong with the women.

"It is obvious," Virginia Woolf says, "that the values of women differ very often from the values which have been made by the other sex" (1929, p. 76). Yet, she adds, "it is the masculine values that prevail." As a result, women come to question the normality of their feelings and to alter their judgments in deference to the opinion of others. In the nineteenth-century novels written by women, Woolf sees at work "a mind which was slightly pulled from the straight and made to alter its clear vision in deference to external authority." The same deference to the values and opinions of others can be seen in the judgments of twentieth century women. The difficulty women experience in finding or speaking publicly in their own voices emerges repeatedly in the form of qualification and self-doubt, but also in intimations of a divided judgment, a public assessment and private assessment which are fundamentally at odds.

Yet the deference and confusion that Woolf criticizes in women derive from the values she sees as their strength. Women's deference is rooted not only in their social subordination but also in the substance of their moral concern. Sensitivity to the needs of others and the assumption of responsibility for taking care lead women to attend to voices other than their own and to include in their judgment other points of view. Women's moral weakness, manifest in an apparent diffusion and confusion of judgment, is thus inseparable from women's moral strength, an overriding concern with relationships and responsibilities. The reluctance to judge may itself be indicative of the care and concern for others that infuse the psychology of women's development and are responsible for what is generally seen as problematic in its nature.

Thus women not only define themselves in a context of human relationship but also judge themselves in terms of their ability to care. Women's place in man's life cycle has been that of nurturer, caretaker, and helpmate, the weaver of those networks of relationships on which she in turn relies. But while women have thus taken care of men, men have, in their theories of psychological development, as in their economic arrangements, tended to assume or devalue that care. When the focus on individuation and individual achievement extends into adulthood and maturity is equated with personal autonomy, concern with relationships appears as a weakness of women rather than as a human strength (Miller, 1976).

The discrepancy between womanhood and adulthood is nowhere more evident than in the studies on sex-role stereotypes reported by Broverman,

Vogel, Broverman, Clarkson, and Rosenkrantz (1972). The repeated finding of these studies is that the qualities deemed necessary for adulthood—the capacity for autonomous thinking, clear decision making, and responsible action—are those associated with masculinity and considered undesirable as attributes of the feminine self. The stereotypes suggest a splitting of love and work that relegates expressive capacities to women while placing instrumental abilities in the masculine domain. Yet looked at from a different perspective, these stereotypes reflect a conception of adulthood that is itself out of balance, favouring the separateness of the individual self over connection to others, and leaning more toward an autonomous life of work than toward the interdependence of love and care.

The discovery now being celebrated by men in mid-life of the importance of intimacy, relationships, and care is something that women have known from the beginning. However, because that knowledge in women has been considered "intuitive" or "instinctive," a function of anatomy coupled with destiny, psychologists have neglected to describe its development. In my research, I have found that women's moral development centres on the elaboration of that knowledge and thus delineates a critical line of psychological development in the lives of both of the sexes. The subject of moral development not only provides the final illustration of the reiterative pattern in the observation and assessment of sex differences in the literature on human development, but also indicates more particularly why the nature and significance of women's development has been for so long obscured and shrouded in mystery.

The criticism that Freud makes of women's sense of justice, seeing it as compromised in its refusal of blind impartiality, reappears not only in the work of Piaget but also in that of Kohlberg. While in Piaget's account (1932) of the moral judgment of the child, girls are an aside, a curiosity to whom he devotes four brief entries in an index that omits "boys" altogether because "the child" is assumed to be male, in the research from which Kohlberg derives his theory, females simply do not exist. Kohlberg's (1958, 1981) six stages that describe the development of moral judgment from childhood to adulthood are based empirically on a study of eighty-four boys whose development Kohlberg has followed for a period of over twenty years. Although Kohlberg claims universality for his stage sequence, those groups not included in his original sample rarely reach his higher stages (Edwards, 1975; Holstein, 1976; Simpson, 1974). Prominent among those who thus appear to be deficient in moral development when measured by Kohlberg's scale are women, whose judgments seem to exemplify the third stage of his six-stage sequence. At this stage morality is conceived in interpersonal terms and goodness is equated with helping and pleasing others. This conception of goodness is considered by Kohlberg and Kramer (1969) to be functional in the lives of mature women insofar as their lives take place in the home. Kohlberg and Kramer imply that only if women enter the traditional arena of male activity will they recognize the inadequacy of this moral perspective and progress like men toward higher stages where relationships are subordinated to rules (stage four) and rules to universal principles of justice (stages five and six).

Yet herein lies a paradox, for the very traits that traditionally have defined the "goodness" of women, their care for and sensitivity to the needs of others, are those that mark them as deficient in moral development. In this version of moral development, however, the conception of maturity is derived from the study of men's lives and reflects the importance of individuation in their development. Piaget (1970), challenging the common impression that a developmental theory is built like a pyramid from its base in infancy, points out that a conception of development instead hangs from its vertex of maturity, the point toward which progress is traced. Thus, a change in the definition of maturity does not simply alter the description of the highest stage but recasts the understanding of development, changing the entire account.

When one begins with the study of women and derives developmental constructs from their lives, the outline of a moral conception different from that described by Freud, Piaget, or Kohlberg begins to emerge and informs a different description of development. In this conception, the moral problem arises from conflicting responsibilities rather than from competing rights and requires for its resolution a mode of thinking that is contextual and narrative rather than formal and abstract. This conception of morality as concerned with the activity of care centres moral development around the understanding of responsibility and relationships, just as the conception of morality as fairness ties moral development to the understanding of rights and rules.

This different construction of the moral problem by women may be seen as the critical reason for their failure to develop within the constraints of Kohlberg's system. Regarding all constructions of responsibility as evidence of a conventional moral understanding, Kohlberg defines the highest stages of moral development as deriving from a reflective understanding of human rights. That the morality of rights differs from the morality of responsibility in its emphasis on separation rather than connection, in its consideration of the individual rather than the relationship as primary, is illustrated by two responses to interview questions about the nature of morality. The first comes from a twenty-five-year-old man, one of the participants in Kohlberg's study:

> [*What does the word morality mean to you?*] Nobody in the world knows the answer. I think it is recognizing the right of the individual, the rights of other individuals, not interfering with those rights. Act as fairly as you would have them treat you. I think it is basically to preserve the human being's right to

existence. I think that is the most important. Secondly, the human being's right to do as he pleases, again without interfering with somebody else's rights.

[How have your views on morality changed since the last interview?] I think I am more aware of an individual's rights now. I used to be looking at it strictly from my point of view, just for me. Now I think I am more aware of what the individual has a right to.

Kohlberg (1973) cites this man's response as illustrative of the principled conception of human rights that exemplifies his fifth and sixth stages. Commenting on the response, Kohlberg says: "Moving to a perspective outside of that of his society, he identifies morality with justice (fairness, rights, the Golden Rule), with recognition of the rights of others as these are defined naturally or intrinsically. The human's being right to do as he pleases without interfering with somebody else's rights is a formula defining rights prior to social legislation" (pp. 29-30).

The second response comes from a woman who participated in the rights and responsibilities study. She also was twenty-five and, at the time, a third-year law student:

[Is there really some correct solution to moral problems, or is everybody's opinion equally right?] No, I don't think everybody's opinion is equally right. I think that in some situations there may be opinions that are equally valid, and one could conscientiously adopt one of several courses of action. But there are other situations in which I think there are right and wrong answers, that sort of inhere in the nature of existence, of all individuals here who need to live with each other to live. We need to depend on each other, and hopefully it is not only a physical need but a need of fulfilment in ourselves, that a person's life is enriched by cooperating with other people and striving to live in harmony with everybody else, and to that end, there are right and wrong, there are things which promote that end and that move away from it, and in that way it is possible to choose in certain cases among different courses of action that obviously promote or harm that goal.

[Is there a time in the past when you would have thought about these things differently?] Oh, yeah, I think that I went through a time when I thought that things were pretty relative, that I can't tell you what to do and you can't tell me what to do, because you've got your conscience and I've got mine.

> [*When was that?*] When I was in high school. I guess that it just
> sort of dawned on me that my own ideas changed, and because
> my own judgment changed, I felt I couldn't judge another
> person's judgment. But now I think even when it is only the
> person himself who is going to be affected, I say it is wrong to the
> extent it doesn't cohere with what I know about human nature
> and what I know about you, and just from what I think is true
> about the operation of the universe, I could say I think you are
> making a mistake.
> [*What led you to change, do you think?*] Just seeing more of life,
> just recognizing that there are an awful lot of things that are
> common among people. There are certain things that you come
> to learn promote a better life and better relationships and more
> personal fulfilment than other things that in general tend to do
> the opposite, and the things that promote these things, you would
> call morally right.

This response also represents a personal reconstruction of morality following
a period of questioning and doubt, but the reconstruction of moral
understanding is based not on the primacy and universality of individual rights,
but rather on what she describes as a "very strong sense of being responsible
to the world." Within this construction, the moral dilemma changes from how
to exercise one's rights without interfering with the rights of others to how "to
lead a moral life which includes obligations to myself and my family and people
in general." The problem then becomes one of limiting responsibilities without
abandoning moral concern. When asked to describe herself, this woman says
that she values "having other people that I am tied to, and also having people
that I am responsible to. I have a very strong sense of being responsible to the
world, that I can't just live for my enjoyment, but just the fact of being in the
world gives me an obligation to do what I can to make the world a better place
to live in, no matter how small a scale that may be on." Thus while Kohlberg's
subject worries about people interfering with each other's rights, this woman
worries about "the possibility of omission, of your not helping others when you
could help them."

The issue that this woman raises is addressed by Jane Loevinger's fifth
"autonomous" stage of ego development, where autonomy, placed in a context
of relationships, is defined as modulating an excessive sense of responsibility
through the recognition that other people have responsibility for their own
destiny. The autonomous stage in Loevinger's account (1970) witnesses a
relinquishing of moral dichotomies and their replacement with "a feeling for
the complexity and multifaceted character of real people and real situations"
(p. 6). Whereas the rights conception of morality that informs Kohlberg's

principled level (stages five and six) is geared to arriving at an objectively fair or just resolution to moral dilemmas upon which all rational persons could agree, the responsibility conception focuses instead on the limitations of any particular resolution and describes the conflicts that remain.

Thus it becomes clear why a morality of rights and non-interference may appear frightening to women in its potential justification of indifference and unconcern. At the same time, it becomes clear why, from a male perspective, a morality of responsibility appears inconclusive and diffuse, given its insistent contextual relativism. Women's moral judgments thus elucidate the pattern observed in the description of the developmental differences between the sexes, but they also provide an alternative conception of maturity by which these differences can be assessed and their implications traced. The psychology of women that has consistently been described as distinctive in its greater orientation toward relationships and interdependence implies a more contextual mode of judgment and a different moral understanding given the differences in women's conceptions of self and morality, women bring to the life cycle a different point of view and order human experience in terms of different priorities.

The elusive mystery of women's development lies in its recognition of the continuing importance of attachment in the human life cycle. Woman's place in man's life cycle is to protect this recognition while the developmental litany intones the celebration of separation, autonomy, individuation, and natural rights.

References

Broverman, I., Vogel, S., Broverman, D., Clarkson, F., and Rosenkrantz, P. "Sex-role Stereotypes: A Current Appraisal." *Journal of Social Issues* 28 (1972): 59-78.

Chodorow, Nancy. "Family Structure and Feminine Personality." In M. Z. Rosaldo and L. Lamphere, eds., *Woman, Culture and Society*. Stanford: Stanford University Press, 1974.

————. *The Reproduction of Mothering*. Berkeley: University of California Press, 1978.

Edwards, Carolyn P. "Society Complexity and Moral Development: A Kenyan Study." *Ethos* 3 (1975): 505-527.

Freud, Sigmund. *The Standard Edition of the Complete Psychological Works of Sigmund Freud*, trans. and ed. James Strachey. London: The Hogarth Press, 1961.

————. *Three Essays on the Theory of Sexuality* (1905). Vol. VII.

————. "Some Psychical Consequences of the Anatomical Distinction Between the Sexes" (1925). Vol. XIX.

Holstein, Constance. "Development of Moral Judgment: A longitudinal Study of Males and Females." *Child Development* 47 (1976): 51-61.

Kohlberg, Lawrence. "The Development of Modes of Thinking and Choices in Years 10 to 16." Ph.D. Diss., University of Chicago, 1958.

————. "Stage and Sequence: The Cognitive-Development Approach to Socialization." In D. A. Goslin, ed., *Handbood of Socialization Theory and Research Chicago*: Rand McNally, 1969.

————. "Continuities and Discontinuities in Childhood and Adult Moral Development Revisited." In *Collected Papers on Moral Development and Moral Education*. Moral Education Research Foundation, Harvard University, 1973.

————. *The philosophy of Moral Development*. San Francisco: Harper and Row, 1981.

Kohlberg, L., and Kramer, R. "Continuities and Discontinuities in Child and Adult Moral Development." *Human Development* 12 (1969): 93-120.

Lever, Janet. "Sex Differences in the Games Children Play." *Social Problems* 23 (1976): 478-487.

Loevinger, Jane, and Wessler, Ruth. *Measuring Ego Development*. San Francisco: Jossey-Bass, 1970.

McClelland, David C. *Power: The Inner Experience*. New York: Irvington, 1975.

Mead, George Herbert. *Mind, Self, and Society*. Chicago: University of Chicago Press, 1934.

Miller, Jean Baker. *Toward a New Psychology of Women*. Boston: Beacon Press, 1976.

Piaget, Jean. *The Moral Judgment of the Child* (1932). New York: The Free Press, 1965.

————. *Structuralism*. New York: Basic Books, 1970.

Simpson, Elizabeth L. "Moral Development Research: A Case Study of Scientific Cultural Bias." *Human Development* 17 (1974): 81-106.

Stoller, Robert, J. "A Contribution to the Study of Gender Identity." *International Journal of Psycho-analysis* 45 (1964): 220-226.

Woolf, Virginia. *A Room of One's Own*. New York: Harcourt, Brace and World, 1929.

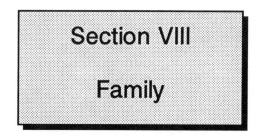

Section VIII

Family

The Children of Narcissus

Christopher Lasch

Are contemporary changes in family life and child rearing beneficial or detrimental to children?

With more than a hint of satisfaction, a feature story in the Toronto *Globe and Mail* announced in February 1981 that the "parent-hood mystique has gone into an irrevocable decline." The feminist movement, improved contraceptives, and the "necessity of the two-income family" have allegedly made the financial and emotional burdens of child rearing increasingly unattractive to a new generation of adults eager to savour the joys of leisure, travel, and sexual self-discovery. No longer defensive about their choice not to have children, the educated professional classes, according to this account, see through "pro-natalist" ideologies and put the "burden of proof" on those who plunge recklessly into parenthood, not on those who sensibly abstain.

A schoolteacher, quoted in this report, notes that "children can be fun, in small doses, but they can also be unrelentingly demanding. They don't have much time for anyone's fantasies but their own." A university instructor points out that children "turn your partner into a mother, one of the most depressing forms a human being can assume."

In his study of the baby-boom generation, published in 1980, Landon Jones attributed the abandonment of the "procreation ethic" to feminism, consumerism, and the emergence of a new set of public attitudes toward children, which "vary between benign neglect and [outright] hostility." Children have fallen "out of favour," according to Jones. Neither parenthood nor marriage commands the unthinking acceptance that produced the baby boom in the first place. At best, they appear to present two "options" out of many. The devaluation of the family, Jones thought, would prove "one of the most enduring and irreversible acts of the boom generation."

Today things no longer look quite so simple. Not that the demographic trends of the 1970s have reversed themselves. People continue to marry later than they married twenty-five years ago. They have fewer children. Many have no children at all. Wives continue to work. The divorce rate continues to climb. What has changed is that people have begun to understand the costs of the new way of life, especially the cost paid by children.

Glib optimism no longer commands automatic assent. A few years ago, authorities on the family assured us that children are better off when their parents divorce than when they bicker endlessly; that divorce disrupts children's lives no more painfully than the death of a parent, which used to break up families, allegedly, at the same rate; and that nuclear families in any case produce neurotic, acquisitive, and overly competitive children. Such reassurance no longer carries much conviction. People have lost the illusion that they can have the best of everything. Instead of talking about "options," they talk about "trade-offs." This kind of talk has a glibness of its own, since it tends to give equal weight to alternatives that are often incommensurable and to assign this weight a cash value. But at least it recognizes the need to choose between competing sets of desirable goods.

Thus although it may be a good thing for women to achieve economic independence from men, it is also a good thing for children to have mothers, not a series of casual caretakers. It may be a good thing for a man and a woman to break up an intolerable marriage, but it is also a good thing for children to have two parents. Thanks to a number of sensible reports on family life and child rearing, including the new books by Vance Packard and Marie Winn, and to the general climate of diminishing expectations, we have reached the point where it is possible to make such observations without inviting accusations of anti-feminism and reactionary "nostalgia."

Without indulging in alarmism or deploring the gains made by women, we can nevertheless say that children have paid a heavy price for the new freedom enjoyed by adults. They spend too much time watching television, which adults use as a baby sitter and as a substitute for parental guidance and discipline. They spend too many of their days in child-care centres, most of which offer the most perfunctory kind of care. They eat junk food, listen to music, read junk comics, and spend endless hours playing video games, because their parents are too busy or too harried to offer the proper nourishment for their minds and bodies. They attend third-rate schools and get third-rate moral advice from their elders.

Many parents and educators, having absorbed a therapeutic morality and a misplaced idea of egalitarianism, hesitate to "impose" their moral standards on the young or to appear overly "judgmental." According to a psychiatric study cited by Marie Winn in her book *Children Without Childhood*, "The majority of the parents shy away from firmly stating that they, rather than children, should set the rules, and some parents state that *everyone* should be equal." The parents of an eleven-year-old boy who pushed his mother into a door, broke one of the bones in her back, and kicked her in the face while she lay on the floor told an interviewer who asked for a moral judgment on the child's action, "It was neither right nor wrong."

Needless to say, these attitudes are by no means universal. In a comparative study of day-care centres, Valerie Polakow Suransky includes a chapter on a low-income nursery school that caters largely to black children, where the black teachers, assisted by three grandmothers, practice a "traditional discipline of firmness and love," as the director puts it. Their supervision combines physical affection and unambiguous moral guidance. The adults do not hesitate to break up fights among the children, to label actions right or wrong, or to insist on the respect due themselves as adults; but neither do they hold themselves pedagogically aloof from the children or attempt to set a model of emotional restraint. The following scene provides a vivid glimpse of a moral atmosphere worlds apart from the atmosphere that prevails in many middle-class schools and households: One morning, Cedric and Benjamin were hitting each other, pulling hair and punching hard. They were left to "fight it out." However, when the fight escalated, Teacher Pat walked to the closet and brought out a box of beanbags. She threw one at each child and said: "Here, throw this at each other." Within minutes the children were laughing, engaged in a boisterous "beanbag fight." They were joined by other children, partitions were drawn back, and soon all thirty children, the staff, and three seventy-five-year-old grandmothers were ducking, throwing, and whooping with laughter.

Compare the contrasting situation Suransky found in a Summerhillian school, where the children are allowed to bully each other and the teachers and where, accordingly, "the 'survival of the fittest' appeared to be the norm." Dogmatically committed to "creativity" and "free expression," the adults in this experimental, progressive school never offered an opinion of their own or even an emotional response that might help the children find their bearings in a confusing world. These adults "appeared to be intimidated," Suransky writes, by their anti-authoritarian ideology.

Even more disturbing than permissive ideologies, as a sign of the prevailing indifference to the needs of children, is the growing inclination to exploit them sexually in movies and advertising, perhaps also in actual practice. There is some evidence that incest is on the rise. Whether it is or not, "a whole flock of sex researchers, academic sexual radicals, and other influential individuals and groups have been pushing the idea," as Vance Packard notes in *Our Endangered Children*, that incest may lead to "real intimacy within the family at a time when our world is becoming increasingly depersonalized" and that "antiquated ideas about incest today are comparable to the fears of masturbation a century ago."

The idea of "salutary incest" is one of the most revealing signs of the fatalism about children that runs through our culture today: the feeling that adults are helpless in dealing with children, powerless to offer them a sheltered space to grow up in or to protect them from the devastating impact of the adult world, and therefore not responsible for failing to protect them or even for exploiting them in ways that make nineteenth-century child labour look almost benign by comparison.

Our society's fatalism about children tries to disguise itself as a liberation of the child from oppressive adult authority, just as the weakening of marital ties attempts to masquerade as a healthy new diversity of family types and "alternative life styles." Betty Friedan expresses the consensus of enlightened opinion when she urges her readers to reject the "obsolete image of the family," to "acknowledge the diversity of the families people live in now," and to understand that a family, after all—in the words of the American Home Economic Association—consists simply of "two or more persons who share values and goals, and have commitments to one another over time." This anaemic, euphemistic definition of the family reminds us of the validity of George Orwell's contention that it is a sure sign of trouble when things can no longer be called by their right names and described in plain, forthright speech. The plain fact of the matter—and this is borne out of the very statistics cited to prove the new pluralism of family types and the expanding array of choices—is that all these so-called alternative arrangements, the ones that matter anyway, arise out of the ruins of the family, not as an improvement on it. "Blended" or "reconstituted" families, so called, result from divorce, as do "single-parent families."

As for the other "alternative" forms of the family, so highly touted by enlightened ideologues—single "families," gay "marriages," and so on—it is absurd to consider them as families and would still be absurd if they were important statistically, as they are not. They may be perfectly legitimate living arrangements, but they are arrangements chosen by people who prefer not to live in families at all, with all their unavoidable constraints.

The attempt to redefine the family as a purely voluntary arrangement (one among many "alternative" living arrangements) grows out of the modern delusion that you can keep all your options open all the time, avoiding any constraints or demands as long as you don't make any demands of your own or "impose your own values" on others, and moreover that you can not only avoid the "trap" of involuntary association but enjoy its advantages at the same time.

Just as we try to excuse marital breakdown as social progress and cultural pluralism, so we try to minimize the effects on children. Contrary to progressive orthodoxy, however, children experience the divorce of their parents, according to recent studies, as a "devastating blow." Recent studies present a great deal of evidence that ought to disconcert those who refuse to acknowledge the traumatic effect of divorce on children. According to Winn's summary of recent research, divorce "causes men and women to regress to a child-like state of helplessness and dependence" and puts a double burden on children. "Not only must they cope with their own painful feelings of loss and resentment, but they must at the same time deal with the helplessness and misery that their parents cannot successfully hide from them." After summarizing the evidence documenting the devastating effects of divorce on children, Packard concludes that the "reduction of our spectacularly high rate of divorce where the children are involved should be considered as a national challenge."

Children suffer not only from the divorce epidemic and from all the other tangible and immediate forms of neglect documented in recent books but from a subtle change in the cultural climate—a new "coolness toward child-raising," as Packard puts it, that expresses itself in the decision not to have children but also in a persuasive cultural prejudice against the young, which has replaced the sentimentalism of earlier times.

Packard speaks of an "anti-child movement," an attempt to ban children from apartment houses and restaurants, to replace family outings with cocktail parties restricted to adults, and to keep children and adults in "different worlds." The anti-child movement, Winn thinks, has the effect of abrogating childhood. Social conditions today encourage a "new precocity." A great many social and cultural changes combine to plunge children into the adult world before they are ready to understand it or deal with it. Packard, on the other hand, stresses the segregation of a childhood, the prolonged dependence of children in industrial societies, and the lack of useful work available to young people.

The conclusions are not necessarily incompatible. As Bruno Bettelheim explains in his book on fairy tales, *The Uses of Enchantment*, misguided attempts to substitute a more realistic and enlightened morality for the vindictive, punitive sense of justice embodied in fairy tales or to overcome fairy tales' loathsome picture of adult sexuality by propaganda about "healthy" sex actually increase the emotional distance between children and adults. To confront children with information for which they are emotionally unprepared, according to Bettelheim, undermines children's confidence in adult authority. "The child comes to feel that he and they live in different spiritual worlds." Premature exposure to modern scientific rationalism and to adult sexuality "makes for a discontinuity between the generations, painful for both parent and child."

If Bettelheim is right, the question of whether children suffer from a "new precocity" or from an unnecessarily prolonged period of economic and emotional dependence—equally plausible interpretations of contemporary childhood, advanced by critics of current child-rearing practices—is probably misconceived. Neither way of thinking about the condition of children captures the quality of childhood in a society that appears indifferent to the needs not merely of children but of future generations in general. The neglect of children is part of a broader pattern of neglect that includes the reckless exploitation of natural resources, the pollution of the air and water, and the willingness to risk "limited" nuclear wars as an instrument of national policy.

Instead of achieving the best of everything, we have managed to devise a set of family patterns of which it can fairly be said that they combine the worst features of earlier systems of child rearing, the repressive systems that we thought we had successfully put behind us. Our new patterns of child rearing reinforce the social segregation of the young that has always been so characteristic of bourgeois society, thereby depriving children of exposure to adult conversation, of practical experience of the world, and of participation in the community's work life.

On the other hand, the new arrangements expose the child all too early to the sexual life of adults, sometimes in the misguided hope of spreading a scientifically based sexual enlightenment, sometimes (as in the case of the mass media) with the deliberate intention of titillating a youthful audience. In many preindustrial societies, children are similarly confronted very early with the "facts of life," but seldom with such complete disregard for their capacity to absorb them. The promiscuous sociability described by historians of the old regime in Europe may have awakened a precocious sexual curiosity in children, but modern education and mass culture probably go much further in plunging children into the sexual dimension of adult experience before they are ready to understand it or deal with it. Nor does this sexual indoctrination succeed in its object—the object avowed by educators, anyway—of easing the child's transition into the adult world.

If we pay attention to honest reports of the facts about contemporary family life and child rearing, I think we have to admit that they undercut the complacent assumption that modern society, having freed itself from the provincial moralities of the past, is entering a new age of enlightenment. The attempt to combine careers and family life, to achieve "open marriage," and to raise sexually liberated and non-sexist children has turned out to be far more difficult than the liberators of the 1960s and 1970s imagined. Thus a number of communes have discovered, as the director of one of them puts it, that "when responsibility is divided up among so many individuals no one is responsible and chaos ensues." The leader of another commune declares, "We don't go along with the idea that kids are supposed to be raised by a whole bunch of other folks. That makes for crazy kids."

The "parenthood mystique," the "irrevocable decline" of which appeared certain only a few years ago, seems to be enjoying something of a revival, often in the most unlikely places. Let us hope that it soon spreads from Steve Gaskin's communal farm in Tennessee to Scarsdale and Shaker Heights.

Thinking About the Future

Meg Luxton

While few would disagree that the family in North America is in transition, there is considerable debate about the significance of these changes and the future of families. In this article Luxton points out that the debate over the family is bound up with the deeper question of how society generally should be organized. The debate has also been heavily influenced by an ideology of familialism. If we liberate the discussion from this prevailing ideology and look more carefully at the reality of families today, what does the future hold?

Introduction

There is no question but that families are now in a state of very rapid transformation. Since the early 1960s there have been dramatic increases in divorce rates, the number of single-parent families, teenage pregnancies, individuals co-habiting without getting married, openly lesbian and gay couples, the ages at which people are having their first child, the number of people having only one or two children, and married women's employment. All of these changing statistical patterns reflect profound changes in people's experience of daily life. As a result, much effort is devoted to the task of interpreting the significance of these changes. Why are they occurring? Will they continue to occur, and will they in turn provoke further, as yet unanticipated, changes? What will the consequences be? All of these changes raise important questions about the future of families.

These questions get raised in a range of different ways, from individuals contemplating their personal future to government legislators and policy analysts designing legislation that can shape the course of an entire nation for several generations. So these are not abstract academic issues but life-and-death concerns affecting everyone. Questions that are asked about what is happening to families today and what such changes will mean for the future reflect both deep confusion about what is possible and profound social disagreement about the way society *should* be organized. Contending visions are at stake, of how we want our future to be.

In this section I explore a number of questions about family life in the future. Because the shape of the future results from developments in the present, I argue that in thinking about families of the future, we must determine first what we include in the concept of "family." Then we can assess what currently exists, what the trends are, and where they might lead. We can uncover varying visions of the future, and anticipate what the world might look like if those visions came to pass.

The Ideology Of "The Family"

One of the reasons why it is so difficult for people to discuss visions of future family life is that there is little consensus about what "the family" actually is. As Michele Barrett and Mary McIntosh (1982) have shown, to understand "the family" we have to differentiate between *ideology* and the actual ways in which people interact, co-reside, have sexual relations, have babies, marry, divorce, raise children and so on. In other words, "the family" exists in two quite distinct forms: as "familialism," a widespread and deeply embedded ideology about how people *ought* to live; and as economic and social groups which in fact organize domestic and personal life (Gittins, 1985). The ideology of "familialism" is a belief system which argues that the best way for adults to live is in nuclear families; that is, as a socially and legally recognized heterosexual couple (a woman and man) who normally expect to have children (Rapp, 1978). The ideal way for children to be raised is in such a family, according to this belief system (Bloom 1976; Blumenfeld 1976), the nuclear family being thought to provide the most stable, intimate, loving environment possible (Spock, 1968). The more people live in ways that deviate from this idealized model, the less likely they are, again according to this ideology, to get intimacy, love, and stability, and the more likely they are to be in some way socially unstable (Riley, 1983). This ideology also assumes that the prevailing organization of family life profoundly affects the total organization of society. Thus, it is argued, the more that people deviate from the nuclear family, the more the fundamental organization of contemporary society is undermined.

Basic to the ideology of familialism are patriarchal definitions and ideals of how men, women, and children should behave. While men are defined primarily by their occupation (the origin of many surnames, e.g., in English, Smith, Taylor, Steward), women and children have for centuries been defined by their relation to the kinship system through men (taking the surname of their fathers and husbands) (Gittins, 1985: 35). Because "the family," by definition, has referred to the authority of the male head over his wife and children, the ideology of the nuclear family implies male power over women and children and a wife's subordination to her husband (Weber, 1967).

This ideology about the way we *should* live shapes our lives profoundly. First, most individuals carry some form of that belief system around with them throughout their lives, and it affects the way they assess their own circumstances (Barrett and McIntosh, 1982). Too often, people marry and have children, not because they are certain that is what they want, but because they feel they should. Other people who have clearly chosen a different route are still affected by this ideology, and may have residual anxieties about whether their decision was actually the right one.

Second, the ideology of familialism permeates the assumptions made about and for other people. So young women will be asked by their well-intentioned relatives whether they have found "Mr. Right" yet, and young men will be asked when they are going to find a nice "girl" and settle down. A daughter's husband who she has married after a short acquaintance will be much more welcome at family gatherings than another daughter's female lover and companion of 20 years. Someone in hospital for a major illness is permitted to have "immediate family" visit, while friends are excluded, even though these friends may in fact provide the only real love and caring in the patient's life and the "proper" family may be estranged and uncaring. In schools it may be assumed that children who do not live in nuclear families will be less able to perform well and more likely to present behaviour problems. Children who actually do have problems may find them attributed to their "abnormal" domestic situation rather than to perceptual difficulties (Griffith, 1983).

Third, the ideology of familialism has shaped social policy and government legislation for much of the 20th century (Eichler, 1983). For example, in many workplaces employees are able to obtain benefits for spouses of the opposite sex but not for those of the same sex. Women can get maternity leave if they give birth or adopt but not if their woman partner gives birth and both are going to be closely involved in raising the child. Married individuals cannot obtain a mortgage without their spouse's involvement, even when the couple keep entirely separate finances. Income tax laws are similarly based on certain assumptions about family. Neighbourhood zoning laws and building codes, as well as the types of housing constructed, impose material constraints on domestic arrangements (Hayden, 1981). For example, in certain areas, *by law*, only people legally related to each other are allowed to share a house. Though a married woman and man and their children can share a dwelling in such areas, three friends cannot.

Controversies About "The Family"

The prevailing ideology of familialism, or the concept of "the family," has recently become a centre of major controversy. The most serious challenge to it comes from reality—the way people actually organize their domestic and personal lives. Yet, while we have quite exact figures on the number of people employed in the labour force and what their earning are, we have very little information about the actual relations between co-habiting individuals (Rubin, 1976), about how housework is done, or who pays for what in a household

(Luxton, 1980; Luxton and Rosenberg, 1986). Precisely because such information on how people actually live is so difficult to obtain, the myths about family life are hard to challenge. However, increasing evidence reveals that, while it is most likely that the greatest number of people will live in a nuclear family for some part of their lives, they may well do so for only a few years; at any given time the majority of the population does not live that way.

Another challenge to the prevailing ideology has emerged with the revelation that the nuclear family is often not the centre of love and security its proponents claim. For example, one of the most prevalent myths about "the family" is that young children grow best when raised exclusively by their (biological) parents and that other ways of raising children, in group daycare, for instance, are only second best. And yet there is no evidence to support this myth at all (Gallager Ross, 1978). Indeed, the few studies that have been done suggest that daycare is excellent for children (Zigler and Gordon, 1983); and there is evidence to show that the nuclear family is too often the site of violence against children, of sexual assault and psychological deformation (Guberman and Wolfe, 1985). Similarly, the idea that women will find their greatest pleasure and satisfaction as wives and mothers has been undermined by women articulating needs for additional sources of self-worth (Friedan, 1963), and is overtly contradicted by the evidence of violence against women in the home (MacLeod, 1980) and by married women's persistent economic vulnerability (Wilson, 1986).

Another powerful challenge to the prevailing family ideology comes from increasing numbers of women who, in their personal lives, have challenged the authority of patriarchal ideology and domination and are insisting on their rights to equality both in the paid workplace within their families (FitzGerald et al., 1982; Briskin and Yanz, 1983). Collectively, the feminist movement has played a part in revealing the differences between the ideology of the ideal family and the lived reality of daily life (Luxton and Rosenberg, 1986: 10-11). Feminists demand that society as a whole provide quality social services (such as health care and childcare) for all people, rather than expecting individuals or families (usually, in practice, women) to bear these costs themselves. Many feminists demand that the term "family" be stretched to include any adult-child groupings such as single parents, lesbian or gay parents, and all intimate co-habitating or self-consciously committed support groups including childless couples, communes, or networks of friends. Such demands raise the issue of public legitimization for people whose existence in the past was always private, sometimes secret. All of them challenge the concept of family which dominates ideologically.

In reaction, conservatives have organized to defend the legitimacy of familial ideology and to attempt to enforce conformity to it. These anti-feminist "backlash" movements, the so-called "pro-family" movements (such as REAL

Women), derive some popular appeal from fears evoked by the new definitions of the family, especially as most people's experience with these ideas come through the media's distorted images.* But today's anti-feminism (like its earlier versions) is also closely linked with hostility to the principle of government provision of social services; it disguises a call for cutbacks by claiming that "the family" (meaning unpaid women) is the best group for providing care. They oppose government intervention in business decisions (e.g., regarding affirmative action and equal pay, health and safety) and in education; they are even averse to the promotion of sexual and racial equality. Indeed, conservatives have used family politics to call for a re-privatization which is a wholly political project, and which demonstrates the links between support for private property and free enterprise on the one hand, and support for the nuclear family's structure of breadwinner husband/dependent wife on the other. It includes not only bolstering the authority of the husband/father as family head, but also increased autonomy for corporate heads—whose control over their private domains in each case has been in dispute for at least a decade (Gordon and Hunter, 1978).

It is worth noting that, though current, conservative politics of "the family" are not new. Concerns about the future of the family are often used to mask various political intentions. They have reappeared with regularity in the history of Western Europe, the United States and Canada, especially at times when "underclasses" (such as women, working-class people, socialists or communists, blacks, or people of the First Nations in Canada) are perceived as politically mobilized and therefore dangerous. The discontent of such groups is often attributed to failures in their family life, rather than to the material conditions that motivate their rebellion. In the past several centuries there has been constant flux in *all* social institutions, including families. Equally constantly, community leaders, both religious and secular, have worried about the implications of aspirations for change, and have predicted general doom as a result.**

At present, a dual concern, about the apparent "crisis of the family" and about the "future of the family," prevails in much of contemporary political discourse. The Canadian government formally recognized the importance of

---

* For a critique of media representations of the women's movement, see the 1981 video *Rising Up Strong* by Lorna Weir and Linda Briskin, DEC Films, Toronto).

** For a powerful fictionalized projection of that position into the future, see Margaret Atwood's novel, *The Handmaid's Tale*. Toronto: McClelland and Stewart, 1985).

this controversy in the 1986 Speech From the Throne, which promised to place "the family" on the formal political agenda. "The family" is at the centre of a major social controversy, as various interest groups compete to ensure that their model of the family wins widespread acceptance and is legislated into social policy. The future of "the family" depends on the outcome of their struggles.

Sociology and the Future of the Family

Sociology is a science which studies human interaction, social organization, and social structure. It provides both an analytic framework and methods of study which can interpret the influence of the past in shaping the present, analyse the present, identify and assess current developments, and project their potential consequences. In this way sociology can help in the combined effort to both predict the future and formulate realistic visions of what might be.

However, "the family" is one of the most problematic and difficult areas to study (Morgan, 1975). First of all, families are relatively private, and it is very difficult for an investigator to study what actually goes on in family relationships. Whereas a researcher can get hired on in a factory and learn fairly accurately on the job what that work experience is like (Westwood, 1984), her colleague hoping to study families will have to rely on interviews in which people describe their family life (Rubin, 1976). The discrepancies between what people say about their families (and often even genuinely believe) and the actuality of family life may never be caught by the research (Luxton, 1980: 142).

Second, everyone has had an experience of family life, and therefore each of us brings a certain expertise to the topic. Because family experiences are so important and the emotions generated by them are so deeply felt, people often find it very difficult to separate their personal experiences and feelings from their analysis of "the family." While individuals may be very clear that their experiences with paid work are quite specific, and that it is not possible to generalize to all paid work situations from that one particular experience, they may find it much more difficult to remember when talking about families that generalizing from their own family life is not appropriate in that case, either. Individual sociologists are just as vulnerable as everyone else's to myths of "family," and that vulnerability can affect their analysis. As Karen Anderson and Margrit Eichler have demonstrated, instead of investigating the reality of "family" life, historians and sociologists have all too often developed contending theories of the family which correspond to the contending popular ideologies (Segal, 1983).

These problems become even more difficult when sociology tackles the future. The task requires cutting through the ideology of familialism, dispelling the myths surrounding "the family," and holding our personal dreams and fears in careful perspective as we investigate current trends and their implications for the future.

Defining "The Family"

Before we can begin to think about the future of families, we must determine how to think about the differences between myth and reality, between how we think people should live and how they actually do. Once we have some sense about what "the family" actually is and why it is that way, we can begin to assess the implications of the competing models of family currently advocated and begin to develop realistic visions of what it might be. Central to that task is the problem of clarifying what is meant by "the family." In everyday language, the term "family" is used variously to refer to a number of different groupings. A "single-family dwelling" is intended for a married woman and man and their children; when a university student living in residence says he is going home to his family at Thanksgiving, we usually assume he means his parents; when a mature adult talks about missing her family she is probably referring to her grown-up children. But when someone says that most of her family were killed in the holocaust, she is referring to a wide range of extended kin; and when a man invites a group of friends to celebrate his success and tells them they are his real family, he means those from whom he receives loving support and encouragement.

The flexibility with which the term "family" is used in regular conversation reflects the complexity of social relations and activities which are commonly included in the term. What is assumed in these usages are notions of "blood" or kinship and strong emotional bonds; family is associated with belonging—those people who have to take you in no matter what.

In academic discourse, "the family" is a term used widely and often uncritically. There are several problems with it. First, it assumes that there is, and has been, and in the future will be one single phenomenon that can be called "the family." So adult sexual and emotional relations get lumped with parent-child relations, or kinship is merged with emotional caring. And it is assumed, despite profound historical changes in all those relationships, that there is something common to all of them throughout time.

Second, it presents a variety of different family forms as though they were really the same thing. For example, an extended matrilineal kin network of immigrants from the Caribbean is equated with a white, middle-class, nuclear family from Ottawa, and both are seen as being the same as a Métis kin group in Saskatchewan; a wealthy factory owner and his heirs in Vancouver and considered in the same light as a single welfare mother in a fishing village in

Nova Scotia. Third, the notion of "the family" tends to assume that all individuals within "the family" are in a similar situation sharing similar resources and life chances (despite extensive research which shows that men and women, boys and girls, do not have equal access to family resources, nor do they share equal life chances). Assuming one identical family form throughoutdenies important differences based on class, race, ethnicity, age, and gender (Thorne and Yalom, 1982). Finally, such usage tends to imply that the model of the nuclear family represented by familial ideology is normative, and actually exists in real life. As a result, other family forms and relationships appear to be deviant. Thus the term "the family" both obscures reality and contributes to the maintenance of familial ideology, instead of recognizing the multiplicity of relationships and activities that are actually subsumed by the terms (Collier, Rosaldo, and Yanagisako, 1982).

Analytically, sociologists include within the definition of family such relations and activities as kinship and marriage, economic inheritance, pooling and sharing, conceiving and bearing children, raising children, domestic labour, sexuality, love and caring, and forms both of power and domination and of intimacy. So, when people talk about the future of the family, they are actually discussing the ways in which that whole range of relations and activities might be organized. And when others advocate that certain legal and social practices be implemented in relation to any one of those items, they are shaping the future of families in Canada.

Kinship and Marriage

Throughout the history of capitalist societies, kinship and marriage have decreased in importance as primary forms of social organizing. Increasingly through the 20th century, adult men have been able to arrange their lives independently of kin and marriage relationships (Ehrenreich, 1983). More recently, increasing numbers of women have also been able to get jobs which pay enough to allow them to live independently as well. However, kinship and marriage still form the basis for one of the main ways in which groups or networks of people are organized. Kinship is a system which demarcates socially recognized and legitimated relations between people. Marriage is a legal relationship which links two different kinship groups and regulates gender relations between men and women. Together, kinship and marriage operate on a number of somewhat distinct levels.

For many people, their kinship and marriage connections form an extended family from which they receive an important sense of identity and belonging. The vast majority of children are raised by kin, and those relationships are among the most significant in their lives. For many adults, the commitment represented by marriage signifies a dedication to the partner greater than any an individual is willing or able to make to other people. For many people, kinship and marriage are the main, most stable, enduring, and committed of relationships. As a result, many people hold a very strong attachment to family and are very suspicious of any criticisms raised over it.

For subordinated social groups, extended family ties are often the means by which cultural, political, religious, and language traditions are maintained and preserved (Stack, 1974; Lamoureux, 1987). When such groups are subject to discrimination or persecution, extended family ties may provide a basis for defence and resistance (Caulfield, 1974).

Politically, kinship and marriage systems are one of the most important ways by which nation states—national governments—control and regulate individuals. First and foremost, kinship establishes an individual's right to citizenship and hence to access to national resources, (rights which vary enormously from country to country but in Canada include such things as the right to seek paid employment; access to social security benefits like unemployment insurance, mother's allowance, old age pensions and welfare; the right to certain legal protections; and the right to vote). The legal citizenship of the newborn child is derived from its kin, that is, from the citizenship of one or both of its parents. While immigration laws determining which adults can acquire Canadian citizenship are constantly changing, kinship or marriage ties are usually regarded as the significant grounds for admitting immigrants.[***]

The regulation of marriage is one way the state exerts social control over individuals. Legal marriage both enforces and privileges heterosexuality and regulates interpersonal relationships. The legal structure of marriage traditionally has reinforced male power and privilege over women and, although in recent years pressure from feminists has forced certain legal changes in family law which gesture in the direction of equality in marriage, its current structure is still fundamentally unequal. More significantly, marriage and kin relations are used by the state to hold certain individuals economically and socially responsible for others (i.e., their family) as a way of avoiding demands that the government provide adequate social services for everyone.

Kinship and marriage are also central to the ways in which individuals have access to and are required to provide certain kinds of economic resources. On a more structural level, kinship and marriage relations are fundamental to the

---

[***]   One terrible exception to this rule occurs when women (usually non-white women) are admitted as domestic workers and are expressly forbidden to bring their children, even after they have established themselves in Canada (Brand, 1984).

organization of certain kinds of property relations and, consequently, as will be seen in what follows, are the chief way in which classes and class hierarchies are maintained and reproduced.

Family Economics: Inheritance, Pooling and Sharing

Because family is one way to organize access to economic resources, family patterns vary by class. One of the features of a capitalist economy is that wages or salaries are paid to individuals and legally belong to those individuals. Similarly, investment income is usually owned either by large corporate organizations or by individuals. However, there are well-established patterns of pooling and sharing by which wealth owned privately is redistributed among kin and household relations.

The economic resources of their family of birth largely shape the opportunities available to children, and therefore profoundly influence their class location as adults. Children from well-off families will have a much easier time establishing themselves as well-to-do adults than will the children of poor families (Porter, 1965). Class privilege and class disadvantage are seen most clearly with the passing of wealth from one generation to the next through inheritance. For poor working-class families, the wealth may be simply some jewellery or treasured mementos; for better-off working-class families it may be a house or a nest egg sufficient to provide the heir with a down payment. Within the ruling class, an individual's inheritance may be the ownership of a business or controlling shares in a multinational corporation.

For many people, the economics of daily subsistence are organized through families. A family is a pooling, sharing group through which individuals obtain much of their food, clothing, and shelter. Legal obligations, cultural values, and common social practices assume that the economic support for individuals unable to support themselves should come from "their family." So governments resist giving greater access to welfare or social services, on the grounds that families have the "real responsibility" for such care. One of the most common of such patterns is found in the particular family form advocated as ideal by familial ideology; that is, a family in which the male is the breadwinner who takes on financial responsibility for the other members of his nuclear family and the female is the housewife-homemaker who takes responsibility for domestic labour including the raising of the children. Under the law the man is required to share his (privately owned) income with his wife and their children.

The fact that women are supposed to be wives and mothers supported by their husbands has been used since the 19th century to justify excluding women from many paid jobs, particularly the most skilled and best paid (Armstrong and Armstrong, 1983; Connelly, 1978). Young women are discouraged from obtaining the education and training that would enable them to qualify for such work, on the grounds that their main occupation will be as wife and mother (Russell, 1987). Jobs held primarily by women (especially in clerical work, sales, and services) are systematically paid less than jobs which require the same or even less training but are held predominantly by men; this discrimination is explained by claiming that women are secondary wage earners (Abella, 1984).

This economic discrimination in the paid labour force provides a major economic compulsion on the part of women toward marriage. Because they are unlikely to earn enough to support themselves very well, and definitely cannot support children on a typical woman's wages, women need marriage to provide them with basic economic resources (Ehrenreich, 1983). As a consequence, married women, whether they are employed or not, are economically dependent on their husbands. If the marriage is a loving and co-operative one, this economic dependency may seem insignificant, but the minute the marriage breaks down, through death, separation, or divorce, the economic consequences reassert themselves. Many women living comfortable lives have suddenly found themselves plunged into poverty when their breadwinner is gone. It is this economic inequality which results in the harsh reality of contemporary Canadian life that poverty is female; the vast majority of poor people in this country are either women with young children to support or older women trying to get by on their old-age pensions (Canadian Advisory council on the Status of Women, 1983; National Council of Welfare, 1979).

The major social change of the last 20 years has been the dramatic increase in married women's participation in the paid labour force. In 1970, 38.3 percent of women were in the labour force and constituted 33.6 percent of it. By 1980, 50.4 percent of women were in the labour force, and they constituted 40.1 percent of the total. By (December) 1986 this had increased to 55.1 percent of women, becoming 49.7 percent of the total (Labour Force Annual Averages, Statistics Canada Catalogue 71-001; Historical Labour Force Statistics, Statistics Canada Catalogue 71-201). Most significantly, the greatest increase of women in the labour force has been amongst women with pre-school children, 58.2 percent. While such shifts mean that women have some independent income, which begins to alleviate the negative consequences of their economic dependency on men, their lower incomes mean that the problem still remains.

This economic basis for family relations means that the future of family life depends more than anything else on what happens economically. Changing patterns of male and female employment will have profound economic consequences for households. As long as women are unable to earn enough to support themselves and their children, they will be subject to strong economic pressures to marry and thus to be dependent on and hence subject to men. Only when women have equal training, equal access to all jobs, equal pay, and equal pay for work of equal value will they be able to genuinely choose whether or not to marry. Hours of work, levels of pay, parental-leave benefits, security of employment, childcare arrangements, and access to housing all affect the way people organize their personal lives and their ability to care for children. So debates about the economy (on issues such as free trade, unemployment insurance, "acceptable" levels of unemployment, a guaranteed annual income, and a shorter work week) and about government spending (who should provide economic support for those unable to support themselves: children, the disabled, the elderly, the ill, and the unemployed) are also debates about family life. At the heart of those economic debates are contending visions of how social life "should" be organized; more than anything else, future economic developments will shape constraints and possibilities for future families.

Conceiving and Bearing Children

While conceiving and bearing children appear to be private individual actions, rooted in biological processes, they are in fact profoundly social. Individual women have children for a variety of reasons, but in so doing they are reproducing the human species and their own particular population. The proportion of women who have children, and the numbers of children they bear, are determined by numerous complex social forces (Gittins, 1982), and in turn shape the population profile of the next generation (Seccombe, 1983).

Familial ideology has prescribed and proscribed appropriate behaviour for conception and child bearing. Fundamental to familial ideology is the assumption that adults marry to have children and that children should only be born to married couples.

> Heterosexuality, marriage, and having children are thus all part
> of the western patriarchal parcel of rules for appropriate sexual
> relations and behaviour between men and women. Indulging in
> one without accepting the rest of the "parcel" has been, and still
> is, widely condemned (Gittens, 1985: 92).

Until recently, because women's economic survival depended on marriage, and because of male power over women's sexuality, having children was, in part, a price women paid for economic security. However, as increasing numbers of women have gained relative economic independence from men, it has become possible for them to exercise greater control over their biological reproduction. This control has been dramatically increased by developments in medical knowledge and reproductive technology.

Relatively effective (though not entirely safe nor cheap) birth control and abortions have made it possible for those fertile women who have access to them to choose when and if to have children. Increasing knowledge about human fertility has increased the chances of conceiving and carrying a pregnancy to term for people who might previously have been unable to do so. Childbirth itself, which was often extremely dangerous for both mother and child is now, for those who have access to modern medical knowledge and technology, much safer (McLaren and Tigar McLaren, 1986). Amniocentesis, genetic testing, fetal monitoring, and *in utero* surgery provide enormous possibilities for control over the types of children who are born.

The new knowledge and the reproductive technology which accompanies it has opened up tremendous possibilities for the future. What is at present completely unclear, however, is what that future might look like. On the one hand, these new developments have offered great hope for people previously unable to have children. On the other hand, a preference for male children has prompted the abortion of some female babies, a practice which could result in dramatic imbalances in future population (Mies, 1986). While genetic testing and manipulation have eliminated for some parents the grief of producing genetically abnormal children, the various drugs and surgical techniques connected with this research are often tested on poor, immigrant, black, native, or third-world women before they are deemed safe for white, middle-class, Western women (Melrose, 1982). For some lesbians, the new knowledge has permitted them to use donated sperm to impregnate themselves without either having intercourse or seeking the intervention of the medical profession. Some people have called for the creation of a "super" population, and have established sperm banks to preserve the genes of (usually white) middle-class professional men. On the other hand, some women have become concerned that, with surrogate mothering, women will be reduced to being merely egg farmers (Murphy, 1984).

At present we simply do not have enough experience to know what the future consequences of such developments might be, but a number of issues have already emerged. There is a complex politics which determines what kind of research gets done and what does not get done. Evidence indicates that the large pharmaceutical companies determine what research is done into birth control, because they fear the loss of their profits if cheaper, more effective methods were to be found. Some of the recent research into genetic engineering was prompted by military strategies for limited nuclear war. At present this knowledge, and control over access to it, is in the hands of the medical profession, a predominantly white, male, middle-class group. They can decide what kinds of people receive certain medical treatment. So, for example, most of the doctors currently able to do artificial insemination insist that prospective parents be a heterosexual couple. Infertile women unattached to a man are refused assistance. The type of genetic counselling offered to parents whose fetus has been shown to have abnormalities varies according to the race and class of the parents (Rapp, 1987).

Concerns about the future consequences of these developments have prompted some people to call for a moratorium on reproductive research. The Roman Catholic Church has declared all aspects of reproductive technology unacceptable for its members. In contrast, feminist groups have called for increased access for all, and have challenged the control of the medical profession, advocating clinics under the control of the community.

The larger question underlying all these debates is who should have the right and the power to make decisions about if, when, and how women give birth (Petchesky, 1985; Gavigan, 1987). Do individual (white male) doctors have the right to decide which women can benefit from medical reproductive techniques? Should governments have the right to legislate (as China does currently) the number of children women can have? Should religious organizations have the right to impose compulsory motherhood on their members? Should individual women have the right to abort a fetus because they don't like its sex? Does anyone have the right to force women to have babies if they do not want to—the logical extension of making abortion illegal or restricted. At present, there are major political struggles over these questions, with some people arguing that the medical profession, the churches, the government, or some combination of all three have the right to determine and control women's biological reproduction. Others argue instead that, as it is individual women whose bodies are involved, and whose lives are most profoundly affected by pregnancy and birth, they must be the ones to make the final decisions. At issue are contending visions of women's place in society and opposing concepts of future family life.

Raising Children

The bottom line in debates about the future of family life is always the question, "But what about the children?" The promoters of the ideology of familialism respond to proposals for alternative family forms by arguing that only the nuclear family can provide the best environment for raising children, and that mothers are the best caregivers for infants and young children. In practice, lived experience and systematic research (Zigler and Gordon, 1983) demonstrate over and over that this is not necessarily the case.

In the same way, women are not innately more skilled at childcare than men, nor are biological parents automatically good parents. What all the research shows is that many different forms of childcare can be equally effective. What matters is that the child is both emotionally and physically nurtured and stimulated, and that the caregivers are not isolated and lacking in support. What we know is that making mothers primarily responsible for their children without providing supporting social services such as daycare renders those women vulnerable to poverty (because they cannot take paid work), extraordinary stress (when they take paid work and juggle two jobs while worrying about childcare), and burnout from bearing too much responsibility in isolation (Rosenberg, 1987).

A current political issue revolves around the question of who should bear the cost of raising children. On the one hand, feminist and daycare activists call for free, universal daycare funded by the government and controlled by the parents, the staff, and the community. They argue that childcare is a social responsibility to be shared by all. In contrast, conservatives insist that the costs of caring for young children should be born by the individual parents. The outcome of this struggle could result in a continuation of current practices of ad hoc, unregulated, and often unsatisfactory childcare arrangements whose cost may keep a couple from having more children; or, on the other hand, if a system of quality daycare centres were to become available across the country, parents could have a much wider range of options available to them.

The question of who cares for the children is a much larger one than that, however. It is really about whether children are the private property and responsibility of their individual parents or whether a larger community of involved and concerned adults will share the work, the responsibility, and the joy of them. Why, for example, should people only have intimate access to children if they are their actual parents? Can we imagine a future society where the choice about who cares for children (and by extension, all those needing special care such as the handicapped, the ill, and the elderly), is not restricted to either their "family" (read "woman") or an institution (the horrors of which have been well documented) but is shared collectively by their community?

Domestic Labour

Domestic labour is the work of looking after the home and the people living in it (which is one reason why it is so easily assumed that anyone primarily responsible for domestic labour will provide caregiving to all who need it). It includes housework (activities such as cooking, cleaning, and laundry), childcare, care of disabled, sick, or elderly people, and a whole series of vital but intangible loving and nurturing tasks which go into "making a home." Overwhelmingly, domestic labour is primarily a woman's responsibility (Oakley, 1974, 1976; Luxton, 1980). It is usually private, individual, and unpaid.

The ideology of familialism offers an explanation for why domestic work should be done on a private, volunteer basis by individual women in their own homes. Because it claims that the best family form is a combination of a male, breadwinner husband/father and a female housewife/mother, it implies that women are "naturally" the best qualified to do domestic labour, and argues that the home and the activities which go on inside it are a world apart from the spheres of economics and politics. To reinforce that argument, this ideology claims that women have always worked in the home and that homemaking is women's "traditional" occupation.

That myth obscures the reality that the work done in the home for "love" rather than pay is indeed influenced by economic pressures and political decisions. Sociologists have shown that the structure of private family households and all the work activities which have historically gone on inside them have been transformed by corporate decisions made to ensure profitability (Strasser, 1982). For one thing, production and marketing strategies develop in the home. Moreover, future changes in tax structures, social service provisions, housing policies, and in the relative wages of women and men will all combine to profoundly affect the supposedly private sphere of the family household.

Intimacy and Sexuality

In contemporary Canadian society "family" is at the heart of emotional life and is understood to be the centre of personal life. Family life establishes our expectations and promises to fulfil our deepest, most fundamental needs. As a result, family relations are among our dearest and most important. At the same time, precisely because of the way familial ideology results in privileging one type of social relationship—the nuclear family—over any others, it is very difficult for people to get intimacy elsewhere and, when they do, it is hard for them to get those alternative relationships validated or supported. As Barrett and McIntosh point out:

> It is the overvaluation of family life that devalues these other lives. The family sucks the juice out of everything around it, leaving other institutions stunted and distorted (1982: 78).

Because family relations are supposed to provide love and intimacy, and because it is so difficult to get these elsewhere, family relations give us strength and undermine us simultaneously. The contradictory nature of the demands placed upon family life mean that those dynamics are also often the most harmful and damaging (Wilson, 1983). When family relations cannot provide what the ideology claims they should, when families are the site of violence, murder, sexual assault, or psychological terrorism, the disappointment generated may be nearly as damaging as the violence itself.

Familial ideology restricts sexuality to the heterosexual adult relations of marriage, claiming that other types of sexual relations are immature, inappropriate, or degenerate. Such notions first of all deny the reality experienced by, on the one hand, thousands of people who enjoy alternative sexual practices. On the other hand they also deny the misery and pain experienced by those people who remain in a heterosexual marital relation because they believe they must. Such compulsory heterosexuality is essential in maintaining the nuclear family in which men control women's sexuality and children are identified as the "property" of particular individuals (something that is absolutely critical in societies where wealth is redistributed through kin-based inheritance).

So, when thinking about the future, we need to focus on how people can best be assured of getting the secure, long-term, committed relationships they need. What the sociological evidence shows is that by restricting sexuality and intimacy to a small family group, and

> ...in privileging the intimacy of close kin, it has made the outside
> world cold and friendless (Barrett and McIntosh, 1982: 80).

By undermining the potential for community-based love and caring, the pressures on the individual family are enormous and the potential for pain and disappointment great. This suggests that unless other kinds of relations are strengthened and given legal, economic, and social support, "the family" will continue to appear to be a "haven in a heartless world" (Lasch, 1977), an appearance which masks the actual extent to which "the family" is anti-social:

> Caring, sharing and loving would be more widespread if the
> family did not claim them for its own (Barrett and McIntosh,
> 1982: 80).

The way society is currently organized, many needs formerly provided by communities are now offered for sale: childcare, therapy, even giving birth and affection. At the same time, anything which is wanted but is outside of a cash nexus or cannot be afforded is now redeposited in "the family." So "the family" is simultaneously the place where one gets what is not available elsewhere and a structure which prevents people getting those things elsewhere except for payment.

Developing New Visions: Strategies for Change

The activities, needs, and satisfactions that are usually embodied in the term "family"—security, affection, sexuality, love, parenting, who we live with and how our households are managed—are centrally important aspects of life. But, as I have tried to suggest, the ways they are actually met at the present time are highly problematic. Some people respond to these problems by reinforcing familial ideology and attempting to compel uniform social compliance to that ideology (Harding, 1981). Arguing that the family is in crisis and that the future of the family is threatened, they urge total social compulsion, from individual behaviour through to government legislation. They are particularly threatened by efforts to legitimize alternative sexual, emotional, economic, and parenting practices.

But attempts to impose universal conformity to an idealized model of how "the family" should be will not solve the problem, precisely because the source of the problem lies in the ideology of familialism and the way its associated practices restrict and limit how needs for love and sustenance are met.

Instead, we must develop a vision of the future in which more people can more easily rely on having those needs met regularly. However, our capacity to envision such a future is shaped and limited by our present experience. Because "the family" is currently one of the few places where people can hope to find security, love, intimacy, and so on, people tend to cling to it tenaciously, fearing that to let go would be to usher in something far worse—a cold, unfeeling, individualized, and competitive world. An analysis of familial ideology and of current practices of family life suggest that:

> ...the iniquities of the family and its appeal are closely related—they are two sides of the same coin. The benefits of family life depend upon the suffering of those who are excluded. The idea of the family life brings in its train many a bitter marriage and disappointed parents. If the family were not the only source of a range of satisfactions, were it not so massively privileged, it would not be so attractive (Barrett and McIntosh, 1982: 133).

So what does an analysis of the present suggest for the future? First, it illustrates the problems inherent in familial ideology and the social practices that go with it. Compulsory conformity to a single model creates situations where people cannot ensure that their needs are met. Instead, we need multiple options which permit people to make real choices about how they will live their lives, and which allow people to live differently at different times of their lives. And those options need to be based on collectivities or communities, networks of people living and working together who can contribute, collectively, to the support needed by each of them.

Second, such an analysis suggests that we need to appreciate that social change occurs in many ways, and that families are changed by forces which may appear to be quite remote. And yet human agency, the actions of individuals organizing together, can play a major role in shaping how that change occurs. Social change involves the complex interaction of many forces, of which a good number are unintentional, but it can also be affected by deliberate intervention such as social policy legislation or political organizing by special interest groups. For example, economic forces lead to changing patterns in labour force participation for women and men; developments in science and technology such as birth control or abortion affect biological reproduction; new ideologies, social norms, and expectations can lead to new practices (for example, the growing involvement of men in the care of young babies); the underlying assumptions shaping various legislative policies can profoundly affect family life (for example, through income taxes, zoning laws, and building codes); and, finally, large social movements and organized political campaigns can either win new possibilities or constrict and limit them (for example, the inclusion of sexual orientation in the human rights code or the current battle over whether to remove abortion from the Criminal Code). The point is that social change occurs; our only hope for shaping a future we want to live in will come from committing ourselves to understanding the implications of contemporary issues and acting on that understanding.

References

Abella, Rosalie. 1984. *Equality in Employment: A Royal Commission Report.* Ottawa: Minister of Supply and Services Canada.

Anderson, Karen. 1987. "A Gendered World: Women, Men and the Political Economy of the Seventeenth Century Huron." In *Feminism and Political Economy: Women's Work, Women's Struggles,* Heather Jon Maroney and Meg Luxton, eds. Toronto: Methuen Publications.

Armstrong, Pat and Hugh Armstrong. 1983. *A Working Majority: What Women Must Do for Pay.* Ottawa: Canadian Advisory Council on the Status of Women.

Barrett, Michele and Mary McIntosh. 1982. *The Anti-Social Family.* London: Verso.

Bloom, Lynn. 1976. "'It's All For Your Own Good': Parent-Child Relationships in Popular American Child Rearing Literature, 1820-1970." *Journal of Popular Culture* 10.

Blumenfeld, Emily. 1976. "Child Rearing Literature as an Object of Content Analysis" *The Journal of Applied Communications Research,* November.

Brand, Dionne. 1984. "A Working Paper on Black Women in Toronto: Gender, Race and Class." *Fireweed* No. 19 Summer/Fall: 26-43.

Briskin, Linda, and Lynda Yanz, eds. 1983. *Union Sisters: Women in the Labour Movement.* Toronto: The Women's Press.

Canadian Advisory Council on the Status of Women. 1983. *As Things Stand.* Ottawa: Canadian Advisory Council on the Status of Women.

Caulfield, Mina. 1974. "Imperialism, the Family and Cultures of Resistance." *Socialist Revolution 4,* No. 20, October.

Collier, Jane, Michelle Rosaldo and S. Yanagisako. 1982. "Is There a Family? New Anthropological Views." In Thorne and Yalom, *Rethinking the Family.* New York: Longmans.

Connelly, Pat. 1978. *Last Hired, First Fired: Women and the Canadian Work Force.* Toronto: The Women's Press.

Ehrenreich, Barbara. 1983. *The Hearts of Men: American Dreams and the Flight from Commitment.* London: Pluto.

FitzGerald, Maureen, Connie Guberman and Margie Wolfe. 1982. *Still Ain't Satisfied: Canadian Feminism Today.* Toronto: The Women's Press.

Friedan, Betty. 1963. *The Feminine Mystique.* New York: Dell.

Gallager Ross, Kathleen. 1978. *Good Day Care: Fighting for It, Getting It, and Keeping It.* Toronto: The Women's Press.

Gavigan, Shelley. 1987. "Women and Abortion in Canada: What's Law Got To Do With It?" In Heather Jon Maroney and Meg Luxton, eds., *Feminism and Political Economy: Women's Work, Women's Struggles.* Toronto: Methuen Publications.

Gittins, Diana. 1982. *Fair Sex, Family Size and Structure in Britain, 1900-39.* London: Hutchison.

————. *The Family in Question: Changing Households and Familiar Ideologies.* London: Macmillan, 1985.

Gordon, Linda and Allen Hunter. 1978. *Sex, Family and the New Right: Anti-feminism as a Political Force.* Somerville, Mass.: 1978 (reprinted from Radical America, Nov. 1977-February 1978.)

Griffith, Alison. 1983. "Skilling for Life, Living for Skill: The Social Construction of Life Skill in Ontario Schools," unpublished Ph.D thesis, University of Toronto, Toronto, Ontario.

Guberman, Connie and Margie Wolfe, eds. 1985. *No Safe Place: Violence Against Women and Children.* Toronto: The Women's Press.

Harding, Susan. 1981. "Family Reform Movements: Recent Feminism and its Opposition." *Feminist Studies,* vol. 7, No. 5:57-75.

Hayden, Delores. 1981. *The Grand Domestic Revolution: A History of Feminist Designs for American Homes, Neighborhoods and Cities.* Cambridge: MIT Press.

Lamoureux, Diane. 1987. "Nationalism and Feminism in Quebec: An Impossible Attraction." In Heather Jon Maroney and Meg Luxton, eds. *Feminism and Political Economy: Women's Work, Women's Struggles.* Toronto, Methuen Publications.

Lasch, Christopher. 1977. *Haven in a Heatless World.* New York.

Luxton, Meg. 1980. *More Than Labour of Love: Three Generations of Women's Work in the Home.* Toronto: The Women's Press.

Luxton, Meg and Harriet Rosenberg. 1986. *Through the Kitchen Window: The Politics of Home and Family.* Toronto: Garamond.

Maroney, Heather Jon and Meg Luxton, eds. 1987. *Feminism and Political Economy: Women's Work, Women's Struggles.* Toronto: Methuen.

McLaren, Angus and Arlene Tigar McLaren. 1986. *The Bedroom and the State.* Toronto: McClelland and Stewart.

Meis, Maria. 1986. *Patriarchy and Accumulation on a World Scale: Women in the International Division of Labour.* Atlantic Highlands, New Jersey: Zed Books.

Melrose, Dianna. 1982. *Bitter Pills: Medicines and the Third World Poor.* Oxford: Oxfam.

Morgan, D.J.H. 1975. *Social Theory and the Family.* London: Routledge & Kegan Paul.

Murphy, Julie. 1984. "Egg Farming and Women's Future." In *Test-Tube Women,* Rita Arditti, Renate D. Klein, Shelley Minden, eds. New York: Methuen Publications.

National Council of Welfare. 1979. *Women and Poverty: A Report.* Ottawa: National Council of Welfare.

Oakley, Ann. 1974. *The Sociology of Housework.* Bath: Martin Robinson.

————. 1976. *Women's Work: The Housewife Past and Present.* New York: Vintage Books.

Petchesky, Rosalina. 1988. *Abortion and Women's Choice.* Boston: Northeastern University Press.

Porter, John. 1965. *The Vertical Mosaic: An Analysis of Social Class and Power in Canada.* Toronto: The University of Toronto Press.

Rapp, Rayna. 1987. "Moral Pioneers: Women, Men and Fetuses on the Frontiers of Reproductive Technology," lecture at York University, North York, Ontario, February 25.

————. 1978. "Family and Class in Contemporary America: Notes Toward an Understanding of Ideology," *Science and Society* 42 Fall, pp. 278-301.

Riley, Denis. 1983. *War in the Nursery: Theories of the Child and the Mother.* London: Virago.

Rosenberg, Harriet. 1987. "Motherwork, Stress and Depression: The Costs of Privatized Social Reproduction." In Heather Jon Maroney and Meg Luxton, eds. *Feminism and Political Economy: Women's Work, Women's Struggles.* Toronto: Methuen Publications.

Rubin, Lilian. 1976. *Worlds of Pain.* New York: Basic Books.

Russell, Susan. 1987. "The Hidden Curriculum of Schools: Reproducing Gender and Class Hierarchies." In Heather Jon Maroney and Meg Luxton, eds. *Feminism and Political Economy: Women's Work, Women's Struggles.* Toronto: Methuen Publications.

Seccombe, Wally. 1983. "Marxism and Demography." *New Left Review No. 137.* pp. 22-47.

Segal, Lynn, ed. 1983. *What Is To Be Done About the Family?* Harmondsworth: Penguin.

Spock, Benjamin. 1968. *Baby and Child Care.* Reprint. Markham, Ontario: Simon and Schuster of Canada.

Stack, Carol. 1974. *All Our Kin: Strategies for Survival in a Black Community.* New York: Harper & Row.

Statistics Canada Catalogue 71-529: 71-201.

Strasser, Susan. 1982. *Never Done: A History of American Housework.* New York: Pantheon.

Thorne, Barrie and Marilyn Yalom, eds. 1982. *Rethinking the Family: Some Feminist Questions.* New York: Longmans.

Weber, Max. 1967. *The Protestant Ethic and the Spirit of Capitalism.* London: Allen and Unwin.

Westwood, Sallie. 1984. *All Day Every Day: Factory and Family in the Making of Women's Lives.* London: Pluto.

Wilson, Elizabeth. 1983. *What is to be Done About Violence Against Women?* London: Penguin.

Wilson, Sue. 1986. *Women, the Family and the Economy.* 2nd edition. Toronto: McGraw-Hill Ryerson.

Zigler, Dr. Ed and Edmund Gordon, eds. 1983. *Daycare: Scientific Issues and Social Policy.* Dover, Mass.: Auburn House.

The Family

Claude Levi-Strauss

In this article Levi-Strauss explores the universality and origins of the family institution. Drawing on anthropological studies of various marriage and family arrangements around the world, he argues that the origins of the family are not essentially natural, as we generally assume, but social. Levi-Strauss finds that a recognizable structure underlies the diverse family patterns and that it involves a division of labour among the sexes and an incest taboo among members of the family grouping. The morality always associated with both of these indicates that, like the family itself, they are not based in nature even though we customarily explain both in naturalistic terms. Levi-Strauss concludes that both function to establish conditions of reciprocity in which groups are forced to establish relationships of interdependency and exchange with one another, thereby making human society possible.

The word *family* is so plain, the kind of reality to which it refers is so close to daily experience that one may expect to be confronted in this chapter with a simple situation. Anthropologists, however, are a strange breed; they like to make even the "familiar" look mysterious and complicated. As a matter of fact, the comparative study of the family among many different peoples has given rise to some of the most bitter arguments in the whole history of anthropological thought and probably to its more spectacular reversal.

During the second half of the nineteenth century and the beginning of the twentieth, anthropologists were working under the influence of biological evolutionism. They were trying to organize their data so that the institutions of the simpler people would correspond to an early state of the evolution of mankind, while our own institutions were related to the more advanced or developed forms. And since, among ourselves, the family founded on monogamic marriage was considered as the most praiseworthy and cherished institution, it was immediately inferred that savage societies—equated for the purpose with the societies of man at the beginning of its existence—could only have something of a different type. Therefore, facts were distorted and misinterpreted; even more, fanciful "early" stages of evolution were invented, such as "group marriage" and "promiscuity" to account for the period when man was still so barbarous that he could not possibly conceive of the niceties of the social life it is the privilege of civilized man to enjoy. Every custom different from our own was carefully selected as a vestige of an older type of social organization.

This way of approaching the problem became obsolete when the accumulation of data made obvious the following fact: the kind of family featured in modern civilization by monogamous marriage, independent establishment of the young couple, warm relationship between parents and offspring, etc., while not always easy to recognize behind the complicated network of strange customs and institutions of savage peoples, is at least conspicuous among those which seem to have remained on—or returned to—the simplest cultural level.

There are two ways of interpreting this preeminence of the family at both ends of the scale of development of human societies. Some writers have claimed that the simpler peoples may be considered as a remnant of what can be looked at as a "golden age," prior to the submission of mankind to the hardships and perversities of civilization; thus, man would have known in that early stage the bliss of monogamic family only to forgo it late until its more recent Christian rediscovery. The general trend, however, except for the so-called Vienna school, has been that more and more anthropologists have become convinced that familial life is present practically everywhere in human societies, even in those with sexual and educational customs very remote from our own. Thus, after they had claimed for about fifty years that the family, as modern societies knew it, could only be a recent development and the outcome of a slow and long-lasting evolution, anthropologists now lean toward the opposite conviction, i.e., that the family, consisting of a more or less durable union, socially approved, of a man, a woman, and their children, is a universal phenomenon, present in each and every type of society.

These extreme positions, however, suffer equally from oversimplification. It is well known that, in very rare cases, family bonds cannot be claimed to exist. A telling example comes from the Nayar, a very large group living on the Malabar coast of India. In former times, the warlike type of life of the Nayar men did not allow them to found a family. Marriage was a purely symbolical ceremony which did not result in a permanent tie between a man and a woman. As a matter of fact, married women were permitted to have as many lovers as they wished. Children belonged exclusively to the mother line, and familial as well as land authority was exercised not by the ephemeral husband but by the wife's brothers. Since land was cultivated; by an inferior caste, subservient to the Nayar, a woman's brothers were as completely free as their sister's temporary husband or lovers to devote themselves to military activities.

There are a large number of human societies which, although they did not go quite as far as the Nayar in denying recognition to the family as a social unit, have nevertheless limited this recognition by their simultaneous admission of patterns of a different type. For instance, the Masai and the Chagga, both of them African tribes, did recognize the family as a social unit. However, and for the same reason as the Nayar, this was not true for the younger class of adult men who were dedicated to warlike activities and consequently were not allowed to marry and found a family. They used to live in regimental organizations and were permitted, during that period, to have promiscuous relations with the younger class of adult girls. Thus, among these peoples, the family did exist side by side with a promiscuous, non-familial type of relations between the sexes.

During recent years anthropologists have taken great pains to show that, even among people who practice wife-lending, either periodically in religious ceremonies or on a statutory basis (as where men are permitted to enter into a kind of institutional friendship entailing wife-lending among members), these customs should not be interpreted as survivals of "group marriage" since they exist side by side with, and even imply, recognition of the family. It is true enough that, in order to be allowed to lend one's wife, one should first get one. However, if we consider the case of some Australian tribes as the Wunambal of the northwestern part of the continent, a man who would not lend his wife to her other potential husbands during ceremonies would be considered as "very greedy," i.e., trying to keep for himself a privilege intended by the social group to be shared between numerous persons equally entitled to it. And since that attitude toward sexual access to a woman existed along with the official dogma that men have no part in physiological procreation (therefore doubly denying any kind of bond between the husband and his wife's children), the family becomes an economic grouping where man brings the products of his hunt and the woman those of her collecting and gathering. Anthropologists, who claim that this economic unit built upon a "give and take" principle is a proof of the existence of the family even among the lowest savages, are certainly on no sounder basis than those who maintain that such a kind of family has little else in common than the word used to designate it with the family as it has been observed elsewhere.

The same relativistic approach is advisable in respect to the polygamous family. The word polygamy, it should be recalled, refers to polygyny, that is, a system where a man is entitled to several wives, as well as to polyandry, which is the complementary system where several husbands share one wife.

Now it is true that in many observed cases, polygamous families are nothing else than a combination of several monogamous families, although the same person plays the part of several spouses. For instance, in some tribes of Bantu Africa, each wife lives in a separate hut with her children, and the only difference with the monogamous family results from the fact that the same man plays the part of husband to all his wives. There are other instances, however, where the situation is not so clear. Among the Tupi-Kawahib of central Brazil, a chief may marry several women who may be sisters, or even a mother and her daughters by former marriage; the children are raised together by the women, who do not seem to mind very much whether they nurse their own children or not; also, the chief willingly lends his wives to his younger brothers, his court officers, or to visitors. Here we have not only a combination of polygyny and polyandry, but, the mix-up is increased even more by the fact that the co-wives may be united by close consanguineous ties prior to their marrying the same man.

As to polyandry proper, it may sometimes take extreme forms, as among the Toda where several men, usually brothers, share one wife, the legitimate father of the children being the one who has performed a special ceremony and who remains legal father of all the children to be born until another husband decides to assume the right of fathership by the same process. In Tibet and Nepal, polyandry seems to be explained by occupational factors of the same type as those already stated for the Nayar: for men living a semi-nomadic existence as guides and bearers, polyandry provides a good chance that there will be, at all times, at least one husband at hand to take care of the homestead.

Therefore, it becomes apparent why the problem of the family should not be approached in a dogmatic way. As a matter of fact, this is one of the more elusive questions in the whole field of social organization. Of the type of organization which prevailed in the early stages of mankind, we know very little, since the remnants of man during the Upper Palaeolithic Period of about 50,000 years ago consist principally of skeletal fragments and stone implements which provide only a minimum of information on social customs and laws. On the other hand, when we consider the wide diversity of human societies which have been observed since, let us say, Herodotus' time until present days, the only thing which can be said is as follows: monogamic, conjugal family is fairly frequent. Wherever it seems to be superseded by different types of organizations, this generally happens in very specialized and sophisticated societies and not, as was previously expected, in the crudest and simplest types. Moreover, the few instances of non-conjugal family (even in its polygamous form) establish beyond doubt that the high frequency of the conjugal type of social grouping does not derive from a universal necessity. It is at least conceivable that a perfectly stable and durable society could exist without it. Hence, the difficult problem: if there is no natural law making the family universal, how can we explain why it is found practically everywhere?

In order to try to solve the problem, let us try first to define the family, not by integrating the numerous factual observations made in different societies nor even by limiting ourselves to the prevailing situation among us, but by building up an ideal model of what we have in mind when we use the word *family*. It would then seem that this word serves to designate a social group offering at least three characteristics: (1) it finds its origin in marriage; (2) it consists in husband, wife, and children born out of their wedlock, though it can be conceived that other relatives may find their place close to that nuclear group; and (3) the family members are united together by (a) legal bonds, (b) economic, religious, and other kinds of rights and obligations, (c) a precise network of sexual rights and prohibitions, and a varying and diversified amount of psychological feelings such as love, affection, respect, awe, etc. We will now proceed to a close examination of several aspects in the light of the available data.

As we have already noticed, marriage may be monogamous or polygamous. It should be pointed out immediately that the first kind is not only more frequently found than the second, but even much more than a cursory inventory of human societies would lead to believe. Among the so-called polygamous societies, there are undoubtedly a substantial number which are authentically so; but many others make a strong difference between the "first" wife who is the only true one, endowed with the full right attached to the marital status, while the other ones are sometimes little more than official concubines. Besides, in all polygamous societies, the privilege of having several wives is actually enjoyed by a small minority only. This is easily understandable, since the number of men and women in any random grouping is approximately the same with a normal balance of about 110 to 100 to the advantage of either sex.

Therefore, it is not necessary to wonder a great deal about the predominance of monogamic marriage in human societies. That monogamy is not inscribed in the nature of man is sufficiently evidenced by the fact that polygamy exists in widely different forms and in many types of societies; on the other hand, the prevalence of monogamy results from the fact that, unless special conditions are voluntarily or involuntarily brought about, there is, normally, about just one woman available for each man. In modern societies, moral, religious, and economic reasons have officialized monogamous marriage (a rule which is in actual practice breached by such different means as premarital freedom, prostitution, and adultery). But in societies which are on a much lower cultural level and where there is no prejudice against polygamy, and even where polygamy may be actually permitted or desired, the same result can be brought about by the lack of social or economic differentiation, so that each man has neither the means, nor the power, to obtain more than one wife and where, consequently, everybody is obliged to make a virtue of necessity.

If there are many different types of marriage to be observed in human societies—whether monogamous or polygamous, and in the last case, polygynous, polyandrous, or both; and whether by exchange, purchase, free choice or imposed by the family, etc.—the striking fact is that everywhere a distinction exists between marriage, i.e., a legal, group-sanctioned bond between a man and a woman, and the type of permanent or temporary union resulting either from violence or consent alone.

In the first place, nearly all societies grant a very high rating to the married status. Wherever age-grades exist, either in an institutional way or as non-crystallized forms of grouping, some connection is established between the younger adolescent group and bachelorhood, less young and married without children, and adulthood with full rights, the latter going usually on par with the birth of the first child.

What is even more striking is the true feeling of repulsion which most societies have toward bachelorhood. Generally speaking it can be said that, among the so-called primitive tribes, there are no bachelors, simply for the reason that they could not survive. One of the strongest field recollections of this writer was his meeting, among the Bororo of central Brazil, a man about thirty years old: unclean, ill-fed, sad, and lonesome. When asked if the man were seriously ill, the natives' answer came as a shock: what was wrong with him?—nothing at all, he was just a bachelor. And true enough, in a society where labour is systematically shared between man and woman and where only the married status permits the man to benefit from the fruits of woman's work, including delousing, body painting, and hair-plucking as well as vegetable food and cooked food (since the Bororo woman tills the soil and makes pots), a bachelor is really only half a human being.

This is true of the bachelor and also, to a lesser extent, of a couple without children. Indeed they can make a living, but there are many societies where a childless man (or woman) never reaches full status within the group, or else, beyond the group, in this all-important society which is made up of dead relatives, and where one can only expect recognition as ancestor through the cult, rendered to him or her by one's descendants. Conversely, an orphan finds himself in the same dejected condition as a bachelor. As a matter of fact, both terms provide sometimes the strongest insults existing in the native vocabulary. Bachelors and orphans can even be merged together with cripples and witches, as if their conditions were the outcome of some kind of supernatural malediction.

The interest shown by the group in the marriage of its members can be directly expressed, as it is the case among us where prospective spouses, if they are of marriageable age, have first to get a licence and then to secure the services of an acknowledged representative of the group to celebrate their union. Although this direct relationship between the individuals, on the one hand, and the group as a whole, on the other, is known at least sporadically in other societies, it is by no means a frequent case. It is almost a universal feature of marriage that it is originated, not by the individuals but by the groups concerned (families, lineage, clans, etc.), and that it binds the groups before and above the individuals. Two kinds of reasons bring about this result: on the one hand, the paramount importance of being married tends to make parents, even in very simple societies, start early to worry about obtaining a suitable mate for their offspring and this, accordingly, may lead to children being promised to each other from infancy. But above all, we are confronted here with that strange paradox to which we shall have to return later on, namely, that although marriage gives birth to the family, it is the family, or rather families, which produce marriage as the main legal device at their disposal to establish an alliance between themselves. As a New Guinea native put it, the real purpose of getting married is not so much to obtain a wife but to secure brothers-in-law. If marriage takes place between groups rather than individuals, a large number of strange customs become immediately clearer. For instance, we understand why in some parts of Africa, where descent follows the father's line, marriage becomes final only when the woman has given birth to a male child, thus fulfilling its function of maintaining her husband's lineage. The so-called *levirate* and *sororate* should be explained in the light of the same principle: if marriage is binding between two groups to which the spouses belong there can be without contradiction a replacement of one spouse by his brothers or by her sisters. When the husband dies, the levirate provides that his unmarried brothers have a preferential claim on his widow (or, as it is sometimes differently put, share in their deceased brother's duty to support his wife and children), while the sororate permits a man to marry preferentially in polygamous marriage his wife's sisters, or—when marriage is monogamous—to get a sister to replace the wife in case the latter remains childless, has to be divorced on account of bad conduct, or dies. But whatever the way in which the collectivity expresses its interest in the marriage of its members, whether through the authority vested in strong consanguineous groups, or more directly, through the intervention of the State, it remains true that marriage is not, is never, and cannot be a private business.

We have to look for cases as extreme as the Nayar, already described, to find societies where there is not, at least, a temporary de facto union of the husband, wife, and their children. But we should be careful to note that, while such a group among us constitutes the family and is given legal recognition, this is by no means the case in a large number of human societies. Indeed, there is a maternal instinct which compels the mother to care for her children and makes her find a deep satisfaction in exercising those activities, and there are also psychological drives which explain that a man may feel warmly toward the offspring of a woman with whom he is living, and the development of which he witnesses step by step, even if he does not believe (as is the case among the tribes who are said to disclaim physiological paternity) that he had any actual part in their procreation.

The great majority of societies, however, do not show a very active interest in a kind of grouping which, to some of them at least (including our own), appears so important. Here, too, it is the groups which are important, not the temporary aggregate of the individual representatives of the group. For instance, many societies are interested in clearly establishing the relations of the offspring with the father's group on the one hand, and with the mother's group on the other, but they do it by differentiating strongly the two kinds of relationships. Territorial rights may be inherited through one line, and religious privileges and obligations through the other. Or else, status from one side, magical techniques from the other.

In most of contemporary India and in many parts of western and eastern Europe, sometimes as late as the nineteenth century, the basic social unit was constituted by a type of family which should be described as *domestic* rather than *conjugal*: ownership of the land and of the homestead, parental authority and economic leadership were vested in the eldest living ascendant, or in the community of brothers issued from the same ascendant. In the Russian *bratsvo*, the south-Slavic *zadruga*, the French *maisnie*, the family actually consisted of the elder or the surviving brothers, together with their wives, married sons with their wives and unmarried daughters, and so on down to the great-grandchildren. Such large groups, which could sometimes include several dozen persons living and working under a common authority, have been designated as *joint families* or *extended families*. Both terms are useful but misleading, since they imply that these large units are made up of small conjugal families. As we have already seen, while it is true that the conjugal family limited to mother and children is practically universal, since it is based on the physiological and psychological dependency which exists between them at least for a certain time, and that the conjugal family consisting of husband, wife, and children is almost as frequent for psychological and economic reasons which should be added to those previously mentioned, the historical process which has led among ourselves to the legal recognition of the conjugal family is a very complex one: it has been brought about only in part through an increasing awareness of a natural situation. But there is little doubt that, to a very large extent, it has resulted from the narrowing down to a group, as small as can be, the legal standing of which, in the past of our institutions, was vested for centuries in very large groups. In the last instance, one would not be wrong in disallowing the terms joint family and extended family. Indeed, it is rather the conjugal family which deserves the name of *restricted family*.

We have just seen that when the family is given a small functional value, it tends to disappear even below the level of the conjugal type. On the contrary, when the family has a great functional value, it becomes actualized much above that level. Our would-be universal conjugal family, then, corresponds more to an unstable equilibrium between extremes than to a permanent and everlasting need coming from the deepest requirements of human nature.

To complete the picture, we have finally to consider cases where the conjugal family differs from our own, not so much on account of a different amount of functional value, but rather because its functional value is conceived in a way qualitatively different from our own conceptions.

As will be seen later on, there are many peoples for whom the kind of spouse one should marry is much more important than the kind of match they will make together. These people are ready to accept unions which to us would seem not only unbelievable, but in direct contradiction with the aims and purposes of setting up a family. For instance, the Siberian Chukchee were not in the least abhorrent to the marriage of a mature girl of let us say about twenty, with a baby-husband two or three years old. Then, the young woman, herself a mother by an authorized lover, would nurse together her own child and her little husband. Like the North American Mohave, who had the opposite custom of a man marrying a baby girl and caring for her until she became old enough to fulfil her conjugal duties, such marriages were thought of as very strong ones, since the natural feelings between husband and wife would be reinforced by the recollection of the parental care bestowed by one of the spouses on the other. These are by no means exceptional cases to be explained by extraordinary mental abnormalities. Examples could be brought together from other parts of the world: South America, both highland and tropical, New Guinea, etc.

As a matter of fact, the examples just given still respect, to some extent, the duality of sexes which we feel is a requirement of marriage and raising a family. But in several parts of Africa, women of high rank were allowed to marry other women and have them bear children through the services of unacknowledged male lovers, the noble woman being then entitled to become the "father" of her children and to transmit to them, according to the prevalent father's right, her own name, status, and wealth. Finally, there are the cases, certainly less striking, where the conjugal family was considered necessary to procreate the children but not to raise them, since each family did endeavour to retain somebody else's children (if possible of a higher status) to raise them while their own children were similarly retained (sometimes before they were born) by another family. This happened in some parts of Polynesia, while "fosterage," i.e., the custom whereby a son was sent to be raised by his mother's brother, was a common practice on the Northwest Coast of America as well as in European feudal society.

During the course of centuries we have become accustomed to Christian morality, which considers marriage and setting up a family as the only way to prevent sexual gratification from being sinful. That connection has been shown to exist elsewhere in a few scattered instances; but it is by no means frequent. Among most people, marriage has very little to do with the satisfaction of the sexual urge, since the social setup provides for many opportunities which can be not only external to marriage, but even contradictory to it. For instance, among the Muria of Bastar, in central India, when puberty comes, boys and girls are sent to live together in communal huts where they enjoy a great deal of sexual freedom, but after a few years of such leeway they get married according to the rule that no former adolescent lovers should be permitted to unite. Then, in a rather small village, each man is married to a wife whom he has known during his younger years as his present neighbour's (or neighbours') lover.

On the other hand, if sexual considerations are not paramount for marriage purposes, economic necessities are found everywhere in the first place. We have already shown that what makes marriage a fundamental need in tribal societies is the division of labour between the sexes.

Like the form of the family, the division of labour stems more from social and cultural considerations than from natural ones. Truly, in every human group, women give birth to children and take care of them, and men rather have as their specialty hunting and warlike activities. Even there, though, we have ambiguous cases: of course men never give birth to babies, but in many societies, as we have seen with the couvade, they are made to act as if they did. And there is a great deal of difference between the Nambikwara father nursing his baby and cleaning it when it soils itself, and the European nobleman of not long ago to whom his children were formally presented from time to time, being otherwise confined to the women's quarters until the boys were old enough to be taught riding and fencing.

When we turn to activities less basic than child-rearing and war-making, it becomes still more difficult to discern rules governing the division of labour between the sexes. The Bororo women till the soil while among the Zuni this is man's work; according to tribe, hut-building, pot-making, weaving, may be incumbent upon either sex. Therefore, we should be careful to distinguish the fact of the division of labour between the sexes which is practically universal, from the way according to which different tasks are attributed to one or the other sex, where we should recognize the same paramount influence of cultural factors, let us say the same artificiality which presides over the organization of the family itself.

Here, again, we are confronted with the same question we have already met with: if the natural reasons which could explain the division of labour between the sexes do not seem to play a decisive part, as soon as we leave the solid ground of women's biological specialization in the production of children, why does it exist at all? The very fact that it varies endlessly according to the society selected for consideration shows that, as for the family itself, it is the mere fact of its existence which is mysteriously required, the form under which it comes to exist being utterly irrelevant, at least from the point of view of any natural necessity. However, after having considered the different aspects of the problem, we are now in a position to perceive some common features which may bring us nearer to an answer than we were at the beginning of this chapter. Since family appears to us as a positive social reality, perhaps the only positive social reality, we are prone to define it exclusively by its positive characteristics. Now it should be pointed out that whenever we have tried to show what the family is, at the same time we were implying what it is not, and the negative aspects may be as important as the others. To return to the division of labour we were just discussing, when it is stated that one sex must perform certain tasks, this also means that the other sex is forbidden to do them. In that light, the sexual division of labour is nothing else than a device to institute a reciprocal state of dependency between the sexes.

The same thing may be said of the sexual side of the family life. Even if it is not true, as we have shown, that the family can be explained on sexual grounds, since for many tribes, sexual life and the family are by no means as closely connected as our moral norms would make them, there is a negative aspect which is much more important: the structure of the family, always and everywhere, makes certain types of sexual connections impossible, or at least wrong.

Indeed, the limitations may vary to a great extent according to the culture under consideration. In ancient Russia, there was a custom known as *snokatchestvo* whereby a father was entitled to a sexual privilege over his son's young wife; a symmetrical custom has been mentioned in some parts of southeastern Asia where the persons implied are the sister's son and his mother's brother's wife. We ourselves do not object to a man marrying his wife's sister, a practice which English law still considered incestuous in the mid-nineteenth century. What remains true is that every known society, past or present, proclaims that if the husband-wife relationship, to which, as just seen, some others may eventually be added, implies sexual rights, there are other relationships equally derived from the familial structure, which make sexual connections inconceivable, sinful, or legally punishable. The universal prohibition of incest specifies, as a general rule, that people considered as parents and children, or brother or sister, even if only by name, cannot have sexual relations and even less marry each other. In some recorded instances—such as ancient Egypt, pre-Columbian Peru, also some African, southeast Asian, and Polynesian kingdoms—incest was defined far less strictly than elsewhere. Even there, however, the rule existed, since incest was limited to a minority group, the ruling class (with the exception of, perhaps, ancient Egypt where it may have been more common; on the other hand, not every kind of close relatives were permitted as spouse: for instance it was the half-sister, the full-one being excluded; or, if the full-sister was allowed, then it should be the elder sister, the younger one remaining incestuous.

The space at our disposal is too short to demonstrate that, in this case as previously, there is no natural ground for the custom. Geneticists have shown that while consanguineous marriages are likely to bring ill effects in a society which has consistently avoided them in the past, the danger would be much smaller if the prohibition had never existed, since this would have given ample opportunity for the harmful hereditary characteristics to become apparent and be automatically eliminated through selection: as a matter of fact, this is the way breeders improve the quality of their subjects. Therefore, the dangers of consanguineous marriages are the outcome of the incest prohibition rather than actually explaining it. Furthermore, since very many primitive peoples do not share our belief in biological harm resulting from consanguineous marriages, but have entirely different theories, the reason should be sought elsewhere, in a way more consistent with the opinions generally held by mankind as a whole.

The true explanation should be looked for in a completely opposite direction, and what has been said concerning the sexual division of labour may help us to grasp it. This has been explained as a device to make the sexes mutually dependent on social and economic grounds, thus establishing clearly that marriage is better than celibacy. Now, exactly in the same way that the principle of sexual division of labour establishes a mutual dependency between the sexes, compelling them thereby to perpetuate themselves and to found a family, the prohibition of incest establishes a mutual dependency between families, compelling them, in order to perpetuate themselves, to give rise to new families. It is through a strange oversight that the similarity of the two processes is generally overlooked on account of the use of terms as dissimilar as *division*, on the one hand, and *prohibition* on the other. We could easily have emphasized only the negative aspect of the division of labour by calling it a prohibition of tasks; and conversely, outlined the positive aspects of incest-prohibition by calling it the principle of division of marriageable rights between families. For incest-prohibition simply states that families (however they should be defined) can marry between each other and that they cannot marry inside themselves.

We now understand why it is so wrong to try to explain the family on the purely natural grounds of procreation, motherly instinct, and psychological feelings between man and woman and between father and children. None of these would be sufficient to give rise to a family, and for a reason simple enough: for the whole of mankind, the absolute requirement for the creation of a family is the previous existence of two other families, one ready to provide a man, the other one a woman, who will through their marriage start a third one, and so on indefinitely. To put it in other words: what makes man really different from the animal is that, in mankind, a family could not exist if there were no society; i.e., a plurality of families ready to acknowledge that there are other links than consanguineous ones, and that the natural process of filiation can only be carried on through the social process of affinity.

How this interdependency of families has become recognized is another problem which we are in no position to solve because there is no reason to believe that man, since he emerged from his animal state, has not enjoyed a basic from of social organization, which, as regards the fundamental principles, could not be essentially different form our own. Indeed, it will never be sufficiently emphasized that, if social organization had a beginning, this could only have consisted in the incest prohibition since, as we have just shown, the incest prohibition is, in fact, a kind of remodeling of the biological conditions of mating and procreation (which know no rule, as can be seen from observing animal life), compelling them to become perpetuated only in an artificial framework of taboos and obligations. It is there, and only there, that we find a passage from nature to culture, from animal to human life, and that we are in a position to understand the very essence of their articulation.

As Taylor has shown almost a century ago, the ultimate explanation is probably that mankind has understood very early that, in order to free itself from a wild struggle for existence, it was confronted with the very simple choice of "either marrying-out or being killed-out." The alternative was between biological families living in juxtaposition and endeavouring to remain closed, self-perpetuating units, overridden by their fears, hatreds, and ignorances, and the systematic establishment, through the incest prohibition, of links of intermarriage between them, thus succeeding to build, out of the artificial bonds of affinity, a true human society, despite, and even in contradiction with, the isolating influence of consanguinity.

In order to ensure that families will not become closed and that they will not constitute progressively as many self-sufficient units, we satisfy ourselves with forbidding marriage between near relatives. The number of social contacts which any given individual is likely to maintain outside his or her own family is great enough to afford a good probability that, on the average, the hundreds of thousands of families constituting at any given moment a modern society will not be permitted to "freeze," if one may say so. On the contrary, the greatest possible freedom for the choice of a mate (submitted to the only condition that the choice has to be made outside the restricted family) ensures that these families will be kept in a continuous flow and that a satisfactory process of continuous "mix-up" through intermarriage will prevail among them, thus making for a homogeneous and well-blended social fabric.

Conditions are quite different in the so-called primitive societies: there, the global figure of the population is a small one, although it may vary from a few dozen up to several thousands. Besides, social fluidity is low and it is not likely that many people will have a chance to get acquainted with others, during their lifetime, except within the limits of the village, hunting territory, etc., though it is true that many tribes have tried to organize occasions for wider contacts, for instance, during feasts, tribal ceremonies, etc. Even in such cases, however, the chances are limited to the tribal group, since most primitive peoples consider that the tribe is a kind of wide family, and that the frontiers of mankind stop together with the tribal bonds themselves.

Given such conditions, it is still possible to ensure the blending of families into a well-united society by using procedures similar to our own, i.e., a mere prohibition of marriage between relatives without any kind of positive prescriptions as to where and whom one should correctly marry. Experience shows, however, that this is only possible in small societies under the condition that the diminutive size of the group and the lack of social mobility be compensated by widening to a considerable extent the range of prohibited degrees. It is not only one's sister or daughter that, under such circumstances, one should not marry, but any women with whom blood relationship may be traced, even in the remotest possible way. Very small groups with a low cultural level and a loose political and social organization, such as some desert tribes of North and South America, provide us with examples of that solution.

However, the great majority of primitive peoples have devised another method to solve the problem. Instead of confining themselves to a statistical process, relying on the probability that certain interdictions being set up, a satisfactory equilibrium of exchanges between the biological families will spontaneously result, they have preferred to invent rules which every individual and family should follow carefully, and from which a given form of blending, experimentally conceived of as satisfactory, is bound to arise.

Whenever this takes place, the entire field of kinship becomes a kind of complicated game, the kinship terminology being used to distribute all the members of the group into different categories, the rule being that the category of the parents defines either directly or indirectly the category of the children, and that, according to the categories in which they are placed, rules of kinship and marriage have provided modern anthropology with one of its more difficult and complicated chapters. Apparently ignorant and savage peoples have been able to devise fantastically clever codes which sometimes require, in order to understand their workings and effects, some of the best logical and even mathematical minds available in modern civilization. Therefore, we will limit ourselves to explaining the crudest principles which are the more frequently met with.

One of these is, undoubtedly, the so-called rule of cross-cousin marriage, which has been taken up by innumerable tribes all over the world. This is a complex system according to which collateral relatives are divided into two basic categories: "parallel" collaterals, when the relationship can be traced through two siblings of the same sex, and "cross" collaterals, when the relationship is traced through two siblings of opposite sex. For instance, my paternal uncle is a parallel relative and so is my maternal aunt; while the maternal uncle on the one hand, the paternal aunt on the other, are cross-relatives.

Now, the startling fact about this distinction is that practically all the tribes which make it claim that parallel relatives are the same thing as the closest ones on the same generation level: my father's brother is a "father," my mother's sister a "mother," my parallel-cousins are like brothers and sisters to me, and my parallel-nephews like children. Marriage with any of these would be incestuous and is consequently forbidden. On the other hand, cross-relatives are designated by special terms of their own, and it is among them that one should preferably find a mate.

All these distinctions (to which others could be added) are fantastic at first sight because they cannot be explained on biological or psychological grounds. But, if we keep in mind what has been explained in the preceding section, i.e., that all the marriage prohibitions have as their only purpose to establish a mutual dependency between the biological families, or, to put it in stronger terms, that marriage rules express the refusal, on the part of society, to admit the exclusive existence of the biological family, then everything becomes clear. For all these complicated sets of rules and distinctions are nothing but the outcome of the processes according to which, in a given society, families are set up against each other for the purpose of playing the game of matrimony.

The female reader, who may be shocked to see womankind treated as a commodity submitted to transactions between male operators, can easily find comfort in the assurance that the rules of the game would remain unchanged should it be decided to consider the men as being exchanged by women's groups. As a matter of fact, some very few societies, of a highly developed matrilineal type, have to a limited extent attempted to express things that way. And both sexes can be comforted from a still different (but in that case slightly more complicated) formulation of the game whereby it would be said that consanguineous groups consisting of both men and women are engaged in exchanging together bonds of relationships.

The important conclusion to be kept in mind is that the restricted family can neither be said to be the element of the social group, nor can it be claimed to result from it. Rather, the social group can only become established in contradistinction, and to some extent in compliance, with the family.

Society belongs to the realm of culture, while the family is the emanation, on the social level, of those natural requirements without which there could be no society and indeed no mankind. As a philosopher of the sixteenth century has said, man can only overcome nature by complying with its laws. Therefore, society has to give the family some amount of recognition. And it is not so surprising that, as geographers have also notice with respect to the use of natural land resources, the greatest amount of compliance with the natural laws is likely to be found at both extremes of the cultural scale: among the simpler peoples as well as among the more highly civilized. Indeed, the first ones are not in a position to afford paying the price of too great a departure, while the second have already suffered from enough mistakes to understand that compliance is the best policy. This explains why, as we have already noticed, the small, relatively stable, monogamic restricted family seems to be given greater recognition, both among the more primitive peoples and in modern societies, than in what may be called (for the sake of the argument) the intermediate levels.

Section IX

Deviance
and
Social Control

Working Philosophies of a Professional Fence

Carl B. Klockars

This case study examines deviance from the frame of reference of an individual engaged in the criminal activity of selling stolen goods. Prompted by the researcher, the individual provides a "defence of his life" (apologia pro vita sua). As it unfolds, we are called upon to question the meaning of deviance and the basis by which we differentiate between a deviant and "legitimate" career.

> The more weakened the groups to which [an individual] belongs, the less he depends on them, the more he consequently depends only on himself and recognizes no other rules of conduct than what are founded on his private interests.
>
> *Emile Durkheim, Suicide*

It is my purpose...to report and analyse Vincent's *apologia pro vita sua*.[1] It is not my contention that all fences see or justify their behaviour as Vincent does, any more than I maintain that they all do business exactly as he does. I do contend, however, that Vincent's explanations are something more than the rationalizations of one particular man with a particular life history. Vincent is neither neurotic nor psychotic. His apologia is persuasive, successfully mitigating the seriousness of his criminality not only to himself but to some others as well. To discard his explanations as simply fragments of illogic, defence mechanisms, or rationalizations would seem at minimum a wasteful use of rather precious testimony.

Vincent is an especially good source for an elaborate apologia. On the one hand he loves his work, knows no other business, and has worked at criminal receiving for more than thirty years. He also has a substantial stake in his identity in this document. On the other hand, he is getting old, has seen a number of his peers die, and is wealthy enough to pack in the business immediately and never want for anything. He is still an Italian Catholic who once took the good sisters' warnings seriously. He has been extraordinarily successful all through his life in persuading people to do what they ought not to do.

One of the problems involved in securing a professional criminal's account for his life is that the only time he need offer it is when he comes into contact with curious or critical members of legitimate society who know he is a criminal. Consequently, one can probably not credit the apologetics of most professional criminals as authentic "working philosophies." But I think the situation with Vincent is different. He is a public, professional criminal; almost everyone he knows is aware that he is a fence. His friends and acquaintances include both upperworld and underworld types. In addition, part of his business includes giving off the impression that what he is doing is not "really bad" even though everybody knows it is illegal. The "public" fence always straddles the boundary between the insiders and outsiders in society. His success depends upon getting insiders to cooperate with outsiders through him. I do not believe that the apologia I present...was constructed just for me. I know that Vincent has explained his mode of life to many others in the same way, and I am further convinced that this is in fact the way he sees what he does.

Although there are no hard data on the subject, it is clear that there is a substantial trade in stolen property.[2] This trade requires, at least in part, the knowing participation of otherwise law-abiding citizens. I venture to suggest that a good many of those who would buy stolen property would be outraged at the thought of committing robbery, burglary, or larceny themselves. Vincent's apologia inevitably plays on themes which support trade in stolen property in the society at large. His explanations are thus cultural artifacts, configurations of sentiment, reason, and perspective which are frequently effective in the rhetoric of our culture in defining the buying of stolen property as acceptable or excusable behaviour. This view of Vincent's testimony suggests that the criminologist seeking to understand the role of the fence in society and the sociology of the trade in stolen goods may begin to do so by considering not only the truth of Vincent's apologia (that is, the extent to which it approximates his actual behaviour and its effect), but also its capacity to assuage the norms which prohibit buying stolen property (and thus free men to do so if the situation presents itself).[3]

Vincent Swaggi: Apologia Pro Vita Sua
Part I—"I Don't Do Nothing Wrong"

Legally, Vincent's acts constitute criminal receiving of stolen property. In the state in which Vincent works, a conviction carries the penalty of imprisonment for up to five years plus a fine of as much as $1,000. With the state's indeterminate-sentence law operating so as to perfunctorily reduce all sentences to one-half the maximum penalty, the maximum time Vincent would serve would be two and one-half years. Vincent correctly considers his conviction exceedingly unlikely and his serving a maximum sentence impossible. In more than thirty years of criminal receiving, Vincent has spent only eight months in jail; his only conviction for receiving was more than twenty years ago. The judgment of the law, except insofar as it codifies certain normative evaluations, is irrelevant to Vincent.

Only Vincent's buying and selling of stolen property threatens his respectability. At first glance, such a statement seems a truism; certainly the reason Vincent is of interest to criminology is that he is a fence. Yet, the context in which otherwise deviant or criminal behaviour occurs enormously affects society's evaluation of that behaviour. Consider the words with which our language reflects a social evaluation of those who violate an identical law in the case of prostitution. Is a "kept woman" a "slut"? Is an "escort" a "whore"? Is a "lady of the evening" a "hooker"? Certainly no poet, a specialist in meaning and impression, would use such words interchangeably. Homosexuality, generally regarded as deviant, seems infinitely more acceptable to society when it is packaged in respectable speech and attire than when it appears in lisping drag. Likewise, it seems easier for society to regard the addiction of the physician or the alcoholism of the housewife as "disease" than to accept the same affliction in the street addict or skid-row bum. Although other factors are also effective in shielding the white-collar criminal from the social and legal definition of his acts as crimes rather than as civil or administrative violations, it would seem that his face of respectability saps our enthusiasm to class and house him with "real" convicts.[4]

The apparatus and behaviour of the fence are not especially different from that of the legitimate businessman. They exist as synecdochical evidence of respectability and affirm that, with the exception of the fact that the fence buys and sells property which is stolen, he is no different from his legitimate-businessman counterparts. For Vincent, his store, his customers, and his legitimate associates simplify his apologia pro vita sua. He need not contend with offensive side effects of his deviance on his presentation of self for they are absent or minor. Instead, he can get right on to the business of showing why his buying and selling stolen goods ain't really that bad after all.

Denial of Responsibility

> The way I look at it, I'm a businessman. Sure I buy hot stuff, but I never stole nothin' in my life. Some driver brings me a couple of cartons, though, I ain't gonna turn him away. If I don't buy it, somebody else will. So what's the difference? I might as well make money with him instead of somebody else.

In the above statement Vincent (1) denies that he ever stole anything in his life. He then asserts either directly or by implication (2) that there is an important distinction between stealing and receiving stolen goods; (3) that the criminal act of receiving would take place even if he were not the one to do it; and (4) that he does not cause the goods to be stolen. Let us consider each of these defences separately.

He never stole anything in his life. In two rigorous senses Vincent has stolen. First, in a number of anecdotes about his childhood...Vincent has described his juvenile industry at theft. He dismisses those events as irrelevant to the above statement, explaining that although he says "never in my life," his childhood does not count. This is illogical in a strict sense of the words used. However, biographical claims are often intended more as moral advertisements than historical descriptions. When such is the intention, it is quite acceptable social form to exclude from public reflections on "true character" those moments of one's life when one was not in full control of one's self. Consider such statements as, "All my life I've followed the Golden Rule." (From age 2? 7? 19? 21?) Or, "He really is a gentle man, but watch out when he's drunk."

Second, according to a strict legal interpretation of his adult behaviour, Vincent does steal. He does, as the common-law definition of theft provides, "take the goods of another, without permission, with the intent to permanently deprive that person of his rightful property." However, the law makes distinctions between theft and receiving (often attaching a lower penalty to receiving), and I suspect that few readers are troubled by Vincent's simultaneous claim both that he has never stolen anything and that he does buy stolen property. It is, for most of us, an understandable social distinction. What Vincent means is that he is not a thief.

There is an important distinction between stealing and receiving. Vincent claims not to be a thief, and we understand what he means. For Vincent himself, there are differences not only between thieves and receivers, but also between thieves and drivers.

> See, Carl, what you gotta understand is when I say "driver" I don't mean "thief." I don't consider a driver a thief. To me, a thief is somebody who goes into a house an' takes a TV set and the wife's jewellery an' maybe ends up killin' somebody before he's through. An' for what? So some nothin' fence will steal the second-hand shit he takes? To me that kind a guy is the scum of the earth.
> Now, a driver, he's different. A driver's a workin' man. He gets an overload now an' then or maybe he clips a carton or two. He brings it to me. He makes a few bucks so he can go out on a Friday night or maybe buy his wife a new coat. To me, a thief an' a driver is two entirely different things.

Those things which distinguish the driver and the thief in Vincent's estimation may point to distinctions that the larger society makes between receiving stolen goods and actually stealing them. The fence, like the driver, does not enter homes or stores to remove property; there is no danger of violence in his presence. A thief, on the other hand, could do anything; he may well be a drug addict, rapist, robber, burglar, or assaulter, or, if the situation arose, a murderer. Society has not clear expectations about the limits of criminality involved.

On the other hand, a fence, Vincent claims, is a businessman who buys an sells stolen property. Like the driver, the fence commits his crime in the course of behaviour which differs only minutely from that of legitimate members of his trade. And like the driver, the fence has a relatively stable social identity: the driver will presumably be at work again tomorrow; Vincent is in his store every day of the week. Vincent buys and sells things, waits on customers, and walks public streets openly. Truck drivers perform public tasks as well. Thieves are shadowy figures, sneaking around behind the scenes and even hiding their right names behind aliases.[5]

In sum, when Vincent begins his apologia by saying "I never stole nothin' in my life," he magnifies a common distinction between a receiver and a thief. He means, first, that he does not actually take merchandise from its owners. But second, and more importantly, he means that the fear, disgust, and distaste which "thief" connotes to some people should not and do not properly apply to him. The law, his customers, his friends, and his neighbours know there are differences between thieves and receivers, and so does Vincent.

Receiving would take place even without him. By saying "If I don't buy it, somebody else will." Vincent attempts to minimize his responsibility by pointing to the presumed consequences of his private refusal to buy. They are, he asserts, nil; therefore his responsibility is nil. This is a patently attractive moral position, and one which is echoed frequently. Let us first examine the accuracy of the assertion before evaluating the moral position which Vincent derives from it.

Would someone else buy the merchandise if Vincent refused? I think they probably would. Although Vincent is able to dispose of some merchandise which other fences might have great difficulty selling (e.g., dental supplies), the vast majority of merchandise in which Vincent trades could be handled by many other fences. The related question, of course, is whether or not the particular thief or driver who approached Vincent with stolen property would be able to locate another fence to sell to if Vincent refused. This is problematic. In my estimation, many would find another outlet almost immediately, some would find one after a bit of looking and asking, and a very few might not be able to find another buyer. Depending on the character both of the merchandise and of his friends and neighbours, the thief or driver might well be able to sell stolen merchandise to them at a better price than he could get from Vincent.

If the accuracy of Vincent's statement is conceded, its moral implications remain to be considered. Certainly one can find examples of the same form of rationalization being offered in quite disparate social situations. The physician on trial for performing a criminal abortion claims that he performed the requested operation rather than have the woman find another, possibly less competent, conspirator. The arms manufacturer claims that he cannot be held responsible for a war because if he had not sold weapons to the participants they would have bought them elsewhere. Likewise, the conscripted soldier who opposes war but fights anyway may take comfort in the knowledge that his participation will not affect the waging of a given war or its outcome.

The moral position upon which such arguments rest is that a person's culpability for participation in an immoral or illegal act disappears or is mitigated if the act is likely to occur even if he does not participate in it. Such a position can be extended to cover situations even less pleasant than those listed above. For example, it removes responsibility in almost all incidents of mob violence. Is no one in a lynch mob responsible because others are also willing to string the victim up? Is looting at a riot scene excusable because others are looting, too? Is vandalism blameless when it is a group affair? To push a position harder still, one could envision a small team of paid professional killers who always shoot their victims simultaneously so that no one gunman feels guilty. Even firing squads, so legend has it, reject such nonsense by actually loading the gun with blanks.

Responsibility for action is responsibility for action. Whether or not an act is likely to occur without one is simply irrelevant to the evaluation of one's own conduct. To surrender that elementary premise of simple moral philosophy is to abandon the responsibility to refuse to participate when one believes that others are doing wrong. Middle-class mothers everywhere, sensitive always to the seductions of the world, have correctly admonished their children who "went along with the crowd": "Just because everybody else jumps off a cliff doesn't mean you have to." It is an admonition of considerable rhetorical sophistication which has absolutely nothing to do with jumping off of cliffs, but gets instantly to the heart of patently attractive denials of responsibility like "If I don't buy it somebody else will."

He does not cause the goods to be stolen. With this statement Vincent suggests his relationship to drivers (and, by extension, thieves) who supply him with stolen merchandise. In Vincent's consideration he is merely a commercial respondent to theft whereas it is thieves and drivers who must bear responsibility for it.

For Vincent, the etiology of theft is a considerably less difficult problem than it is for criminologists: people steal because they want money. Why else should anyone steal? In general, why they want money is their own business, but Vincent, like most small businessmen, is close enough to those he works with to reflect on their motives. For most thieves, Vincent finds that drugs, gambling, and "high living" (Cadillacs for blacks is Vincent's most frequent example) are the main incentives for illegal earnings. Drivers, on the other hand, often use the proceeds from what they sell to add "a little extra" to the family income. To Vincent, it is preposterous to suggest that it is he, rather than the factors which thieves and drivers themselves cite, that is responsible for theft.

Some recent criminology, at least, claims otherwise:

> This coaching (in methods of theft) by the fence in rational criminal techniques may lead to a re-evaluation of the risks involved in criminal activity, which can be an important escalating career contingency.... Additionally, this same effect is achieved merely by meeting the fence and concluding a successful transaction with him.
>
> If we can argue...that we will always "produce" deviants so long as we have an established machinery for processing them, then it might also be legitimate to suggest that the same can be said about the impact of supporting elements. Thus the continued existence of fences, tipsters, and similar types will tend to assure that we will always produce new deviants.[6]

Thus, Shover contends that fences encourage thieves and drivers by approving of their stealing and advising them how to steal successfully. In addition, fences may, simply by their continued existence and availability as fences, tend to assure the continuing existence of a population of drivers and thieves.

Shover's argument is compelling, and with a few technical reservations... Vincent is inclined to agree with this sophisticated sociological rendition of the old adage "If there were no receivers, there would be no thieves." However, Vincent's sense of his own personal responsibility for the stealing by thieves and drivers is quite a different matter. It is at this individual level that the norms of Vincent's world and Shover's sociology part company.

In the same way that Shover's argument suggests that the continued existence of public bars assures the continued existence of a population of alcoholics, or the manufacture of high-powered cars "produces" highway speeders, or the existence of gambling casinos "escalates the career contingencies" of compulsive or intemperate gamblers, Vincent concedes that fences are a part of the machinery that sustains and encourages theft. But with a logic that I suspect is familiar to, at least, bartenders, high-powered-car manufacturers, and casino owners, he argues that "I don't force anybody to do business with me who doesn't want to." Vincent further insists that adults are adults and "should know what they are doing."

Vincent views his own life history with a similar sense of individual responsibility. He can see how some of his early experiences—street hustling, his orphanage term, his association with his Uncle Hoppo—may have encouraged his becoming a fence. ("I guess I picked up a lot of my ideas from hangin' around with Hoppo and those guys.") But there is no sense in which Vincent would blame anyone else for where he is and what he does today. To do so would strike Vincent as unmasculine, the mark of a weak person or a crybaby.[7]

In denying his responsibility for theft in this way, Vincent takes the question of his responsibility to an area with which he is most familiar—one in which moral and legal grounds for establishing responsibility are constantly shifting. Consider the case of the vendor of alcoholic beverages. One can state categorically that if there were no alcohol there would be no abuse of alcohol, no alcoholics, no drunken driving, no public drunkenness. Nevertheless, it is generally conceded that vendors of alcohol ought not to be held responsible for their customers' abuse of it. Normally, the consumer bears the total responsibility for his use or misuse of what he buys. However, in particular circumstances, the vendor may acquire both legal and moral responsibilities for his customers. He cannot, for example, sell liquor to minors, nor, according to the law in many states, can he sell it to an obviously intoxicated person. In still other states, the law requires that he provide transportation home for a patron who is unfit to drive. In each of these special cases the loss or absence of the consumer's adult capacities may legally if not morally oblige the vendor to assume them. There is some point beyond which legal responsibility cannot be extended for practical reasons, but how far ought one to extend moral responsibility? Should a bartender serve a customer who has cirrhosis? Or, are even the above laws too morally and legally paternalistic, denying one's right to get drunk in public if he wants to?[8] There are no certain grounds, legal or moral, upon which to settle such questions.

Similar problems, both moral and legal, are involved in many transactions between buyers and sellers. The question is always "Who is responsible?" and, ultimately, it must be resolved in favour of one party or the other. The bartender must know if he is obliged to serve the intoxicated person who demands another drink or if he is obliged to refuse him and call a taxi to take him home. When Vincent argues that it is the thief or driver and not he who is responsible for theft he employs a notion of responsibility which is derived from and is peculiar to business transactions. For Vincent, responsibility is an either/or proposition, as it must be in relations between buyers and sellers. It works on the principle of subtraction: if the thief is responsible for his stealing then Vincent is not.

The highly peculiar quality of Vincent's subtractive sense of responsibility becomes apparent when one takes it out of the context of business transactions. Elsewhere, the notion of responsibility is governed not by a principle of subtraction but by a principle of addition. It is perfectly normal to refer to two, three, ten, or even hundreds of, people as being responsible for a given act or event. Ant it is, of course, with this additive concept of responsibility that the law prohibiting criminal receiving is justified and the moral responsibility of the criminal receiver established. Simply stated, the thief is responsible for his stealing and the criminal receiver is responsible for encouraging that theft.

Denial of Victims

The first line of defence in Vincent's apologia is his denial of responsibility for theft and his argument that for him to refrain from buying stolen goods would be inconsequential. His second line of argument is to deny that his activities have any meaningful victims or inflict any significant injury. To appreciate Vincent's second defence one must consider some of the experiences from which he reasons.

More than most people, Vincent witnesses extensive violations of the law against receiving. He sees respectable society, including police and judicial officials, coming to him for bargains that they know are suspect. Because of his reputation, he is often solicited by otherwise legitimate businessmen interested in buying something that they deal in should he come across it. He also encounters respectable types who find something romantic about his being a fence. For example:

> I got to know my doctor real good when I was in for my last operation. Somebody told him about me, I guess. Well, I started tellin' him about stuff, you know, buyin', sellin', thieves, boosters. He just couldn't get over it. He wanted me to get him some hot suits. You know, have him pick out the suits and send some booster in to get 'em. He really wanted to do it. You shoulda seen how excited he was talkin' about swag. Imagine a guy like that, a big doctor an' all, getting so excited about hot stuff.

This widespread trafficking with him, and occasional fascination for his work, have consequences for the way Vincent sees his own behaviour. First of all, he is conscious of a certain hypocrisy in society's attitude toward dealing in stolen property. He is aware of the legal prohibition against receiving, yet sees frequent evidence of wilful, guilt-free violation of it by those who ought to know better. Vincent's recall of occasions when highly respectable citizens bought

stolen goods or what they thought were stolen goods is extremely acute.
Legitimate citizens of high status are truly "significant others" for Vincent.

Indeed, Vincent sees the patronage of such legitimate citizens as a reflection
of his own worth. Their buying from him and maintaining friendly relations with
him are considered by Vincent to constitute an important vindication of the
possibly shady character of what he does. It is true that Vincent is an attractive
and enjoyable person; but even if his friendly acquaintances seek him out only
for this social aspect of his personality, Vincent finds it easy to perceive that
they are not sufficiently offended by his receiving to limit their association with
him.[9]

Given the highly supportive character of Vincent's immediate environment,
he is able to think of his victim and the injury he receives as someone or
something "out there," removed from him physically and normatively, and
separated by the intervening actions and responsibility of the thief or driver.
Only very rarely does Vincent ever confront the victim of a theft. The latter is
likely to direct his rage at the thief, his employee's carelessness, or his faulty
security system rather than at the fence who eventually buys what was stolen
from him.

From this detached perspective, Vincent contemplates the extent of his
victims' losses:

> Did you see the paper yesterday? You figure it out. Last year I
> musta had $25,000 worth a merchandise from Sears. In this city
> last year they could'a called it Sears, Roebuck, and Swaggi. Just
> yesterday in the paper I read where Sears just had the biggest
> year in history, made more money than ever before. Now if I had
> that much of Sear's stuff can you imagine how much they musta
> lost all told? Millions, must be millions. And they still had their
> biggest year ever.

Vincent reads Sears's declaration of success as evidence of the inconsequential
character of his receiving their stolen merchandise. Hence he considers any
possible claim on their part that he or hundreds of others like him are
substantially harming business as at least greedy if not absurd. The logic of such
an analysis is the same, on a larger scale, as the "Ma Bell can afford it"
reasoning invoked by the pay-phone patron who receives a windfall from a
malfunctioning unit. Vincent does not stop there in his consideration of Sears's
success, however.

> You think they end up losing when they get clipped? Don't you
> believe it. They're no different from anybody else. If they don't

get it back by takin' it off their taxes, they get it back from
insurance. Who knows, maybe they do both.

Carl, if I told you many businessmen I know have a robbery every
now an' then to cover expenses you wouldn't believe it. What
does it take? You get some trusted employee, and you send him
out with an empty truck. He parks it somewhere an' calls in an'
says he was robbed. That's it. The insurance company's gotta pay
up. The driver makes a couple of hundred bucks and it's an
open-an'-shut case. You can't do it every year but once in a while
it's a sure thing.

Oh, there's millions a ways to do it. You come in in the mornin'
an break your window. Call the cops, mess some stuff up. Bang!
You got a few thousand from the insurance company. I'm tellin'
ya, it happens all the time.

Thus Vincent denies significant injury to Sears not only because of their net
profits but because they can be seen as recovering most of their loss from
insurance payments or through tax write-offs.[10] The reality for Vincent, in
sum, is the comparatively trivial effect of theft on the insured victim.
Inconvenient, perhaps; devastating, no! Hence: no real injury, no real victim.

The problem remaining is the general effect on pricing that theft produces.
As a businessman, Vincent is in agreement with his counterparts that theft and
shrinkage result in higher mark-ups and higher prices. But Vincent again falls
back on the question of the ultimate consequences of his particular refusal to
buy. Assuming his thieves and drivers could not find anyone else to sell to, the
entire result of Vincent's private refusal to buy might amount to a penny a
person for the entire year, if it were distributed over the total population of the
city. And on the other side of the ledger, Vincent reckons that some of his
other services to the general welfare of the community more than balance what
he takes out.

The questions of the moral responsibility involved in buying stolen goods,
and of the consequences of such an act for any putative victims, would be even
less problematic for Vincent's customers than for Vincent were they to confront
them. Given that a particular item is on Vincent's shelf and is known to be
stolen, a particular purchase will not affect Vincent's survival as a fence. I do
not believe that a rational economic argument can be made against an
individual decision to buy stolen goods. The claim that theft costs everyone as
reflected in higher costs and insurance rates is inadequate. It costs everyone
surely, but those who buy stolen goods manage to offset these higher costs and
rates. In fact, were it simply a question of a personal economic strategy, one
might argue that the only way to beat the consequences of the thieves' market

is to patronize it. The only argument left seems to be to appeal to a responsibility to the general welfare of others.

To legalize receiving stolen goods would legitimize an institution which is intolerable. It would encourage theft and have a pernicious effect on society. Clearly it is an absurd suggestion. But the conflict is still real. The department-store sweater costs $15.99. Vincent is selling it for $10.00. In this particular case it is a question of saving $5.99 or making an economic gesture to the general welfare. All day long Vincent sees the general welfare lose out to bargains.

Vincent Swaggi: Apologia Pro Vita Sua
Part II—"I Think I'm a Pretty Decent Guy"

To this point Vincent's apologia has focused on what he considers to be the particularly benign features of his occupation. He finds no victims and no real injury. He denies responsibility for theft and its encouragement. He maintains that his private refusal to buy stolen property would be inconsequential. Vincent reaches these conclusions about the character of what he does by interpreting his day-to-day behaviour in the most favourable possible way. I have been able to point to these errors in Vincent's analysis because this portion of his apologia was an analysis of concrete events. In short, I could compare Vincent's evaluation of what he does and has done with descriptions of the events themselves.

In this second portion of his apologia Vincent changes the character of his account from a professional, offence-specific defence of his criminal career to a more general evaluation of his character. The assertion Vincent made in Part I of his *Apologia, Pro Vita Sua* was that he didn't do anything wrong; the assertion he makes in Part II is that he is, all things considered, a nice guy.

Because the terms of Vincent's argument change in this second portion of his apologia, it is difficult to criticize what he says. Specific acts, their consequences and interpretation, are not at issue. Hence the critic of Vincent is disarmed, because no particular act of Vincent's will disprove his claims. Contrariwise, the nature of the way Vincent makes his argument ensures that a complete display of evidence in favour of his claim (viz., in spite of everything he has done, he is a decent fellow) need not—indeed cannot—be made. I have called the sensibility within which Vincent comprehends his good character "the metaphor of the ledger."

The Metaphor of the Ledger

> Sure I've done some bad things in my life. Who hasn't?
> Everybody's got a skeleton in his closet somewhere. But you gotta
> take into account all the good things I done too. You take all the
> things I done in my life and put 'em together, no doubt about it,
> I gotta come out on the good side.

As a businessman, Vincent is familiar with the use of a ledger for evaluating the success or failure of enterprise. He knows that there are different ways of setting up and managing accounts. Some entries are puffed a bit more than they deserve; other profits don't show up in the accounting. Occasionally, one shows a loss so as to make things look normal or to prevent having to pay too much in the end. Business accounts, property managed by able accountants, set things in order for the businessman and those who are interested in judging what he has accomplished. When all is said and done, the ledger tells whether or not one comes up in the red or in the black.

A metaphorical ledger is equally useful in evaluating life histories: good in the credit column is balanced against evil in the debit column. Thus, acts of charity and benevolence offset entries of greed or selfishness. It is an attractive metaphor. From the scales of justice to the great Book of St. Peter, the notion of a balancing between good and evil has proven to be a persuasive one for the common comprehension and consideration of penance, indulgence, grace, judgment, atonement, salvation, and contrition.[11]

To Vincent, a businessman all his life, the metaphor of the ledger comes easily. In accounting for his conduct, Vincent considers his criminality and his exemplary behaviour on the same balance sheet.

> When it comes to fences I consider myself in a class by myself. I
> don't consider your street-corner fences, buyin' an' sellin' second-
> hand stuff, to be anything like me at all. For one thing they're all
> no good. They're all cheap, greedy bastards who'd sell their
> mother if they had a chance. I figure I have a certain class, ya
> know, a certain way of doin' things. To me them guys are nothin'.
> They're stupid, ignorant people. I can't even stand bein' around
> 'em.

Thieves and Drivers. In reckoning credits for his self-evaluation, Vincent points to those good things he has done for people which his role did not require him to do. For example:

> Take what I done for Artie, for instance. Now there's a guy, he's
> been a thief for years, an' nothin' to show for it. That year alone
> I musta given him $25,000. One day I'd give 'em a hundred
> bucks, the next day he'd be back askin' for a loan. So I had a talk
> with him. I told him, "Look, you're makin' good money. Why
> don't you put it toward a house?" So we set up a little deal where
> I'd keep a little each time we had a deal; then when he had
> enough we'd put it toward a house.
> Well it took about three months an' he had about $1,500 with
> me. So I got a real estate agent I knew to get him a place, nothin'
> fancy but a pretty good neighbourhood. It was coloured but clean.
> Well, you know what happened? His wife came down with his
> kids an' she couldn't thank me enough. They had been livin' in
> one of those welfare high rises and she hated it. Every now an'
> then she comes by to tell me how things are goin'.
> Don't get me wrong. I made a lot of money off of Artie, but I set
> him straight too.

What places Vincent's efforts in Artie's behalf on the credit side of the ledger
is the fact that Artie and his wife appreciated Vincent's assistance and that
Vincent did not have to give it. Vincent has repeated similar anecdotes to me
frequently.

> I am good to children. You know "Eyeball," right? All the trouble
> I had with him? His wife came in at Christmastime last year.
> When she left she had at least a hundred dollars worth of clothes
> and toys for her kids. I knew Eyeball was in jail an' she didn't
> have nothin'. Carl, if you knew how much stuff I gave to people,
> outright gifts, you wouldn't believe it.
> Would you believe it if I told you that I got a thief who calls me
> "his white father"? It's true. I been good to him. Posted bail for
> him a couple of times. He tells everybody, "Vincent Swaggi, he's
> my white father."

The matter of the posted bail in the second anecdote raises a number of
complications in the matter of crediting Vincent's generosity. One could
interpret Vincent's bailing out the thief as self-serving, since Vincent knew that
once back on the street, the thief would resume bringing him merchandise. The
extent to which such actions should be seen as impelled by generosity becomes
even more problematic in those cases where Vincent benefits more than does
the recipient. Many people turn to Vincent for "help" when they are in a jam
and don't know what to do. Providing alibis, referrals to persuasive lawyers,

loans at high interest, and the kind of encouragement a man occasionally needs to get back to his work are all well appreciated. Just a little bit of help sometimes pays off handsomely.

> I had this guy bringin' me radios. Nice little clock radios, sold for $34.95. He worked in the warehouse. Two a day he's bring me, and I'd give him fifteen for the both of 'em. Well, after a while he told me his boss was gettin' suspicious 'cause inventory showed a big shortage. So I asked him how he was gettin' the radios out. He says he puts 'em in his locker at lunch an' takes 'em to me after work. So I ask him to lay off for a while an' the next time he sees one of the other guys take somethin' to tip off the boss. They'll fire the guy an' clear up the shortage. Well he did it an' you know what happened? They made my man assistant shipper. Now once a month I get a carton delivered right to my store with my name on it. Clock radios, percolators, waffle irons, anything I want, fifty off wholesale.

Though Vincent is reluctant to place such profitable assistance in his credit column, one must consider that matter from the perspective of the newly appointed shipper: Vincent advised him well. He saved him from his suspicious boss, cleared his reputation, got him promoted, probably with a raise, and made it possible for him not only to increase his earnings from theft but to steal with greater security as well. For Vincent, on the other hand, such an incident cancels itself out; it was good advice which paid off. Yet, although such events cannot, because they paid off so well, be offered individually as evidence of virtue, in the aggregate they enhance Vincent's professional self-conception. However, they leave a residual magnanimity which surfaces in statements such as the following:

> I treat the people I deal with right. If they're in a jam an' I can help 'em out, I'll do it. And I don't mean just your high-class types either. I mean, thieves, drivers, police, customers, anybody. I'm known for helpin' people out when I can.
> You don't have to be a bastard to be in this business, you know. You can treat people decent. Some guys, like my brother, never learn that. They think a black man comes into the store, you can push 'em around, call him "coloured" or "boy"; you just can't do that no more. Times have changed.
> I am liked by the people I do business with. No doubt about it. They know I treat 'em right. Look at my window. You see any grate over it? How long have you known me? More than a year

now, right? Did you ever see that window broken? With all the
characters I do business with, how long do you think it would be
before somebody threw a brick through it if they didn't like me?
I am known for bein' good to people. That window's been there
ever since I had this store. Nobody ever touched it.

Vincent is sensitive to the opinions people have of him, even if those people
are only thieves and drivers. When his daughter's home was robbed, he
explained, "You know, Carl, if it's somebody I know, I'm hurt. If not, God bless
'em." This remark, although a bit more sentimental than usual for Vincent, is
interesting. It reveals both an expectation of occupational loyalty and a kind of
professional respect. "God bless 'em" ought not to be interpreted as implying
a passive response, however. Vincent worked very hard at locating the culprits.

The difficulty in finding unambiguously creditable behaviour for the positive
side of the ledger is that in relations with thieves and drivers the roles of "good
fence" and "decent guy" are in part congruent. Self-interest becomes visible in
generosity, and profits make altruism suspect. Such an opinion is possible,
though, only to those permitted a full account of the fence's operations. While
Vincent is aware of the payoffs for him in acts of apparent generosity and
assistance, his thieves are not.... If Vincent is liked, appreciated, and thanked,
he does not advertise his altruism; in fact, he is likely to minimize the
importance of his own acts. ("It was the least I could do. Don't get me wrong,
I made a lot of money off of him.") By doing so he is thus freed to accept the
gratitude and appreciation of those he helped. These responses Vincent
remembers, reminds me of, and credits to the good side of the ledger.

Customers. Vincent's customers provide him with frequent opportunities for
creditable behaviour, but just as with thieves and drivers, questions of self-
interest plague Vincent's accounting. "Bargains," "Just-for-you" prices, and
doing people "favours" by selling them merchandise at 30% below wholesale
evoke favourable attitudes, but just don't qualify as hard evidence of goodness,
because they are too much a part of what is required in a fence's business. The
following incident is clearly creditable to the good side of the ledger, but it also
suggests how difficult it is to be good when self-interest is suspected.

The other day this old lady comes in my store. She's Irish, got a
brogue so thick you could cut it with a knife. I can tell she ain't
got much. I mean her clothes were cheap an' she's got this real
thin cloth coat on. You remember how cold it was last
Wednesday? Well, she's real old-country, kerchief on the back of
her head an' all.

She says she's lookin' for a sweater 'cause it's so cold out. I tell her she don't need a sweater, what she really needs is a good heavy coat. She says she ain't got enough money for a coat now. So I ask her how much she got an' she says six dollars. "Six dollars," I say. "Are you in luck, Mother. I have a special sale on coats today, but you can only get one if you're Irish.
"I'm Irish," she says. "No," I say, "really?" I'm givin' her the whole bullshit, you know.
Anyway, I show her three coats I got in the back. They were samples, retail maybe $45 or $50. "Are you selling these for only six dollars?" she says. "Ya," I say, "but only today and only if you're Irish. Are you sure you're Irish?" "Aye," she says, "I sure am." Then you know what she says to me? She says, "What's wrong with these coats?" Fifty-dollar coats for six dollars and she asks me what's wrong. "The buttons are the wrong colour. They're black an' they should be brown." I gotta tell her somethin' or she wouldn't buy it. So I take her six bucks so she won't think it's charity.
You know, she comes back to shop every so often. Do you know she still doesn't understand I gave her that coat. She thinks I had to sell the coat for six bucks 'cause the buttons were black instead of brown.

It is important to remember that within a few minutes after this incident of generosity Vincent was probably back at his characteristically very sharp trading. There is no illogic in bargaining extremely hard at one moment and virtually giving away goods at the next. The former confirms a professional businesslike self-conception; the latter demonstrates that one is a good man.

Generosity and creditable behaviour are possible only when the motives of Vincent's customers are innocent. To be generous when the recipient of your generosity is an able and aggressive economic foe not only is unprofessional but also leaves one open for being seen as a sucker.

I got this guy who comes in every so often, he's an insurance agent. He walks all over my store—behind the counter, in the back room, everywhere. He's a real tight bastard, a Jew. I can't stand him, you know. One day I got a store full of customers. I'm sellin' like mad. He's pullin' stuff off my shelves an' he comes over with a couple of sweaters. "How much for me, Vince?" he says. I say, "Whaddaya mean, 'how much for me?'" So he says, "You know, what's my price on this stuff?" So I really let him have it. I start yellin', "What the hell makes you think you get a special price? What makes you think you're better than anybody else? Take this old lady here. You think you're better than her? She's the one who really deserves a special price." Well, the whole store gets upset. The guy don't know what to do. "OK, OK, Vince," he says. "Take it easy. I didn't mean nothin'. Take it easy. Tell me what the price is, I'll pay it." "No," I says. "To you it's not for sale; you ain't buyin nothin' in here today." I told him that. Threw him right outta the store. I'll tell you, sometimes I just can't stand that kind a guy.

With those who by definition do not act out of self-interest, on the other hand, charity and generosity are easy to establish.

You know how much I do for children, right? The other day this nun comes in from the House of the Good Shepherd. Oh, I known her for years. If you knew the stuff I gave her—shoes, clothes, toys, everything. Well, she comes in and my brother and Kelly, Happy, an' another hood are all in the store too. Well, I give her a pile of girls' dresses I was savin' up. Then I says, "Wait a minute, Sister, I think we can do a little more for you." So then I turn to everybody in the store an' I say, "When was the last time you gangsters did anything for the children of this world?" I said, I'm gonna give Sister here twenty dollars an' I'm gonna put four tens out on the counter. Each one of you guys puts up a ten, the Sister here gets another ten too." Well, my brother, he runs in the back room, and that fatso, Happy, runs out the door. Both of 'em have more money than they know what to do with, but the're just cheap bastards. So Kelly and the other hood are stuck. They gotta put up the dough or they look bad. Well, I gave the Sister the other twenty, too. On the way out, she says to me, "Are those men really gangsters?" I said, "Ya, they been in rackets all their lives." Then she says to me, "Hmmm, they did look a little shady."

The Police. Sometimes Vincent claims credit for his actions for reasons more subtle than outright charitableness or benevolence. This is particularly so with respect to his acts of cooperation with the police.

I had a computer once, you know. [I respond, "A computer?"] Ya, a computer. Two guys drove up to my store in a truck. They said they had a machine in the truck they wanted me to look at. It was a computer right out of the university. I don't know how they got it out, but it was about as big as that chair [a large recliner]. I said, "Look, there ain't nobody nowhere gonna touch that. It must have a million numbers on it." Well, we talked about it for a while an' they took my advice. I gave 'em fifty bucks an' told 'em to unload it on my platform. Then I called this Inspector I know an' told him what I had. Do you know he got the report it was missin' right while I was talkin' to him on the phone? That machine was worth twenty or thirty thousand dollars. If I didn't take if off those shines, they would'a dumped it in the river. See, the police department knows that I'll help 'em out when I can. An' I never took no reward for doin' that, either.[12]

Vincent's assistance here qualifies as creditable behaviour not so much because it was virtuous in itself (the computer was returned rather than destroyed), but because no special claim for its goodness was made (no reward was taken).

And sometimes Vincent's motives for what would be considered creditable behaviour are more subtle than those of either simple benevolence or simple self-interest or a mixture of both:

I had two guys, black guys, drive up one day. They had rifles. I could tell just by lookin' at 'em they were Army rifles. So I told 'em I'd take all they could get, an' they said they had thousands of 'em. They left, and right away I got on the phone to a guy I knew from the FBI. I told him I didn't want the guys arrested, but I didn't want all these guns gettin' into the hands of Black Power, either. So I got the OK to buy. They found out they were comin' out of a boxcar an' stopped it. I figure I done a good thing there, don't you?

I agreed, as Vincent knew I would. And so did the FBI. Vincent demonstrated not only civic responsibility but also self-sacrifice: he could have made a great deal of money. He also evidenced certain limits on what he will do, apparently owing in this case to his harbouring certain fears and attitudes regarding potential recipients of the weapons. But self-interest is always in dogged pursuit of Vincent. The reader is invited to consider the above anecdotes in light of Simmel's classic understanding of gratitude:

This irredeemable nature of gratitude shows it as a bond between men which is as subtle as it is firm. Every human relationship of any duration produces a thousand occasions for it, and even the most ephemeral ones do not allow their increment to the reciprocal obligation to be lost. In fortunate cases, but sometimes even in cases abundantly provided with counter-instances, the sum of these increments produces an atmosphere of generalized obligation (the saying that one is "obliged" ["verbunden"] to somebody who has earned our thanks is quite apt), which can be redeemed by no accomplishments whatever. This atmosphere of obligation belongs among those "microscopic," but infinitely tough, threads which tie one element of society to another, and thus eventually all of them together in a stable collective life.[13]

Deviant Behaviour and the Metaphor of the Ledger

No one has ever seen a real "ledger" for life. Yet it is an old theme, and one which has caused no small amount of controversy. The theological grounds of the debate between Luther and the Roman Catholic Church were not simply the abuses of the Roman Church in selling indulgences, but whether or not good works (like giving money to the church) could, in the heavenly ledger, balance out sins.[14] However, in no way does the metaphor of the ledger disappear with the Reformation. One finds it equally reflected in the *values weighed* and *balanced* under the *calculus* of *price* in *utilitarian* ethics.[15]

But Vincent's sense of the metaphor of the ledger is neither careful Catholic theology nor neo-Benthamite utilitarianism. It is rather a common-sense perception of the vague standard by which most of us evaluate men—one that is metaphorically embedded in our language almost everywhere we speak of evaluation. Consider "pay off," "dividend," "cost," "value," "price," "good" and "goods," "waste," "profit, "and "debt." The words of business come easily to us in our reflections on morality. The judge declaring that the prisoner has "paid his debt to society" speaks in the moral metaphor society is willing to hear. Vincent—a businessman, Catholic, and self-made man—takes to the metaphor of the ledger naturally. It does not emerge as his instrument of moral evaluation in concrete references to a real book of life or a real ledger kept in heaven. Vincent does not believe in such a real book in any way. Rather, the mechanism of the metaphor of the ledger is hidden in the way he organizes his apologia and the impression he intends from offering his positive anecdotes.

When Vincent says, "You gotta take into consideration all the good things I done, too," the question in response might well be "Why?" To ask it would be to challenge the metaphor of the ledger hidden within it. But Vincent would not understand the question, any more than most of us would think to ask it. The metaphor of the ledger is driven deeply enough in our consciousness that the question would be dismissed as annoying "philosophical meddling" with what everybody knows is "just common sense."

But, as we have seen, Vincent's eye for the loophole works as well with the metaphor of the ledger as it does with the morality (and law) of criminal receiving. His sense for the balance between good acts and bad, for the credit he earns for his charity, and for the existence of a debit column in every man's ledger allows him to make a favourable accounting of his life. In so doing, he manages to preserve his faith in am oral order not notably different from that which most of us accept. However, his sense of the metaphor of the ledger allows him to loosen the restraints of that moral order just enough to emerge from a thirty-year criminal career with a positive, moral, decent self-image.

Endnotes

1. Chapter 26 of John Landesco's *Organized Crime in Chicago*, from *The Professional Fence* by Carl B. Klockars. Copyright 1974 by The Free Press, a Division of Macmillan Publishing Company.

2. There is no way to make a reliable estimate of the total value of goods passing through the hands of fences like Vincent each year. Since 99% of Vincent's merchandise is new, it is certain that most of it comes from wholesale and retail businesses, including manufacturers, distributors, shippers, and warehouses. Business losses are uniformly entered under the category of "shrinkage," which includes employee theft, shoplifting, bookkeeping errors, and some forms of embezzlement. In 1963 the "shrinkage" total for retail stores, estimated at retail prices, was $1,757,000,000. Of this figure, it was further estimated that $1,318,000,000 was due to some form of dishonesty. There is no way of estimating what percentage of this figure represents merchandise that was eventually fenced. One must also remember that this figure applies only to retail businesses and does not include burglary, hijacking, or theft from the cargo industry, including trucking, shipping or air freight. President's Commission on Law Enforcement and the Administration of Justice Task Force on Assessment, *Crime and Its Impact—An Assessment* (Washington, D.C.: Government Printing Office, 1967), pp. 48—49.

3. Essays in the theoretical tradition that this chapter follows include the following: C. Wright Mills, "Situated Actions and Vocabularies of Motive," *American Sociological Review* 5 (1940): 904-13; Marvin B. Scott and Stanford M. Lyman, "Accounts," *American Sociological Review* 33 (1968): 46-62; Gresham Sykes and David Matza, "Techniques of Neutralization," *American Sociological Review* 22 (1957): 556-69; and especially David Matza, *Delinquency and Drift* (New York: John Wiley and Sons, 1964). The full theoretical grounds of this perspective on the

social order as I understand it are best set forth by Kenneth Burke in *A Grammar of Motives* (New York: Prentice-Hall, 1945) and *Performance and Change* (New York: Bobbs-Merrill Co., 1965).

4. Cf.: "Legislators admire and respect business and cannot conceive of them as criminals; that is, businessmen do not conform to the popular stereotype of 'the criminal.'" Edwin H. Sutherland, "Is White Collar Crime Crime?" in *White Collar Criminal*, ed. Gilbert Geis (New York: Atherton Press, 1968), p. 360. See also Richard Austin Smith, "The Incredible Electrical Conspiracy," *Fortune* (April, 1961), pp. 132-80, for an application of Sutherland's observation.

5. The matter of "potential for deviance," by which I mean people's estimations of the probability that one type of deviance implies the capacity for other types, merits systematic criminological examination. As an example, our treatment of the insane by incarceration seems to presume that relatively mild violations of social propriety suggests a capacity for more serious and perhaps violent deviance. Similarly, before the time when long hair was co-opted by an economic establishment willing to capitalize on it, long hair seemed to be regarded by many as a certain sign of the willingness of the wearer to engage in other, non-tonsorial, forms of deviance. Likewise, society may well assume that, all other things being equal, a thief has a greater "potential for deviance" than a fence.

6. Neal Shover, "Structures and Careers in Burglary," *Journal of Criminal Law, Criminology, and Police Science* 63 (1972), pp. 545-49.

7. Or, occasionally, the ploy of criminals hustling those with social-worker mentalities. (Robert Earl Barnes, "The Fence: Crime's Real Profiteer," *Reader's Digest* [September 1973], p. 155).

> My criminal career began when I was ten years old and I stole a bundle of comic books from a drugstore doorstep. When I tried to trade them to the local barber for some in his shop I hadn't read, he wouldn't barter—but he did offer to buy all the comics I could provide for two cents each. He never asked, but I'm sure he knew they were stolen. From that first transaction, I learned what every professional thief must know: there's no use stealing unless you know someone willing to pay for the goods you steal....

8.   A case in point: an article in the London *Times*, for Friday, March 8, 1974, entitled "Publican Criticized over Death of Customer."

A publican served two double measures of Chartreuse and five double Pernods to a customer who had already drunk 11 or 12 pints of beer, an inquest heard today. The customer fell off his bar stool and died.... The coroner said both Mr. Mosley [the publican] and Mr. Lewis [the man with whom the customer was engaged in a drinking competition] were both stupid and irresponsible in their actions. Mr. Ross's [the dead customer's] drinking was incredible and abnormal and Mr. Moseley in particular ought to have realised it was reaching the danger level. Irresponsibility did not amount to manslaughter.

9.   The idea of *innocence by association* raises important questions for researchers in the sociology of deviance. Simply by associating with deviants the field researcher gives tacit reinforcement to them. My association with Vincent was interpreted by him as quite complimentary, and the vast majority of thieves I have interviewed have felt similarly flattered. My generally non-judgmental attitude was uniformly construed as approval. Likewise, I find that a text like my own is easy to interpret as being supportive of deviant careers, in spite of my protestations that it is primarily descriptive and analytical, in the way sociology must be. A similar case can be made regarding the degree of attention paid to militant blacks in the liberal press. (See Nathan Glazer and Daniel P. Moynihan, *Beyond the Melting Pot*, 2nd. ed., rev. [Cambridge: M.I.T. Press, 1970], p. xxxvii.)

10.   Months after Vincent told me about his views on Sears' profits in spite of their losses from theft, I ran across the following obscure news item (John Manning, ed., "No Money Down" [Philadelphia: Publication of the Model Cities Consumer Protection Program, vol. 1, no. 3, p. 3] It is rather perverse to print it here but I cannot resist the irony.

Sears fastbuck: Second Income News relates how Richard W. Sears, founder of Sears, Roebuck, got started in business. Sears was a railroad telegrapher with a sideline business of selling watches. His gimmick was to buy watches at $2 apiece, affix $20 price-tags, and mail them to fictitious locations across the country. When the packages came back "undeliverable," Sears would open them in the presence of fellow employees and palm the watches off as "bargains"—at $10 apiece.

11.   Reference to a Book of Life wherein all of man's deeds are recorded is
        found throughout Scripture. For example, Rev. 20: 11-15 states:

        [11] Then I saw a great white throne and him who sat upon it;
        from his presence earth and sky fled away, and no place was
        found for them. [12] And I saw the dead, great and small,
        standing before the throne, and books were opened. Also another
        book was opened, which is the book of life. And the dead were
        judged by what was written in the books, by what they had done.
        [13] And the sea gave up the dead in it. Death and Hades gave
        up the dead in them, and all were judged by what they had done.
        [14] Then Death and Hades were thrown into the fire; [15] And
        if any one's name was not found written in the book of life, he
        was thrown into the lake of fire.

12.   Maurer notes that pickpockets occasionally return wallets containing
        valuable papers to their owners after the money has been removed.
        Usually this is done by disposing of the empty wallet in a post office box.
        "This is not done," says Maurer, "for reasons of sentiment, for fair play,
        or consideration for the sucker. It is done for reasons of public
        relations...." David W. Maurer, *Whiz Mob* (Gainesville, Fla.: Publication
        of the American Dialect Society, 1955), p. 119. "Public relations" are far
        more essential to the fence than to the pickpocket, and the similarity in
        public relations technique is notable.

13.   George Simmel, "Faithfulness and Gratitude," in *The Sociology of George
        Simmel*, ed. and trans. Kurt Wolff (New York: The Free Press, 1964),
        p. 395.

14.   In 1517 Luther posted his Ninety-Five Theses on the side door of the
        Castle Church at Wittenburg. Theses no. 40 and no. 44 (quoted in John
        Dillenberger, ed., *Martin Luther* [New York: Doubleday and Co., 1961],
        p. 494) are particularly relevant:

        No. 40 A truly contrite sinner seeks out, and loves to pay, the
        penalty of his sins; whereas the very multitude of indulgences
        dulls men's consciences, and tends to make them hate the
        penalties.
        No. 44 Because, by works of love, love grows and a man becomes
        a better man; whereas, by indulgences, he does not become a
        better man, but only escapes certain penalties.

15.   See "Secular Mysticism in Bentham" in Burke, op. cit., pp. 188-94, for Burke's study of the metaphors which seduced Bentham.

The Criminal Justice System

Laureen Snider

Who breaks the law? Who ends up in prison? What is the role of the police and the courts in enforcement and punishment? In this selection Laureen Snider gives a statistical outline of the Canadian criminal justice system and attempts to explain what these facts mean. Her research shows how decisions by police, judges, lawyers and other participants both reflect and influence the wider political and economic system within which crime is "made."

Introduction

The criminal justice system in Canada has been the subject of much discussion in recent years. The media dwell at great length on crimes of violence, on alleged crime waves and on the deficiencies of "the system." Urban Canadians are apparently restricting their activities and modifying their life styles out of a fear of being victimized (e.g., by refusing to use public transportation at night, buying more and heavier locks, etc.). Reports that the police are being handicapped by concern for the rights of prisoners and that courts are too lenient share space with accounts of the results of Royal Commissions into police brutality and prison conditions.

There are certain more or less accepted facts about each stage of the criminal justice system—who breaks the law, what criminal laws are routinely enforced by police, what the role of prosecution and defence is in the criminal courts, who the judges are, and who ends up in prison. This chapter tries to explain what these facts mean and what they tell us about Canadian society in a broader perspective.

The Giant Funnel

If everyone who committed an illegal act in Canada on a given day was actually charged with that offence and taken to court, we would end up with 95 to 98 percent of the population going through the court system. And if these people all received the most common sanction for the offence they committed, well over half would serve time in a jail or prison. It is well known in criminological circles (if not outside them) that nearly everyone has committed one or more Criminal Code offences (LeBlanc, 1975; McDonald, 1969; Vaz, 1966; Gold, 1977; Christie, 1965; but see Tribble, 1975, for a quasi-dissenting view). This does *not* include all those who have committed petty offences against municipal by-laws by parking at an expired meter or building a new bathroom without a permit. Typical Criminal Code offences which people in routine surveys admit having committed are:

> Theft—over and under $200.00
> Assault
> Breaking and entering
> Theft of a motor vehicle
> Fraud—relating to credit card usage and phony cheques
> Driving while impaired
> Possession an/or sale of illegal or prohibited drugs (e.g., marijuana, cocaine) under the Narcotic Control or Food and Drug Act.

While these offences are most often committed by people under 25 years of age, this does not mean that older or middle-class people "mature out" of crime. Rather, it seems that the type of wrongdoing changes, often to so-called occupational crimes—theft from one's employer, the provincial medicare or legal aid plan, theft from employees through violations of minimum wage laws, payoffs and kickbacks, and violations of laws governing occupational safety in mines, factories and business enterprises throughout the nation. (Reiman [1984:63] suggests the people who break these laws in the U.S. are responsible for *five times* as many deaths per year as are murderers. The rate in Canada would probably be higher, simply because our murder rate is so much lower.)

That most people are *not* known to the police, and think of themselves as upright, law-abiding citizens despite this reality, is the result of many factors. In the first place, the vast majority of illegal acts that are committed are never reported to authorities. This is to be expected when we are dealing with white-collar and occupational crimes, for the victims typically do not realize an offence has been committed, as in polluting offences, occupational safety or misleading advertising—and even if they were aware of the offence, and did know to whom to report it, reporting rates would be low because of the wide-spread and well-founded belief that no effective action would be take. However, it is also true of traditional crime. The figures vary somewhat with the time and place the study was done, but generally speaking it appears that only about one-third of burglaries are reported to police; one-quarter or less of rapes and assaults; one-tenth or less of thefts of all kinds; and no more than one in one hundred of "victimless" crimes such as illegal abortion or possession of illegal drugs (Waller and Okihiro, 1978; Courtis, 1975; Biderman and Reiss, 1967; Hood and Sparks, 1970). The most recent Canadian study found that, in the seven cities studied, the percentage of crimes reported to police varied, with average reporting levels of 70 percent for motor vehicle thefts and 64 percent for break and enters, but only 29 percent of personal thefts, 34 percent of assaults and 35 percent of vandalism incidents (Canada, Solicitor General, 1984: 3). Overall, more than half (58 percent) of all incidents of the eight crimes studied (sexual assault, robbery, assault, break and enter, motor vehicle theft, household theft, personal theft and vandalism) never came to police attention. Many of the unreported incidents, however, were trivial or unsuccessful. (Almost half of the unreported incidents in most of the categories were attempts only.) It is reasonable to assume that the vast majority of these "criminals" who have committed date rape, punched someone in a bar or stolen a bicycle think of themselves as decent respectable citizens, far removed from the criminal rabble.

In those cases that are reported, only a small percentage of the offenders are caught and charged by the police. In Canada in 1985, while 84.8 percent of all reported murders and 79 percent of all reported assaults were cleared by charges, only 31.3 percent of all reported robberies and 27.7 percent of all types of theft (motor vehicle theft, theft over and under $200.00, receiving stolen goods, break and enter, and frauds) were cleared (Canada, Statistics Canada, 1986). In the United States in 1965, only 26 percent of all reported Index crimes were cleared by charges (Silberman, 1980: 350). ("Index" crimes are the offences which must be reported to the F.B.I. by all police forces: murder, burglary, rape, larceny theft and auto theft.) In 1985, this meant that, out of 2 283 352 Criminal Code offences reported to the police in Canada,[1] 490 557 or 22.6 percent were cleared by charges (meaning that charges were laid against the presumed perpetrator) and 270 883 or 12.5 percent were cleared otherwise (meaning that the police "solved" the offence, but did not lay charges) (Canada, Statistics Canada, 1986: 2-5, 2-6). The vast majority of these were prosecuted as summary crimes. Summary crimes are either those offences which are not seen by the state as being very serious, such as taking a motor vehicle without permission or being drunk in a public place, *or* offences in which the Crown Attorney in charge of the case has the option of attempting to get a summary conviction with the lighter penalties this carries, or proceeding by indictment. Theoretically, this decision is based on the circumstances of the offence and the characteristics of the defendant. (In crimes where this choice is available, prosecutors typically proceed by summary conviction for first offenders or for "non-criminal" types where losses are small.) Most serious crimes, such as theft or break and enter, *must* be prosecuted as indictable. Because no statistics on sentencing have been gathered since 1973, we must go back to 1970 to obtain information on this aspect of the funnel. This, however, may be less misleading than one would think, since the total number of crimes reported to the police in 1970 was very similar to the number reported in 1985. (In fact, there were 2 757 442 reported in 1970 and 2 724 308 in 1985, making 33 134 *fewer* reported offences in 1985!)

Of the 1 878 172 summary charges laid, nearly a third of these (654 001) were dropped, usually because of insufficient evidence. Of the 1 224 169 convictions entered, 1 148 660 or 92 percent were fined, but 18 598 people ended up serving time in a municipal jail (Silberman and Teevan, 1975: 71). (All sentences under two years duration are served in municipal or provincial institutions; all of more than two years are served in federal prisons.) That leaves us with the indictable offences; some 53 318 in 1970. Nearly 87 percent (45 886) of those charged were convicted. A majority of these received non-institutional sentences such as fines and suspended sentences with or without parole, but 16 337 offences led to a prison sentence. In 1973, 53 964 were charged with indictable offences and 40 761 were convicted (Canada Year Book, 1977-78). Of those convicted, 4.2 percent were sentenced to penitentiary terms, 32.2 percent to provincial institutions, 34.3 percent were fined, 23.5 percent received a suspended sentence with probation, and the remaining 5.8 percent received a suspended sentence without probation (Griffiths et al., 1980: 173). Eventually, everyone sentenced to penitentiaries will be released, either on parole (which is granted only to "good risks" anytime after one-third of their sentence is completed), or, at the end of two-thirds of their sentence, on mandatory supervision. The final one-third of a sentence has traditionally not been served inside the prison; it is used as a device to ensure institutional conformity since prisoners who break rules risk losing varying amounts of this "good time." In either case, ex-inmates are subject to strict regulations (curfews, inability to drink in bars or socialize with ex-inmates) which, if violated, lead to a return to the institution.

This, then, is an overview of the Canadian criminal justice system. Over two and a half million offences are reported annually to the police. The most common offences are related to drinking and driving (82 percent of charges laid in 1977 were automobile-related), and the most common Criminal Code offence is the very minor "theft under $200.00" which made up 27.7 percent of all property crimes in 1985 (Canada, Statistics Canada 1986: 2-3, my computation). Fewer than 1 percent of all the charges laid lead to sentences over two years in length, and only, as we saw, 4.2 percent of all indictable offences do. Does this mean that we are excessively "soft" on criminals? That the courts are hamstrung by an exaggerated respect for the civil liberties of the defendant? That judges are too lenient? Or does it mean, on the other hand, that police are laying unnecessary and trivial charges, or that we have too many laws on the books? We will explore the answer to these questions below.

Policing and the Canadian Legal Code

The vast majority of charges laid under the Criminal code of Canada are laid
by the police. There are three types of police force: municipal, provincial and
federal. Most cities have their own municipal forces (Toronto, Vancouver,
Montreal, etc.), while smaller communities usually have to depend on either the
provincial or the federal police. (Arrangements vary from province to province,
but most population centres are legally obliged to set up or contract for police
services after they reach a certain size.) Since only Ontario and Quebec have
provincial forces, small communities and rural townships and counties in the
other eight provinces are policed by the federal force, the Royal Canadian
Mounted Police. In addition to the Criminal Code, the police are responsible
for enforcing many municipal by-laws and provincial statutes (governing
everything from parking to securities legislation), as well as being responsible,
in the most general sense, for "keeping the peace." In essence, they are
supposed to enforce all laws except those which have other enforcers specified
in the legislation; for example, fish and game laws, or laws regulating safety
standards and working conditions which provide for inspectors to be the normal
enforcement agents. Obviously, no police force can actively enforce all the laws
it is theoretically responsible for—the Criminal Code alone contains 774
different sections, forbidding everything from assisting deserters and committing
acts "intended to alarm Her Majesty" (this indictable offence carries a
maximum penalty of 14 years imprisonment!) to interfering with boundary lines,
injuring cattle or making counterfeit money. Which laws are actively enforced
is a complex matter determined by subjective judgments on what are the most
important laws. These judgments are made by the political authorities
responsible for the force and communicated down through the organizational
hierarchy to the police chiefs and their staff. There they are translated into
working procedures, modes of operation, and rules and regulations which are
meant to ensure that basic priorities (usually phrased in such terms as "the
protection of the community" or "the security of the citizens") will be met. If,
for example, a priority is the protection of private property, then ordinary
police routines will concentrate on patrolling business areas at night, and police
training manuals will focus on how to spot and apprehend potential thieves. If
a basic priority is protection of the state, then the spotting and arresting of
dissidents will be emphasized, and resources will be allocated accordingly.
Priorities such as these, which both underlie and determine procedures, are
usually unstated and unrecognized by police personnel and citizens. They are
taken for granted in the truest sense, and seldom is their crucial role in shaping
the workings of a police force recognized. These priorities are filtered through
the top police personnel. Because they mostly reflect the dominant ideology,
strands of which are deeply engrained in the fabric of Canadian society and

socialized into every child by family, schools and media, no one has to tell the top police officers what kinds of behaviours they must control. However, on a day-to-day basis police chiefs are likely to be kept informed of the immediate concerns of the elite groups in the society (but *not* of the concerns of the poor or the powerless). As Grosman said in his study of police chiefs across Canada,

> His affiliations and sources of information, however, too often relate primarily to service clubs within the community, merchants, and those citizens and groups to whom the Chief accords high status. It is their preferences which quickly become known to him. He then sifts this select external information and utilizes it...(1975: 53).

This is not to suggest, however, that information and power flow only from the top down. We know from a wide variety of sources (Vincent, 1979; Wilson, 1971; Manning, 1977; Reiss, 1971; Bittner, 1970; Skolnick, 1967; Bordua, 1967) that police have a distinctive occupational subculture. This, combined with the fact that the patrol officer on the beat has tremendous freedom and discretion to decide who and what to officially notice, and who and what to ignore, means that the police can in practice modify or even reverse certain types of orders. Moreover, because the police officer never knows when he/she will need his/her peers as back up in a sticky situation—perhaps to save his/her life in a confrontation, or his/her job before a disciplinary board—he/she[2] is highly motivated to respect the values and norms of this subculture. Let us discuss how theses two factors work together to give the average police officer a considerable amount of unofficial power.

The police officer on the beat decides, on his/her own, such things as how to defuse a touchy domestic dispute where the husband is beating the wife, and whether or not to chase that speeding, possibly stolen, car. His/her superior in the station house cannot know the exact circumstances; moreover, an instant decision is often required. But the police officer exercises this discretion within a framework of rules. Some of these rules are imposed "from above" by the bureaucracy of the police force; for example, what activities lead to promotion? What is a "good" arrest? What arrests will "bring down the heat" and get you in trouble? What kinds of initiative are you discouraged from taking? What laws do you have to *justify* invoking to your superiors?

Others are imposed by peers in the police force. Because of the shift work and the strains and tensions associated with being police officers, they tend to associate, both on and off the job, with other police officers. They have their own definitions of a "good cop" and a "bad cop," and they have developed a set of common values and attitudes about the world, the political system, the criminal, human nature, and the job of the police (Vincent, 1979; Bittner, 1970;

Silberman, 1980). They view themselves as high-status people doing an essential but unpleasant task, a role calling for deference from the police. Public perception of the police is usually quite at odds with this self-concept. As a result, police tend to feel persecuted, misunderstood, unloved and unappreciated by the general population, the politicians and their spouses.

A recent study of Canadian police (Vincent, 1979) identified a constellation of behaviours and attitudes which police officers share. They tend to favour capital punishment (witness the recent campaign by the 52 000 member Canadian Police Association to get Parliament to restore it); they believe in gun control; as a group they see parole officers and social workers as "bleeding hearts" or "do-gooders"; and they think the court system and everyone connected with it deals too leniently with criminals. In fact, some think the judges and many of the lawyers are "in cahoots" (Vincent, 1979: 90-110). Police work breeds cynicism and suspicion, so it is no surprise that police officers as a group come to think that people, especially those they deal with in their work, are "assholes" (Silberman, 1980: 323). This jaundiced view of human nature, while understandable in terms of the work they are doing and the reactions they arouse as symbols of the authority of the state, often makes it more difficult to form or maintain relationships with those outside the force. Thus, they tend to stick together, and can be a very cohesive unit. This power has been used to defeat policies that the police do not like; in New York City in 1967, police actions nearly sabotaged an attempt to have prostitution changed from a misdemeanour with a one-year prison sentence to a violation with a 15-day maximum sentence. Until recently, the N.Y.C. police were also successful in invalidating the section of the law which made patronizing a prostitute illegal—simply by not charging the customers when they picked up the prostitutes (Roby, 1976).

Generally speaking, the police subculture calls for strict enforcement not so much of particular laws, but for strict control of particular "types of people." As Silberman has pointed out (1980; also Wilson, 1971; Ericson 1981, 1982) police tend to see themselves as playing cops and robbers. Despite the fact that over 80 percent of their time is spent on serving the public (as social workers sorting out domestic crises, finding lost children, taking people to hospitals, directing traffic, etc.) or on paperwork, police typically see their real work, their only important task, as catching criminals. But their picture of criminals is a very narrow one; it does not encompass 98 percent of all the law breakers we discussed earlier. It focuses on a small number of young, usually lower-class males who are seen as "punks" or troublemakers. These are people who show no respect for the authority of the police and often challenge it, who typically come from families or districts which are known to the police as "bad." They have usually become known to the police over several encounters. They are the people most likely to be noticed, booked, charged, eventually put on probation, and then sent to "reform" school. Their activities, however, will not be so much different from their more respectful middle-class peers. (As pointed out earlier, just about all people, as adolescents, commit illegal acts defined by the law as serious, and change to more specific class-related and occupationally influenced crimes once they are older). However, the "punk's" demeanour, social class, family background, and realistically assessed future prospects have made him into a member of a suspect category. Once he is in reformatory and officially labelled, the police will be keeping an eye on him, and he will be much more likely to be picked up again, charged and end up in prison. He has become an automatic suspect to be checked out whenever certain crimes occur. Nor is this perception necessarily wrong. He may be more likely to commit the kinds of crimes that will eventually lead to prison, as the social network therein (i.e., the prison sub-culture) encourages the rejection of "straight" or conventional values, jobs and people. (It is no accident that, while the vast majority of juveniles who go before juvenile court do *not* become adult criminals, the vast majority of those who *do* were sent away as children.)

Thus, certain kinds of people are precast in the role of potential criminals by police, and the characteristics of these people are taught to all new recruits, as are strategies for dealing with them so they cannot "take advantage." New police officers learn that only certain kinds of crimes are seen as serious. Arrests for these crimes constitute "good busts," whereas arrests for many other illegal acts do not. What are these serious acts? They tend to be property crimes such as bank robbery, break and enter, related indictable criminal code offences, as well as certain crimes of violence (murder; serious, stranger or interclass assaults; or rapes perpetrated against "respectable" women, especially by groups/gangs). And, of course, the people most likely to commit these offences, especially the property crimes, are the very same troublemakers we discussed before! Why not? They have learned the attitude favourable to committing these acts (from peers or reform school); they are cut off from legitimate channels of upward mobility and have no realistic future prospects; they are the last hired and first fired if they do manage, against all odds, to land an unskilled or semi-skilled job; and property crimes are often the only way open to them to survive, let alone "make a fast buck!" After all, no one but a young, unskilled person would choose theft as an occupation—the risks are very high (almost all career criminals end up serving time [Silberman, 1980]), the status is negative and the profits are small. But the vast majority of equally serious crimes being committed by people who do not fit the police stereotype are likely to escape all official notice.

In addition to these underlying and ongoing pressures (the political-economic forces forming overall priorities and the police subculture), more immediate factors influence what laws are enforced at a given time. Pressure groups arise from time to time and try to change either the law itself or the customary enforcement practices in a particular area. For example, in Canada today there are groups attempting to change the enforcement of marijuana laws, abortion laws, laws on homosexuality, on breaking and entering, and on drinking and driving (Law Reform Commission, 1974; Waller and Okihiro, 1978). Business people or hotel owners may spearhead a drive against prostitution or pickpockets. A particularly grisly crime (such as the abduction, sexual assault and murder of Alison Parrot in Toronto in 1986), a race riot or a public meeting which gets out of hand may trigger either crack-downs or a hands-off policy. During such periods, laws on massage parlours or licensing which have not been enforced for 20 years will be dusted off, or enforcement will be relaxed and police will ignore, for a while, public drinking or marijuana smoking offences committed by certain ethnic groups in a certain neighbourhood. After a while, normal enforcement patterns will reassert themselves.

This is not to suggest that policing is predominantly proactive; that is, that police initiate the majority of situations, or that they routinely stumble across crimes in process while on patrol which lead to confrontations and arrests. Indeed, the evidence shows (Silberman, 1980; Vincent, 1979; Wilson, 1971; Manning, 1977; Ericson, 1981, 1982) that much, if not most, of the time police officers are reacting to calls of every sort. One study in Los Angeles figured out that, if present trends continued, the average police officer would come across a burglary once every three months and a robbery once every 14 years (Science and Technology Task Force, 1967). But this does not deny the centrality of police discretion and autonomy. For this is exercised on virtually every call that is made. Even though a victim may have reported an assault, the officer who responds must decide whether the caller is serious or using the police to resolve a personal disagreement; whether the caller is indeed the victim or the aggressor; whether the incident is serious enough to warrant an arrest; and what charges, if any, are justified. He may well decide that the interests of neighbourhood peace and social justice (as he perceives it) are best served by doing nothing. Similar decisions are required in virtually every police-citizen contact.

To sum up: police forces in Canada initiate the criminal justice process by laying the vast majority of charges. To a considerable degree, they choose which of the multitude of laws they are responsible for will be enforced; as Ericson says, they "make crime" (1981). Their choices, in turn, are shaped first by the situation itself on the street and their reaction to/and perception of it; secondly, by the police sub-culture to the degree that they have internalized its values and codes; thirdly, by "middle level" organizational-bureaucratic concerns set forth by superiors in the police hierarchy; and, ultimately, by the basic political and economic forces that shape the intellectual climate (ideology) of the society itself.

Prosecution and Defence

After charges are laid, what is the next step? Most people, basing their knowledge on television shows from the United States, would guess that the accused, still under arrest, proceeds to hire himself a lawyer and eventually repairs to court to appear before a judge and jury. His lawyer conducts a defence while the lawyer for the state (in Canada, the Crown) attempts to prove his guilt. Then 12 carefully chosen members of the jury, after hearing all the evidence, declare his guilt or innocence and the judge passes sentence. This picture is far from the truth. What *is* likely to happen after one is charged with a criminal offence? The scenario goes something like this.

First, much depends on whether one is arrested or summoned. The police make this initial decision, and it varies according to what you are charged with and who you are. General policy is "for the police to charge every person possible with every offence possible...except for the occasional minor charge...not laid in exchange for information." (Ericson and Baranek, 1982: 128). If it is a drug or Criminal Code offence, even a minor or summary one, chances are you will be arrested (67.5 percent of those charged with a summary Criminal Code offence, 79.4 percent of those on indictable charges, and 89.2 percent on drug charges were arrested in a major study of Toronto provincial courts) (Hann, 1973: 196-197). If arrested, your freedom is at least temporarily curtailed; you are taken into custody. You may be kept in a local jail or detention centre until your case is heard, or you may be released after a court date is set, either on bail or on your own recognizance. In either case you must, in law, be brought before a justice of the peace to determine whether you will be subsequently released or kept in custody, no more than 24 hours after the arrest. If you are poor, as the vast majority of those charged with Criminal Code offences are (Ouimet, 1969; Tepperman, 1977), then the hearing must decide whether or not to release you without the posting of bail. Theoretically, a person is released without bail *if* the judge believes that chances are good that he will show up in court when his case is to be heard, will not commit any new offences while free, and will not jeopardized the prosecution's case (by destroying evidence or threatening witnesses, for example). Generally speaking, the first concern is the paramount one, and it works to the advantage of the established citizens since it is considered easier for someone with no fixed address or a room in a rooming house to leave town than for the person with a job and a house.

Prior to 1971[3] when the bail Reform Act was passed, all people who could not post bail were imprisoned until their case came up. This resulted in many people spending three to eight months in jail on charges of which they were then found innocent! (Friedland, 1965; Canadian Civil Liberties Education,

1974). The aforementioned Hann study found that even after the Bail Reform Act, 56 percent of all defendants studied were arrested, and only 53.4 percent of these were released before their first court appearance (Hann, 1973: 196). In a Montreal study, MacKay (1976: 8) found 53 percent of all the accused still in custody at their initial court appearance. The pre-trial detention rate for those in adult prisons, per 100,000, was 12.4 in 1980 (Canada, 1982: 105). Ericson and Baranek (1982), in their study of accused persons in a large Ontario city, found that 74 of the 101 accused people they interviewed believed they were under arrest. They also argue that the treat of holding the accused for bail hearings instead of releasing them on their own recognizance has proven to be a powerful factor in persuading many defendants to sign statements implicating themselves, or to forbear from requesting lawyers during interrogation (1982: 61). The ability of Canadian police forces to add a "resisting arrest" charge to those already laid is no doubt an additional incentive for many to cooperate in incriminating themselves. Bail reform, then, does not appear to have had quite the effect which was originally envisaged in safe-guarding the (poor) defendant.

Once bail has been posted or the person released, the case is sent to the office of the Crown Attorney who, with his or her staff, is responsible for prosecuting cases. Some must be dealt with in a provincial court by a provincial judge (for example, all summary offences, driving with licence suspended, theft under $200.00, common assault); others must go to a higher court as they cannot be disposed of at the low-level courts (examples would be treason, sedition, murder and manslaughter). The remainder of indictable offences fall into a twilight zone, and the accused chooses the court level in which he wishes to be tried (provincial or county court), and elects trial by judge alone or by judge and jury. (In three Maritime provinces and Ontario there is yet another layer of procedure for those choosing trial by judge and jury—a grand jury must be convened in secret to examine the evidence against the accused and see whether trial is warranted.) However, the reality appears to be that fewer than 3 percent of all criminal cases are decided in upper-level courts (Griffiths et al., 1980: 146). To call all of this a real choice made by the accused is then, accurate only in theory. In fact, he or she is usually too well aware of his/her perilous and powerless position, or too confused and demoralized to exercise any choices not suggested by police or defence counsel (Ericson and Baranek, 1982). Studies have documented the fact that heavier penalties are demanded from those who inconvenience the court by insisting upon certain rights; for example, defendants who opt for jury trials receive heavier penalties if found guilty than those who plead guilty before a judge (Uhlman and Walker, 1980). Perhaps this partially accounts for the fact that there are, it is estimated, fewer than 2000 criminal jury trials per year in all of Canada (Hagan, 1977: 158; Griffiths et al., 1980).

However, chances are nearly one in two that the accuse we have been discussing will have had all charges dropped by this time. In Robert Hann's study, a full third of all charges were dropped or withdrawn before any court appearance was made, and another 10 percent were dismissed by the judge at the first court appearance (Hann, 1973: 461); Helder (1979) found that 37.5 percent of all charges were dropped in his study of 100 criminal incidents in 1978-1979. Before this happens, however, if he/she is one of the 53.3 percent of defendants kept in custody, the accused may well have served one to three months in jail, lost his job, deprived his family and children of emotional and financial support, meanwhile having been forced to live in a tiny, dirty cell. And there is, of course, no real legal recourse against the state which the defendant can take to secure compensation for this.

If the case has not been dismissed, it will probably proceed to trial in the provincial court—only 3 percent of all cases in Hann's study went on to the county or supreme court levels—and will be disposed of by a guilty plea, without a jury, in a trial lasting less than 20 minutes (and probably less than ten). The Canadian Civil Liberties study of all major Canadian cities found that 69.7 percent of all cases are disposed of in less than 20 minutes, 37.9 percent in less than ten minutes. The length of time spent per case was not significantly longer for more serious cases; that is, those in which the accused received a lengthy as opposed to a short prison sentence (Canadian Civil Liberties Education, 1973: 182-183). Moreover, from first to final appearance, the process will take an average of two months—more if the defendant is represented by a defence lawyer, less if she-he is not. While the length of time taken, and the number of delays experienced in Hann's study, varied with the type of case, the median time from first to final court appearance for summary, traffic and indictable Criminal Code offences was 50 to 63 days (Hann, 1973 117). While the majority of defendants will have to make several court appearances, one in four can expect to have to show up from four to eight times (Hann, 1973: 134). This, of course, costs defendants a lot of money—people must take time off work, hire babysitters, pay transportation costs and waste long hours waiting for the case to come up. And if the accused has been kept in custody, the expense to the state, as well as the potential injustice to the accused, is further multiplied.

Conclusion

Contrary to appearances and to rhetoric, the criminal justice system represents one of the easiest and most efficient ways of solving the problem of social control of excess and troublesome populations. Lower-class males, with or without criminal records, have virtually no legitimacy and no power. People, generally speaking, will not listen to, believe, or care about their allegations of police brutality, judicial unfairness, or inhuman prison conditions. They are unlikely to be able to hire lawyers to protest and publicize their cases; they are seen as having engineered their own predicament, through the myth of individual as opposed to social responsibility; and they do not have the resources or the sophistication to organize and protest politically.

Moreover, they themselves usually have bought the dominant ideology, and feel that they really are bad human beings who have no discipline and no real value (Shover, 1977). Thus, they can be processed through the system at virtually no cost, and, more importantly, with no loss of legitimacy and no potentially embarrassing and expensive accusations of oppression. As Tepperman said, when discussing alternatives to punishments in controlling "problem" populations:

> The achievement of control through reward places most of the hardship on the person seeking compliance. Control through punishment may not be as certain in the long run, but in the short run it is...less expensive and less demanding of patience. (1977: 84)

In short, these people are paying the price for the type of society we apparently want; for inciting everyone to consume when they can never consume enough; for forcing everyone to work to be recognized as a contributing human being, when there can never be enough jobs to go around; and for motivating everyone to want to be glamorous and successful, when by definition only a tiny minority can ever be recognized as such. This game may produce a high standard of living (as measured by the quantity of goods turned out), but it also produces far more losers than winners. Most of these losers adjust, compensate and outwardly conform; a few strike out in frustration and anger. It is these few we have been discussing.

In conclusion, it is time that criminologist, criminal justice employees, and the general public stopped denying the obvious. Processing vast numbers of poor people and reserving the most punitive sanctions for them, while simultaneously denying that social class has anything to do with the exercise of "justice" in this country, is too ludicrous a claim to be accepted any longer. Surely it is time the burden of proof was shifted onto those who would argue, in the face of such overwhelming evidence, that the criminal justice system aims to deliver even-handed justice to all who break the law.

Endnotes

1. The total number of Criminal Code offences reported in 1977 and 1981 are, respectively, 1 654 020 and 2 168 226 (Canada, 1982).

2. The masculine pronoun is used for much of this article, for the simple reason that the vast majority of officers in the criminal justice system, from police to judiciary, and of people charged and processed, are males. However, to underline the fact that we are not *necessarily* talking about males only, the he/she form has been used where it is appropriate.

3. The Act was tightened up on April 26, 1976, but the changes affect primarily repeat offenders. For anyone who has previously been charges with an indictable offence, the onus is on him/her to show why he/she should be released before trial rather than, as in the case with other offenders, on the police and Crown to show why she/he should *not* be (Powell, 1976).

References

Biderman, A.D. and A.J. Reiss, Jr. 1967. "On Exploring the 'Dark Figure' of Crime," *Annals of the American Academy of Political and Social Science.* 374: 1-15.

Bittner, E. 1970. *The Functions of the Police in Modern Society.* Rockville, Md.: National Institute of Mental Health Center of Studies of Crime and Delinquency.

Bordua, D., ed. 1967. *The Police: Six Sociological Essays.* New York: John Wiley and Sons.

Canada, Statistics Canada. 1986. *Canadian Crime Statistics 1985.* Ottawa: Statistics Canada, Canadian Centre for Justice Statistics.

Canada Year Book, Annual. 197-1978. Ottawa: Supply and Services Canada.

Canadian Civil Liberties Education. 1974. "Due Process Safeguards and Canadian Criminal Justice." In C. Boydell, C. Grindstaff and P.C. Whitehead, *The Administration of Criminal Justice in Canada.* Toronto: Holt, Rinehart and Winston, pp. 155-186.

Christie, N. 1965. "A Study of Self-Reported Crime," *Scandinavian Studies in Criminology*, Vol. 1. London: Tavistock Publications.

Courtis, M.C. 1975. "Victimization in Toronto." In R. Silverman and J. Teevan, *Crime in Canadian Society.* Toronto: Butterworths. pp. 119-127.

Ericson, R. 1981. *Making Crime: A Study of Police Detective Work.* Toronto: Butterworths.

———. 1982. *Reproducing Order: A Study of Police Patrol Work.* Toronto: University of Toronto Press.

Ericson, R. and P. Baranek. 1982. *The Ordering of Justice.* Toronto: University of Toronto Press.

Rriedland, M.L. 1965. *Detention Before Trial: A Study of Criminal Cases tried in the Toronto Magistrates Courts.* Toronto: University of Toronto Press.

Gold, M. 1977. "Undetected Delinquent Behaviour," *Journal of Research in Crime and Delinquency,* 3(1) (January, 1966): 27-46.

Griffiths, C.T., J.F. Klein and S.N. Verdun-Jones. 1980. *Criminal Justice in Canada.* Toronto: Butterworths.

Hagan, J. 1977. *Disreputable Pleasures: Crime and Deviance in Canada.* Toronto: McGraw-Hill Ryerson.

Hann, R. 1973. *Decision making in the Canadian Criminal Court System: A Systems Analysis.* Toronto: Centre of Criminology Research Report, University of Toronto.

Helder, H. 1979. "The Police, Case Negociations and the Para-Legal System." Unpublished M.A. dissertation, Centre of Criminology, University of Toronto.

Hood, R. and R. Sparks. 1970. *Key Issues in Criminology.* Toronto: McGraw-Hill, World University Library.

Law Reform Commission of Canada. 1974a. *Principles of Sentencing and Dispositions.* Working Paper #3. Ottawa: Information Canada.

———. 1974b. *Discovery in Criminal Cases: Report on the Questionnaire Survey.* Ottawa: Queen's Printer.

LeBlanc, M. 1975. "Upper Class vs. Working Class Delinquency." In R. Silverman and J. Teevan, *Crime in Canadian Society.* Toronto: Butterworths, pp. 102-119.

MacKay, E. 1976. *The Paths of Justice: A Study of the Operation of the Criminal Courts in Montreal.* Montreal: Groupe de Recherche en Jurimetrie, University of Montreal.

McDonald, L. 1969. *Social Class and Delinquency.* London: Faber.

Manning, P.K. 1977. *Police Work: The Social Organization of Policing.* Cambridge, Mass.: M.I.T. Press.

Ouimet, R. 1969. *Towards Unity: Criminal Justice and Corrections.* Report of the Canadian Committ on Corrections. Ottawa: Information Canada.

Reiman, J. 1984. *The Rich Get Richer and the Poor Get Poorer.* 2nd ed. Toronto: J. Wiley and Sons.

Reiss, A.J. 1971. *The Police and the Public.* New Haven: Yale University Press.

Roby, P. 1976. "Politics and Criminal Law: Revision of the New York State Penal Law on Prostitution." In G.F. Cole, ed., *Criminal Justice: Law and Politics,* 2nd ed. North Scituate, Mass.: Duxbury Press, pp. 28-51.

Science and Technology Task Force. 1967. *A Report to the President's Commission on Law Enforcement and Administration of Justice*. Washington, D.C.: U.S. Government Printing Office.

Shover, N. 1977. "Criminal Behaviour as Theoretical Praxis." In J.F. Galliher and J.L. McCartney, eds., *Criminology: Power, Crime, and Criminal Law*. Homewood, Ill.: Dorsey Press, pp. 159-174.

Silberman, C.E. 1980. *Criminal Violence, Criminal Justice*. New York: Vintage Books.

Silberman, R. and J.J. Teevan. 1975. *Crime in Canadian Society*. Toronto: Butterworths.

Skolnick, J. 1967. *Justice Without Trial*. New York: J. Wiley and Sons.

Tepperman, L. 1977. *Crime Control*. Toronto: McGraw-Hill Ryerson.

Tribble, S. 1975. "Socio-Economic Status and Self-Reported Juvenile Delinquency." In R. Silverman and J. Teevan, *Crime in Canadian Society*. Toronto: Butterworths, pp. 95-102.

Uhlman, T.M. and N.D. Walker. 1980. "He Takes Some of My Time, I Take Some of His: An Analysis of Judicial Sentencing Patterns in Jury Cases," *Law and Social Research,* 14:2 (Winter).

Vaz, E. 1966. "Self-Reported Juvenile Delinquency and Socio-Economic Status," *Canadian Journal of Corrections*, 8: 20-27.

Vincent, C.L. 1979. *Policemen*. Toronto: Gage.

Waller, I. and N. Okihiro. 1978. *Burglary: The Victim and the Public*. Toronto: University of Toronto Press.

Wilson, J.Q. 1971. *Varieties of Police Behaviour*. New York: Atheneum.

The Body of the Condemned

Michel Foucault

The nature of social control in western industrial societies has changed over the last two hundred years. As this excerpt from Foucault's Discipline and Punish *indicates, the change is most poignantly seen in the shift from the spectacle of punishment to the discipline of the prison. Foucault analyses this shift and examines how our ideas of punishment and justice are related to the human body. Are these ideas also reflected in other examples of social control in modern society?*

On 2 March 1757 Damiens the regicide was condemned "to make the *amende honorable* before the main door of the Church of Paris," where he was to be "taken and conveyed in a cart, wearing nothing but a shirt, holding a torch of burning wax weighting two pounds"; then, "in the said cart, to the Place de Grève, where, on a scaffold that will be erected there, the flesh will be torn from his breasts, arms, thighs and calves with red-hot pincers, his right hand, holding the knife with which he committed the said parricide, burnt with sulphur, and, on those places where the flesh will be torn away, poured molten lead, boiling oil, burning resin, wax and sulphur melted together and then his body drawn and quartered by four horses and his limbs and body consumed by fire, reduced to ashes and his ashes thrown to the winds" (*Pièces originales...*, 372-4).

Bouton, an officer of the watch, left us his account:

> The sulphur was lit, but the flame was so poor that only the top skin of the hand was burnt, and that only slightly. Then the executioner, his sleeves rolled up, took the steel pincers, which had been especially made for the occasion, and which were about a foot and a half long, and pulled first at the calf of the right leg, then at the thigh, and from there at the two fleshy parts of the right arm; then at the breasts. Though a strong, sturdy fellow, this executioner found it so difficult to tear away the pieces of flesh that he set about the same spot two or three times, twisting the pincers as he did so, and what he took away formed at each part a wound about the size of a six-pound crown piece.
>
> After these tearings with the pincers, Damiens, who cried out profusely, though without swearing, raised his head and looked at himself; the same executioner dipped an iron spoon in the pot containing the boiling potion, which he poured liberally over each wound. Then the ropes that were to be harnessed to the horses were attached with cords to the patient's body; the horses were

then harnessed and placed alongside the arms and legs, one at each limb.

Eighty years later, Léon Faucher drew up his rules "for the House of young prisoners in Paris":

Art. 17.   The prisoner's day will begin at six in the morning in winter and at five in summer. They will work for nine hours a day throughout the year. Two hours a day will be devoted to instruction. Work and the day will end at nine o'clock in winter and at eight in summer.

Art. 18.   *Rising.* At the first drum-roll, the prisoners must rise and dress in silence, as the supervisor opens the cell doors. At the second drum-roll, they must be dressed and make their beds. At the third they must line up and proceed to the chapel for morning prayer. There is a five minute interval between each drum-roll.

Art. 19.   The prayers are conducted by the chaplain and followed by a moral or religious reading. This exercise must not last more than half an hour.

Art. 20.   *Work.* At a quarter to six in the summer, a quarter to seven in winter, the prisoners go down into the courtyard where they must wash their hands and faces, and receive their first ration of bread. Immediately afterwards, they form into work-teams and go off to work, which must begin at six in summer and seven in winter.

Art. 21.   *Meal.* At ten o'clock the prisoners leave their work and go to the refectory; they wash their hands in their courtyards and assemble in divisions. After the dinner, there is recreation until twenty minutes to eleven.

Art. 22.   *School.* At twenty minutes to eleven, at the drum-roll, the prisoners form into ranks, and proceed in divisions to the school. The class lasts two hours and consists alternately of reading, writing, drawing and arithmetic.

Art. 23.   At twenty minutes to one, the prisoners leave the school, in divisions, and return to their courtyards for recreation. At five minutes to one, at the drum-roll, they form into work-teams.

Art. 24.   At one o'clock they must be back in the workshops: they work until four o'clock.

Art. 25.   At four o'clock the prisoners leave their workshops and go into the courtyards where they wash their hands and form into divisions for the refectory.

Art. 26. Supper and the recreation that follows it last until five o'clock: the prisoners then return to the workshops.

Art. 27. At seven o'clock in the summer, at eight in winter, work stops; bread is distributed for the last time in the workshops. For a quarter of an hour one of the prisoners or supervisors reads a passage from some instructive or uplifting work. This is followed by evening prayer.

Art. 28. At half-past seven in summer, half-past eight in winter, the prisoners must be back in their cells after the washing of hands and the inspection of clothes in the courtyard; at the first drum-roll, they must undress, and at the second get into bed. The cell doors are closed and the supervisors go the rounds in the corridors, to ensure order and silence (Faucher, 274-82).

We have, then, a public execution and a time-table. They do not punish the same crimes or the same type of delinquent. But they each define a certain penal style. Less than a century separates them. It was a time when, in Europe and in the United States, the entire economy of punishment was redistributed. It was a time of great "scandals" for traditional justice, a time of innumerable projects for reform. It was a new theory of law and crime, a new moral or political justification of the right to punish; old laws were abolished, old customs died out.

Among so many changes, I shall consider one: the disappearance of torture as a public spectacle. Today we are rather inclined to ignore it; perhaps, in its time, it gave rise to too much inflated rhetoric; perhaps it has been attributed too readily and too emphatically to a process of "humanization," thus dispensing with the need for further analysis. And, in any case, how important is such a change, when compared with the great institutional transformations, the formulation of explicit, general codes and unified rules of procedure; with the almost universal adoption of the jury system, the definition of the essentially corrective character of the penalty and the tendency, which has become increasingly marked since the nineteenth century, to adapt punishment to the individual offender? Punishment of a less immediately physical kind, a certain discretion in the art of inflicting pain, a combination of more subtle, more subdued sufferings, deprived of their visible display, should not all this be treated as a special case, an incidental effect of deeper changes? And yet the fact remains that a few decades saw the disappearance of the tortured, dismembered, amputated body, symbolically branded on face or shoulder, exposed alive or dead to public view. The body as the major target of penal repression disappeared.

By the end of the eighteenth and the beginning of the nineteenth century, the gloomy festival of punishment was dying out, though here and there it flickered momentarily into life. In this transformation, two processes were at work. They did not have quite the same chronology or the same *raison d'être*. The first was the disappearance of punishment as a spectacle. The ceremonial of punishment tended to decline; it survived only as a new legal or administrative practice. It was as if the punishment was thought to equal, if not to exceed, in savagery the crime itself, to accustom the spectators to a ferocity from which one wished to divert them, to show them the frequency of crime, to make the executioner resemble a criminal, judges murders, to reverse roles at the last moment, to make the tortured criminal an object of pity or admiration. As early as 1764, Beccaria remarked: "The murder that is depicted as a horrible crime is repeated in cold blood, remorselessly" (Beccaria, 101). The public execution is now seen as a hearth in which violence bursts again into flame.

Punishment, then, will tend to become the most hidden part of the penal process. This has several consequences: it leaves the domain of more or less everyday perception and enters that of abstract consciousness; its effectiveness is seen as resulting from its inevitability, not from its visible intensity; it is the certainty of being punished and not the horrifying spectacle of public punishment that must discourage crime; the exemplary mechanics of punishment changes its mechanisms. As a result, justice no longer takes public responsibility for the violence that is bound up with its practice. If it too strikes, if it too kills, it is not as a glorification of its strength, but as an element of itself that it is obliged to tolerate, that it finds difficult to account for. The apportioning of blame is redistributed: in punishment-as-spectacle a confused horror spread from the scaffold; it enveloped both executioner and condemned; and although it was always ready to invert the shame inflicted on the victim into pity or glory, it often turned the legal violence of the executioner into shame. Now the scandal and the light are to be distributed differently; it is the conviction itself that marks the offender with the unequivocally negative sign: the publicity has shifted to the trial, and to the sentence; the execution itself is like an additional shame that justice is ashamed to impose on the condemned man; so it keeps its distance from the act, tending always to entrust it to others, under the seal of secrecy. It is ugly to be punishable, but there is no glory in punishing. Hence that double system of protection that justice has set up between itself and the punishment it imposes. Those who carry out the penalty tend to become an autonomous sector; justice is relieved of responsibility for it by a bureaucratic concealment of the penalty itself. It is typical that in France the administration of the prisons should for so long have been the responsibility of the Ministry of the Interior, while responsibility for the *bagnes*, for penal servitude in the convict ships and penal settlements, lay with the Ministry of the

Navy or the Ministry of the Colonies. And beyond this distribution of roles operates a theoretical disavowal: do not imagine that the sentences that we judges pass are activated by a desire to punish; they are intended to correct, reclaim, "cure"; a technique of improvement represses, in the penalty, the strict expiation of evil-doing, and relieves the magistrates of the demeaning task of punishing. In modern justice and on the part of those who dispense it there is a shame in punishing, which does not always preclude zeal. This sense of shame is constantly growing: the psychologists and the minor civil servants of moral orthopaedics proliferate on the wound it leaves.

The disappearance of public executions marks therefore the decline of the spectacle; but it also marks a slackening of the hold on the body. Generally speaking, punitive practices had become more reticent. One no longer touched the body, or at least as little as possible, and then only to reach something other than the body itself. It might be objected that imprisonment, confinement, forced labour, penal servitude, prohibition from entering certain areas, deportation—which have occupied so important a place in modern penal systems—are "physical" penalties: unlike fines, for example, they directly affect the body. But the punishment-body relation is not the same as it was in the torture during public executions. The body now serves as an instrument or intermediary: if one intervenes upon it to imprison it, or to make it work, it is in order to deprive the individual of a liberty that is regarded both as a right and as property. The body, according to this penalty, is caught up in a system of constraints and privations, obligations and prohibitions. Physical pain, the pain of the body itself, is no longer the constituent element of the penalty. From being an art of unbearable sensations punishment has become an economy of suspended rights. If it is still necessary for the law to reach and manipulate the body of the convict, it will be at a distance, in the proper way, according to strict rules, and with a much "higher" aim. As a result of this new restraint, a whole army of technicians took over from the executioner, the immediate anatomist of pain: warders, doctors, chaplains, psychiatrists, psychologists, educationalists; by their very presence near the prisoner, they sing the praises that the law needs: they reassure it that the body and pain are not the ultimate objects of its punitive action. Today a doctor must watch over those condemned to death, right up to the last moment—thus juxtaposing himself as the agent of welfare, as the alleviator of pain, with the official whose task it is to end life. This is worth thinking about. When the moment of execution approaches, the patients are injected with tranquillizers. A utopia of judicial reticence: take away life, but prevent the patient from feeling it; deprive the prisoner of all rights, but do not inflict pain; impose penalties free of all pain. Recourse to psycho-pharmacology and to various physiological "disconnectors," even if it is temporary, is a logical consequence of this "non-corporal" penalty.

The modern rituals of execution attest to this double process: the disappearance of the spectacle and the elimination of pain. The same movement has affected the various European legal systems, each at its own rate: the same death for all—execution no longer bears the specific mark of the crime or the social status of the criminal; a death that lasts only a moment—no torture must be added to it in advance, no further actions performed upon the corpse; an execution that affects life rather than the body. Punishment had no doubt ceased to be centred on torture as a technique of pain; it assumed as its principal object loss of wealth or rights. But a punishment like forced labour or even imprisonment—mere loss of liberty—has never functioned without a certain additional element of punishment that certainly concerns the body itself: rationing of food, sexual deprivation, corporal punishment, solitary confinement. Are these the unintentional, but inevitable, consequence of imprisonment? In fact, in its most explicit practices, imprisonment has always involved a certain degree of physical pain. The criticism that was often levelled at the penitentiary system in the early nineteenth century (imprisonment is not a sufficient punishment: prisoners are less hungry, less cold, less deprived in general than many poor people or even workers) suggests a postulate that was never explicitly denied: it is just that a condemned man should suffer physically more than other men. It is difficult to dissociate punishment from additional physical pain. What would a non-corporal punishment be?

There remains, therefore, a trace of "torture" in the modern mechanisms of criminal justice—a trace that has not been entirely overcome, but which is enveloped, increasingly, by the non-corporal nature of the penal system.

The reduction in penal severity in the last 200 years is a phenomenon with which legal historians are well acquainted. But, for a long time, it has been regarded in an overall way as a quantitative phenomenon: less cruelty, less pain, more kindness, more respect, more "humanity." In fact, these changes are accompanied by a displacement in the very object of the punitive operation. Is there a diminution of intensity? Perhaps. There is certainly a change of objective.

If the penalty in its most severe forms no longer address itself to the body, on what does it lay hold? The answer of the theoreticians—those who, about 1760 opened up a new period that is not yet at an end—is simple, almost obvious. It seems to be contained in the question itself: since it is no longer the body, it must be the soul. The expiation that once rained down upon the body must be replaced by a punishment that acts in depth on the heart, the thoughts, the will, the inclinations. Mably formulated the principle once and for all: "Punishment, if I may so put it, should strike the soul rather than the body" (Mably, 326).

During the 150 or 200 years that Europe has been setting up its new penal systems, the judges have gradually, by means of a process that goes back very far indeed, taken to judging something other than crimes, namely, the "soul" of the criminal.

And, by that very fact, they have begun to do something other than pass judgment. Or, to be more precise, within the very judicial modality of judgment, other types of assessment have slipped in, profoundly altering its rules of elaboration. Ever since the Middle Ages slowly and painfully built up the great procedure of investigation, to judge was to establish the truth of a crime, it was to determine its author and to apply a legal punishment. Knowledge of the offence, knowledge of the offender, knowledge of the law: these three conditions made it possible to ground a judgment in truth. But now a quite different question of truth is inscribed in the course of the penal judgment. The question is no longer simply: "Has the act been established and is it punishable?" But also: "What *is* the act, what *is* this act of violence or this murder? To what level or to what field of reality does it belong? Is it a fantasy, a psychotic reaction, a delusional episode, a perverse action?" It is no longer simply: "Who committed it?" But: "How can we assign the causal process that produced it? Where did it originate in the author himself? Instinct, unconscious, environment, heredity?" It is no longer simply: "What law punishes this offence?" But: "What would be the most appropriate measures to take? How do we see the future development of the offender? What would be the best way of rehabilitating him?" A whole set of assessing, diagnostic, prognostic, normative judgments concerning the criminal have become lodged in the framework of penal judgment. Another truth has penetrated the truth that was required by the legal machinery; a truth which, entangled with the first, has turned the assertion of guilt into a strange scientifico-juridical complex. A significant fact is the way in which the question of madness has evolved in penal practice. Already the reform of 1832, introducing attenuating circumstances, made it possible to modify the sentence according to the supposed degrees of an illness or the forms of a semi-insanity. And the practice of calling on psychiatric expertise, which is widespread in the assize courts and sometimes extended to courts of summary jurisdiction, means that the sentence, even if it always formulated in terms of legal punishment, implies, more or less obscurely, judgments of normality, attributions of causality, assessments of possible changes, anticipations as to the offender's future. And the sentence that condemns or acquits is not simply a judgment of guilt, a legal decision that lays down punishment; it bears within it an assessment of normality and a technical prescription for a possible normalization. Today the judge—magistrate or juror—certainly does more than "judge."

And he is not alone in judging. Throughout the penal procedure and the implementation of the sentence there swarms a whole series of subsidiary authorities. Small-scale legal systems and parallel judges have multiplied around the principal judgment: psychiatric or psychological experts, magistrates concerned with the implementation of sentences, educationalist, members of the prison service, all fragment the legal power to punish; it might be objected that none of them really shares the right to judge; that some, after sentence is passed, have no other right than to implement the punishment laid down by the court and, above all, that others—the experts—intervene before the sentence not to pass judgment, but to assist the judges in their decision.

To sum up, ever since the new penal system—that defined by the great codes of the eighteenth and nineteenth centuries—has been in operation, a general process has led judges to judge something other than crimes; they have been led in their sentences to do something other than judge; and the power of judging has been transferred, in part, to other authorities than the judges of the offence. The whole penal operation has taken on extra-juridical elements and personnel. It will be said that there is nothing extraordinary in this, that it is part of the destiny of the law to absorb little by little elements that are alien to it. But what is odd about modern criminal justice is that, although it has taken on so many extra-juridical elements, it has done so not in order to be able to define them juridically and gradually to integrate them into the actual power to punish: on the contrary, it has done so in order to make them function within the penal operation as non-juridical elements; in order to stop this operation being simply a legal punishment; in order to exculpate the judge from being purely and simply he who punishes.

> Of course, we pass sentence, but this sentence is not in direct relation to the crime. It is quite clear that for us it functions as a way of treating a criminal. We punish, but his is a way of saying that we wish to obtain a cure.

Today, criminal justice functions and justifies itself only by this perpetual reference to something other than itself, by this unceasing reinscription in non-juridical systems.

But we can surely accept the general proposition that, in our societies, the systems of punishment are to be situated in a certain "political economy" of the body: even if they do not make use of violent or bloody punishment, even when they use "lenient" methods involving confinement or correction, it is always the body that is at issue—the body and its forces, their utility and their docility, their distribution and their submission. It is certainly legitimate to write a history of punishment against the background of moral ideas or legal structures. But can one write such a history against the background of a history of bodies, when such systems of punishment claim to have only the secret souls of criminals as their objective?

Historians long ago began to write the history of the body. They have studied the body in the field of historical demography or pathology; they have considered it as the seat of needs and appetites, as the locus of processes and metabolisms, as a target for the attacks of germs or viruses; they have shown to what extent historical processes were involved in what might seem to be the purely biological base of existence; and what place should be given in the history of society to biological "events" such as the circulation of bacilli, or the extension of the life-span (cf. Le Roy-Ladurie 1974). But the body is also directly involved in a political field; power relations have an immediate hold upon it; they invest it, mark it, train it, torture it, force it to carry out tasks, to perform ceremonies, to emit signs. This political investment of the body is bound up, in accordance with complex reciprocal relations, with its economic use; it is largely as a force of production that the body is invested with relations of power and domination; but, on the other hand, its constitution as labour power is possible only if it is caught up in a system of subjection (in which need is also a political instrument meticulously prepared, calculated and used); the body becomes a useful force only if it is both a productive body and subjected body. This subjection is not only obtained by the instruments of violence or ideology; it can also be direct, physical, pitting force against force, bearing on material elements, and yet without involving violence; it may be calculated, organized, technically thought out; it may be subtle, make use neither of weapons nor of terror and yet remain of a physical order. That is to say, there may be a "knowledge" of the body that is not exactly the science of its functioning, and a mastery of its forces that is more than the ability to conquer them: this knowledge and this mastery constitute what might be called the political technology of the body. Of course, this technology is diffuse, rarely formulated in continuous, systematic discourse; it is often made up of bits and pieces; it implements a disparate set of tools or methods. In spite of the coherence of its results, it is generally no more than a multiform instrumentation. Moreover, it cannot be localized in a particular type of institution or state apparatus. For they have recourse to it; they use, select or impose certain of its methods. But, in its mechanisms and its effects, it is situated at a quite different level. What the apparatuses and institutions operate is, in a sense, a micro-physics of power, whose field of validity is situated in a sense between these great functionings and the bodies themselves with their materiality and their forces.

One might imagine a political "anatomy." This would not be the study of a state in terms of a "body" (with its elements, its resources and its forces), nor would it be the study of the body and its surroundings in terms of a small state. One would be concerned with the "body politic," as a set of material elements and techniques that serve as weapons, relays, communication routes and supports for the power and knowledge relations that invest human bodies and subjugate them by turning them into objects of knowledge.

It is a question of situating the techniques of punishment—whether they seize the body in the ritual of public torture and execution or whether they are addressed to the soul—in the history of this body politic; of considering penal practices less as a consequence of legal theories than as a chapter of political anatomy.

It would be wrong to say that the soul is an illusion, or an ideological effect. On the contrary, it exists, it has a reality, it is produced permanently around, on, within the body of the functioning of a power that is exercised on those punished—and, in a more general way, on those one supervises, trains and corrects, over madmen, children at home and at school, the colonized, over those who are stuck at a machine and supervised for the rest of their lives. This is the historical reality of the soul, which, unlike the soul represented by Christian theology, is not born in sin and subject to punishment, but is born rather out of methods of punishment, supervision and constraint. This real, non-corporal soul is not a substance; it is the element in which are articulated the effects of a certain type of power and the reference of a certain type of knowledge, the machinery by which the power relations give rise to a possible corpus of knowledge, and knowledge extends and reinforces the effects of this power. On this reality reference, various concepts have been constructed and domains of analysis carved out: psyche, subjectivity, personality, consciousness, etc.; on it have been built scientific techniques and discourses, and the moral claims of humanism. But let there be no misunderstanding: it is not that a real man, the object of knowledge, philosophical reflection or technical intervention, has been substituted for the soul, the illusion of the theologians. The man described for us, whom we are invited to free, is already in himself the effect of a subjection much more profound than himself. A "soul" inhabits him and brings him to existence, which is itself a factor in the mastery that power exercises over the body. The soul is the effect and instrument of a political anatomy; the soul is the prison of the body.

That punishment in general and the prison in particular belong to a political technology of the body is a lesson that I have learnt not so much from history as from the present. In recent years, prison revolts have occurred throughout the world. There was certainly something paradoxical about their aims, their slogans and the way they took place. They were revolts against an entire state of physical misery that is over a century old: against cold, suffocation and overcrowding, against decrepit walls, hunger, physical maltreatment. But they were also revolts against model prisons, tranquillizers, isolation, the medical or educational services. Were they revolts whose aims were merely material? Or contradictory revolts: against the obsolete, but also against comfort; against the warders, but also against the psychiatrists? In fact, all these movements—and the innumerable discourses that the prison has given rise to since the early nineteenth century—have been about the body and material things. What has sustained these discourses, these memories and invectives are indeed those minute material details. One may, if one is so disposed, see them as no more than blind demands or suspect the existence behind them of alien strategies. In fact, they were revolts, at the level of the body, against the very body of the prison. What was at issue was not whether the prison environment was too harsh or too aseptic, too primitive or too efficient, but its very materiality as an instrument and vector of power; it is this whole technology of power over the body that the technology of the "soul"—that of the educationalist, psychologists and psychiatrists—fails either to conceal or to compensate, for the simple reason that it is one of its tools.

References

Beccaria, C. de, *Traité des délits et des peines*. 1764, ed. 1856.

Faucher, L., *De la réforme des prisons*. 1838.

Le Roy-Ladurie, E., *Contrepoint*. 1973.

Le Roy-Ladurie, E., "L'histoire immobile," *Annales*. May-June, 1974.

Mably, G. de, *De la législation,* Oeuvres complètes, IX, 1789.

Pièces originales et procédures du procès fait à Robert-François Damiens, III,
    1757.

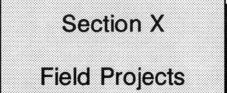

Section X

Field Projects

*In the following four selections, Aaron and Wiseman outline some basic
sociology projects for the introductory student. Each project centres on a
qualitative research method, and can be treated as an individual exercise.
They can also be integrated into broader projects focusing on culture or
social organization.*

Observation

Jacqueline Aaron and Marcia Wiseman

Observation as a Research Tool

Observation as a means of increasing one's knowledge is basic to the
investigation of almost any phenomenon. Some types of social action can only
be truly understood and appreciated when they are actually witnessed—seen
"in the flesh." The pomp and ceremony of rituals, the life conditions of men
in prison, and the subtle nuances of flirting are but a few aspects of social life
best grasped through firsthand observation. Many of the most memorable
sociological studies have been conducted by investigators who used observation
techniques. That such studies are often of interest far beyond the immediate
application of their findings bears witness to the vitality of observation as a
research tool.

Observation of social phenomena is obviously not restricted to the
sociologist. All people observe social situations to which they are privy or about
which they would like greater understanding. Moreover, they offer amateur
reports of such scenes by describing and interpreting them to friends or
relatives who were not present, in order to increase these persons'
understanding of what happened. There is an important difference between the
observations of the sociologist and those of the lay observer, however. Because
the sociologist must organize and analyse his data in terms of sociological
theories and concepts, he is sensitized to attending to human group life in a far
more systematic fashion than the average person is. The layman relies primarily
on his memory, but the researcher attempts to keep written descriptions of
what he sees, for he is interested in more detail than his memory can retain.
For this reason the sociologist is forced to think of systematic ways to conduct
his observations and record what happens as it a happens, or soon after,
without upsetting his subjects or missing significant actions. Such planning is a
part of the observation technique for which laymen seldom have patience or
need.

How to Do Observation Research

Observation research is part craft and part art. Anyone can observe, but it takes practice and careful planning to observe and record a scene accurately and then to analyse perceptively what happened of sociological significance. Such skills improve with experience.

An early decision the observer must make is the setting. He must choose this with the goals of the study in mind. For instance, if the observer is studying strategies of flirting, he must select a setting in which this interaction is likely to occur both openly and frequently. Furthermore, he must think of an unobtrusive way to record his observations in an organized manner. Sometimes it is helpful to set up tally sheets before going into the field.

Professional observers try to blend with others in the settings they are observing. They may dress and act as if they belong to the groups so as not to influence the interactions by their presence. Sometimes an observer also participates in the activities to get a feel for the meaning they have to the persons he is studying. Blending into the scene can make the recording of data a problem. Of course, if the subjects of the research are very young, or if writing is expected in a particular setting, the problem is eliminated. But if writing might seem out of place, the observer must find a private area where he can record events and descriptions of them from time to time, because he cannot rely on memory alone.

Once on the scene the observer must remain alert and flexible. Keeping track of the interactions of even a few persons can be very demanding. An observer must be able to adjust his tally sheets and focus of attention as the situation dictates, because the true gold mined through observation is the unexpected.

At frequent intervals the sociologist observing human group life in action should stop and ponder (usually in private) what he has seen and recorded. What is its sociological significance? What sorts of interactions seem to bring on what kinds of counter moves? What sociological concepts seem to be in play? (The investigator may also discuss his findings with other sociologists to get their insights.) Once he has made some preliminary decisions about these and other questions, the investigator will try to think of ways to confirm his hunches about what is going on in the scene he is watching. Thus sensitized by his introspection, he returns to continue his observations.

Not least among the talents of an observer of human group life is the ability to organize the findings and relay them to a reader via well-written description. Deciding on the central theme of the data often aids its organization. Descriptive passages should aim at reproducing, as closely as subtleties of language will permit, the situations observed. The sociological import of descriptions should be included in order to relate the particular findings to the broader spectrum of theory about human group life.

Advantages and Disadvantages

Observation is particularly useful for gaining insight into a respondent's habitual round of activities. The average person seldom sees these activities as sociologically significant and rarely reports them to the researcher during an interview. The routines and rituals that families develop in the course of living together, for example, can so recede into the background of daily events that they do not seem sufficiently important to the people involved to mention to an investigator. Interactions that are difficult to describe or that people are reluctant to talk about are often amenable to observation, provided they are accessible to an outsider. Techniques of parental discipline, times of personal embarrassment, riots, strikes, and other collective behaviour are but a few such situations.

Of course, observation research can have drawbacks. It is time-consuming and, somewhat like police stake-outs, it is not always rewarding in the type of data desired. Observations cannot be scheduled solely at the convenience of the investigator; instead he must be on the scene when the scene is on! Perhaps the most troublesome problem in observation is researcher bias that can contaminate findings. If the investigator is aware of the following sources of bias, he should be able to neutralize their effects—to some extent, at least.

1. Unlimited selectivity in perception, recording or reporting.
2. Imputation of meaning that the actors themselves do not intend or experience.
3. Mistaking an idiosyncratic event for a recurrent one.
4. Affecting the action by his presence.

It is obvious, of course, that the lay observer also runs afoul of these biasing factors. We are often aware of flaws in the descriptions that other people offer us concerning an event at which we were not present. We know, for instance, that in reporting, some of our friends tend to select only certain features of a situation, or to emphasize certain aspects in a way that distorts it. Then, too, people frequently misinterpret the actions they witness. And we have all experienced the occasion when a person tells us that so and so is always engaged in a certain activity, when we know the speaker has viewed such action by the person in question only once or twice.

Some Applications of This Method

Observation techniques have been used to gather data on the means people employ to ease embarrassing moments—for example, a male doctor's examinations of female patients (Emerson, 1963). Observation has also been used to watch intake procedures at a drug and alcoholism clinic in order to detect unwritten screening principles (Wiseman, 1970); to look at the police in action (Sudnow, 1965); to see how children act and interact in a small town in various natural habitats such as the library and drugstore (Barker and Wright, 1955); and to observe men living on Skid Row to discover what their typical day is like (Wiseman, 1970). These are but a few studies based on observation.

Although many investigators use natural settings and look at whatever develops in the normal course of events, psychologists and social psychologists often use observation techniques to watch people in experimental laboratory situations. In such cases the observers often remain behind mirror-windows, unseen by the subjects—who are often aware, however, that they are taking part in a controlled experiment of some kind (Asch, 1956; Garfinkel, 1963; Lippitt, 1940; Milgram, 1965, and Bales, 1950, 1970).

Before Going into the Field

1. Gain access to the setting. Some settings, like bus depots, are open to everyone. Others are closed and present problems of access. If you do observation research in an educational institution (for example, a classroom), you are likely to need permission. Often you need the recommendation of someone whose name carries some weight. If such is the case, perhaps your instructor can make arrangements for you. Where negotiations fail and the researcher still wishes to pursue the subject, he must locate alternative areas.

2. Narrow your topic of inquiry. Do not be afraid to do something that seems "too simple." Better a simple project elegantly handled than a complex one that is botched.

3. Decide what you want to know about the topic you select. This is actually an additional narrowing of your inquiry.

4. Select a setting that offers an opportunity for the type of social activity you wish to study.

5. Organize your observation and note-taking in advance. Do some preliminary planning on how you will keep track of your data. Set up some sort of tally sheet for the structured portion of the observations that will allow you to keep track of the acts you are interested in, the specific persons acting, and the responses to them. You will

undoubtedly have to revise this after being in the field a short time, but this planning will force you to think of the types of activity to watch for and how you can organize their collection.

6. For the unstructured portions of the observation project, plan to write the details of pertinent social interactions and your interpretation of them at the time. This should include verbatim records of conversations (or as close to verbatim as possible) and descriptions of specific situations.

In the Field

1. Find a location where you can watch without disturbing the interaction.
2. Test your tally and revise as necessary to accommodate what is occurring.
3. If at all convenient, jot down descriptions and sociological interpretations as they occur to you. You may be unpleasantly surprised at the good ideas you will be unable to recall later when you are writing the report unless you note important items while in the field.
4. If you get some special, unexpected insight into your sociological problem, be flexible enough to follow it up in your systematic and descriptive observations even though you did not originally plan for it.

References

Asch, S.E. (1956). "Studies of Independence and Conformity." *Psychological Monographs* 70:9.

Bales, Robert F. (1950). *Interaction Process Analysis: A Method for the Study of Small Groups.* Reading Mass.: Addison-Wesley.

Bales, Robert F. (1970). *Personality and Interpersonal Behaviour.* New York: Holt, Rinehart and Winston.

Barker, Roger and H.F. Wright. (1955). *The Midwest and Its Children.* Evanston, Ill.: Row, Peterson.

Emerson, Joan (1963). "Social Functions of Humour in a Hospital Setting." Unpublished Ph.D. dissertation, University of California. Berkeley.

Garfinkel, H. (1963). "A Conception of, and Experiments with, 'Trust' as a Condition of Stable, Concerted Actions." pp.187-238 in O.J. Harvey (ed.), *Motivation and Social Interaction.* New York: Ronald.

Lippitt, Ronald (1940). "An Experimental Study of the Effect of Democratic and Authoritarian Group Atmospheres." *University of Iowa Studies in Child Welfare* 16 February: 43-195.

Milgram, Stanley (1965). "Some Conditions of Obedience and Disobedience to Authority." pp. 243-262 in Ivan D. Steiner and Martin Fishbein (eds.), *Current Studies in Social Psychology.* New York: Holt, Rinehart and Winston.

Sudnow, David (1965). "Normal Crimes: Sociological Features of the Penal Code in A Public Defender's Office." *Social Problems* 12 (Winter): 255-276.

Wiseman, Jaqueline P. (1970). *Stations of the Lost.* Englewood Cliffs, N.J.: Prentice Hall.

Participant Observation

Participant Observation, a Definition

Now that you are acquainted with the field technique of observation you should be ready to take a turn with its research cousin, participant observation. Both of these techniques are important sociological tools. It is only by observing what people do when they interact with one another, as well as by recording what they say they do, that we can begin to get an understanding of the dynamics of social processes.

The method of research known as participant observation differs from the previous structured and unstructured observations in several important ways. As the name implies, the participant observer is a researcher who becomes a member of the group he is observing, while the non-participant observer tries to remain aloof from it. This distinction is not clear cut since there is a wide range in the level of participation—from the sociologist who stays out of the group and just watches the action to the researcher who is actually a member. Usually a researcher participates to a degree somewhere between these two extremes by either posing as a member or announcing himself as a scientific investigator and hoping to be accepted by the group in that role. Inevitably, a time continuum parallels the degree of participation. The longer an observer stays on the scene, the more likely he is to be drawn into participating in the group's way of life. As a general rule, the participant observer commits himself to a group for a considerable period of time, ranging from several weeks or months to many years.

A second characteristic of the participant observer is that he tries to understand the frame of reference of the group he is investigating. He does this primarily by joining the members in their daily activities in order to experience things as they do. The autobiographies of those who have lived for many years in institutions such as prisons (Black, 1927) or convents (Baldwin, 1959) are particularly insightful studies of these "closed" societies. Though these individuals were not trained sociologists, they were participant observers par excellence.

There is a certain similarity between this approach and espionage. The observer must exist mentally on two levels. Instead of being socialized to the new way of life almost unknowingly, as are most individuals after they join a group, the scientific investigator must learn to be simultaneously "inside" and "outside" the group life he is studying. He must learn the meanings that behaviour has for the members of the group, and he has to become sufficiently involved with the group to be able to understand what makes it tick. At the same time, he cannot be so involved that he is unable to report accurately what is happening and why. He cannot be so far "inside" that everything seems so "normal" as to be not worth reporting. And to top it all off, he must be able to report patterns of behaviour and interrelationships objectively, without moral judgment or bias. The reason for this double frame of reference is that the participant observer wants to understand the group and its actions not only in its own terms—that is, how the members themselves live and feel the culture—but also in terms of a larger and more general set of sociological hypotheses or theories about the nature of human interaction.

Do these sound like impossible tasks? They are difficult, but with practice they can be handled fairly well. Anthropologists occasionally find some of the attitudes, beliefs, and behaviours of the societies they study repugnant or immoral. However, they are trained not to judge, but rather to try to faithfully record and to determine what meaning these behaviour patterns have for the people who practice them.[1] Perhaps an even more common outcome of close contact with a new group over a prolonged period of time is the observer's identification with the group. He starts to accept their behaviour patterns as his own and may find it hard to re-enter his old way of life when he has finished his study. Many Peace Corps volunteers have had this problem after living for a year or two in a foreign culture with a way of life dissimilar from their own. These twin dangers—aversion and over-identification—can be partially neutralized if the researcher is aware that he is not merely a recording machine—and that he is going to have personal reactions to any new group he enters.

How to Do Participant Observation

Traditionally, participant observation requires access to a group or community over a long time period since it is essentially a research technique to learn about and describe a group's total culture or way of life. How long should an investigator stay with a group or community to obtain the information he seeks? Certainly he must remain long enough to observe recurring behavioural patterns. This may mean attendance at all the weekly activities of a small club for two or three months, or living in a community (small town or primitive society) for several years. In the first case, he may be interested in learning how the leadership of the club maintains its power; in the second, whether there is a relationship between child-rearing techniques and achievement motivation.

What should the participant observer notice and record? This depends on the purpose of the study. If it is exploratory, presumably the researcher does not know the culture of the group. Thus he must be careful to keep comprehensive and detailed notes on all that occurs around him. Even behaviour that seems trivial or unimportant should be recorded in his researcher's "diary." The good investigator will record observations as often as possible and not rely on his memory, which more often than not is untrustworthy when it comes to detail. Sometimes it is necessary to record as often as five or six times a day if the observer is living with the group. No matter how difficult the circumstances, he should keep his diary current.

If the researcher is only interested in one particular aspect of a group—for example, the leadership pattern—then it would seem permissible for him to limit his observations and note-taking to those actions of the participants that exhibit "leadership" qualities. Even here, however, seemingly unimportant behaviour patterns (speech, facial expressions, gestures) may offer clues that aid in giving insight into the research problem.

Because the participant observer attempts to understand how the people he is studying feel about their situation, he is trying to do more than simply describe the distinctive behaviour patterns of the individuals interacting in a particular group. He is also trying to explain why they, as individuals, are behaving as they are.

Whether the researcher is aware of it or not, whenever he enters a group as a newcomer he is assigned a role by the old members. He may be accepted as an "observer" or as a "member." but in whatever role he is cast, he has altered the previous structure of role-relationships. Thus he is a potential, if not an actual, disturbance in existing schizoid patterns. It is only when the observer has been "placed" by the other members and is interacting with them in a "normal" way that his is able to start collecting information without arousing fear and hostility (Blau, 1967). After this normalizing has occurred will members of the group feel comfortable and act naturally.[2]

The degree to which a participant observer can bias his results by his mere presence can probably never be fully known. The effect of his presence varies with the size of the group (the smaller the group, the greater the effect), how deeply entrenched previous patterns of interaction were, and whether the group knows it is being studied. Because you already have a place in the group and a role to play, your research efforts will probably not change previously established patterns of behaviour and the biasing effect of your presence presumably will not be a problem.

Advantages and Disadvantages

A major advantage of participant observation is that the investigator need not rely totally on "empathetic insight" or intuition to understand the perspective of his research subject, as he might from observation alone. He sees the world, at least part of the time, in the same way other members of the group see it because he is living their kind of life with them. Therefore, personal introspection will provide him with clues for understanding his data. Also, as with non-participant observation, he watches human group life as it is lived, not as it is reported to an interviewer. All the contradictions between what people say they believe in doing and what they actually do, their consistencies and inconsistencies, are played out before the observer. Also, as a participant he can often casually ask for the types of explanations that an interviewer arriving "cold" on the scene cannot. He can ask, "Hey, what's so funny?" or "Why did everyone look so glum just then?" and it will not sound inappropriate. The method offers great flexibility in the field. If the observer notes some activity that seems significant to the problem he is investigating and that he knew nothing about before he began his study, he can arrange his observation efforts to encompass this behaviour.

Participation has one other major advantage—a built-in validity test. If the participant who is trying to "pass" as a member in the group he is studying misinterprets some bit of interaction and then acts on the basis of his misinterpretation, the group will soon show him the error of his ways!

Participant observation has its disadvantages too. It is time-consuming. Also, the investigator is not usually able to control the action (although this depends to a large extent on his role in the group), so that he must wait for events that are of interest to him to occur. Sometimes he will have to spend hours watching interaction he has already seen while waiting for some new data. Because of the "ongoing" nature of the happenings in the group, a participant observation project cannot be planned so completely in advance as can a survey research project.

Being a participant in some groups can be very demanding. Sociologists have performed in dance bands (Becker, 1963), successfully faked the symptoms and problems of mental illness (Claudill, 1958), and worked with the police on stake-outs (Skolnick, 1966). Often those who participated with some deviant groups found themselves faced with the choice of either joining what they considered to be immoral or illegal actions or severing their ties with the group.

Finally, one of participant observation's greatest virtues can also be one of its most troublesome areas (we mentioned this before, but it deserves repeating). The deeper the participant investigator immerses himself in the group's culture, the more difficult he finds it to study it "objectively," and the more likely he is to miss the sociological significance of action that becomes increasingly "normal" to him.

Some Applications

Participation in the normal life of a community or group to understand its social processes better has a long and interesting history in social investigation. One of the first important studies using this technique was conducted by Frederic LePlay (1808-1882), who studied the family life of European workers by actually living in their homes. His major interest was the interrelationships between geographical location, type of work, and a family's way of life.

Anthropologists have found this method of investigation particularly useful in studying primitive communities, and it is often associated with this branch of the social sciences. Most of what we know today of non-literate societies has been because of excellent anthropological field studies. Sociologists have found participant observation particularly valuable for the study of groups that the average American—including the investigator himself, usually—does not understand. It has been used to study mental hospitals (Goffman, 1961), delinquent gangs, and gamblers (Scott, 1968), to name but a few. Sociologists have also used the technique to study small towns (Withers, 1945; Lowry, 1965), industrial plants (Warner and Lew, 1947), and other more conventional settings.

Before You Go into the Field

1. Determine what particular aspect of the group you want to study. Since you have limited time available to complete this assignment, it is essential that you determine the kinds of group interaction you want to know more about. Here are a few suggestions:
    a. Focus on the communication patterns of the group. All groups develop a "secret language" by using both vocal and non-vocal gestures.
    b. Examine the leadership patterns. Who are the leaders, and how do they maintain their position?
    c. Look at this group's problems. How does it solve them?
    d. Discover the modes of cooperation, or the exchange processes. Who does what for whom?
    e. Identify the sanctions or punishments of members who violate the rules or norms or who try to change their expected role-behaviour. (You as a member could deliberately change your accustomed behaviour in order to test whether other members attempt to bring you back into line. If this tack is taken, it would first be necessary to observe the group in your "normal" role so that you could make a comparison.)
2. Specify more clearly the dimensions of your topic. Think out the kinds of social phenomena you will use as real-life examples of problems. For example, if you are interested in how the group solves problems, what will you regard as a problem? Will it be the necessity to make a decision—such as to charge non-members for tickets to a play? Or will it be the necessity to ease tensions arising from arguments? Or would both of these different kinds of interactions be

considered as problems you want to study? What will you consider as "solutions" to these problems?

3. Go into the field only after giving considerable time and thought to 1 and 2 above.

In the Field

It is essential that your retire to privacy from time to time or as soon as possible after your observation to write up your description. Keep a diary of events, separating your observations from your interpretations.

Endnotes

1.   The diary of Bronislaw Malinowski, the famous English anthropologist, was published recently and a great many people, including social scientists, were shocked at the disclosures he made of his personal feelings about the Trobriand Islanders (Malinowski, 1967)

2.   Anything that is out of the ordinary can affect the status quo of a group, and there may be less danger that a single observer will contaminate (or bias) the group's identity and integrity than would the artificiality of a laboratory experiment.

References

Baldwin, Monica (1959). *The Called and the Chosen*. New York: New American Library.

Becker, Howard S. (1963). *The Outsiders: Studies in the Sociology of Deviance*. New York: The Free Press.

Black, Jack (1927). *You Can't Win*. New York: Macmillan.

Blau, Peter (1967). "The Research Process in the Study of The Dynamics of Bureaucracy." pp. 18-57 in Philip E. Hammond (ed.), *Sociologists at Work: The Craft of Social Research*. Garden City, N.Y.: Doubleday.

Caudill, William (1958). *A Psychiatric Hospital as a Small Society*. Cambridge, Mass.: Harvard University Press.

Goffman, Erving (1961). *Asylums: Essays on the Social Situation of Mental Patients and Other Inmates.* Garden City, N.Y.: Doubleday.

LePlay, Frederic (1879). *Les Ouvriers Europeans.* Paris: Alfred Mame et Fils.

Lowry, Ritchie P. (1965). *Who's Running This Town?* New York: Harper and Row.

Malinowski, Bronislaw (1967). *A Diary in the Strict Sense of the Word.* New York: Harcourt, Brace and World.

Scott, Marvin B. (1968). *The Racing Game.* Chicago: Aldine.

Skolnick, Jerome H. (1966). *Justice Without Trial.* New York: Wiley.

Warner, William Lloyd, and J.O. Lew (1947). *The Social System of the Modern Factory.* New Haven, Conn.: Yale University Press.

Withers, Carl [James West, pseud.] (1945). Plainville, U.S.A. New York: Columbia University Press.

The Depth Interview

The Depth Interview, a Definition

One of the major tools of the social scientist—the depth interview—is also a favourite of the average citizen. Everyone at one time or another has used this technique to learn more about a subject of interest. A person will start by asking someone general questions. As he receives answers, he follows up on certain points with increasingly specific questions until he has acquired "an understanding" of the topic.

Depth interviewing, as generally conducted by sociologists, has the same pattern as that used by a curious non-professional. The major difference is that the answers social researchers receive are usually carefully recorded and reviewed in terms of concepts and theories of concern to the discipline. As an exploratory tool, depth interviewing is a way to locate important information for further study. It can also become an end in itself—that is, a way to get detailed descriptions or even explanations of certain types of social behaviour.

The depth interview enables the investigator to probe the intensity of an individual's feelings about a given social phenomenon-, the intricacies of his definition of it, and how he relates it to other areas of his social life.

Respondents will often give their judgments of what the attitudes of others are and how these affect their own attitudes and behaviour. Memories of past events (technically called retrospective longitudinal data) can be obtained through depth interviews, especially when respondents are allowed adequate time to recall past events and place them in proper order or perspective.

Depth interviewing can be viewed as a fishing expedition, because the sociologist does it to get information when he has so little knowledge on a subject that he cannot ask structured questions. He also uses it to obtain more detail than a formal questionnaire normally makes available. The depth interview is a major tool in the social sciences, one that every competent researcher should be able to handle.

How to Do Depth Interviewing

The researcher attempting a depth interview is initially faced with the problem of creating and maintaining personal rapport with the respondent. This is essential if the interviewee is to be able to express in detail his deepest thoughts and feelings. To obtain the rapport he needs, the depth interviewer must assure the respondent that his identity will be kept confidential, and that he is collecting the information as part of a legitimate research project. Throughout the interview, the social investigator must take pains to be as neutral as possible. He must resist the temptation to moralize, to give advice, or to otherwise indicate how he feels about the information given. Above all, he must encourage his respondent to keep talking. A nod of the head once in a while, to indicate understanding, is sufficient after a relationship has been established and answers are forthcoming. More reaction might interrupt the respondent's train of thought and elaboration of various points.

Because a depth interview will often last for over an hour, recording detailed answers can present problems. The tape recorder is often used, but it is by no means necessary. In fact many researchers avoid using it because of the time involved in typing tapes—approximately two to three times the length of the interview. There is also the fear that respondents may feel inhibited if they know they are being recorded, though most people forget the machine is there. Seasoned depth interviewers learn to write rapidly (using abbreviations and bits of shorthand) during an interview. They also find that respondents, far from being annoyed at the time it takes to write down their comments, are flattered that the investigator is taking pains to get what they say correctly.

Because depth interviewing is used to develop categories and hypotheses, the interviewer usually asks very general questions. "What's going on?" or some variation of this question was a favourite query of Howard Becker and his associates when they interviewed respondents for their study of the medical student world (Becker and Geer, 1960). Other examples of general questions (depending on the subject) are:

Would you describe a typical day here to me?
Tell me about the thoughts and reasons you had before doing
_____.
In general, how do you feel about _____?

The investigator may gradually focus a depth interview on those portions of the material about which he would like further information. To do this, he must be alert at all times for clues that could be pertinent to his problem. He may then ask more non-directive questions about these specific areas; for example:

You say that a typical day here always includes _____ activity?
Why is that? Do you participate? Why or why not?

A spot analysis of previous interviews will often reveal clues about the subject matter under investigation that can be followed up in greater detail in subsequent interviews. The more rechecking the interviewer does of past responses, the more he is able to determine areas that he has not covered or where he has only scratched the surface. Thus as the research progresses, the questions tend to become increasingly focused (Merton and Kendall, 1946).

Eventually the investigator returns to the field with a short list of topics to cover. For instance, a typical list of focused topics for a depth interview concerning the respondent's job might include:

> Describe a typical day here. (This is always a good opening question.)
> What is your job here? What do you do? How do you feel about your job?
> Why?
> Describe various supervisors (or top ranking employees) you see during the day. What are they like?
> What are the other employees like? What do you think of them? Why?

Note that even when the questions are concentrated on a special topic, the *tone* of the questions is as neutral and open as possible so as not to suggest answers. A questions like, "What do you think of it here?" is preferable to "Do you like it here?" The same principle applies to "probing"—that is, pursuing the answer to a question to be certain you have a complete understanding of it. The best probes do not suggest answers:

> Can you think of anything else to tell me about that?
> What are your reasons for feeling this way?
> Why do you think others do that?

The interviewer usually inserts a hash-mark "/" where he probed for more detail. A short excerpt from his verbatim notes of the respondent's answers might look like this:

> Well, this job pays well, but that's about all I can say for it. It's just a job, that's all./ Well, I can support my family, keep up on my bills. We aren't wanting for anything./ Well, what I mean about that's all that's good about the job is that it is boring. It's the same thing day after day and there is not real hope for advancement to something more challenging./ Oh, you know, challenging to the mind, something that really interests me and makes me think about it and makes me feel proud of what I do. It doesn't offer that.

Advantages and Disadvantages

A researcher uses depth interviews rather than observation techniques when he decides that the only way to know what is on the subject's mind is to ask him. As we mentioned earlier, the researcher uses depth interviewing rather than the standard structures survey interview (especially those with fixed-choice answers) when he wants detail on social interactions and interrelated attitudes that he does not have and therefore cannot "build into" his questionnaire.

A major advantage of depth interviewing is its flexibility. Instead of going into the field with a narrow and specific hypothesis that he assumes to be the best approach to the study area, the researcher goes in with the idea of developing hypotheses and categories in the course of the investigation. He can, of course, narrow the topical scope of his inquiry to the subject of his interest; but the interview framework must not be so rigid as to prohibit consideration of all material a respondent offers on this subject. The goal, then, of this unstructured approach is to obtain information that cannot be anticipated.

Obviously depth interviewing, like observation, is time consuming. Often, in order to establish or maintain rapport, the investigator must allow the respondent to tell him many things he already knows about a given phenomenon- before he can work his way to new material.

As with observation, the major disadvantage of depth interviewing is the difficulty of quantifying—or even organizing—data that was collected in semi-haphazard ways. There comes a time, however, when the mass of material must be put into some kind of logical order so that the investigator can present what he has learned in an understandable fashion. Usually this is accomplished by analysing the respondents' remarks for content that will become the focus of the report. The goal of the study offers some guidance here, but many of these decisions depend on the insight of the researcher.

Among the other arguments used against depth interviewing is the presumed inability of the average person to verbalize the "true" reasons for his decisions and actions. Researchers who believe people act for reasons they are not consciously aware of will use depth interviews—if they approve use of them at all—only to get at what they call "rationalizations." On the other hand, researchers who advocate depth interviews as a tool to study motivation are convinced that people do know why they act in certain ways. Therefore, they say, it would be less than professional to ignore a viable, worthwhile avenue to a respondent's thought processes.

Some Applications

A person in a social grouping will ordinarily have complex feelings of satisfaction and dissatisfaction about his role there. He is also usually concerned about the judgment of his "performance" by others, and about the possibilities of gaining friends and making enemies. Depth interviewing is applicable to topics where the actor's point of view and inner feelings are important to the research goals.

The depth approach has been used as a means of interviewing deviants such as prostitutes (Bryan, 1965), alcoholics (Wiseman, 1970), homosexuals (Hoffman, 1968), and felons (Irwin, 1970; Sykes, 1965). In the area of family interaction, where attitudes and emotions are crucial, the depth interview has also proved valuable (Hess and Handel, 1959). On an institutional level, students' feelings about their curricula, their instructors, and their classmates (Werthman, 1963) have been probed through the depth interview, as have the attitudes of employees toward their jobs and bosses (Roethlisberger and Dickson, 1939).

Depth interviews are also used in combination with observation techniques as an approach to data collection. Often the information obtained through these two methods will stimulate the researcher to conduct a broader survey on a larger sample of respondents using a structured questionnaire.

Before You Go into the Field

1. Select your specific topic of inquiry.
2. Think out a small number of neutral questions—six at most—that will lead your subject to talk about your topic. Jot these down in your interviewing notebook.
3. Decide whom you will need as respondents.

In the Field

1. As usual, you must gain access to subjects who have had experience with the topic of your interest. Tell a prospective respondent you are doing research on a given subject (make your description very general) and that you would appreciate interviewing him.
2. Once you have gained permission to interview a subject, it is important to gain rapport so that he will talk freely and comfortably with you. The best way to do this is to be courteous, interested in

what he says, and non-judgmental regardless of your own feelings or beliefs.
3. Get repondent's answers as nearly verbatim as possible. This means in his own words, not in a summary composed by you. If you try to summarize his thoughts, there is a danger that you will give them meaning they did not actually possess.
4. If you feel you are holding up the interview by writing the answers, it often helps to say, "I hope you don't mind the delay. I want to be certain to get all of your answer." An alternative is to write up the interview as soon as you are alone, counting on your memory for details, but this has definite liabilities.
Where you probe for more detail, insert a hash-mark to indicate that you interjected a "Why?" or "What are your reasons for feeling this way?" at that point in the interview.
5. Read over each interview before embarking on the next. Watch for points that you will want to follow up in this and subsequent interviews.

References

Becker, Howard S., and Blanche Geer (1960). "Participant Observation: The Analysis of Qualitative Field Data." pp. 267-289 in Richard H. Adams and Jack J. Preiss (eds.), *Human Organization Research.* Homewood, Ill.: Dorsey.
Bryan, James H. (1965). "Apprenticeship in Prostitution." *Social Problems* 12 (Winter): 287-297.
Hess, Robert D., and Gerald Handel (1959). *Family Worlds.* Chicago: University of Chicago Press.
Hoffman, Martin (1968). *The Gay World: Male Homosexuality and Social Creation of Evil.* New York: Basic Books.
Irwin, John (1970). *The Felon.* Englewood Cliffs, NJ.: Prentice Hall.
Merton, Robert K., and Patricia L. Kendall (1946). "The Focused Interview." *American Journal of Sociology* 51 (May): 541-557.
Roethlisberger, F.J., and W.J. Dickson (1939). *Management and the Worker.* Cambridge, MA: Harvard University Press.
Sykes, Gresham M. (1965). *The Society of Captives.* New York: Atheneum.
Werthman, Carl (1963). "Delinquents in Schools: A Test for the Legitimacy of Authority." *Berkeley Journal of Sociology* 8:39-60.
Wiseman, Jaqueline P. (1970). *Stations of the Lost.* Englewood Cliffs, N.J.: Prentice Hall.

Role Analysis

Role Analysis, a Definition
Role analysis is concerned with the effects of fairly well-established social structures and their concomitant role relationships on the behaviour of participants. Just as social life is not carried out in a vacuum but reflects the characteristics of its physical settings, so it is also affected by the expectations that people have developed concerning the proper role behaviour for themselves and others. Thus, if a researcher can draw a map of socially important ecological elements such as barriers, pathways, hiding places, and conversation areas in a setting, he can also chart the role and counter-role relationships in society.

Sociologists have borrowed the term "role" from the theatre. It refers to a cluster of behaviour norms (rules) that apply to a given position in the social structure. These norms consist of a set of expectations by others that include not only how one should perform the role itself, but also how one should act toward others while performing it, and even how one should feel at the time. The term also includes the role occupant's expectations about how others should act toward him. These reciprocal norms usually remain consistent over time. Such interrelationships of role activities and the expectations it created mean that a noticeable deviation in behaviour is upsetting. Such complaints as "He doesn't act at all as a minister (or teacher, father, etc.) should act toward a parishioner (student, son)" reflect this disappointment in role enactment. The speaker is essentially arguing that the cluster of behaviours toward others by a minister and from others to a minister form a coherent whole that has social-psychological boundaries, so far as the expectations of others are concerned. This includes a minister's mode of dress, his behaviour and demeanour toward others, and his status vis-à-vis them.

Society is possible, in part, because people go about quietly fulfilling the role expectations of the different positions they occupy. Often we become consciously aware of what those role expectations are only when someone transgresses them. When a child "smarts off" to an adult, for instance, or a professor arrives at class "inappropriately" dressed, or a low-ranking employee gets "too friendly" with the boss at a company picnic, the discomfiture signals a digression from role expectations.

Role analysts believe the concept of "internalization" of role obligations can explain much of people's behaviour, and the motivations for this behaviour. We have all witnessed the socializing effect of roles on their occupants: the flighty young girl who marries and slowly takes on the role of "matron" because she believes it is expected of her; the vice president who is suddenly catapulted to power by the death of the president and begins to show qualities of statesmanship no one knew he possessed; the contestant who bravely acts the role of the gracious loser, because this is part of playing the game. Some of the most dramatic illustrations of the socializing effect of acquiring a social position with accompanying role expectations are to be found in literature and the theatre. In *Pygmalion*, and its musical counterpart, *My Fair Lady*, a lower-class woman is socialized to the role of "lady" and surprises everyone by feeling like one as well as acting the part. *Becket* is the story of a medieval playboy whose appointment to the position of Archbishop of Canterbury gradually socializes him to the point where he acts as is expected of a man in this position. Thus we often act to fulfil the expectations we believe others have of us.

How to Do Role Research and Analysis

Role analysis is not a method of data-gathering per se, but a conceptual and analytic tool. In action, it is an excellent illustration of the interplay between theory and method in research, because its concepts circumscribe the data to be gathered and direct the analysis.

The concept "role" is only one in a constellation of related terms used in role analysis to study the behaviour of individuals. These terms are:

> **Position:** One's "situation" in the social structure.
> **Role:** The dynamic or behavioural aspect of position.
> **Status:** The evaluative aspect of position—whether others see it as "high" or "low."
> **Counter role:** A role that is complementary to the role (that is, "completes" the dyadic interaction), allowing, by its existence, the enactment of the role. Teacher-pupil, parent-child, and clerk-customer are three pairs of counter roles that reinforce and make possible each other's performance.
> **Rights and obligations:** Every role carries with it certain actions owed by others and to others. These are the shared expectations or ideal patterns of our own and counter role enactments that we carry in our heads.
> **Role perception:** How one thinks of his social role, what he thinks he should be doing.
> **Role behaviour:** Actual performance in a role. (Sometimes we fall below our own role expectations, or those of others. Sometimes we are gloriously successful—we "carry it off.")
> **Role conflict:** A situation in which a person finds that his proper enactment of one role results in falling below expectations in another. Thus, no matter what he does, he has some guilt feelings. (Women who are trying to be good mothers and good students too often experience such role conflict.)

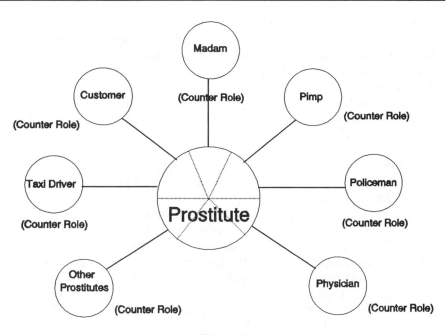

Figure 1

Using these concepts as guides for data-gathering, the social scientist is able to take the information he obtains and map out a "role system" that can in turn be a useful device to alert the researcher to other areas of interaction that might be fruitfully investigated. For instance, Gross et al. (1958) suggested that one way to understand the pressures experienced by a school superintendent was first to map out the counter roles of positions relative to his, such as principles, teachers, school-board members, and students. In an analogous discussion of role and counter role, Merton (1957) uses as his illustration the student physician and focuses on persons who share the same small world—what he refers to as a "status set." In Merton's status set of the student physician, one finds physicians, nurses, social workers, medical technologists, and so on. Each of these, though fundamentally in the same "world" as the student physician (the "medical world"), looks at him from a different perspective and thus interacts with him in somewhat different ways and has somewhat different expectations of him as well.

Following Gross's or Merton's lead, in Figure 1 we have charted the counter roles of a prostitute. (It should be clear that the designations "central role" and "counter role" depend upon the researcher's interests. One man's counter role could be another's central role; thus the pimp could be in the focal position and the prostitute in a counter role if the pimp were the major research interest. Furthermore, counter-role occupants also interact with each other. These interactions may be included in or excluded from a research efforts, depending upon the goal of the study.)

Once the researcher has mapped out (literally and figuratively) the significant counter roles that are a part of the social situation under study, he can examine the behaviour of persons occupying these roles with the following questions in mind:

1. How do individuals in a counter-role relationship interact with each other? (Specific emphasis would be placed on interaction with the designated "central role.")
2. What unspoken expectations do they seem to have of each other? (As mentioned, moments of obviously violated expectations—noted because of the outrage expressed by one person in a role dyad—are very revealing in this area.) For instance, what is expected of a school superintendent? What happens if he falls below expectations?
3. How does each person in the role apparently see himself? How does he see others? For instance, how does a pimp see himself? How do others view him?
4. What expectations must be fulfilled for a role to be properly played? How much leeway in performance is permitted? For instance, how must a student physician act toward others in his set?
5. Is there any difference in the status of the roles under study? (Here look for signs of deference shown by one role occupant for another.) For instance, does one call the other "Sir?"
6. What sorts of sanctions, positive or negative, do role players use on each other? What does this reveal about variations in power of the roles (and status as well)? For instance, what threats can a superintendent use to keep teachers in line? And vice versa?
7. Are some roles more insulated from observation than others? How can such private areas be penetrated? Where, for instance, can interns relax together?
8. What sorts of "props"—clothing, language, demeanour, general appearance—do persons use to maintain themselves in their roles? How does a prostitute dress, for example?
9. What sorts of conflicts does a person with multiple role expectations experience? What, for example, happens when a school superintendent is torn between the expectations of the teachers and those of the school board?

How Can the Researcher Obtain Such Information?

1. *Observation* of persons enacting a role. This would include noting how persons in counter roles talk and act toward each other and attempting to catch their mutual expectations.
2. *Participant observation* in a role set. Here the investigator notes role players' reactions to him and other persons in roles, and from these experiences (and his reactions to others in the situation) he draws some descriptions of role enactment and expectations.
3. *Depth interview* with some persons in roles pertinent to the study. How do they see the role? What kinds of behaviour would they include in a proper enactment of it? The same sort of questions can be asked of pertinent counter-role occupants. This gives the investigator a feeling for the cluster of *normative expectations and counter expectations* found in constellations of role sets.

Advantages and Disadvantages

Perhaps the major advantage of role analysis is that a search for roles, counter roles, and the normative expectations incumbent upon each imposes an order on social life. Such organization aids the investigator to pull into a meaningful whole data about human group life that might otherwise appear to be bits and pieces of unrelated social behaviour. The very act of mapping roles and counter roles helps to locate explanations for such phenomena as patterns of deference and manipulation and brings possible areas of social conflict and other problems of interaction to the investigator's attention.

Role analysis furnishes clues to motivation that may not be physically evident to the sociologist in an interactional situation; yet he know these motives should be considered because people mentally refer to the expectations of others before acting. For instance, a person may think, "If I do something to satisfy Person A (in the counter role), what will Person B (in another counter role) think of me?" In other words, role analysis expands the boundaries of the investigation into the social-psychological histories of the actors involved.

As with all approaches to the understanding of social life, role analysis has its limitations. It can lull the investigator into perceiving a rather static social structure in which persons fulfil one role at a time for the continued successful existence of the social system. Some role theorists forget that social life is actually in a constant flux and that people may be able to play several roles simultaneously (an age role, a sex role, an occupational role, in addition to unique interpersonal roles with people). A single counter role may also have several, often contradictory, aspects rather than being the simple unity some researcher depicts.

Conceptually, the term "role" has become so popularized in sociology that almost any cluster of normative expectations has been called a role. These roles are not always tied in the same way to an actual position in the social structure, nor are their behavioural expectations equally formalized. For example, there are conventional occupational roles generally associated with employment that are well demarcated in the social structure and have rather well-defined behavioural expectations. On the other hand, age and sex roles have more nebulous behavioural boundaries, and the positions associated with them are quite loosely defined. Interpersonal roles (Shibutani, 1961: 323-366) established by the idiosyncratic relationships of people—such as the "fool" (Klapp, 1962) or the "tension manager" (Bales, 1950)—are so unusual that they have no formalized place in most social structures, but they still develop behavioural expectations among significant others.

The role analyst's most dangerous pitfall is to assume that all behaviour is role behaviour. People do act for other reasons than role expectations, and other types of theoretical approaches are often better for capturing these activities.

Some Applications

Role analysis is a useful approach to the study of how an individual is incorporated into any social structure, from the family and informal peer groups to such highly bureaucratized organizations as educational institutions and businesses. Social dilemmas can often be pinpointed through attention to problems of role conflict or role discontinuities. For instance, Komarovsky (1957) noted that college girls are expected to show an interest both in a career and in marriage, and that these two demands often cause problems and indecision about proper action, especially since it is considered impossible for a girl to be feminine and intelligent simultaneously. Role analyses of "middle-management" positions reveal the conflicting pressures exerted on their occupants. The foreman in a factory, for instance, deals simultaneously with executives and assembly-line workers. In attempting to cope with the problems of each, he often finds his loyalties torn, because he is in the difficult position of trying to fulfil the often conflicting demands of groups whose interests and perspectives frequently do not coincide (Roethlisberger, 1957).

Because a role can be viewed as a conceptual link between personality structure and social structure, a number of sociologists and social psychologists have been interested in the "fit" or "congruence" (or lack of it) between role demands and the personality of the individual in the role. Are bureaucratic personalities or organization men recruited, or are they created by the roles available to them? Are such roles eventually "internalized" to become the fulcrum of the person's outlook on life—the centre of his self-concept? Are people pushed into roles incompatible with their self-images? Erving Goffman (1961) has suggested that in such cases the social actor will display "role distance"—that is, public disdain for the role he is forced to play.

Some sociologists (called functionalists) are interested in what each role does to help maintain the social system, and how roles in a given system support each other. The roles in small social systems such as the family or some other primary group are often analysed—especially when there is a deviant member. Such analyses (Dentler and Eriksons, 1959) may indicate that the deviant person is actually functional to the system, because his bad behaviour is the one thing other members can agree upon and rally against! Occupational roles in bureaucracies can also function to reduce strain for people who must work together despite personal animosity. This is because the occupant of a position in the social system can fill a role requirement without putting his total "self" into the performance.

Social psychologists are interested in how people apprehend what their actual behaviour in a role should be, and how they adjust and readjust their behaviour to the expectations and counter roles of others when the standards of acceptable role behaviour are nebulous. In pursuit of answers to these questions, researchers have looked at how people emulate role models (other people already in the role). Such studies often focus on mass media—movies, television, popular magazines, and newspapers—as the sources of models for individuals who wish to become something other than what they are.

Some psychologists feel that the measure of a person's successful socialization is his ability to stay in a role—that is, to act appropriately—regardless of inner tension (Sarbin, 1954). Children gradually develop this ability, a fact to which any parent who has given birthday parties over a period of years can testify. It has also been suggested (Brim, 1960) that the measure of a mature person is his ability to shift roles as the occasion demands—from boss at the office to loving husband at home, etc.

Before You Go into the Field

1. Decide on the role and counter-role interaction you wish to study.
2. Decide on the best setting for this study in terms of the role sets usually found there.
3. Decide on your method of gathering data. You may use more than one method if you wish. (Interviewing and observation complement each other nicely, for instance.) Remember, in asking questions the sociologist does not use technical terms, but devises laymen's substitutes. Therefore, you should not ask, "How do you see the role

of mother as properly handled?" but rather, "What do you think makes for a good mother? A bad mother?" and so on.

References

Bales, Robert F. (1950). *Interaction Process Analysis.* Reading, MA: Addison-Wesley.

Brim, O.G. (1960). "Personality Development as Role Learning." pp. 127-159 in Ira Iscoe and Harold Stevenson (eds.), *Personality Development in Children.* Austin, Texas: University of Texas Press.

Dentler, Robert A., and Kai T. Erikson (1959). "The Functions of Deviance in Groups." *Social Problems* 7 (Fall): 98-107.

Goffman, Erving (1961). *Encounters.* Indianapolis, Ind.: Bobbs-Merrill.

Gross, Neal, W.L. Mason, and A.W. McEachern (1958). *Explorations in Role Analysis.* New York: Wiley.

Klapp, Orrin E. (1962). *Heroes, Villains, and Fools.* Englewood Cliffs, N.J.: Prentice Hall.

Komarovsky, Mirra (1957). "Cultural Contradictions and Sex Role." pp. 230-234 in R.W. O'Brien, C.C. Schrag, and W.T. Martin (eds.), *Readings in General Sociology.* Boston: Houghton Mifflin.

Merton, Robert K. (1957). "Role Sets." *British Journal of Sociology* 8 (June): 106-120.

Roethlisberger, F.J. (1957). "The Foreman." pp. 243-249 in R.W. O'Brien, C.C. Schrag, and W.T. Martin (eds.), *Readings in General Sociology.* Boston: Houghton Mifflin.

Sarbin, Theodore R. (1954). "Role Theory." pp. 223-258 in Gardner Lindzey (ed.), *Handbook of Social Psychology.* Reading, MA: Addison-Wesley.

Shibutani, Tamotsu (1961). *Society and Personality.* Englewood Cliffs. NJ: Prentice-Hall. pp. 323-366.

Printed in Canada